STANISLAVSKI:

HIS LIFE AND ART

a biography by

JEAN BENEDETTI

METHUEN DRAMA

Published by Methuen Drama

1 3 5 7 9 10 8 6 4 2

First published in Great Britain in 1988
by Methuen Drama
First published in paperback in 1990
by Methuen Drama

This newly revised and expanded edition published in 1999
by Methuen Drama

Copyright © 1988, 1990 and 1999 by Jean Benedetti

The right of Jean Benedetti to be identified as the author of
this work has been asserted by him in accordance with the
Copyright, Designs and Patents Act, 1988

A CIP catalogue record for this book
is available from the British Library

ISBN 0 413 52520 1

Photoset by SX Composing DTP, Rayleigh, Essex

No one has had a greater influence on acting as we know it than Stanislavski. Director of the first productions of Chekhov and Gorki, co-founder of the Moscow Art Theatre, and, above all, inventor and teacher of the Stanislavski system of actor training, he has inspired and guided actors and theatre lovers throughout the world. Yet in spite of his stature, much of the material relating to Stanislavski's life and career has remained untapped in Russian archives, with the result that a comprehensive account of the man and his work has been impossible.

In preparing this life of Stanislavski, Jean Benedetti has had unprecedented access to the original Russian material – letters and production notes never previously translated – which brings to life Stanislavski's most famous productions and provides extraordinary insights into his career and personality.

In this fully revised edition of the biography, Jean Benedetti includes much new and fascinating material only recently made available as a result of *Glasnost*, notably a long letter from Stanislavski to Stalin on the state of the Art Theatre, and a letter from Stalin himself concerning Nikolai Erdman's play, *The Suicide*.

'Jean Benedetti retrieves a full-fleshed man whose life begins under the rule of tsars and ends creating a system for, among others, Hollywood stars . . . he also gives us the man's voice, vivid, passionate and totally unpompous. Humorous, too . . .' *Guardian*

'Jean Benedetti has provided a book that was badly needed.' *The Listener*

Jean Benedetti was born in 1930 and educated in England and France. He trained as an actor and teacher at the Rose Bruford College of Speech and Drama, returning in 1970 as Principal of the College until 1987.

He is author of a number of semi-documentary television plays. His published translations include Brecht's *Edward II* and *A Respectable Wedding* and Georges Michel's *A Sunday Walk*. His first book was a biography of Gilles de Rais. In 1982 he published *Stanislavski: An Introduction*, which has been reprinted many times. *Stanislavski: A Biography* was first published in 1988 and then revised and expanded in 1990. He subsequently published *The Moscow Art Theatre Letters* in 1991 and *Dear Writer . . . Dear Actress*, the love letters of Anton Chekhov and Olga Knipper, in 1997. *Stanislavski and the Actor*, an account of Stanislavski's teaching in the last three years of his life, followed in 1998.

From 1979 to 1987 he was chairman of the Theatre Education Committee of the International Theatre Institute (UNESCO). He is currently Honorary Professor at both Rose Bruford College and Queen Margaret University College.

CONTENTS

PART I: AN OPEN THEATRE

PART II: THE BIRTH OF THE 'SYSTEM'

PART III: THE REVOLUTION AND AFTER

ILLUSTRATIONS

AUTHOR'S NOTE

The agreed international system for the transliteration of Russian words, used by scholars, is not familiar to most readers. Names have therefore been transliterated as directly as possible. The arbitrary usage of /y/ and /i/ which does not correspond in any consistent way with the two /i/ sounds in Russian, has been avoided.

It has not, however, been possible to be entirely consistent. Certain names, particularly of musicians, are so familiar that they have been left in the form readers will know best. Thus, while Chekhov is current, so is Tchaikovski, although both names in Russian begin with the same letter.

Russian pronunciation does not always coincide with spelling. In certain instances the letter /g/ is pronounced as /v/. In transliterating I have therefore tried to make sure that the non-Russian speaker is able to pronounce names and book titles correctly.

All dates up to February 1, 1918, are given according to the Old Style Julian Calendar. Dates thereafter are given in the New Style Gregorian Calendar. By a decree of the Bolshevik government of January 22, 1918, February 1 became February 14. The dates given, therefore, correspond to those which appear on the documents quoted.

PREFACE TO THE
THIRD EDITION

It is now ten years since the second, enlarged and revised, edition of this biography appeared. At the time I indicated that doubtless a great deal of new material would become available. Such has proved to be the case.

I was gratified by the reaction of specialist Russian colleagues to the earlier editions of this book and their assurances that my account of Stanislavski's development is a correct and balanced one. What the new material provides is an opportunity to clarify obscure areas and to understand better the context in which Stanislavski had to work, both at a professional and at a political level. A major problem has always been to escape from the sanitized image carefully fostered by Stalin. It is now possible to give a fuller account of the personal difficulties Stanislavski encountered as a writer, his battle to get his ideas in coherent form on paper, his struggle with communist ideologues over the terminology of the 'system'. It is also possible to chart the history of the American editions of his works and the consequences of the contracts he signed on the publication of his works world-wide.

I have drawn on material from three books I have published since 1988, *The Moscow Art Theatre Letters, Dear Writer . . . Dear Actress, Stanislavski and the Actor* and also on a number of articles. In particular, I have made extensive use of material from *The Moscow Art Theatre Letters*, much of it still unpublished in book form in Russia. Since 1988 I have also discovered a copy of the typescript of *An Actor Prepares* sent in 1935 and 1936 to Elizabeth Hapgood for translation and have therefore been able to see the changes that were made for the 1938 Russian edition of *An Actor's Work on Himself: Part One*.

A number of studies and books of memoirs have appeared in Russia to which I am greatly indebted. These include, notably, Anatoly Smeliansky's detailed account of the relationship between Bulgakov and the Art Theatre (published in English as *Is Comrade Bulgakov Dead?*, trans. Arch Tait, Methuen, 1993), Vadim Shverubovich's *Memoirs* in which he describes the life of the Art Theatre in the crucial years following the Revolution, in particular the European and American tour 1922–1924, and Sobolevskaia's memoir of her work as a young singer with Stanislavski. More recently, Olga Radishcheva has published a detailed account of the first ten years of the collaboration between Stanislavski and Nemirovich-Danchenko. No less important has been the publication, thanks to the efforts of Anatoly Smeliansky, of the correspondence between Stanislavski and his translator, Elizabeth Hapgood, and his literary adviser, Liubov Gurevich, covering the writing, publication and translation of his major works on acting.

One aspect of Stanislavski's personal life that remains obscure is his relationship to the Stalinist regime. We shall have to wait for Anatoly Smeliansky's study of that period based on documents discovered in the Art Theatre archives by himself and Inna Soloviova.

As in earlier editions, references have been kept within the body of the text rather than placed in footnotes or endnotes. References to the *Moscow Art Theatre Letters* are placed in brackets with *MATL* and the letter number. A revised bibliography is also provided.

Jean Benedetti, December 1998

PREFACE TO THE
SECOND EDITION

Even as the first edition of this book was coming off the presses, new information was becoming available. A series of Stanislavski seminars, two in Paris, at the Théâtre de Chaillot and the Centre Georges Pompidou, and another in Moscow provided opportunities to meet a group of international specialists and I am indebted to Sharon M. Carnicke of the University of California, Laurence Senelick of Tufts University and to three colleagues from the Centre National de la Recherche Scientifique in Paris, Claudine Amiard-Chevrel, Marie-Christine Autant-Mathieu and Béatrice Picon-Vallin, for many useful exchanges.

A great deal of new material is being released from Soviet archives and this has now been incorporated into the text. I am grateful to Anatoly Smeliansky, Secretary General of the Theatre Workers' Union of the USSR, for making material from the new Complete Works available in advance of publication and for many private communications, also to Inna Soloviova of the editorial board of the new Complete Works for her comments on the first edition and to the Curator and Deputy Curator of the Stanislavski House-Museum for their elucidation of points of detail. It is certain that the new edition of the Complete Works, with the additional material it contains, will necessitate further modifications at a subsequent date.

J. Benedetti, April 1989.

INTRODUCTION TO THE
FIRST EDITION

The year 1988 marks the 125th anniversary of Stanislavski's birth and the 50th anniversary of his death. The moment seems opportune for a reappraisal of his life.

The Stanislavski 'system' is known and used in one form or other throughout the world. It remains the only fully worked-out method of acting available. Though aspects of it are much disputed, no one has come forward with an equally well-organized alternative. As Lee Strasberg commented in his autobiography:

> 'The teachings of Constantin Stanislavski and his disciples changed not only my life, but that of the entire twentieth-century theatre. Just as our understanding of human behavior and modern physics is still turning on the revelations of Freud and Einstein, so our contemporary knowledge of the actor's craft is still heavily indebted to Stanislavski's 100-year-old discoveries.'

The 'system' is taught in the form codified by Stanislavski's pupils in the Soviet Union, Eastern Europe, China and parts of the Third World. Its modified form, the Method, has been instrumental in shaping some of the finest American actors. In England its history has been slightly more chequered, for although Stanislavski's methods and practice were familiar to the likes of Harley Granville-Barker, the theatrical profession at large did not have an opportunity to see the Art Theatre until 1958, long after Germany, Austria, Czechoslovakia and France. Much information was gleaned second-hand from émigrés like Fiodor Komissarzhevski, whose version of the 'system' by no means met with Stanislavski's approval, or Michael Chekhov, who developed his own related but independent method. Perhaps the only major English actor of the twentieth century to have applied the 'system' consistently was Michael Redgrave.

The production methods which Stanislavski and the Art Theatre pioneered have been absorbed into theatre practice world-wide and are now accepted as the norm. Yet Stanislavski himself remains for the most part a shadowy figure. For that he is, to some extent, responsible. One of the greatest obstacles to a proper understanding of the complexity of his character is his own book, *My Life in Art*. Written in haste at a time when his ideas and practice were under attack in Russia it is less autobiography than an *apologia*. It is a justification of the 'system' and a demonstration of his path through failure to it. Many of his early achievements are played down. The reader can get no idea of his immense fame and reputation even before the creation of the Moscow Art Theatre. A further problem is that it does not deal with his last, highly productive years. The first American edition stops in 1922 and the Russian edition does not go beyond 1924 – that leaves the years up to 1938 to evaluate. English-speaking readers are at a double disadvantage because of the poor quality of the translation by J. J. Robbins, who had to cope against the clock with Stanislavski's prevarications and delays. The result seems at times to be written in an English of Robbins' invention. Its worst fault is to betray the tone of Stanislavski's voice. Purple passages apart – and Stanislavski was prone to them even when speaking in public – the Russian text is much more easy-going, more directly conversational than the unidiomatic English text would suggest. Generations have grown up thinking of Stanislavski as alternatively naïve and po-faced.

The 1926 and 1928 Moscow editions differ substantially from the American edition. Much material was added, in particular the critical penultimate chapter in which Stanislavski described his response to developments in Russian theatre during his two-year foreign tour. The revised Russian version, not currently available in English, still contains errors of memory, telescoping of events, misdating of performances. For that reason I have tried to avoid too heavy a reliance on *My Life in Art* and to approach Stanislavski's life through other documentary sources. In the last forty years a considerable amount of published material has become available, notably the eight-volume Complete Works, soon to be replaced by a twelve-volume edition, four volumes of Production Plans, two volumes of extracts from the *Notebooks*, exhaustive studies by scholars of Stanislavski's career as actor and director, and innumerable Memoirs by individual actors or critics.

Studying these works, it becomes still more apparent how incomplete a picture *My Life in Art* gives. Stanislavski appears to be living in a void without contact with the artistic, social and intellectual movements of his time. One of the tasks of this book is to describe the development of a creative mind in its artistic and historical context and specifically in its Russian context. There are aspects of Russian thinking on art, politics and society which are essential for a full understanding of Stanislavski and the aesthetic position he adopted. In *My Life in Art*, Stanislavski was able to assume a common culture and a common frame of reference with his Russian readers. Much was therefore left implicit. As a non-Russian, writing for non-Russian readers, I have tried to make what was implicit, explicit.

Given that much of the material I have used is not easily available and has not been previously translated I have tried, within the limitations of space, to quote the texts rather than summarize them, in the hope that the original voice will be heard. All source references and dates are included in the body of the text so that the reader may immediately see the origin of the information.

Some published works deserve particular mention. Any contemporary biographer of Stanislavski must be indebted to Vinogradskaia's monumental four-volume documentary biography, *Zhizn i Tvorchestvo K. S. Stanislavskovo*, which took some fifteen years to compile. It provides invaluable archive material and press reviews. It also directs attention to many original sources. Other important studies to which I am indebted are M. M. Stroeva's detailed two-volume study of Stanislavski's productions at the Art Theatre and Elena Poliakova's study of his career as an actor, *Stanislavski Aktior*. Poliakova is also the author of a well-researched and eminently readable recent biography, published in Moscow in 1977, and available in an English translation. For the discussion of individual productions I must acknowledge my debt first, to Laurence Senelick for his indispensable account of the Craig–Stanislavski *Hamlet*, and, second, to A. Smeliansky for his authoritative account of the much disputed production of Bulgakov's *Molière*.

I would like to thank Professor Brian Jarman of St Mary's Hospital, Paddington, for his advice on medical terminology and on the possible interpretation of such medical evidence as is available. Finally I would like to express my deep and continuing gratitude to Aleksei Bartoshevich, Professor at the State Institute for Theatre Arts (GITIS) and the State Institute for Research and a member of the executive committee of the Theatre Workers' Union of the USSR, for his help in directing my attention to certain essential reading, and his patient elucidation of questions of cultural context. Any errors of judgement are, of course, entirely my own.

PART ONE

AN OPEN THEATRE

CHAPTER ONE

ALEKSEIEV

Stanislavski was born on January 5, 1863, into what Lady Bracknell described as the purple of commerce. Baptized Konstantin Sergeievich Alekseiev, he was the son of Sergei Vladimirovich Alekseiev and Elizaveta Vasilievna Alekseieva. He came into the world at the family mansion at 29, Great Alekseievskaia Street, which was named, not as many have supposed, after his family but after the local church. Yet such a mistake is understandable, for this palatial building with its giant portico, classical façade and imposing interior staircase was visible proof of the advance the Alekseievs had made since the mid-eighteenth century, their progress from starving peasants to one of the richest families in Russia. If, in the United States one could be 'rich as Rockefeller', in Moscow the corresponding expression was, and is, 'rich as Alekseiev'.

Most of what we know of the Alekseiev family and of Stanislavski's early life comes from accounts left by his brother, Vladimir, two of his sisters, Zinaïda and Anna, and Anna's son, Georgi, who wrote a history of the family business.

Where their fortune originally came from no one knew for certain. Family legend had it that Stanislavski's great-great-grandfather, known as Petrov the Younger, had made money as a street vendor, selling peas; it was suggested that he might have been a money-lender but no proof of this story exists. All that is clear is that Petrov made an extremely rapid rise up the social ladder. Born a serf in Yaroslavl, in 1724 he made enough money to buy his freedom and go some 150 miles south-west to Moscow. In 1746, at a mere twenty-two, he was legally registered by the magistrates as belonging to the merchant class. In 1785, Semeon, his son, went into the textile business, a growth industry in the Moscow area. He decided to specialize in gold and silver thread. It was an astute choice. The product was at the top end of the market and demand constant. It was needed for church vestments, court dress and uniforms both civil and military. Thanks to the government's policy, dating from Peter the Great, of granting absolute monopoly in manufacture, the field was open. He prospered and by 1812 was able, in common with other leading citizens, to make a contribution of 50,000 roubles towards the war effort against Napoleon.

His associates were by this time seriously worried that so respectable and solid a citizen did not possess a real surname. Alekseiev was no more than a patronymic – son of Aleksei. A proper and more respectable name was therefore manufactured for him. Since he dealt in silver goods – *serebriani* – he would be known as Serebrenikov. The name, however, never caught on and he and his descendants continued to be known as Alekseiev without loss of prestige.

Stanislavski's grandfather, Vladimir Semeonovich, married a woman of superior culture and refinement, Elizaveta Aleksandrovna, and the family's life-style underwent a change. The virtues of application and hard work remained – as they were always to remain, no matter how much money the family made – but time could now be found for the arts of living. Grandfather Vladimir lived like a gentleman, though without ostentation, and it was he who built the house in which Stanislavski was born. It was situated, for all its grandeur, in an industrial suburb, next to the family's factory. For the Alekseievs, industry and art went together.

Stanislavski's father, Sergei Vladimirovich, came up the hard way. He was born in 1836 in the new family mansion. Like his father before him he learned every aspect of the business before finally becoming Chairman of the Board. As a boy he cleaned the office and ran errands. As in the rest of Europe, however, the rising bourgeoisie was beginning to adopt the manners and customs of the aristocracy. Thus Sergei, apart from acquiring the necessary competence in mathematics and book-keeping, learned to speak reasonable French and German, indispensable accomplishments for anyone with social pretensions. He also had a good knowledge of Russian literature, Gogol being his particular favourite. Like most educated people he subscribed to the major literary journals of the time, the so-called 'thick' magazines which were so important in shaping progressive opinion. Not that he sympathized with the radical tendencies that lay behind much of the writing; Sergei Vladimirovich's sense of social responsibility expressed itself in terms of paternalism and philanthropy. He was a good employer and a skilled fund-raiser. Hospitals and orphanages benefited from his efforts.

The choice this mild-mannered, conventional man made for a wife sent shock-waves of disapproval through the family. They wanted him to marry someone with a good solid background in Moscow society. Instead he fell in love with an eighteen-year-old girl from Petersburg, who had no position, was half-French, illegitimate and, to complete the catalogue of social disasters, the daughter of an actress. Elizaveta Vasilievna Yakovlieva and her sister, Marie, were the result of a liaison between a wealthy Petersburg merchant, Vasili Abramovich Yakovliev, and a French actress of small talent and less brain, Marie Varley. Yakovliev was famous for erecting the memorial to Aleksandr I in front of the Winter Palace. Elizaveta's godfather was Sosnitiski, a leading player at the imperial Alexandrinski Theatre. She was christened Adèle and brought up as a Catholic.

Marie Varley very soon found her children an encumbrance and, when Elizaveta was eleven, abandoned them. Yakovliev acknowledged them legally as his own, which he need not have done, and took them into his home. He then married a rich wife, Aleksandra Bostanzhoglo, but unfortunately omitted to warn her that she was to be presented with two ready-made daughters. One of the step-mother's first acts was to have them baptized into the Orthodox church. Adèle thus became Elizaveta.

Relations between the two girls and their step-mother were, understandably perhaps, never good. When her sister married and went to Moscow, Elizaveta followed her by overnight train, properly chaperoned by her governess. She was by no means destitute in Moscow. She was taken in by her step-mother's family, the Bostanzhoglos, who played a leading role in social life. It was in their house that Sergei Vladimirovich met her. It is easy to understand the attraction. Elizaveta was bi-lingual in Russian and French and widely read in the literature of both languages, although her preference was for French. She was also an exceptionally good pianist. The great virtuoso, Nikolai Rubinstein, often expressed regret that she would not allow him to teach her. As to Marie Varley, she invented her own romanticized version of events, claiming that her daughters had been abducted. She later tried to re-establish contact but she was never admitted to the Alekseiev home. None of her grandchildren ever met her.

This was uncharacteristically harsh of Elizaveta Vasilievna as she was essentially generous and warm-hearted by nature. Much as she wanted, however, to exclude her mother from her present life she nonetheless shared the same volatile temperament. If Marie Varley created drama in the theatre, her daughter created drama in the home, shouting at the servants one minute and begging their pardon the next. She never changed and was as tempestuous at sixty as she had been at twenty.

Despite the family's initial misgivings and the differences of temperament between the partners, the match proved ideal. No one in later years could recall a single quarrel, they complemented each other so perfectly. They had ten children in all; nine survived. Vladimir, Konstantin, Zinaïda, Anna and Georgi were born in the 1860s. Boris, Liubov, Pavel and Maria followed in the 1870s. Stanislavski was the second child of the marriage.

Grandfather Vladimir had died in 1862. This marked the end of an era and a further stage in the upward progress of the family. A few months after Stanislavski was born, the family decided to leave the house near the factory and the industrial slums that surrounded it and move to central Moscow. They bought a mansion at Red Gates, on Sadovaia Street, a fashionable district some half-an-hour's walk north-east of Red Square. The new house was large enough to accommodate three generations of Alekseievs with their attendant staff and it was here that Stanislavski lived until he was forty. The old house, on Great Alekseievskaia Street, was donated in the late 1860s as a home for the widows and orphans of the merchant class.

Sergei Vladimirovich had no intention of imposing the stern regime he had known on his own children. Elizaveta Vasilievna, for her part, having been handed on from a mother who gave her little affection to a step-mother whose main concern was to play the society hostess, made her family her life. Neither parent was willing to abandon their children in order to participate in the frantic social life around them. In the season Sadovaia Street witnessed an endless succession of carriages, of glittering jewels and dresses; armies of flunkeys attended the people who arrived for the nightly round of balls and receptions given by their neighbours. Sergei and Elizaveta preferred to enjoy the company of their children. When the Alekseievs went out it was as a family; when they received, it was as a family.

What was important to them was their proximity to the artistic life of the city. The mid-nineteenth century was a period of unprecedented cultural richness. Russia was in the process of discovering a new artistic identity in almost every domain – music, opera, ballet, literature, theatre, painting. Educated and affluent families like the Alekseievs lived within the ambit of the artistic world. Savva Ivanovich Mamontov, a railway magnate, a near neighbour and Stanislavski's cousin by marriage, spent a considerable amount of his fortune indulging his passion for the theatre, mounting performances, particularly of opera, which set new standards of production, and musical soirées and concerts. Actors from the Mali, dancers from the Bolshoi, musicians and writers were regular visitors to the house and became family friends.

The children grew up in this materially and artistically privileged environment. They were, of course, spoiled, although it does not seem to have done any of them ultimately very much harm. Each child was individually considered. Each had its own special kind of sweets and its own kind of bread at breakfast. There was no early rising. Nine o'clock was quite soon enough. Elizaveta Vasilievna took an active part in their upbringing, her insistence on supervising almost every aspect of their lives leading to regular and spectacular quarrels with Nanny Fiokla. A heated exchange would invariably end in Nanny packing her meagre belongings and storming out of the house while the children set up a collective wail. Ten minutes later she would be back and order would be restored – until the next time.

Much less beneficial to the children's welfare was their mother's fanatical obsession with health. In the country she would sleep over the stables on the pretext that the fumes of horse manure were beneficial. The children were not allowed to walk past hospitals for fear of infection; before they were allowed out in bad weather they were wrapped up to the point of suffocation lest they catch cold. These precautions produced the opposite effect to the one desired. Bathed in perspiration before they got beyond the front door they immediately caught chills. From his early childhood Stanislavski retained two things – a disposition towards colds and flu and an indisposition to get up in the morning.

Sergei and Elizaveta Alekseiev had the gift of drawing others into their magic circle. Loyalty and affection extended beyond the immediate family. Nanny Fiokla and Elizaveta Vasilievna's elderly governess had their own rooms and their place at table. It was a house of nicknames. Normal diminutives in which Russian abounds were abandoned in favour of a family version. Thus Vladimir, instead of being known as Volodia, became Vovosia; Konstantin was not Kostia but Kokosia. The coachman was known as Pirozhok (Meat-pie) and the children's governess, Evdokia Snopova, as Papusha.

True to their determination not to relinquish their children's company but to watch and help them grow, Stanislavski's parents insisted they be educated at home. A fully equipped gymnasium was installed to ensure adequate physical development. As each child grew up he or she was handed on from Nanny Fiokla to Papusha, or her successor, and thence to a series of tutors – a Swiss tutor for gymnastics, a Swedish tutor for music and a certain Mademoiselle Adeline Schmitt for French. French was spoken regularly in the home but the formal study of grammar began at the age of five. Mathematics were taught by a young man named Lvov, who was rumoured to be something of a revolutionary. There were, in addition, dancing lessons from members of the Bolshoi company and in particular from Ermolov, uncle of Stanislavski's favourite actress, Ermolova. There was also, for a period, a young, rather eccentrically dressed musician, a pupil of Nikolai Rubinstein, who came to play the piano, which he appeared to do day and night, throwing off a cascade of scales, studies and exercises. All these diverse personalities were welded into a small private community. When the family made a trip to Kiev in 1877, two complete railway carriages were taken; the first, a ministerial coach, including a sitting-room for the family and their doctor, the second for the servants, the nursemaids and the tutors.

Stanislavski was by no means the 'star' of the family. On the contrary. Nanny Fiokla remembered him as 'nothing much'. His early years were dogged by almost continuous ill-health. As a baby he had difficulty in holding his head up; it would loll forward. This caused a minor accident when he was nine months old. The family doctor was attempting to inoculate him against smallpox when his head suddenly fell forward on to the lancet, cutting his lower eye lid. The scar remained with him for the rest of his life. He also suffered from scrofula which meant various forms of medicated baths. When he learned to speak he had problems with the sounds 'l' and 'r'.

Zinaïda recalled that she and her brother were the 'Cinderellas' of the family. It was a condition of Elizaveta Vasilievna's self-esteem as a mother that her children should be 'showable'. This meant that though she loved them all dearly, her special favour was reserved for those among them who, like Vladimir and Anna, would most readily perform their party pieces, playing the piano or reciting poems. Stanislavski felt intimidated by Elizaveta and her demands and, although he was lively enough in the nursery, in the presence of adults he withdrew into himself. Much as he adored his governess, Papusha, he resisted all her attempts to make him learn little verses to speak for guests. The sudden improvement in his general health at the age of seven made little difference. There was now colour in his cheeks and he began to gain in strength. The physical education sessions in the family gymnasium, the dancing and fencing lessons developed his body and at the same time laid the foundations of his technique as an actor. When, in 1869, his father bought an estate in Liubimovka, a short distance from Moscow, he was able to pass the hot summer months in outdoor pursuits such as boating and riding which helped him grow in strength. He soon became an excellent horseman. But he still did not shine. His mother's unreserved approval was only forthcoming when he achieved a reputation as an amateur actor but by then it was too late. The older he grew the more constrained he felt in her presence, although in middle age he was able to write to Chekhov about her with a degree of amused detachment. It was his father who provided the background of security and his brothers and sisters who gave him the affection and support he needed.

Outside the family he only ever had one close friend, Fedia Kashkadamov, known as Fif, the son of his tutor in Russian. Fif was the model companion, someone who could enter Stanislavski's world on equal terms. He was highly intelligent, musical, playing both the piano and the violin; he wrote good poetry. Later, he took the lead with Stanislavski in organizing amateur theatricals. Stanislavski loved and respected him but Fif suffered from a weak heart and died at the age of twenty-four. Stanislavski never again had a friend who was his contemporary.

A reserved boy, Stanislavski could, however, turn into an obstinate demon. Just as he refused to learn even simple poems, he resisted his piano lessons, although he was extremely musical. He refused to play duets with his teacher and would time his lesson to the second, declining absolutely to go one instant over the allotted hour. He even managed to drive his tolerant and mild-mannered father into a quite exceptional rage one day by endlessly repeating 'I will not let you go to Aunt Vera's'. He was at first requested and then ordered to stop but would not or, rather, could not. Something had taken possession of him. His outraged father eventually stormed out of the room. Only then did the young Konstantin relent. Stanislavski regarded this incident as the first manifestation of his will to succeed. It was, in his view, this obstinacy that enabled him to get things done.

Play, make-believe and fantasy played a large part in the Alekseiev children's early education. For this Papusha was responsible. She was barely nineteen when she was engaged. She was well educated with an instinctive understanding of children's needs ahead of the conventional wisdom of her time. She used creative play as part of the learning process. She used fantasy to explain away fears and anxieties and encouraged the children to act out situations or characters from history. At other times they would improvise small scenes to entertain the family on special occasions. It was thanks to her that Stanislavski made his stage 'debut'.

In great secrecy she rehearsed the children in a series of tableaux vivants, *The Four Seasons*, a conventional subject for the period, which were intended as a surprise offering in honour of Elizaveta Vasilievna's name-day, September 5. The performance took place in a dilapidated out-building at Liubimovka. A small stage had been constructed and a curtain improvised out of tartan rugs. Stanislavski played Winter, or Grandfather Frost.

He found it, if we are to believe *My Life in Art*, a puzzling experience. His account, however, is homiletic rather than historically accurate. In the first American edition he states that he was two or three at the time; in the Russian edition he changes this to three or four, but neither is possible. Liubimovka was not purchased until 1869 and the earliest date a performance could have taken place there was 1870, when he was seven. He claims that this was the first occasion on which he experienced the embarrassment of being on stage with no motivation for what he was doing. It was an omission he quickly remedied.

His little scene was so successful that it was considered he merited an encore:

'They put a lighted candle in front of me, hidden in brushwood, to represent a bonfire and gave me a stick which I was to pretend to put into it.

"You understand? Pretend. Don't really do it," they explained to me. And so I was strictly forbidden to put the stick into the fire. All this seemed quite senseless to me. "Why pretend if I really can put the wood in the fire?"

As soon as the curtains opened for the encore I stretched out my hand with the stick towards the fire with considerable interest and curiosity. It seemed to me that this was a completely natural and logical action, one with thought behind it.' (*Sobranie Sochinenii*, i, p. 9.)

The stick went up in flames, setting light to the cotton wool that covered the set. Stanislavski was grabbed from the stage and taken straight up to bed in tears.

This sixty-year-old man's account of the reasoning processes of a child of seven is far too sophisticated but, placed as it is in *My Life in Art* side by side with the Aunt Vera incident, it indicates his determination to see his later life and personality in terms of his earliest experiences. This performance marked for him the beginning of his preoccupation with the problem of illusion and reality on stage.

Theatre was the Alekseiev family passion, be it the Punch and Judy men and clowns who roamed the streets and came knocking at the door, the circus, the Mali or the Bolshoi. The children were taken to the theatre and concerts almost as soon as they could walk. On the whole they were resistant to the weightier dramatic and musical works. They made it clear to their parents that if their treats were to be limited in number, the 'heavy stuff' was not to count.

Stanislavski's favourite was the circus – 'the best place in the world', he declared aged nine. He liked to sit where he could see the artists preparing to come on. The physicality, the speed, the colour of the spectacle carried him away. His parents were amazed when, one day, this boy, normally so reserved in public, seeing his particular favourite, Elvira, an equestrienne, jumped out of the family box, ran to her and kissed the hem of her skirt. When he ran back to his seat his parents registered a mild protest – 'Kostia, qu'as-tu fait?' – but he just sat, all unheeding, staring into space.

Other great occasions included visits to the ballet. Ermolov's dance classes had awakened Stanislavski to the expressive possibilities of his own body. He went to the Bolshoi, therefore, with active interest. The glory of the Tchaikovski ballets and the full development of a choreographic style were yet to come. The children's favourites were works like *The Corsair*.

The Alekseiev family descended on the theatre *en bloc*. Picnic refreshments were provided and they took with them a board that could be placed across the seats so that the children could have a proper view. The parents preferred No. 14, next to the Imperial Box, so as 'to be seen'. The children preferred boxes 1 or 2, at the side, so that, as at the circus, they could see the artists preparing in the wings. All had their own favourite ballerina; Kostia's was Stanislavskaia. During the intervals the children were allowed to run and play in the theatre's hallowed corridors. Their noisy antics were smiled upon both by the theatre's venerable and bewhiskered officials and by the lackeys whose magnificent blue livery was decorated with silver braid which had doubtless come from the Alekseiev mills. After the performance the children were gathered up by the nursemaids, lifted into the carriage by the servants and taken home.

For a time Zinaïda and Anna could think of nothing else but being sent away to ballet school. Their father, indulgent as ever, preferred not to confront them with a direct refusal but dutifully wrote a letter of application which he assured them he had sent. His closing sentence was, however, sufficiently tongue-in-cheek to indicate his request would be granted over his dead body. No answer was ever received.

Theatre visits provided material for play. Scenes from the ballet – usually those involving death and destruction – were performed. With Fif, Stanislavski created the Konstantino Alekseiev Circus. The children were by turns jugglers, clowns, acrobats. Since they could not always reproduce the more spectacular acts they resorted to puppets. They persuaded the family carpenter to construct a special table complete with trap-doors, footlights and overhead lighting. Notebooks and pencils were taken along to theatre visits and sets and costumes were duly noted to be reproduced at home. Everyone in the household was drawn in to help. Performances were given for sympathetic friends and a sell-out was not unusual. Sometimes Vladimir, who confined himself to accompanying the performance on the piano, would sabotage the occasion by shouting, 'The Idiots! They imagine it's a real circus.' Stanislavski would be momentarily angry but nothing could destroy for long his belief in the world of illusion he had created.

Papusha left the family service in 1874, when Stanislavski was eleven. She had been with him for seven formative years. He was always grateful to her. Dedicating a photograph in 1928 he described her as his 'second mother'. Her departure presaged more radical changes.

The following year, Sergei and Elizaveta, much against their will, were obliged to send the two older boys to school; compulsory military service had been introduced and to qualify for exemption young men needed to demonstrate an approved level of education. This meant taking public examinations. Vladimir and Konstantin took the entrance examination for the grammar school at 4 Pokrovka Street and passed. Vladimir entered the Third Form and Konstantin, the Second. The school was considered one of the best although Stanislavski's comments are distinctly unflattering.

The young Kostia cut a strange figure. Although only twelve he was exceptionally tall. According to Vladimir, he stood among his contemporaries like Gulliver among the Lilliputians. As an adult he stood six feet six inches tall and in group photographs can be seen towering above the people around him. This caused problems of coordination which took many years of effort to resolve.

He showed the same reserve at school as he showed with adults. He made no friends in his own form. Such companions as he had were drawn from his brother's year. He was always, as his headmaster recalled, unfailingly courteous to masters and pupils alike, but no more. He remained polite but distant.

Learning at school had none of the excitement and stimulation of lessons at home. Instead of Papusha and lively-minded tutors he had a pompous master who peppered his remarks to his pupils with endless deferential 'Excellencies'. He was, as Stanislavski put it, 'a bit dotty'. School meant boredom and frustration. The authorities had decided to emphasize the importance of classical languages. They hoped that concentration on Latin and Greek would keep young minds away from Russian literature and hence from subversion. Try as he would the young Kostia could not master irregular Latin verbs. He copied them out, page after page, in his attempt to get them by heart but to no avail. He failed Latin regularly.

Stanislavski never had any capacity for parrot-learning or the mechanical acquisition of facts, nor, conversely, did he have any gift for abstract or conceptual thought. He learned when confronted with concrete problems or when his imagination or, as he later put it, his will to create, was aroused. Motivation was everything and it was the theatre that provided the stimulus. Theatre could unblock his obstinate memory. This is illustrated by two incidents which occurred in his mid-teens. The boy who could not learn Latin verbs surprised his parents during a public dress rehearsal of Molière's *Le Mariage Forcé* at the Mali by reciting one of Pancrace's long speeches from memory. On another occasion he took advantage of the master's absence from the classroom to act a whole scene, playing all the parts, from Griboiedov's *Woe from Wit*. Unfortunately he was so absorbed in his performance that he did not notice the master's return. He was punished for indiscipline. Playacting would not enhance his examination prospects or his career.

CHAPTER TWO

STANISLAVSKI

The year 1877 marked a turning-point in Stanislavski's life. His father was elected head of the merchant class in Moscow, one of the most important and influential positions in the city. He could rise no higher, for while the aristocracy might be mortgaged to the state for two-thirds of its wealth, all important posts in central government, the army and the church were still reserved, by law, for its members. One of his first acts was to raise 1,000,000 roubles for the families of casualties in the latest Russo-Turkish war.

Sergei Vladimirovich had always been fond of his estate at Liubimovka. Soon after buying it he had created a medical centre in the village and named it after his wife. Now he decided to convert the out-building which had been used for the tableaux vivants into a proper theatre for the enjoyment of family and friends. Amateur theatricals were a popular pastime among the summerfolk at their dachas and estates. Few, however, apart from Mamontov, could aspire to a fully equipped theatre. The finished building was handsome with a dressing-room each for the gentlemen and ladies, a wardrobe and a prop-store. The footlights could be covered by lowering a board over them when a blackout was required. Guests could either spend the intervals on the verandah or in a specially provided sitting-room when the weather was bad.

Elizaveta Vasilievna's name-day, September 5, was selected for the gala opening. Guests were asked to present themselves at Yaroslavl station from where they were to be taken by special train to Liubimovka to arrive in time for dinner before the performance. The entertainment was to consist of four short pieces, directed by the mathematics tutor, Lvov. Stanislavski appeared in two of them, *A Cup of Tea* and *The Old Mathematician*.

He was in such a state of tension and excitement that he could scarcely contain himself and almost fell out of the carriage. It was to be his great day. In the event it proved more problematic than he could have anticipated. He was confronted for the first time with the contradiction between what an actor and an audience feel about a performance. In *A Cup of Tea* he had felt comparatively at ease but the audience had not responded. In *The Old Mathematician*, however, where he had felt less secure, he was declared by director and audience alike to have played much better. He was thoroughly confused.

An immediate consequence of the grand opening was the creation of the Alekseiev Circle which consisted of the immediate family, Fif Kashkadamov and his brother, and various cousins. A further, and, in the long-term, more significant consequence was Stanislavski's decision to note down and analyse his performance. He had kept a series of notebooks from his earliest childhood on subjects that interested him. He now began the first of a new set in which he described and analysed his work from role to role and performance to performance. He continued this practice for the next sixty years. The last of the books was at his bedside on the day he died. The notes he so carefully and assiduously made provided the basis for much of his published work.

The first entry, written on the evening of the performance, runs:

'In the role of the Mathematician I played coldly, lifelessly, without talent, although I was no worse than the others but I in no way showed talent. The audience said the part did not suit me. . . .

'In *A Cup of Tea* I was successful, the audience laughed – not at me, however, but at Muzil whom I copied, even down to the voice.' (*SS*, V, p. 85.)

He noted, too, that he gabbled his lines and waved his arms about like a windmill.

This entry, like later examples, must be read with caution. In common with many talented actors who are only concerned with improvement, Stanislavski tended to see only the negative side of his work. His sister, Zinaïda, rejected his account of the gala evening:

'In his Notes Kostia writes, "I was not successful in *The Old Mathematician*". That is not quite true, rather he himself was dissatisfied but at the same time even in that first production he distinguished himself from the rest by the naturalness of his playing and it was not at all evident that he was nervous or shy.' (Z. Sokolova in *K. S. Stanislavski*, Moscow, 1955, p. 382.)

Whatever the actual quality of his performance may have been, the fact that at the age of fourteen, he was able to analyse the technique of a leading character actor, Muzil, and consciously copy it is evidence of an insight and understanding beyond his years.

The standards by which Stanislavski judged his own work were drawn principally from the performances he saw at the Mali Theatre, his 'university', as he put it. The Mali was the home of psychological realism. At the time it was founded, in 1823, Pushkin was struggling with the problem of verisimilitude. What is believable in the theatre? How does the spectator enter the world of the play? The reader can lose himself in a book, to the exclusion of the world around him, but how can a member of a theatre audience, sitting with 2000 other people, in a space which is divided in two parts, one for those watching, the other for those performing, believe in the reality of what is going on? Since, at this period, the auditorium remained fully lit during performances there was no surrounding darkness in which he could lose himself.

For Pushkin it was not historical authenticity that made a play credible since classic authors like Shakespeare, Racine, Corneille and Calderon were manifestly anachronistic. Does not a clock strike in *Julius Caesar*? What then is verisimilitude? Wherein does it lie? Pushkin came to the conclusion that the only truth which interested classic authors was truth of character and situation: credible behaviour in believable circumstances. In an unfinished article on the history of drama, drafted in 1830 but not published until after his death, he summarized his findings in what came to be known as his Aphorism:

'The truth concerning the passions, verisimilitude in the feelings experienced in the given circumstances, that is what our intelligence demands of a dramatist.' (Pushkin, *Sobranie Sochinenii*, VI, Moscow, 1976, p. 318.)

Gogol developed the notion of psychological probability further. In his *Notes on how to Act The Inspector General*, he enjoined the actor to go first to the core, the kernel of the character, before concerning himself with externals:

'The intelligent actor, before seizing on the minor quirks and superficial oddities of his role, must endeavour to capture those features which are *common to all mankind*. He must reflect on the purpose of his role, the principal, the primary concerns of the character, what it is that rules his life and continually occupies his thoughts, the immovable nail planted in his head. Having grasped this the actor must assimilate it so thoroughly that the thoughts and strivings of his character seem to become his own and never leave his mind for the length of the performance. . . . One should first grasp the soul of a part, not its trappings.' (Gogol, *Izbrannie Stati*, Moscow, 1980, p. 324.)

Caricature, pointing up, demonstrating were to be avoided. The actor, as he wrote in another context, 'must not *present* but *transmit*'.

The insistence on the primacy of inner psychological truth radically distinguishes the concept of realism from subsequent notions of naturalism if naturalism is defined, as Stanislavski came to define it, as the undiscriminating replication of the surface of life. Shakespeare and Molière are realist writers. Griboiedov's comedy *Woe from Wit*, written in an elaborate stanza form, is a realist play. Tchaikovski could describe himself as a realist composer. The task of the actor is to create a characterization which is both individual and typical, not merely idiosyncratic and contingent.

Pushkin and Gogol found their ideal actor in Mikhaïl Shchepkin. He insisted that an actor get into the skin of a character, that he should identify with his thoughts and feelings. The actor had two sources of material: knowledge of his own nature and observation of life. Writing to the actress Aleksandra Shubert on March 27, 1848, he said:

> 'It is so much easier to play mechanically – for that you only need your reason. Reason will approximate to joy and sorrow just as an imitation approximates to nature. But an actor of feeling – that's quite different. . . . He just begins by wiping out his own self . . . and becomes the character the author intended him to be. He must walk, talk, think, feel, cry, laugh as the author wants him to. You see how his efforts become more meaningful. In the first case you need only pretend to live – in the second you really have to live. . . .' (Shchepkin, *Zhizn i Tvorchestvo*, I, Moscow, 1984, pp. 199–200.)

By this attack on the theory of the consciously calculating, objectively cool performer advanced by Diderot in his *Paradoxe sur le Comédien* Shchepkin drew up the battle-lines for later conflicts concerning the nature of the actor's art.

In a short time the Mali came to be known as the House of Shchepkin, just as the Comédie Française was known as La Maison de Molière. He passed on his methods, training young artists, as was the practice at the time, by taking them into his home. His influence would have been confined to his immediate circle had not Pushkin bullied him, much against his will, into writing his biography. Pushkin drafted the first sentence himself, daring the actor to refuse to continue. The resulting *Memoirs of a Serf-Actor* became the bible of all actors whose ambition it was to achieve a naturalness of style. It charts Shchepkin's battle with himself. Trained in his early days in the prevailing school of rant and rhetoric it was many years before he could behave like a recognizable human being on stage. Stanislavski's own heavily annotated copy survives in the archives and the story it contains forms the prototype for his own struggle to master truth and banish theatrical cliché.

By the time Stanislavski began attending performances the Mali was already in decline. Shchepkin died in August 1863, eight months after Stanislavski was born. There was no school to teach his methods and all attempts to establish a systematic approach to the education of the young actor failed. Ostrovski's well-thought-out training programmes were shelved. The company drifted and standards fell. Nonetheless there were still some members of the company who had been trained by Shchepkin and continued his tradition. Some, like Medvedeva, were friends of the family with whom Stanislavski could spend an evening and ask advice.

The company was revitalized from time to time by actors of out-standing talent and none more gifted than Aleksandr Pavlovich Lenski who arrived from Odessa in 1876. At twenty-nine, with his good looks, elegance of movement and well-modulated voice, he was not only the perfect example of the romantic lead but, as a painter, sculptor and writer, a model of the literate, cultivated artist Stanislavski wanted all actors to become.

Lenski dealt in subtlety and nuance. He used as little make-up as possible, transforming himself from within. He looked for the inner logic of the character's psychology. Not until he had created a mental image of the character did he learn the lines or concern himself with external appearance. His silences were proverbial, filled with thought and inner action. His great gift was his ability to show the slow, organic growth of an emotion. When playing Benedick in *Much Ado About Nothing* he took a long pause before the soliloquy, 'Ha! Against my will I am come to bid you in to dinner; there's a double meaning in that.' A twitch was seen at the corner of the mouth which developed slowly into a radiant smile enveloping the whole face. The audience burst into a delighted round of applause before he had uttered a word. For the external appearance of his characters he went to paintings, turning for Victor Hugo's Hernani to Velasquez.

Apart from the leading artists of the Mali, Stanislavski drew his notions of acting from the foreign artists touring in Moscow, mostly during Lent, when Russian actors were forbidden, for religious reasons, to appear. In March and April 1877 the great Italian actor Ernesto Rossi appeared as Hamlet, Othello, Romeo, Macbeth and Lear. For Stanislavski it was a revelation. He was presented with a virtuoso display of natural talent: physical and vocal freedom, free-flowing emotion, clarity of expression, all apparently achieved without effort. It was with these performances in mind that he made his appearance at Liubimovka and began his notebook.

He prepared for his theatre visits carefully. The texts were read in advance – in the case of French classics, Racine, Corneille and Molière, in the original language. At the same time he was building up a scrapbook in which he collected pictures and sketches of possible models for characterizations.

No such energy and enthusiasm, however, went into his school work which remained a problem. In 1878 both he and Vladimir had been transferred to the Lazarev Institute for Oriental Languages. The grammar school had deteriorated to such an extent under a headmaster known as 'the human beast' that many parents were taking their children away. Besides, Stanislavski's father calculated that given the family business's connections with the east, a knowledge of oriental languages would be useful. Konstantin's Latin, however, remained a stumbling block. If he did not pass he could not go on to higher study. Even though his father promised him an English horse if he passed he failed again in 1879, but got the horse anyway. In 1881 he took the easy way out. He scribbled as much as he could on his shirt cuffs, prepared a number of cribs and cheated his way through. The notion of going on to Moscow University, like Vladimir, held no attraction for him. He decided that his formal education must come to an end and persuaded his father to let him join the business. His academic failure shadowed him all his life. He might have been comforted had he known that Chekhov had failed his school examinations twice. There are more ways for an artist to cultivate the mind than through formal education, not least direct contact with other artists, which Stanislavski enjoyed all his life. His was a creative, not a critical intelligence. He could nevertheless be intimidated by men of obvious learning and would plead ignorance rather than attempt to compete. No one, however, took him for a fool or doubted that he was a man of wide culture and refined sensibility.

For the moment any disappointment he felt was more than compensated by his sense of freedom. Liberated from his school books, he could do what he liked. He enjoyed the new role of the active young business executive and acted it out to the full. Once he had fulfilled his duties at the office he was his own man. He could devote himself to the theatre. His father converted two rooms in the house at Red Gates into a second family theatre. It was lavishly decorated in red plush and gilt and could seat 300 people. The house more than ever became a focus of artistic and cultural life with musical soirées and literary evenings. Stanislavski could make theatre all year round. He was now also a complete balletomane and suffered the inevitable infatuation with one of the Bolshoi dancers, Pomialova. This adolescent passion worried his parents particularly when on February 19, 1881, while yet at school, he did not come home all night.

In the following year Stanislavski was provided with another demonstration of theatrical mastery. The great Italian tragedian, Tommaso Salvini, gave an Othello which combined minimum effort with maximum emotional impact. Stanislavski was shaken and stunned. Salvini's talent obsessed him. He followed his idol around for days, striking up a conversation with anyone who knew him, trying to discover the basis of his technique. All he learnt was that Salvini arrived at the theatre two hours before curtain-up to think himself into the role.

Living a part was now Stanislavski's major concern. It seemed to him that the test of the truth of a characterization was the ability to maintain it in real life. While at Liubimovka the members of the Alekseiev Circle disguised themselves as tramps and drunks in the evenings and went down to make a nuisance of themselves at the railway station. The startled reaction of the passengers on the platform gave them great satisfaction and when the porters chased them away they knew they had succeeded. On another occasion they dressed up as fortune-telling gypsies and played an elaborate hoax on a visiting cousin who was completely taken in.

In the summer of 1883 Stanislavski decided to apply the principle of living the role to a production of Diachenko's comedy, *The Practical Man*. He insisted that the cast should sustain their characterization outside rehearsals in their daily life and maintain the relationships laid down in the script. The young actors found the task of improvising their own dialogue difficult at first but gradually acquired greater facility. Stanislavski undermined the value of his own experiment, for while he was improvising he was also busy aping Mikhail Sadovski's performance as Meliusov in Ostrovski's *Artists and Admirers*. His characterization, which was much praised, owed less to his own creative imagination than to his skill in absorbing another actor's technique and mannerisms.

Stanislavski found he could not build up a sound and independent technique by imitation or by trying to develop scraps of information about other actors' work habits. He needed a teacher. He had failed to make contact with Salvini, but when the German actor Ernst Possart came to Moscow on tour in 1884 Stanislavski called on him and asked for lessons. Possart possessed a fine voice and a graceful body. His somewhat bizarre method of teaching, however, consisted of making his pupils recite to piano accompaniment, using note values to denote the rhythm of the words. As Stanislavski's German was poor, the whole exercise was reduced to a farce.

Opera now claimed Stanislavski's attention. Thanks to the Bolshoi and touring Italian companies he acquired a knowledge of the standard repertoire – *La Traviata*, *Aida* (Verdi), *I Puritani* (Bellini), *L'Africaine*, *Les Huguenots* (Meyerbeer), *Le Roi de Lahore* (Massenet), *La Gioconda* (Ponchielli), *Carmen* (Bizet), *Lucia di Lammermoor* (Donizetti), *Faust* (Gounod) and *Evgeni Onegin* (Tchaikovski). For a wider knowledge of the Russian repertoire he had to turn to Mamontov's Private Opera, launched in 1885, which premiered Rimski-Korsakov's operas, *The Tsar's Bride* and *The Golden Cockerel*, both of which Stanislavski later directed. Mamontov also championed the much-criticized Moussorgski and rescued Chaliapin from provincial obscurity.

In January, 1884, Stanislavski decided that he should develop his vocal technique. It was typical of him that he should turn to the best teacher in Moscow, Fiodor Komissarzhevski, a leading member of the Bolshoi company and professor at the Conservatoire. Stanislavski, who had a pleasant, light bass-baritone voice and natural sense of phrasing, made a great impression on Komissarzhevski who saw a combination of dramatic ability and musical talent worth developing. The lessons went well, so well that Stanislavski toyed with the idea of an operatic career. On April 8, 1886, he appeared as Ramfis in extracts from Verdi's *Aida* given as part of a concert by pupils from the Conservatoire and presented at Red Gates. Plans were made to stage extracts from Gounod's *Faust* and Dargomizhski's *Rusalka*.

Stanislavski had been fascinated by Gounod's opera ever since he first saw it in January 1881. The *Notebook* for 1885 contains an entry, *Dreams of How I Would Direct and Play the Role of Mephistopheles in Gounod's Faust*; it consists of a description of the opening scene in Faust's study. The emphasis is on the realism of the setting, on the creation not of a conventional stage-set constructed out of wings and flats but of a specific room. The furniture and props are exactly described. Illustrations of the characters, taken from books, are pasted in, with small pen sketches in the margins. This approach to the problem of design owed much to Mamontov. All Stanislavski needed to do was to take a short walk along Sadovaia Street and he could see leading artists, scene-painters and carpenters at work on sets considerably more realistic than the drops, flats and wings in current use. Mamontov selected his designers among those painters who, like the Itinerants, were concerned to give a more accurate picture of Russia past or present. What applied to Russia could be made to apply to medieval Germany.

Stanislavski came to the *Faust* project, therefore, with clear ideas but they were never to be realized. He began to experience serious vocal problems. His voice gave out under pressure. Komissarzhevski was convinced that the cause was not technical but physiological:

'I am more and more convinced that all the problems with the voice stem from the pharyngeal catarrh. The purity of all sounds *piano* indicates that the laryngeal mechanism is more or less in good order but the catarrh impedes the proper exertion of the vocal cords. And that's a pity because you are a very gifted man with an excellent musical memory and an active theatrical understanding . . . in every rehearsal I saw that you had great gifts and for that reason we must hope for an improvement in your throat.' (K. K. Alekseieva Archive.)

Komissarzhevski continued to give him lessons and even when he cut down drastically on his work offered private classes between 6.30 and 7.30 in the evening. Stanislavski continued his studies well into 1887. But the hoped-for improvement did not occur. Stanislavski's voice was always described as muted and later problems with vocally taxing classical roles, such as Othello, may have had their roots in this basic medical condition. He did not help himself, it must be said, by smoking heavily.

Stanislavski's work with Komissarzhevski extended beyond pure questions of vocal technique. Together they explored the problem of coordinating voice and body. Stanislavski hired a pianist to improvise while they moved, sat, stood or were simply silent in time and rhythm to the music. Feeling that he had found a sympathetic collaborator, in August 1884, barely six months after they had started working together, Stanislavski suggested the creation of a musical-dramatic group, within the ambit of the Alekseiev Circle, where young people could develop their talents more 'scientifically'. Komissarzhevski agreed that a well-organized private group would probably be more effective than the sprawling and unwieldy Conservatoire. His own participation, however, would have to be discreet, given his post at the Conservatoire. The project had to wait three years before coming to fruition.

Stanislavski could not wait for proper training until he was able to start his own school. He was twenty-two and in a hurry. In September 1885 he auditioned for the Moscow Theatre School. He prepared conscientiously. While the rest of the family went to Liubimovka, he spent the summer alone in Moscow working on voice, diction and movement, mainly in front of a mirror. He would start at seven in the evening and go on well into the night. For his audition he gave a stirring rendering of the poem, 'Napoleon', and was accepted.

His experience at the school was short-lived. He left within three weeks. Any illusions he might have had about receiving insights into the actor's creative process were quickly dispelled. He was asked to copy his masters' interpretations, their manner of playing a role, their tricks. This was not the logical, 'scientific' training he wanted but imitation of the worst kind. The only person who might have been of real help to him was Glikeria Fedotova, a pupil of Shchepkin, and the mother of one of his schoolfriends, but she left the school a week before he did. The last thing he needed, in any case, after his experience of school, was another institution with formal structures. He was led by nature and upbringing to demand exclusive, individual attention.

Sergei Vladimirovich did not seem averse to his son's attending theatre school as he had been, earlier, to his daughters' going to ballet school. Doubtless he believed the whole idea was impractical. It would be impossible for his son to work full-time at the office and attend classes. Lack of time was, indeed, the reason Stanislavski gave for quitting the school.

It never for one moment occurred to Sergei Vladimirovich that his son harboured ambitions to become a professional actor. Such a notion was unthinkable. The status of the professional actor was even lower in Russia than in the rest of Europe. Actors, including the great Shchepkin, had been serfs within living memory, the property of the nobility, humiliated and beaten when they did not come up to standard. To be an actor was to be legally disqualified from any form of public office. The taboo against turning professional was absolute.

The future pattern of Stanislavski's life was, whether he liked it or not, being laid down for him. With his father head of the merchant class and his highly ambitious cousin, Nikolai, now Mayor of Moscow at the early age of thirty-one, the path he would be expected to take was obvious. He had proved himself more dynamic and able at the factory than his brother, Vladimir, who was altogether a softer personality. He must, therefore, take his proper place in society and assume power and responsibility.

He was soon caught up in the inevitable round of committees which, on the whole, he found tedious. Relief came in 1886, when his cousin invited him to take over as Chairman of the Russian Music Society and Conservatoire. He was duly elected on February 17 and immediately began working with leading composers such as Tchaikovski and his pupil Taneiev, and patrons of fine art like Tretiakov. Tchaikovski found him *très sympathique* and was sufficiently impressed with his singing voice to consider writing a one-act opera for him on the subject of Peter the Great.

The Society benefited considerably from Stanislavski's energy and business experience, while he acquired experience of the problems of programme-planning and the negotiations of artists' contracts. The Society's school also attracted his attention. He found its facilities inadequate and said so. In October 1887 he was invited to work out a scheme for improvement and cost it. The plan he put forward was accepted early the following year.

The Alekseiev Circle had, in the meantime, continued to offer its programmes of light pieces and vaudevilles. In 1882, Stanislavski made his directorial debut with something a little more serious, a production of Molière's *Le Mariage Forcé*, which he had seen at the Mali with Lenski. Stimulated by his studies with Komissarzhevski, he decided that the Circle should launch into operetta. Vladimir, who had always been diffident about appearing on stage, now came into his own both as a musician and a translator. The first work he adapted was Hervé's *Lili*, which the family had seen in November 1883 when the celebrated French actress, Anna Judic, was on tour. The rehearsal period was exceptionally long by contemporary standards. While Mamontov did not care much about the standard of acting in his productions, Stanislavski did. The play finally opened at Red Gates on February 18 and was well received.

The Circle had now been in existence for ten years and had achieved a level of performance which set it well above other amateur groups. Stanislavski decided to stage the Russian première of *The Mikado* which Zinaïda and Anna had seen in Paris and Vienna. Once again Vladimir grappled with the problem of translating the libretto not, it must be assumed, from the English original. As with *Lili* the preparation period was long. Work began in the summer of 1886 and went on until the following April. Stanislavski's developing ideas of realism came into play. He sent to Paris for costume material which was cut in the authentic manner. By chance a group of Japanese acrobats were appearing at the Moscow Circus. They became regular visitors at Red Gates, instructing the cast in movement, gesture and deportment. Even the giant Stanislavski managed to make himself look small.

The opening night on April 18, 1887 was a huge success and earned Stanislavski his first professional review. The *Moskovski Listok* reported that a performance had taken place in the home of one of Moscow's most respected businessmen.

'. . . the soloists . . . were so vital and witty that even the best of our artists could learn something from them. First honours must go to the beautiful voice and sensitive phrasing of K. A———v.' (*Moskovski Listok*, May 3, 1887.)

The absence of the full name and the use of 'K. A———v' was a necessary gesture, a clear indication of amateur status.

By the time he came to *Lili* and *The Mikado* Stanislavski had formalized an acting method based on a series of articles the actor Nikolai Struzhkin had published in the magazine *Teatralnaia Biblioteka* in 1879 and 1880. In the *Notebook* for 1885, Stanislavski notes thirteen 'aspects' which need to be considered:

1. What is the temperament of the role.
2   To what nationality or period it belongs.
3. The physiological aspect of the role.
4. The psychic aspect of the role.
5. Relationship to other roles.
6. Age.
7. Maturity.
8. What type (*emploi*) of role.
9. The most recent presentation of the character.
10. The author's intention.
11. Opinions of other characters concerning this role.
12. The most outstanding passages in the role.
13. The outward appearance of the role. (SS, V, pp. 83–4.)

Stanislavski was still thinking in conventional categories, of temperament (sanguine, melancholic, etc.), role-types (romantic lead, heavy, etc.); and still concerned with other actors' performances. The notion of individuated psychology, was, as yet, beyond him. Unfortunately he had little opportunity to put even this limited discovery into practice.

The life of the Alekseiev Circle was coming to a natural end. Fif had died in 1886, brothers and sisters were growing up, marrying, acquiring responsibilities for family and children. The Circle no longer enjoyed pride of place in their lives. Productions were fewer and farther between. Stanislavski's appetite for acting, however, was as insatiable as ever and wherever he could K. A———v appeared with respectable amateur groups, performing in plays of quality such as Gogol's *Marriage* and *The Gamblers*. At the same time a 'Mr Stanislavski' was appearing with various groups outside the family's circle of acquaintance. Many of the plays he appeared in were not only inferior but risqué by contemporary standards. They were thrown on, sometimes half improvised. Performances often took place in dirty and unkempt premises and with companions whom the Alekseiev family would have considered to be definitely *louche*. The company consisted of men whose only object was to get the actresses into bed and women whose virtue had long ceased to be a matter of concern to them.

Stanislavski had to keep this double life secret from his parents. The easiest solution was to take a stage name. He inherited 'Stanislavski' from another amateur, Dr Mako, a friend at Liubimovka, and an admirer, as he had been as a boy, of the ballerina Stanislavskaia. It was a safe name to adopt. Of Polish origin, it suggested humble status and was unlikely to be associated with one of Moscow's most eminent bourgeois families. Stanislavski used it for the first time on March 3, 1884, when he appeared in a comedy by the popular dramatist Ivan Krilov. His sister, Zinaïda, now married, was in on the secret as he sometimes used her flat to change costume when the theatre could not provide proper dressing-rooms.

The deception could not last for ever. One evening when appearing in a three-act French vaudeville, which included rather daring love scenes that would never be allowed at Red Gates, he made his first entrance only to be confronted by his father, mother and her elderly governess sitting in the large box centre. He froze. Any pretence at characterization disappeared. No longer a dashing dandy, he turned into a shy, respectable young man. He managed to avoid his family that night but had to confront his father in the morning. Sergei Vladimirovich greeted him with the brief sharp sentence, 'If you really want to act in your free time start a proper dramatic circle with a decent repertoire but stop appearing in muck with God knows who.'

It has not been possible to date this incident precisely, nor discover the title of the play in question but it was crucial to Stanislavski's development.

Stanislavski's father may be regarded as the major moral and ethical influence in his life. Sergei Vladimirovich was a generous, loving man of strong principles. Like his father and grandfather before him, he had a strong sense of social responsibility and disliked display, including self-display. Whatever one did, should ideally be done for others. It is perhaps for this reason that Stanislavski, who as a young man longed to play romantic juveniles, was never really able to play himself, or be a personality actor. There was a deeply embedded inhibition.

His father's words had their effect and in late 1887 Stanislavski set about creating the Moscow Amateur Music-Dramatic Circle which he had discussed with Komissarzhevski three years earlier. Its first production, Ostrovski's *The Forest*, was presented on December 6.

Early in the following year the Alekseiev Circle went out in style. On January 9, 1888, it staged a revival of *Lili*, which, like *The Mikado*, drew an appreciative notice in the press. Zinaïda was praised, as was Stanislavski.

> 'The gifted Mr K.S.A. was very good indeed, both as actor and singer, in the role of the soldier Antoine Planchard . . . and . . . especially in the third act when he really was a crusty old soldier.' (*Russkii Kurier*, January 13, 1888.)

The season ended well. He felt he was making progress as an actor. On February 29 he appeared as Freze in a production of Krilov's *Spoiled Darling* and, for once, took his characterization from life. One evening, while at the Mali, he saw a foreigner who was just the type he needed. He managed to change seats so as to be next to his chosen model, engaged him in conversation and then invited him to return to the theatre on another occasion. A dash to the box office resulted in two adjacent seats for the next production. He thus had another evening in which to study his companion's voice, movements, intonations and facial expressions. The consequence was a highly successful performance in a role that was to remain one of his favourites.

Spoiled Darling was also important for more personal reasons. In the cast was his future wife, Maria Petrovna Perevostchikova. She came from a respectable professional background: her grandfather had founded the Moscow Astronomical Centre, while her father was a well-known lawyer. To avoid her family's blushes she acted under the stage-name Lilina.

Stanislavski's last appearance before the summer break flattered his self-esteem. On April 3 he took part in an evening of excerpts which included scenes from the production of Ostrovski's *The Forest* which he had presented the previous December. Two stars from the Mali, Ermolova and Yuzhin, were on the same bill. It was a sign of his growing reputation that he should have been invited to appear in such company. He was able to approach his next venture with confidence.

CHAPTER THREE

THE BROAD PATH TO THE
TRUE WAY

Even as he launched the Moscow Amateur Music-Dramatic Circle Stanislavski knew it had been overtaken by events. In January 1887 he had been invited to take part in a semi-professional production of Gogol's *The Gamblers*, to be directed by Aleksandr Fedotov, the estranged husband of Glikeria Fedotova. Like his wife, Fedotov had been a member of the Mali theatre and trained in the realist school of Shchepkin. His youthful ambition had been to create a people's theatre, with seats at prices ordinary people could afford. In 1870 he had got together with a number of friends and drawn up a plan for a company, run more or less as a collective, based at a theatre that would include not only a stage and an auditorium but a reading-room, a school, a tea-room and a dining-room. He eventually found a venue in the new building created for the Technical Exhibition in Moscow. He had no intention of putting on the cheap farces supposed to be the staple diet of the lower orders and the proper repertoire for 'popular' theatres. He wanted to produce classic plays such as *The Inspector General* or *Georges Dandin* which experience had shown working-class audiences enjoyed. True to Gogol's precepts he demanded simple truthful ensemble acting from his company, without false declamation or exaggerated 'business'.

A major obstacle in his path was the state monopoly of theatres, deliberately designed to keep a tight grip on what was performed and to obstruct projects such as this. Eventually, after long and tortuous negotiations, the theatre was launched on June 4, 1872, with a programme which included *The Inspector General*. The choice of play was as much political as artistic; Gogol had once described the theatre as a platform from which to give a living lesson to the masses, a point the authorities were not slow to understand.

On July 10 Tsar Alexander II, who was visiting the exhibition, attended part of the performance. He arrived in the middle of Act Two and left in the middle of Act Three so that he might be in time for Gluck's *Orfeo*. On July 15 *The Inspector General* was banned. A confidential telegram to the Governor of Moscow stated that the play was not conducive to the public good. It did not fulfil the 'wholesome objectives for which popular performances had been started, namely to mollify and ennoble the people's temper'. The theatre did not reopen after the summer break.

Not wishing to return to the Mali, Fedotov had readily accepted an offer to stage foreign-language performances in St Petersburg only to find that the performances in question were not of plays but operetta. Despairing of even modest change in Russia, like so many intellectuals of the period, he left for Paris where he made a successful career. Now forty-six, though looking much older, he felt the time had come to return home and re-establish himself. He had no job to come back to, no offers from the Mali or any other imperial theatre. He would have to make his mark through amateur or semi-professional companies. Hence his invitation to Stanislavski whose name may well have been suggested to him by his son, Aleksandr.

Stanislavski has left no account of the rehearsals or the performance of *The Gamblers* which opened on February 6, 1888, but the impact of Fedotov's disciplined, rigorously professional methods was decisive in determining his own future development. For the first time he encountered a director with an organic sense of the structure and purpose of the play. Fedotov understood the dramatic function of individual characters and their contribution to the plot-line. He forbade self-indulgence and eliminated gratuitous effects. The company was unanimous that some way must be found of staying together though no one could see how it could be done.

After working with Fedotov, Stanislavski realized there could be no going back to old ways, that he could never again be satisfied with amateur methods. The Moscow Amateur Music-Dramatic Circle was now no more than a temporary group with which to work.

While, for the most part, Stanislavski displayed the characteristic Alekseiev caution when it came to money, he was capable of extravagant gestures when his enthusiasm was aroused. Then it was all or nothing. As chance would have it, 1887–1888 had been an exceptionally profitable period for the Alekseiev factory and he suddenly found himself with 25,000–30,000 roubles more than he expected. It was the first time he had ever possessed such a sum and it went to his head. In the spring of 1888 he decided to spend it all on an ambitious scheme, which would bring together artists of all kinds – writers, musicians, painters, actors – into an organization which would be known as the Society of Art and Literature. Not only would the Society become the focal point of the arts in Moscow, it would be suitably accommodated. He rented the Ginzburg House on Tverskaia Street and proceeded to convert it into a luxurious clubhouse with a large stage and several exhibition rooms. The problem of meeting year-by-year running costs once his money had run out did not enter his mind.

Friends and relations did their best to discourage him. Glikeria

Fedotova spelled out the difficulties he was bound to encounter but he attributed her warning to resentment of her ex-husband. His cousin Nikolai was distinctly put out when, in order to have more free time, he resigned as Chairman of the Russian Music Society. To abandon so prestigious a post in favour of some hare-brained scheme was non-sensical. Young Kostia 'had something wrong up top' and, moreover, he was spending much less time at the factory than he should.

Stanislavski, Komissarzhevski and Fedotov began drafting the statues both of the Society and of the School which was to be attached to it. As the Society and the School came under separate Ministries two sets of negotiations had to be conducted simultaneously. All three men were determined that the training the school offered would be systematic. Fedotov began work on a manual, setting out a rigorous, logical programme of study.

Stanislavski at the same time addressed the question of repertoire. His first thought was to open with an adaptation of Dostoievski's novella, *The Village of Stepanchikovo*. He had learned from Dostoievski's widow that her husband had originally conceived the work as a play but had decided finally that the material was too complex to be staged. He wrote to Dostoievskaia asking permission to create his own version and on March 7 received a favourable response. It was a bold and unexpected choice for an opener but his showman's instinct convinced him of the importance of making an impact. A Dostoievski première would be an event nobody could ignore.

While waiting for the script to be completed work began on the second play of the season, Pushkin's *The Miserly Knight*. Stanislavski was still basking in the afterglow of his evening of glory when he had appeared side by side with the great Ermolova. He had developed an entirely false idea of himself as a romantic actor in the Lenski mould. Excellent as Lenski was as an example of technical accomplishment and inner truth, he was a different type of actor altogether. Handsome Stanislavski certainly was – 'an Adonis' Knipper later called him – and attractive to women, but he was not a personality actor. His admiration for certain dashing, swashbuckling singers did nothing to help him towards a more balanced view. Before rehearsals even began he decided that the character of the Knight would be based on Saint-Bris in Meyerbreer's opera, *Les Huguenots*, which he had seen at the Bolshoi. His com-placency was shattered when he learned that Fedotov and the designer, Sollogub, intended him to play the part as a decrepit old man. Neither was prepared to listen to his objections. Both poked merciless fun at his conventional, 'theatrical' notions. It was, on the face of it, a surprising decision to ask a handsome twenty-five-year-old to play a crumbling wreck of a man, yet it may be that Fedotov, with his wide experience, realized Stanislavski's potential as a character actor long before he did himself.

Fedotov was not interested in the bundle of imitative tricks Stanislavski had acquired over the years and so began what Stanislavski later described as 'a surgical operation' to cut away his theatrical airs and posturings. Fedotov suggested that they spend a night in the same room together. There, in his nightshirt, Fedotov, who was already crooked and bent, with thinning hair, demonstrated how an old man moves. He outlined his interpretation of the play and the role. Stanislavski noted, copied and allowed himself to be more or less choreographed into the role, trying to achieve, by trial and error, a facsimile of what Fedotov demonstrated. Yet despite his earlier work with Komissarzhevski he could not coordinate his thoughts and actions. When concentrating on the physical aspects of the role, he was reduced to a mechanical delivery of Pushkin's lines. When rehearsals came to an end for the summer break in May he was no nearer to a satisfactory solution and the conflict between his own idea of the part and Fedotov's was still unresolved.

The summer was overshadowed by a family tragedy. In June Stanislavski was called to a small village near Samarik where his brother Pavel, who was suffering from tuberculosis of the bone-marrow, was seriously ill. On June 10 he died, aged thirteen. The emotional impact on the close-knit Alekseiev family was considerable. Stanislavski was deeply marked by the incident. Tuberculosis was in the family and, in later years, he himself had to cope with the illness of his own son, Igor, and finance his treatment one way or another.

Stanislavski's characteristic reaction to grief was to travel. On July 3, with his brothers Boris and Georgi, he left for Vichy, stopping over in St Petersburg, where he saw a performance of *Carmen*, and in Berlin and Paris. In Vichy, on the 22nd, he saw *Mademoiselle Nitouche* with Anna Judic, one of the family's favourites, in the lead.

His battle with *The Miserly Knight* continued. In a desperate attempt to get inside the role he reverted to one of his earlier experiments: living the role in real circumstances. He persuaded the proprietors of a château not far from Vichy to allow him to spend two hours alone locked up in its vast dungeons. The intention was to get the feel of the conditions in which the knight lived, to absorb the atmosphere. All he got was a cold. He ran the lines in the dark, among the scurrying rats, but the exercise seemed pointless. Lived experience does not transfer to the stage unless mediated by a creative, or a re-creative, process.

On July 28 he moved to Biarritz keeping up a regular correspondence with Komissarzhevski and with D. N. Popov who had been appointed as the Society's assistant administrator. On July 24 Komissarzhevski wrote outlining his ideas for the School and asked Stanislavski to find out all he could first about the rehearsal methods at the Comédie Française and, second, the teaching methods at the Paris Conservatoire. Which subjects were taught and how much time was allotted to each of them? Stanislavski moved on to Paris and spent most of August and September observing classes and attending performances at the Comédie Française where he was impressed, once again, by the restrained acting style, the economy of gesture and the use of pauses. He was equally and less usefully taken with the elaborate bows and flourishes which accompanied Molière's comedies.

Popov wrote on August 3 describing the progress of the conversion work on the Society's premises and again on August 8 with the news that the day before the Ministry of the Interior had given permission for the Society to be set up. Permission for the School was granted by the Ministry of Education on September 29. The Society's Board was formed at the beginning of October, with Komissarzhevski as chairman, Fedotov as deputy chairman and Stanislavski as administrator and treasurer. Departmental heads were nominated for each of the other sections, music, literature and design.

By now Stanislavski had changed his mind about the opening play for the season. He wrote to Zinaïda that he had now thought it best to put *Stepanchikovo* second and start with *The Miserly Knight* and another classic. *Georges Dandin* seemed the obvious choice. Two reasons dictated this change of mind. In the first place the script of *Stepanchikovo* had still not been submitted to the censor and was not, in fact, sent until October 13. It was presented under the title 'The Village of Stepanchikovo and Its Inhabitants. Scenes in Three Acts from the Story by Dostoievski. Adapted for the Stage by K.A.' Twelve days later it was banned. This was the first of Stanislavski's many battles with the Tsarist censorship, which had the distinction of banning or mutilating, either for political or religious reasons, every major work of Russian literature in the nineteenth century. Even Pushkin's *Boris Godunov* was not played complete until after the Revolution. A second, more practical reason, was that Fedotov knew *Dandin* well and it was better for him to start with that than tackle a new and untried script with an inexperienced company.

The Society of Art and Literature was ceremonially inaugurated on November 3. All the intelligentsia were invited. Chekhov and Lenski were present. Two days later, on the 5th, the hundredth anniversary of the Shchepkin's birth was celebrated with readings from his works and lectures on his place and importance in the development of acting. The next day the *Moskovskii Listok* reported that almost the entire company of the Mali had attended.

The school was already in operation, having opened on October 8. The atmosphere there was described as 'serious' and 'hard-working'. From time to time Stanislavski would attend Fedotov's acting classes and pass on some of the work he had seen at the Paris Conservatoire. He was particularly excited by exercises which required actors to play characters who were in contradiction with themselves – a queen who is, in fact, a beggar-woman who sells matches, a devoted wife who is forced to send her beloved husband to the war.

Yet while he was happy to pass on the knowledge he had acquired, he still had his own problems to solve. Rehearsals for the opening presentation began in October. It had been decided finally to present a triple-bill consisting of excerpts from one of Fedotov's own plays, *The Miserly Knight* and *Georges Dandin*. The role of Claudine in *Dandin* was offered to Lilina after Stanislavski learned that she had recently been sacked from her job as a schoolmistress at the Catherine Institute for offending against good taste by appearing in public as an amateur actress.

Fedotov was as ruthless with the Molière as he had been with the Pushkin. Stanislavski arrived at the first rehearsal with the whole battery of tricks he had picked up during the summer. 'My God,' Fedotov remarked, 'you've brought the whole orchestration with you.' Out went the bows, the swoops, the flourishes, the whole Molière 'style'. In its place Fedotov wanted something much more difficult, the simple, relaxed playing he had learned from Shchepkin. But Stanislavski, like the young Shchepkin himself, could only offer a loud, rapid delivery accompanied by a multitude of gestures. He was, in truth, producing neither the best in French acting nor in Russian. The most he was able to achieve, as he ultimately recognized, was a passable imitation of the role which Fedotov step-by-step demonstrated to him. He did not act on the basis of his own experience or on the observation of real-life models but on the basis of a reality mediated by Fedotov's personality and skill. What there was of himself in the part came, as was so often the case at this time, by accident. Right up to the first dress rehearsal he was caught between Fedotov's demands and his own natural inclinations until, while making up, he suddenly realized that his face looked silly. Everything then fell into place. His own personality was released and the part came alive.

The Society's opening performance on December 8 was a glittering occasion with an audience of actors, artists, professors and dukes. Stanislavski scored a great personal success, a success that would not have been possible had he been no more than Fedotov's puppet. *The Miserly Knight* attracted the most attention. The critic of the *Novosti Dnia* reported:

'Until *The Miserly Knight* . . . I did not know who this Mr Stanislavski was. When the curtain fell it was obvious to me that Stanislavski is a splendid actor, thoughtful, hard-working, with a great gift for dramatic roles.' (*Novosti Dnia*, December 14, 1888.)

The correspondent of the St Petersburg *Novoe Vremia* of December 17 admired his sincerity, his capacity to capture the right tone, his ability to wear costume, his elegant gestures and his talent for creating a real, living character. He was, the article added, although an amateur, 'obviously experienced and gifted and superior to the average Moscow professional'.

In his notes, Stanislavski set down his own reactions: a slow start in scene one, with too many long pauses, picking up in scene two, the monologue, with more fire and energy. But there was still the paradox he had experienced at his début in Liubimovka:

> 'It's strange, when you feel you are right inside it, audience reaction is not so good; when you are in control of yourself and don't let the part take you over, it is better. I am beginning to understand how a role moves forward. I have tested out the technique of acting without gestures (in the last scene there were only two). I know how to wear costume, I really feel that. My powers of physical expression are developing, I am beginning to understand pauses. Facial expression progressing. They say I died well, good body and truthfully'. (*SS*, V, p. 90.)

He noted the comments of the professionals on both the Pushkin and the Molière. Most, including Fedotov, were favourable and were able to point to passages where he had been technically and emotionally right. The next day he was the talk of the Mali.

Three days later he appeared as Ananias in Pisemski's *Bitter Fate*. The play was more or less thrown on in three rehearsals. Stanislavski just did as he was told although, like the rest of the company, he was convinced the evening would be a disaster. When he made his entrance on the first night he had no idea how to play Act One. The evening was nonetheless a success and in his *Notebook* he was able to point to real progress in his understanding of his craft:

> 'I remember that while I was acting I consciously considered where I wanted to hold back, where I wanted to pick up the level if it dropped. I watched the others. When it came to a dramatic passage I let fly for a few moments and got carried away. Only during the performance itself did I understand how to play Act One and I carried it off so well that I got four curtain calls. . . .
>
> The second act went well and without a single gesture. The audience was amazed at the calm and truthfulness of the acting. . . .
>
> The moment after the murder must have gone well. At least suddenly I pulled out a gesture I had never made in rehearsal and I felt that the audience went along with me.' (Ibid., p. 91.)

He was showered with compliments both during the intervals and after the performance. One enthusiastic critic called him a future Salvini.

He slowly relaxed into the part and began introducing spontaneous changes. On February 5 he noted progress both in emotional depth and technical control. The following day, at the barber's, he met the actor Yuzhin whose wife had been at the performance:

'He said to me . . . "Tell me, why don't you come to the Mali? Is it your family circumstances?" I answered that I had no wish to be an insignificant artist and that I dare not compete with Yuzhin and Lenski. "What do you mean? The more good artists there are, the better."' (Ibid., p. 101.)

Flattering as the offer was, for the Mali, whatever its shortcomings, was still the foremost theatre in Russia, Stanislavski was right in feeling that, quite apart from the social problem to which Yuzhin referred, he was not ready to take the leap into full-time professional work. It was one thing to come up with one or two good performances under the watchful eye of a demanding but helpful director, another to perform regularly and in competition with other highly experienced actors.

His technique was not yet secure and the battle with his romantic self-image was by no means won as his next important role demonstrated. In January the Society presented Pushkin's *The Stone Guest*, in which he played the minor role of Don Carlos. Prince Kugushev, who was playing Don Juan, was evidently not up to it. The production had somehow to be rescued and Stanislavski was asked to take over. He prepared the part carefully and felt before the first rehearsal that he understood the text and what was needed. He loved himself in the role, peacocking about in front of the mirror, with his sword and shiny boots, going through the entire part to see how he looked physically. Parading about at home did not, however, necessarily produce a convincing performance. He consoled himself with the thought that even if he was not very good at least he would please the ladies, a remark which he immediately realized said little for his integrity as an artist. The ladies did indeed love him and that, as he had anticipated, was good for his self-esteem even if it did nothing for his acting. He asked his brother Vladimir to make notes on his performance and also asked Fedotova for her frank opinion. As usual she gave it.

'She took me to task for being too emotional and too theatrical. She said that the last two scenes should be taken more lightly, that I should show fake, not real, emotion – in a word, I should adopt the same tone I had used in the scene when I was waiting for Doña Anna in the graveyard. That scene, to use her own words, I had played perfectly, just like the scene with the Commendatore.' (Ibid., pp. 87–98.)

Fedotova's remarks stuck in his mind and when he next played the part on February 16 he changed his interpretation completely. On his way to the theatre he decided that Juan was no longer the fiery passionate suitor he had been but a man fascinated by women and interested only in deceiving them. He presented this new reading without rehearsal and without telling the rest of the cast. Their reactions are not recorded.

A few weeks after his flashy first appearance as Don Juan,

Stanislavski made his breakthrough as an actor in Fedotov's play, *The Rouble*. He drew his characterization, as Obnovlenski, from his knowledge of the behaviour of his own class, the merchants and entrepreneurs of Moscow. He still had to wait for the dress rehearsal and the make-up for everything to come together but once on stage he felt that he had lived the role. He presented not the usual theatrical stereotype but a genuine, natural villain who could have been seen in any drawing-room in Moscow. He was in control. The pauses came easily and naturally. Fedotov realized that his pupil had finally found his feet, he was dependent no longer:

> "You gave me great pleasure because this character was your own; it was *your* creation. In other interpretations it was just me playing." (Ibid., p. 102.)

This new-found independence was demonstrated in his first production for the Society. In March he directed a one-acter, *Burning Letters*. He intended to reproduce the sober style he had seen in Paris, a style, which he assured the company, would be new to Russian audiences. He insisted that everything should be 'simple, natural, elegant and, above all, artistic'. The actors were not to push their voices. Critical and audience response was divided between the intelligentsia who were delighted, and the solid bourgeois who wanted the old, familiar approach. Nikulina, an actress from the Mali, was particularly pleased when one of the characters turned his back to the audience, an innovation unheard of at a time when everyone played out front. Stanislavski had noted as far back as March 1885:

> 'It is very truthful and life-like on stage when two people are talking in the doorway with their profile to the audience. . . .' (Ibid., p. 77.)

Reaction to his own performance was equally mixed but his reply was uncompromising: the actor's task is to educate an audience, not pander to its tastes for the sake of cheap success. There is a new note of seriousness in the voice and a new sense of purpose. The search for theatrical truth had become a moral issue. In a diary entry for April he noted his fear of falling victim to theatrical cliché, to routine. Yet what was 'routine'? What is the genuine theatricality? What is the difference between theatre and 'Theatre'? Was routine a particular, a conventional way of speaking and moving? Should there not be a distinction between that kind of convention and the essential, inescapable demands that the theatre, the performing space, by its very nature imposes and which distinguish it from real life? The problem was to transpose life, truth on to the stage without falling victim to routine but at the same time remaining, in the true sense, theatrical. It was a problem he had to solve if he was to make progress. He felt he had acquired a basic technique, a basic 'grammar' as he put it. An actor must be able to feel at home on stage and in front of an audience. He needs to be able to control his nerves, to develop self-confidence. This, by and large, he had done. But it was only a beginning:

> 'It seems to me . . . my work is only just beginning, work for the intelligence and spirit, only now the creative process is beginning to open up the broad path to the true way. This is the task, to find that true way. Of course that path is the most proper which leads to truth and life. To achieve it one must know what truth and life are. This then is my task: to study both. In other words, one must educate oneself, one must think, one must develop in the moral sense, one must keep pulling at one's intelligence.' (Ibid., pp. 115–16.)

Stanislavski's contact with Fedotov had done more than revolutionize his acting technique. It had forced him out of the confines of the Alekseiev family and their friends into a wider world. As prominent members of the establishment the Alekseievs worked within the constraints of the prevailing order. Their interest in the arts was, in the non-pejorative sense of the word, dilettante, for pleasure. But to go beyond personal pleasure, to take the arts seriously in nineteenth-century Russia meant coming to terms with the nexus aesthetics-politics-morality-ethics. In a country where the discussion of politics was not possible, where, indeed, the names of dissident philosophers could not even be printed, literary and dramatic criticism became the vehicles whereby fundamental social issues were treated. In evaluating a work of art the content took precedence over form, since discussion of content, for those who understood the code, meant discussion of the political realities with which the work of art dealt.

Fedotov was a member of the intelligentsia, that group of artistically, intellectually and socially aware people who came together, irrespective of social class, to form an élite whose task it was to modernize and liberalize a stagnant and repressive society. The word 'intelligentsia' had been coined by the polemicist and critic Vissarion Belinski and it was from him that Stanislavski derived his concept of the artist. Belinski dominated the intellectual life of his period. Gogol declared that his name was known in every village in Russia. Herzen and Turgenev left affectionate portraits of this difficult and choleric man who by the time he died in 1848 at the age of thirty-seven had set the agenda for all discussion on the relationship between art and society for a century or more.

Belinski had a vision of the artist as missionary whose task was to declare the poetic nature of the world itself. Contemporary literature, written in an age of science, had to abandon the realm of myth and legend and the subjective expression of emotion to address itself to the problem of describing the world of external reality as it impinged on human consciousness and experience. To describe the sun as a natural phenomenon, a star travelling through infinite space rather than as Phoebus' chariot driving across the sky was not to abandon poetry as such but to exchange one kind of poetry for another, more mature kind – the poetry of the real. The role of the contemporary artist was to present the world 'in all its truth and nakedness'. The drama, Belinski noted, was less able to provide those significant touches of detail and local colour which the novel and the short story could offer.

Belinski demanded that the artist see the general in the particular. He must find the truth beneath the surface but in imaginative not in political terms; for while science and art tend to the same end, the improvement of society, they use different means which must not be confused. An economist may, by the use of statistics, convince the intellect that the condition of a particular social class has deteriorated but a novelist like Dickens, by appealing to the imagination, makes the reader feel that it is so:

> '[The artist's] mind must penetrate to the heart of things; he must apprehend the secret motives which led the characters to act the way they did, he must understand the critical moments in events which make them unique, whole, complete, self-sufficient. Only a poet can do that. . . .' (Belinski, *Sobranie Sochinenii*, VIII, Moscow, 1982, p. 359.)

> '[He must not] be the instrument of this or that party or of that sect, which might be ephemeral and disappear without trace, but the instrument of the profound and secret thoughts of a whole society, the instrument of aspirations of which they may only as yet be dimly aware. In other words, the poet should express not the particular and the contingent but the general and the necessary which give the age in which he lives its flavour and meaning.' (Ibid., p. 362.)

The artist thinks and works in images, not in philosophical concepts:

> 'In the final analysis [the artist] will be guided mainly, perhaps exclusively, by his instinct . . . the poet is only effective . . . as long as he follows . . . instinctively, unconsciously, the promptings of his own talent. As soon as he starts to reason and embarks on philosophy he trips and falls, indeed he does . . .!' (Ibid.)

Charged by nature with a sacred mission to speak for his times and for people as a whole, the artist must, above all else, himself conform to the highest moral and ethical standards. He must not delude himself that he could live like a devil and write like an angel. The truthful artist must be a truthful man.

In Belinski's philosophy Stanislavski found a moral justification for his own passion to perform and ideas which were consonant with his family's sense of social responsibility and the ethical standards by which he had been brought up. The humanitarian and libertarian values to which he was now committed went beyond his father's notions of philanthropy but stopped well short of a revolutionary ideology.

By the spring of 1889 he had formed a view of the theatre and its function that was a combination of ideas drawn from Belinski and Gogol. So much is evident from a letter he wrote on April 23 to Lilina, three days after he had set out his need for moral education in his diary. The two were playing opposite each other in Schiller's *Kabale und Liebe*. The production was a great success and Stanislavski's dashing, elegant Ferdinand widely praised, producing fresh invitations to join the Mali. On the other hand, Lilina's simple, unaffected interpretation of Luisa was coolly received by the audience. This made Stanislavski angry. In an attempt to comfort her, he wrote a long letter on the mission of the artist in terms that come directly from Belinski. 'The artist', he wrote, 'is a prophet who appears on earth to bear witness to purity and truth. . . . He must be an ideal man'. His strictures on audiences also demonstrate a clear knowledge of Gogol's *Petersburg Notes* of 1836. An undiscriminating public, Stanislavski wrote, looking only for amusement or a chance to wallow in the mire of everyday life, destroys artistic ideals and reduces the theatre to a plaything. But a serious, thinking public finds satisfaction in the natural, the real. A noisy, spectacular success under those circumstances is to be treated with suspicion. It is no good looking to audiences for help or guidance if progress is to be made. They even begrudge paying proper prices for their seats. The best course for the true artist is constant self-criticism and dedication.

Few people were privileged to share Stanislavski's innermost thoughts in this way. Normally they were confided to the privacy of his diary and *Notebooks*. What he had written, in his own special way, was a declaration of love. Only someone who shared his ideals could share his life. Everyone in the cast of *Kabale und Liebe*, watching the way the two acted together, realized how deep their affections ran. No one was surprised, therefore, when they were married at Liubimovka on July 5, 1889.

CHAPTER FOUR

SAXE-MEININGEN IN MOSCOW

Stanislavski and Lilina spent their honeymoon in Biarritz, returning to Moscow at the end of September. Stanislavski was as fortunate as his parents in his marriage. Lilina was a remarkable woman, always supportive yet never offering blind adulation, offering criticism where needed and going her own way artistically if she had to. They occupied the ground floor of the house at Red Gates in an apartment that was comfortable but not lavish, a curious mixture of stage-set and home. The thick wooden door to Stanislavski's study with its great iron studs had been taken from Sollogub's set for *The Miserly Knight*. Throughout his married life there was a continuous to and fro of furniture and objects from flat to theatre and back again.

While away Stanislavski had been studying a new role, Imshin in Pisemski's *A Law unto Themselves*. The role of an ageing general, betrayed by a lecherous brother and deceived by a young wife, was perhaps a curious one for a good-looking young man on his honeymoon but it did allow him to continue his exploration of the movement of old men begun in *The Miserly Knight*. He studied the effect of the removal of dentures on the speech mechanism. He started to develop Imshin's imperious, autocratic manner. He had taken the precaution however of providing himself with a photograph of Samarin who had played the role at the Mali, probably because he was to work for the first time with a new director and was uncertain how much help he would get.

It had taken less than a year for jealousies and rivalries to appear at the Society. Komissarzhevski and Fedotov did not get on, each suspecting the other of receiving more favourable treatment, each demanding more time and money. Stanislavski bore the expense. In October, Fedotov resigned. His limitations as a director were becoming plain. He was excellent at dealing with comedy, especially French comedy, but he had no real feeling for serious drama. Riabov of the Mali was invited to replace him.

Stanislavski found Riabov less talented than Fedotov but no less exacting. He was stopped on every line, which he found highly frustrating. Riabov shaped and coloured the whole interpretation. The result of their combined efforts was a performance of almost unremitting grimness. When the play opened on November 26 the audience found the evening hard going but appreciated the actors' skill. Stanislavski scored a critical success. Riabov called him a 'gold-mine' and was reported by his son to have declared 'if you took Possart, Salvini and Rossi and rolled them into one they would not amount to half a Stanislavski.'

Others were more critical. Fedotova, as was her wont, poked gentle but pointed fun at him:

> 'We adored you, my dear. You played beautifully, my dear fellow. Such wild animals, these autocrats. Such stupid people! You know, I have a watch-dog just like that, he gets angrier and angrier and then suddenly stops. . . . It's not easy to play tragedy . . . I was so frightened! Thank you, my dear, dear boy, but watch your voice.' (*SS*, V, p. 566.)

Riabov had to agree finally that the performance had been all on one note.

How then, Stanislavski asked himself, is an actor to find light and shade within the broad lines of an interpretation? He found the answer to this problem, as it were, under his nose. In *My Life in Art* he relates that he attended rehearsals for one of the Society's other productions in which he was not involved. He found a certain monotony in his colleagues' work and he realized that if a role calls for a great deal of weeping you must do something other than weep. There must be a counterbalancing element. It was at this moment, he states, that he formulated his famous dictum: when you play a villain look for what is good in him, when you play a good man look for what is evil in him. Not for the last time his memory appears to have played him false. His notes suggest that he only arrived at this principle of opposites many years later when recalling comments Fedotova had made to him. The more Stanislavski worked on the role of Imshin, and the more he thought about the production, the more pedestrian it appeared. When the play was given again on December 6 he had redirected it completely.

Still determined to stage his adaption of *Stepanchikovo*, he had reworked it, changed the name to *Foma* and, on the advice of friends, altered the names of the central characters in an effort to disguise the work still further. The script was resubmitted to the censor on December 16, 1889, and passed the following January. Dostoievski's name, however, still worried the authorities, for although his early radicalism had long since changed to religious conformity, he remained politically suspect right up to his death. They insisted that the work appear as Stanislavski's own. Stanislavski refused to lend himself to such a paltry deception and, when the play was performed, no author's name appeared on the posters. Everyone, in any case, knew who the real author was. At the end of February Stanislavski sent the revised script to Dostoievskaia and received her final approval on April 10. He was less fortunate with his own one-acter, *Monaco*, which he had submitted to the censor at the same time as *Foma*. It was banned.

Stanislavski's final role of the season, Paratov in Ostrovski's *The Girl Without a Dowry*, obliged him to recognize finally that he was a character actor. Paratov is a Don Juan type, an obvious temptation for him once more to indulge in superficial swaggering as in *The Stone Guest*. Only by creating a character other than himself could he avoid the obvious pitfalls. To be a personality actor one must have absolute confidence, on stage at least, in oneself. He had no such confidence. He was not entirely certain he liked himself. His struttings and posturings were a front. His deep-seated natural reserve prevented him from exploiting his own personality. He needed the protection of another individual's identity and the mask of make-up.

> 'Deprived of the typical characteristics of a role I felt completely naked on stage and it was pure embarrassment for me to stand in front of an audience as myself, so shamelessly exposed.' (*SS*, I, p. 125.)

The highly-charged condemnation of the personality actor which accompanies his account of this role in *My Life in Art* is a product of his later crusading zeal rather than his thinking at the time.

His resolution never again to indulge in egotistical display was reinforced when in April 1890 the company of the Duke of Saxe-Meiningen came on its second tour to Russia. Stanislavski had, unaccountably, not seen them on their first tour five years earlier. They brought a repertoire of Shakespeare and Schiller: *Julius Caesar*, *The Merchant of Venice*, and *Twelfth Night*, *Die Verschwörung des Fiesco*, *Wallensteins Tod*, and *Der Jungfrau von Orleans*. Stanislavski prepared himself by rereading Shakespeare. He appears to have ignored Schiller.

The Meiningen company was a director's company. In March 1885 Ostrovski had recorded that he had attended a performance of *Julius Caesar* but he had seen neither *Caesar* nor Shakespeare but a well-drilled group of actors who were essentially nondescript and often cast merely because they resembled the characters they played. It was the crowd scenes which impressed. The extras were as strong as the leads. Here was an ensemble of clockwork precision. Much of the impact, however, came from the lighting and sound. Any well-equipped theatre, Ostrovski remarked, could do the same. But the imperial theatres were not so equipped and much of the asperity of his remarks may be due, in part at least, to his inability to push through the reforms he wanted.

Stanislavski later denied that the acting was as mediocre as Ostrovski had claimed but there is no doubt that the interest for him lay less in the performances than in the production style. The Meininger, for all their limitations, offered a coherent approach. Everything hung together. The sets, costumes and props were historically accurate and, while Ostrovski and Lenski may have found this concern with authenticity excessive and not necessarily theatrical, it was a salutary corrective to prevailing Russian practice where the same stock sets and stereotyped costumes were brought out time and time again. What the Meininger demonstrated was the artistic level even a mediocre group of performers could achieve if properly drilled and presented in productions that were through-designed.

Stanislavski went to the theatre armed with notebooks and pencils. He made sketches and recorded his impressions. He was particularly struck by the use of off-stage sound, as in *Der Jungfrau von Orleans* where the illusion of a battle was created by two or three actors with trumpets blaring in the background. In *Fiesco*, Act Four scene seven, he noted, the entry of each character was preceded by distant knocking, the bass voice of the sentry, a response, the officer's voice, stating 'Advance', the opening of the gates and chains being dragged over a stone floor. Once the character had made his entrance there was the noise of the gates being relocked. Dramatic tension was increased by the way in which the on-stage characters listened, in silence, to the off-stage action. The impression created was of real space, in a real world, in real time.

Of *The Merchant of Venice* Act Two scene four he noted:

'The gondolas run very smoothly on rails. One gondola sets off, is stopped by people standing on a bridge. It returns. Conversation between the people on the bridge and the people in the gondola. Characters appear, for the most part in gondolas. Finale – carnival. The people riding in the gondolas ask for money.' (K.S. Archive.)

Reminiscences of this moment occur, forty years later, in his production plan for *Othello*.

Stanislavski was fascinated by the personality of the Meininger's director, Chronegk. Autocratic, precise, he marshalled his company like a military commander. Rehearsals were orderly, beginning and ending precisely on time. Discipline was absolute. An actor who arrived late found that his part had been given to someone else, while he was assigned elsewhere. Chronegk drilled and timed everything to a split second. No variations were allowed. It was thus possible to cover up the deficiencies of the actors. They had merely to execute the set pattern. Seeing Chronegk look at his watch and begin work exactly on the hour, Stanislavski was reminded of his childhood when he would do the same to his piano teacher.

Much has been made of the influence of the Meininger on Stanislavski, perhaps too much. He never denied his debt, or the fact that his own method as a young director, working with inexperienced casts, was modelled on Chronegk, but the impact was something less than a theatrical Road to Damascus. What Stanislavski found was a working tool that would help him along the path he was already travelling. The vague ideas he had, the sketchy notions, the 'dreams' of staging Gounod's *Faust* were crystallized with diamond-like precision by the Meininger. His ideas were not so much radically changed as pushed several steps further. The task that remained was to bring together the creative, imaginative actor as defined by Shchepkin and Gogol and the organically conceived production as staged by the Meininger 1890.

On May 1 his first child Xenia, who had been born in March, died of pneumonia. The effect was devastating. In June he and Lilina retreated to Liubimovka, spent three weeks in Finland in July and in October went down to the Caucasus. They did not return to Moscow until the beginning of November 1890.

The Society of Art and Literature was now in serious financial difficulties. Subscriptions did not cover costs and Stanislavski could not go on endlessly subsidizing its activities out of his own pocket. All his 30,000 roubles had been spent. Some members, mainly the painters, had already left. They had objected to being pressed into painting sets for the Society's productions when all they wanted to do was play cards.

Stanislavski resisted the obvious temptation to wind up the whole enterprise and found a compromise solution. The house on Ginzburg Street was taken over by the Sporting Club. The Society's school and music section had to close but the theatre company survived and was allowed access to the stage on condition that it put on a play a week. This was a treadmill and far from ideal but Stanislavski was forced to admit that it gave the company much needed experience in tackling a variety of roles and increased their confidence on stage. The Society gave its last performance at Ginzburg Street on January 3, 1891. On the night of January 10 the building burned down.

Stanislavski decided the time had come to take full control both of repertoire and production. His first choice was Tolstoi's *The Fruits of Enlightenment* which the censor had just passed for performance. He approached the production methodically, casting with great care, preparing everything in advance, planning all the moves and drilling his cast in true Meininger fashion until they got it right. His account of the play dates from November 1891, ten months after the opening performance. In it he refers confidentially to 'my usual production method' which included close work with individual actors who were having difficulty.

Stanislavski was now concerned with more than the quality of individual performances. He wanted the production to show the pattern of social relationships. He saw three distinct strata, like the storeys of a house – gentry, peasants and servants – whom he wanted played not according to established theatrical stereotypes but truthfully, as in life. He did not find his own characterization as Zvezdintsev easy. While adept at playing the very old, he discovered, as Fedotov had once told him, that it is more difficult, to play a middle-aged man than an old one. The physical difficulties of the aged are more obvious and easy to demonstrate. The production was awaited with considerable interest. On January 29 the *Novosti Dnia* reported:

'The amateur Society of Art and Literature is preparing the play very thoroughly. They have already had ten rehearsals and intend to have the same number more.'

In the event there were fourteen or fifteen rehearsals.

The opening night, February 8, was a triumph both for the production and Stanislavski's own performance. In his review in *Novosti Dnia* on the 10th, Nemirovich-Danchenko said it was the finest amateur performance he had seen. Indeed, had he not been told he was watching amateurs he would not have believed it. Here was ensemble acting, *intelligent* acting. The *Moskovski Listok* of February 16 reported:

'A brilliant future awaits [the Society] if in its future activities it follows the path it has taken in its presentation of this play of L. N. Tolstoi.'

As to Stanislavski's own performance:

'This talented artist carried through his difficult role so thoughtfully, so truthfully that his whole interpretation emerged as a great *chef d'oeuvre* of dramatic art.' (*Moskovskaia Illustranovannaia Gazeta*, February 12, 1891.)

Nemirovich wrote:

'If I were the theatre editor I would devote a whole article to him as would many others. He put so many subtle details into the role. . . .'

In December of the same year the same play was staged by the Mali; writing to his friend Suvorin in March 1892, Chekhov noted, 'they say these amateurs played *Fruits* far better than it is currently being performed at the Mali.'

The Society's final performance for the season took place on February 18 and a fancy-dress ball was given on March 2. In April, Komissarzhevski, having no real function any longer, left the Society. Glikeria Fedotova agreed to become Chairman of the Board and quickly introduced stricter standards of professional discipline. During the Lent break Anna Judic returned to Moscow once more with a season of operetta at the Paradiz Theatre. In May, Duse was on tour with Dumas' *La Dame aux Camélias*, Shakespeare's *Antony and Cleopatra* and Sardou's *Odette*. The summer was a period of private happiness following the birth on July 21 of a second daughter, Kira.

In the new season Stanislavski fulfilled his ambition to stage *Stepanchikovo (Foma)* which opened on November 14. He found the production rewarding from every point of view. He felt a natural affinity with the role of Rostanev (Uncle), a man hounded on one side by a mother whose approval he cannot win and duped on the other by the Tartuffe-like figure of Foma who gradually takes control materially and morally of the entire household. In Dostoievski's grotesque satire it is gentle, mild-mannered, much-put-upon Uncle, who finally in an outburst of rage drives Foma from the house only to relent and readmit him to the fold.

The technical challenge of the role was to pull violent emotion 'out of the bag', with no build-up. The December number of *Artist* was particularly impressed by Stanislavski's skill in negotiating the double transition from a mild-mannered almost spineless character to a figure of towering animal-like fury and back again. The *Artist* also noted the accuracy of the sets and costumes which conveyed the Russia of the 1830s. It was better than the Mali.

Critics noted, though not with universal approval, Stanislavski's use of silences, or, as he called them, 'vibrant pauses'. At the end of Act Two he delayed the curtain:

'The stage remains empty for some time. A shaft of moonlight picks out the edge of a bench on which a forgotten scrap of paper is lying. Aleksandr snuffs out the candle and there is total silence, broken only by the distant sound of late-night merry-makers and occasional trills from a nightingale. Somewhere, far off, a night-watchman reminds us of his presence with his rattle, then once again silence falls after a particularly turbulent day, with the expectation of storms to come. . . .' (*K. S. Stanislavski*, Moscow, 1955, p. 514.)

The influence of the Meininger is evident but there is a significant difference. The Meininger effects were grandiose. What Stanislavski introduces are the ordinary, mundane elements of life, common sights and sounds which, Belinski had noted, gave prose literature its distinctive quality but were absent from drama. Stanislavski uses the theatre and its technical possibilities as an instrument of expression, a language, in its own right. The dramatic meaning is in the staging itself.

The critic Nikonov, writing in the paper *Razvlechenie* on December 1, noted that it was a pity that Stanislavski's talent was denied to the imperial theatres. His was one of many voices now urging Stanislavski to turn professional, but he was again made aware of the limitations of acting technique when in March of the following year he participated for the first time in a full-length professional production at a benefit performance of Nemirovich-Danchenko's play *The Lucky Man* for the actor Levitski. It was to be given first in Riazan on the 23rd and then four days later at Red Gates. The only amateurs in the cast were Stanislavski and Fedotova's son, Aleksandr. The rest, including Fedotova herself and

Sadovskaia, were almost all members of the Mali where the play was already in the repertoire. Although familiar with the play they set about rehearsal with a business-like professionalism, a commitment and a degree of energy which Stanislavski found difficult to match. He had never been required to work on a daily basis, maintaining a regular level of competence, controlling his imaginative and emotional resources at will. He tried to bluff his way through, pretending to understand when he was, in fact, completely bewildered. He confided his difficulties to Fedotova who told him kindly but firmly that he was a mess, a talented and promising mess, but a mess all the same. He had to improve his working method by more regular contact with professionals. She passed on one or two key notions that she had learned from Shchepkin. He must not work in isolation. He must look into the eyes of the person he was speaking to. He must never lose vital touch with the other people on stage.

As the rehearsal period drew to a close he became a bundle of nerves. He travelled to Riazan on the 22nd. He spent a sleepless night and could not eat anything the next day. As he reached the theatre his legs were giving way beneath him. As usual he was critical of his own performance: Act One was under-energized, Act Two sagged in the middle and in Act Three he had another attack of nerves and lost control. He was, as he wrote in his *Notebook*, not at all happy with his début with actors of the Mali. Fedotova told him that the beginning and end of Act Two were good. Other colleagues and friends, who were not necessarily uncritical, thought highly of his performance. As one wrote to Lilina:

> 'Tell Konstantin Sergeievich not to be down-hearted or to imagine he was a failure. Everyone I know is in raptures over his performance.'
> (*SS*, V, p. 576.)

Wisely, he preferred to believe Fedotova.

On April 3 he and Lilina travelled to Lyons partly for pleasure but mainly to buy new machinery for the factory. They stopped over in Warsaw, Vienna and Mulhausen, reaching Lyons in May. Stanislavski surprised himself when he discovered a genuine interest in the machines he was shown and congratulated himself on having done a good job as a buyer. He stopped over in Paris on the return journey but saw little of interest outside the Comédie Française and the can-can which he saw for the first time. He arrived back in Moscow on May 14 to find Aleksandr Fedotov waiting on the station platform. There was a crisis. A performance of *The Happy Man* was scheduled to be given by the Mali at the Civic Theatre in Yaroslavl. Yuzhin, who was playing Bogucharov, had fallen ill. Could Stanislavski take over? He travelled to Yaroslavl immediately and went on without a rehearsal.

The Society's new season could not offer comparable excitement. It consisted mainly of revivals performed for the most part in the Sporting Club's new premises. The year 1893, too, was a fallow period artistically. Family concerns predominated. On January 17 Stanislavski's father, Sergei Vladimirovich, died, and in March his cousin Nikolai was assassinated, gunned down outside the Town Hall, not for political reasons but as an act of personal revenge by a jealous fiancé. Stanislavski was now in charge of the family firm and realized that some reorganization was necessary. New plant was needed and this, given the poor state of Russian technology, had to be imported from abroad. In April he returned with Lilina to Lyons to look at the latest developments in textile machinery. On their return he negotiated a merger between the Alekseiev and another company, P. Vishnaikov and A. Shamshin. This did not receive government approval until January of the following year.

This unwelcome period of exclusive attention to business was relieved by a meeting on October 29 with Lev Tolstoi. Stanislavski was so overawed that he was scarcely able to utter a word. He felt that he had appeared totally stupid. This was a characteristic response to great men of letters whom he regarded with almost religious awe. And, indeed, to come into Tolstoi's presence was to encounter a mixture of a saint and a demi-god. Tolstoi is the final great influence on Stanislavski's views on aesthetics. In 1898 he published his essay, *What Is Art?*, in which he advanced the notion that a work of art must be immediately intelligible and of moral use to simple, unsophisticated minds, without the need for commentary or explanation. It must be 'transparent'. This led him to a number of extreme conclusions. Many classic writers, Shakespeare included, were found wanting and consigned to oblivion. Nonetheless the idea of 'transparent action' became central to Stanislavski's thinking and he consistently opposed theatre which revealed its truth to theatre which proclaimed its message.

The following February the Society mounted a production of Ostrovski's *The Last Sacrifice*. Reviewing the production on the 22nd, the *Moskovski Vedomosti* saw the Society as the one bright spot in an otherwise depressing theatrical landscape. The Mali appeared to be in terminal decline. Shortly afterwards Stanislavski was invited to make a guest appearance in Nizhni-Novgorod playing opposite Ermolova in a special performance of *The Girl Without a Dowry*. This was the most significant tribute so far to his talent and he collected excellent notices for a performance distinguished for its fire, precision and originality. No one now thought to mention the fact that he was an amateur. The word no longer had any meaning.

The Society, or what was left of it, still had no permanent home and during the summer Stanislavski began negotiations with the Sporting Club. Confident now in his reputation and his mission as artistic director, he was prepared to lay down a number of essential demands. In early August he wrote a long letter to the Sporting Club's directors pointing out that artistic results could only be achieved through efficient management and discipline. He required better working conditions than he had enjoyed so far and he also required respect. A performance needed to be accompanied by a sense of occasion. If the theatre was to be more than a bear-garden and fulfil its civilizing mission, actors, technicians and audience had to approach a performance in the right frame of mind.

'. . . can you play any kind of serious part when not a yard away from an actor who is trying to get into the mood there is a door creaking and his voice is drowned by the shuffling feet of members of the audience still coming in? Can one surrender to the mood when a step away from the people acting on stage there are drunken technicians stamping about, whispering or openly swearing at each other? If an actor cannot believe in his feeling under such conditions what can you expect of the audience who can see nothing of what is happening on stage because of the stream of people going in and out and hear nothing because of the shuffling feet and creaking door?' (*SS*, VII, p. 86.)

He detailed the kind of equipment he wanted and the conditions under which rehearsals and performances were to be conducted. He insisted that once the curtain had gone up no one was to be admitted until the interval, an ambition he was only to achieve at the Moscow Art Theatre and even then not immediately. The letter is an advance warning of what he would require when he had the requisite power.

On September 14, his son, Igor, was born just as Stanislavski started work on his most ambitious production to date, *Uriel Acosta*, a now-forgotten play set in the Jewish quarter of Amsterdam in the seventeenth century. It is the story of an intellectual outsider, Acosta, and his battle with the rigid mentality of his community.

It was a bold choice. The play was immensely popular and had long been in the repertoire at the Mali, with Lenski and Ermolova in the lead roles. Stanislavski knew what he was taking on. The Society's productions had often been compared favourably with the Mali's but *Acosta* would be a trial of strength. Stanislavski was now inviting open comparison with the idol of his youth, Lenski.

Work began immediately after Igor's birth and went on into the new year. The company was drawn from the worlds of business and education. Rehearsals began in the evening after work and went on until midnight. One observer described them as sheer torture. Stanislavski was now the complete director-dictator. Every word, every gesture was criticized, repeated, discussed. Nothing, not the most minute detail, was allowed to deviate from the prepared production plan. Thus, the crowd scene in Act Two:

> 'As the curtain rises there is a noise of high spirits. Everyone on stage must laugh 3 times. Those entering bow to the ladies. The gentlemen offer their arms to the ladies who place their hands on them near the elbow. Those entering bow to Manasse. They offer both hands. They talk to him. The conversation lasts 10 seconds. Absolutely no gestures. *Cue for silence when N. D. Popov and A. S. Shteker quit the rostrum and go off* . . . the crowd must be reminded not to stop talking all at once and to disperse on different sides. Music as soon as N. D. Popov and A. S. Shteker have gone. After 15, 20 seconds . . . Simon and Manasse come right down stage . . .' (*Uriel Acosta* Production Plan, K.S. Archive)

In order to avoid the somewhat mechanical acting of the Meininger crowds Stanislavski gave every extra specific dialogue drawn either from the script itself or rhythmically consistent with it. There was to be no rhubarb, rhubarb. Conversations were established in couples or small groups followed by moments when the entire stage was gripped by silent emotion. All gestures were strictly choreographed.

The first dress rehearsal was not without its comic side. When the cast appeared in costume for the first time they were a sorry sight, 'a motley collection of ragamuffins' Stanislavski called them, as useless as a row of coat-hangers. By 4 a.m. he had transformed them, thanks to a painstaking series of individual demonstrations, into an authentic-looking group of seventeenth-century Dutch Jews.

Acosta, perhaps, established the myth that all the props in Stanislavski's productions were real. Certainly Stanislavski's insistence on accuracy, his excursions inside and outside Russia to buy materials, clothes and furniture could easily give rise to such a notion. But the fact was that much of what appeared on stage, if only for reasons of cost, was created in the props-room. The 'authentic' goblets, which caused such excitement at the time, were made of gas-brackets and wood.

Acosta was the first of Stanislavski's productions to be analysed by the critic Nikolai Efros, who was to chronicle the artistic development of the Society and then the Moscow Art Theatre for twenty-five years. He was always very open in his criticisms and in the early years Stanislavski resented his comments deeply, suspecting him, without just cause, of personal animosity. Writing years later, Efros noted that the historical authenticity of the production went beyond surface detail to the very psychology of a closed Jewish community:

> '. . . you could feel the Hebrew way of life, dominating, swamping the personality, the binding force of centuries-old tradition of religious and national fanaticism.' (Nikolai Efros, *The Moscow Art Theatre*, Moscow, 1923, pp. 68–9.)

In his review in January 1895 he noted the terrifying impact when Acosta is torn limb from limb by an angry mob:

'. . . the fiendish delight of the crowd which cannot endure "exceptional intelligence" grew; passions flared, a single, wild emotion seized the crowd, thirst for revenge on this audacious madman. And when Acosta, unable to endure the shameful rite of recantation to the very end, ran back into the synagogue shouting that everything he had just been reading was a lie, the frenzy of the crowd reached its uttermost limit and toppled over into *delirium*, into some sort of collective madness. The crowd rushed at the man who had dared oppose it and tore him to pieces. . . . It was frightening to be sitting there in the theatre.' (N. Efros, *Artist*, January, 1895.)

The careful orchestration had not restricted the display of emotion.

Praise for the production was almost universal but Stanislavski's own performance was criticized. It ran counter to the accepted interpretation of the character established by Lenski. Lenski opted for the sublime, concentrating on the expression of poetic feeling. His Acosta was a dreamer, a man set apart, a transcendental being. Stanislavski, on the other hand, was more low key, concentrating on the human dilemma. Efros found this difficult to take and said so, laying the foundations of Stanislavski's dislike of him. This Acosta:

'. . . was neither a philosopher nor a thinker for whom the truth of ideas is above everything else and for whom contemplation of truth is the highest pleasure . . . on the contrary, before us stood a man who was oppressed by his own reputation as an outcast and did not bear it with pride, someone who even had doubts about the probity of his conduct – not his ideas but precisely his conduct. It was as though someone had loaded an impossible burden on his back, which he had to bear, whether he would or no, to the bitter end. . . . The finer qualities of the hero disappeared in such an interpretation; his halo was tarnished.' (Ibid.)

This 'tarnished halo' upset other people. Stanislavski was accused of creating a 'non-hero', of failing to exploit his own dramatic gifts. Other critics, however, responded positively:

'Most people were disappointed because for all the means he has at his disposal to make Acosta a hero, Stanislavski did not do so. . . . This condemnation of the non-heroic which Stanislavski offers springs from intellectually short-sighted attitudes, backward thinking where everything that is old and hackneyed seems great and everything that is rational, living, fresh is a failure and to be rejected. . . .' (S. Dudishkin, *Russkii Listok*, January 13.)

Fedotova was overwhelmed. According to Stanislavski's mother she wept uncontrollably during the performance. Afterwards she went up to the dressing-room, called Stanislavski out to her, and kissed him repeatedly. Nothing Stanislavski had done before had provoked such controversy. Earlier criticism had been concerned with technical competence not with basic interpretation. Now, with his performance in this role Stanislavski nailed his colours to the mast and challenged received ideas.

The intellectual origins of this new challenge may well lie in Belinski. In an article on the Russian short story, written in the mid-1830s, Belinski made a radical distinction between drama which is a lyrical outpouring of the poet's own personal feelings and drama which is dictated by the outer form and inner logic of the character's behaviour. He took as an example the long tirade which Karl Moor delivers, in Schiller's *Die Räuber*, over his father's body:

'Some people . . . say that a man in Karl Moor's situation, when he speaks to the brigands about his father, would have found one or two words sufficient rather than a long speech. I think he would not have uttered a single word but simply shown his father in silence. . . . In actual fact it is not the character who is speaking but the writer: this work does not contain the truth of life but the truth of feeling; there is neither reality or drama but a deep well of poetry; attitudes are false, situations unnatural but the feeling is correct and the thought profound. . . . Karl Moor's speech cannot be considered as the ordinary, natural expression of a character in a real situation but as an ode, designed to express anger. . . .' (Belinski, *SS*, I, Moscow, 1976, pp. 147–8.)

In making this radical distinction, Belinski set out one of the modern actor's greatest problems: how to resolve the contradiction between the stylistic demands of a rhetorical text and the obligation to present plausible, probable behaviour. Stanislavski attempted to achieve such a resolution with his still more controversial next role, Othello.

Othello had haunted him ever since he had seen Salvini play it. It was a hurdle he had to jump. The whole production was intended as a vehicle for himself. He wanted to shine, to demonstrate his virtuosity as director, actor and designer in a classic play.

He spent the summer as usual at Liubimovka, working on the production plan. A reading of Shlosser's *Universal History* convinced him that he should give the Cyprus scenes an oriental flavour as the island had been for so long under Turkish domination. When the plan was ready he invited a few friends down so that he could outline his ideas to them. Nikolai Popov registered it as an important event in Stanislavski's development as a director. He went through the whole play in a completely different way, not relying on the text as such, with quotes from important speeches, not providing a 'literary' explanation, but speaking in terms of the play's dynamic, its action, the thoughts and feelings of the protagonists, the world in which they lived. His account flowed uninterruptedly from moment to moment.

Stanislavski decided to create his own designs to ensure his concept of the play's dynamic was carried over into the action. He showed his colleagues a rough model representing the eastern quarter of the town. A number of narrow streets ran into a small square. Houses with flat roofs, two storeys high, were piled on top of each other. On the roofs were lines of ragged washing, tubs with trees in them, carpets and rush mats.

Just how this set was used is illustrated in the production plan for Act Two scene three:

> 'A shot, then a single cry, shouting grows, clash of sabres. All leap up, music stops. Noise and shouts. All run on stage. There the shouting grows stronger. Trumpets. Bells ringing. Soldiers run from the palace. Turks run on from the wings left and off up the street right. Noise fades.
>
> The stage is empty. Rodrigo runs down the street right, no sword, crying help with all his might. Cassio runs after him, carrying a sword. Iago who has hidden himself at the street corner near the turning on the left, stops Cassio, Montano overtakes him and also restrains Cassio.
>
> Another shot, trumpets, shouts off-stage grow louder. Soldiers run down the street right and hide at the angle of one of the houses. Left a group of Turks runs in and collides with them. A fight. At the climax Othello's powerful voice is heard and he rushes into the midst of the mêlée.' (Production Plan, K.S. Archive.)

Stanislavski went to Paris in August to buy books on costume and select material for Desdemona's outfits. There he had a chance encounter reminiscent of his meeting with the young foreigner at the Mali. Seated at a café terrace was a handsome Arab in full robes. Stanislavski engaged him in conversation and invited him to dinner. During the meal he was able to observe his guest's movements and gestures. He was even allowed to try on his robe. Back at his hotel half the night was spent in sheets and bath-towels reproducing the pattern of physical behaviour he had observed. Thus Othello the 'Moor' was born. In early October, after a stay in Biarritz, Stanislavski visited Venice where he bought rapiers, chain-mail, leg-padding and hats, and made copious notes and architectural sketches. He saw the interaction of canals and buildings which gives Venice its special character. The stage direction for Act One scene one reads:

> 'Curtain. Ten seconds. The distant chime of a bell or clock. A peal of bells. Five seconds. The distant splash of an approaching boat. Rodrigo and Iago enter right, in a gondola. . . .' (Ibid.)

The set, however, with its canal crossed by a bridge, owes as much to the Meininger set for *The Merchant of Venice* as to his own drawings.

Rehearsals began immediately after his return on October 16. The production plan was detailed and elaborate, with the text marked up in different colours in a code to which the key has been lost. Stanislavski was well aware that everything depended on the quality of the production and not on the modest talents of the cast. Busy as he was with other productions – notably a much-improved revival of *A Law unto Themselves* – and with his business and family, he needed quick results. Those who could not deliver the goods had to be dragooned into doing what he wanted. He had not yet acquired the ability to draw out performances from his actors. When all else failed he followed the old dictum: when an actor is weak, create a diversion. His Iago, although a professional, was just such a case. During one of his more important soliloquies he found himself practically unlit while Stanislavski brought on a doorkeeper with a lantern to distract the audience's attention from a tedious moment.

The play opened on January 19 and was received with almost universal acclaim. Efros commented:

'I do not offend against truth if I say that Moscow has never witnessed such a production of this Shakespeare play. The décor, props, costumes were distinguished by great taste, originality, living truth and, so experts in these matters tell me, absolute historical accuracy.' (*Novosti Dnia*, February 2, 1896.)

The twenty-two-year-old Meierhold noted in his diary on January 29:

'The Society of Art and Literature's production of *Othello* made a great impression on me. Stanislavski has enormous talent. I have never seen such an Othello, not even Rossi. . . . The ensemble is splendid. Really, every minor role lives on stage.'

Meierhold's positive assessment of Stanislavski's performance was shared by other critics, in contradiction to what Stanislavski writes in *My Life in Art*. He was dissatisfied with his voice which did not have the range, pitch and flexibility demanded by the text. The vocal mechanism gave way under pressure just as it had in opera and his obsession with this difficulty clouded his reaction to the whole performance. For his contemporaries, however, it was the deep psychological realism which mattered:

'It is a long time since I have experienced the aesthetic pleasure which Stanislavski provides at the beginning of Act Four, at the moment where he is listening to Iago's slanders yet still not believing them. As far as I can remember everyone who has played Othello, apart from Salvini, starts to shout at this point and plays the "hero". Stanislavski at this point was simply a man. He listened to Iago but his soul, the soul of a child, was still calm. He adores his Desdemona, he speaks tenderly about her clothes, her desire to please. . . . He is just a man. This is magnificent. What you see is not the way jealousy takes hold of his soul all at once but how passion, little by little, takes possession of his whole being.' (V. Marov, *Russkii Listok*, January 22, 1896.)

The shadow of Salvini certainly hung over the performance, his legendary restraint and his barely audible *andiamo* which reduced audiences to jelly. But another influence is discernible here, Lenski. Stanislavski had mastered his capacity for conveying the slow, inward progress of an emotion which only gradually expresses itself in outward, physical terms.

The judgement that mattered to Stanislavski was that of Ernesto Rossi who saw the play on January 22 and applauded warmly. The next day he sent a congratulatory note 'to the amateurs who discharged their roles with the intelligence and love of real artists.' Encouraged by this, Stanislavski called on him a few days later, in the hope of receiving more detailed criticism. Rossi cut through the elaborate paraphernalia of the production; this was a useful device to conceal the weaknesses of the cast but an unwelcome distraction when it comes to actors of talent, such as Stanislavski himself. Rossi was tactful and judicious, suggesting that Stanislavski was not perhaps quite ready for the great classic roles. He had considerable ability but 'there must be art. That will come of course.' Where, Stanislavski asked, was he to learn this art? Rossi answered, if there was no great teacher available – and there was none – he would have to teach himself.

Rossi had indicated the next crucial step in Stanislavski's development as an actor. In avoiding the pitfalls of personality acting, in opting for the 'mask' behind which he could hide, he had become nothing but the mask. He had developed a polished external technique and knew how to calculate his effects but what he offered on stage was a shell. Something deeper was required: the integration of the actor's personality into the role and the release of personal, creative energy so that actor and character became indistinguishable.

Stanislavski accepted Rossi's brief, elliptical comments without argument. He was much less accommodating with his friend, the distinguished French theatre critic, Lucien Besnard, who was spending two months in Moscow. On December 18, he had seen *A Law unto Themselves* and wrote a letter congratulating the company on a good performance of a bad play. He looked forward to *Othello* but the production proved a bitter disappointment to him. Writing on the same day that Rossi was offering his encouraging comments, Besnard criticized Stanislavski's interpretation as being too edgy, too modern. It was not in the 'tradition'.

Stanislavski did not answer the letter for almost a year and a half. When he did so he provided what amounts to an artistic credo, a clear statement of his thinking on the eve of the creation of the Moscow Art Theatre. At the heart of his reply is a long discussion of Hamlet's speech to the Players. This he sets against the 'tradition', which is no more than a miscellany of the most impressive moments in past performances by great actors, cobbled together without regard to the way they corresponded to the actor's own personality. A creative discovery becomes a prescription. Tradition of this kind provides a safety net for the mediocre performer – if he follows the rules he cannot fail – but offers no opportunity for the real artist to create afresh. It produces a dead uniformity. He had seen two famous French actors, Coquelin Fils and Leloire, in Molière's *L'Avare*. Their 'traditional' performances were indistinguishable from one another, and dull. He had, in fact, seen livelier, funnier performances of Molière in Germany and in his own native Russia, particularly by Lenski, because the material was created afresh to suit contemporary taste. Nature and an apprehension of human conduct must be the guide.

'It was Ben Jonson – Shakespeare never – who loved pathos, affectation, the picturesque and pseudo-theatrical effects, in fact, heroics. He made fun of Shakespeare because his passion was for everyday characters. In every one of his plays Shakespeare was carried away by the specific traits of a role but thanks to his extraordinary gifts he not only portrayed his characters vividly but they acquired universal significance. If Ostrovski in our time has been called the writer of the ordinary then so was Shakespeare in his. I am not for a moment comparing their talents, I am merely saying that they are very close in their attitude to art. Not for nothing does Hamlet say in Act Two, in the scene with the Players: "They are the abstracts and brief chronicles of the time." (*SS*, VII, pp. 114–17.)

Critics and commentators also come under attack. They, too, are part of this false 'tradition'. They smother a text with notes and glosses until it disappears from view. In terms too reminiscent of Tolstoi to be accidental, he insists that art must be simple, direct and immediately accessible to audiences. Shakespeare can reach audiences. He needs no apparatus.

'Shakespeare is life itself, he is simple and therefore can be understood by everybody. If you pick away at every word and look for every kind of hidden meaning then Shakespeare loses all his brilliance, his passion, his beauty . . . and all that remains is a philosopher and talker, who is only of interest to scholars. . . .' (Ibid.)

If the French theatre, which he admires, would jettison its false tradition and take a lead he would gladly follow for, he concluded:

'. . . it is the task of our generation to liberate art from outmoded tradition, from tired cliché and to give greater freedom to imagination and creative ability. That is the only way to save art.' (Ibid.)

He was by now convinced that if anyone was to save art it was himself.

CHAPTER FIVE

NEMIROVICH

Stanislavski was approaching a crisis. He was proving a more than efficient head of the firm. In the years following his father's death, as well as negotiating the merger, he modernized the plant, bringing in new, metal machinery from France. He also proved to be a model employer: at the factory he provided not only ideal working conditions – clean buildings and a large sick-bay – but a reading-room as well. He was respected and, thanks to the merger, richer than before, but it was all ashes in the mouth. What he wanted was theatre. He confided his ambitions to his diary as early as 1890. The entry for March 21 records the factory accountant's reaction to his indifference:

> 'The old man is astonished at the indifference with which I glance at the annual reports. "What's this," he says to himself, "I work the whole day and he can't spare so much as a glance. . . . What's it to me? I don't get anything out of it. His money comes easy! . . . If God takes his capital away then he'll sing another tune."
>
> Maybe he doesn't know it but perhaps the old man is right. I put little value on the gifts God has given me and I would honestly not be afraid to lose my money. If there were no money I could go on to the stage. I would go hungry, it's true, but I would be able to act to my heart's content. Yes, my work at the factory is pointless and therefore of no interest.' (K. K. Alekseieva Archive.)

His ideas on the function of theatre had taken firmer shape. Building on Fedotov's example, in conversation with friends, he outlined a scheme whereby touring companies would be set up in selected towns and would bring plays of quality to the surrounding area. His intention was to create theatres which would be 'open', a term which the authorities would find less alarming than the subversive-sounding 'popular'. Early in 1896 he discussed his plans with Efros and engaged in active preparations for the launching of a professional company and a popular theatre.

Pressure was now mounting on all sides for him to take the initiative. Russian theatre had to move forward and reach new audiences. Young actors had to be trained. During the 1890s a number of drama schools sprang up but no one could guarantee their quality. There was a movement in the making but it needed a leader. Stanislavski had created the Society of Art and Literature and had turned it into the most powerful and original theatre group in Moscow. The intelligentsia now considered that his talent, energy, and influence needed to be applied on a wider scale.

What was considered desirable by the artistic community, however, was not necessarily attractive to the family. Lilina's parents in particular were worried. Their daughter had married well in their terms but they were only too aware that the success of the Alekseiev factories also depended on Stanislavski's talent and energy. His brothers did not seem capable of taking real responsibility. If he were to devote himself exclusively to the theatre, business might decline, income drop off. What would happen to the family then? For the first time, too, there were tensions within the marriage. Although an actress herself, Lilina felt her husband's continual absences acutely and became ill. The children saw little of him although it was always exciting when he did go to the nursery. He would tell them stories from Shakespeare on which they would then improvise.

An enforced separation brought matters to a head. In April 1896 the house at Red Gates was commandeered by the government to house the German delegation who were attending the coronation of Tsar Nicholas II. Lilina and the family were sent to stay with relatives in Kharkov while Stanislavski took another apartment.

The separation was painful but gave them both a little space for reflection. In his letters Stanislavski seems to be pleading with her to accept the inevitable. Trying to sort out his confusion, on May 1 he went to see his old friend, the actress Medvedeva. He wrote to Lilina:

'As yesterday was a public holiday I got up at about 12. The house was empty so where would I go? I thought about it and thought about it . . . then I went to see Medvedeva. I stayed from 2 till 8, had lunch, drank tea and talked for the whole six hours . . . about theatre, of course. She wanted to get to the bottom of everything. Why were you ill? Was it perhaps because you were jealous of my love for the theatre? I wondered how she could possibly know. It turned out she has gone through the same thing with her husband all her life. Forgive me but I did confess to her that part of the reason for your illness was due to the fact that you see so little of me. Medvedeva understands how I am torn between being an artist and being a husband and how difficult it is to reconcile both forces. She understands this duality in an artist. Love for one's wife is one thing; love for the theatre another. They are two completely different feelings. One does not exclude the other. . . . I think she talked very well. I decided that when you return we'll both have a talk with her. It seems to me that, as a woman, she will understand you and, as an actress, will understand me. All the time, no matter what the subject she came back to the idea that *I have a duty* to do something for the theatre, that *my name must go down in history.*' (*SS*, VII, p. 98.)

In other letters he describes himself as leading the life of the typical businessman, dividing his time between the factory and evenings of boring conversation during which most of his companions got drunk. He would return home with a bad headache and a worse temper. Another letter describes a tedious evening spent discussing finance with a government minister. Behind all these accounts is the implicit question: is this the way you want me to live? By the early summer they appear to have reached some sort of compromise. On May 27 he wrote:

> 'I am terribly happy that you are beginning to understand that artists have to be a little different. That is their charm and their misfortune.' (K.S. Archive.)

Stanislavski's intention was to develop and expand the Society into a professional company and he planned the new season with that in mind, selecting plays which would give him an opportunity to display his skills as an actor and as a director. He scored great success as Matthias in *The Polish Jew*, better known in English-speaking countries in Irving's adaptation as *The Bells*, and as Benedick in *Much Ado About Nothing*.

In *The Polish Jew*, which opened on November 19, he gave free rein to his new-found love of lighting effects, and demonstrated his ability to play upon an audience's feelings:

> 'We must give credit to Stanislavski: he put all his directorial and artistic talent into making the audience experience "a night of horror". He kept the audience in darkness for half an hour – dark in the auditorium, dark on the stage. A beam of electric light picked out Matthias' face from the gloom as he stretched to his full height in the pillory. In the surrounding shadows and gloom a voice read the indictment. Stanislavski, with exceptional "realism" conveyed the agonising delirium of a man who is suffering a terrible nightmare.' (*Russkii Listok*, November 22, 1896.)

In the first-night audience was the German actor Ludwig Barnay, a member of the Meininger company. *The Polish Jew* and *Uriel Acosta* were both in his repertoire. On December 4 he sent a letter of warm congratulations for both performances.

The Polish Jew was followed in February 1897 by *Much Ado About Nothing*. Stanislavski's dismissive comment on his own Benedick – that it had been liked only by 'nice, uncritical schoolgirls' – is belied by the reviews:

> 'The soliloquy at the end of the second act when Benedick changes his mind about love and marriage was simply a masterpiece and could serve by itself alone as a clear model of Stanislavski's talent for

economy.' (*Russki Listok*, February 13, 1897.)

On February 15 he met Anton Chekhov. He had been playing *The Miserly Knight* as part of a literary-musical evening. After the performance:

> 'A[nton] P[avlovich] came up to me and thanked me . . . not for *The Miserly Knight* but for my part . . . in his play *The Bear* which I had performed not long before. "Listen, they say you acted wonderfully in my play. I didn't see it, you understand. I'm just an author . . . someone to chuck out."' (*SS*, V, p. 615.)

The next day the two men participated in an open discussion on creating a popular theatre, which was reported in the *Russkaia Misl*. In February and March, with a group of other artists, including Ermolova, Stanislavski set up yet another literary-artistic circle. At the same time he was heavily involved in organizing the first all-Russian conference on the theatre.

His future intentions were still vague when he and Lilina went abroad in the middle of April, and they would have remained so had he not been propelled into action by two letters which were waiting for him when he went to Red Gates on June 18. They were from a man he hardly knew but who had desperately been trying to contact him, Vladimir Ivanovich Nemirovich-Danchenko. The first, written on June 7 from his wife's estate in the country, was brief:

> 'Dear Konstantin Sergeievich,
> Are you in Moscow? I drafted a huge long letter to you but as I shall soon be in Moscow myself I shan't send it. . . .
> If this letter finds you away from Moscow I will send the longer one I wrote earlier. But where?
> I will be in Moscow between June 21 and 26.' (*Izbranie Pisma*, I, p. 89.)

The second, dated June 17 when Nemirovich tried again, was written on the back of a visiting card:

> 'Did you get my letter?
> I hear you will be in Moscow tomorrow, Wednesday. I will be at the Slavianski Bazar at one o'clock – could we meet? Or let me know at the enclosed address when and where.' (Ibid., p. 90.)

Stanislavski replied by telegram, suggesting lunch at 2 o'clock on the 22nd.

Stanislavski knew of Nemirovich-Danchenko as a successful dramatist and critic whose plays were in the repertoire at the Mali and who had twice won the coveted Griboiedov Prize for Play of the Year, the second time in competition with Chekhov's *Seagull*, a judgement which Nemirovich described as senseless.

Nemirovich came from a military family and his brother Vasili had a considerable reputation as a war correspondent. He did not enjoy the benefit of private means, and earned his living mostly as a professional writer and critic. He was an elected member of the Russian Society of Authors and of the Russian Society of Psychology and had been appointed to the Repertoire Committee of the Imperial Theatres which brought him into close contact with the Mali. In 1891 he had taken over the drama department of the Philharmonic School where he gave courses in actor training that were as rigorous and intelligent as anything Stanislavski could have wished. Among his pupils were Meierhold and Olga Knipper.

Nemirovich, too, was at a turning-point in his career. He had virtually ceased to write plays. He had seen enough at the Mali to make him realize that radical changes were necessary. Year after year he presented programmes of reform but always came up against the same bureaucratic inertia. He, too, was committed to the notion of popular theatre. In 1897, shortly before contacting Stanislavski, he had submitted two schemes to the government, the first for the creation of an 'opera' theatre, the second for the total reorganization of the Mali. His hope was that one or the other would result in his being given an official appointment. He was in Moscow to press his case.

There was no harm, however, in killing two birds with one stone. If he could make no headway with the authorities it might be possible to create a privately backed theatre. He already had a scheme to form a company from his ex-pupils and take it to the provinces. He was aware – as who was not? – from gossip and the press of Stanislavski's plans for a professional theatre. He was also aware that nothing had yet been decided. Might not the two of them work in collaboration?

Later correspondence, when the two men were no longer on good terms, reveals what Nemirovich meant by 'collaboration'. As a writer he believed in the absolute supremacy of the dramatist. Theatre consisted in the translation of the author's intentions into stage terms. Unfortunately he was, by his own admission, a conservative not to say pedestrian director. His productions were worthy rather than inspired. He did, on the other hand, possess an outstanding ability to analyse a play and reveal its hidden meanings. No one could rival him in this field and successive generations of young directors benefited from his teaching. Stanislavski, on his side, possessed the directorial flair Nemirovich lacked. He had demonstrated his skill in creating vivid theatrical images, in selecting significant detail. What Nemirovich was looking for was not only someone who would put up the money but someone who would give his literary insights theatrical life. Such was his hidden agenda for the meeting on June 22.

Nemirovich was not certain what sort of man he was lunching with. Would he be confronted by an egocentric 'star', a would-be *monstre sacré*, who would insist on playing every leading role, on directing everything, on hogging the limelight? Stanislavski had to pass a character test. Nemirovich's description, in his autobiography, of his approach to the meeting is unconsciously patronizing in tone. He portrays himself as the practised professional giving the gifted amateur the once-over. At all events his fears proved groundless. The person he encountered was both modest and distinguished, no over-resonant actor's voice, no extravagant gestures, but an elegant, graceful, quiet-spoken man who made no attempt to mark himself off from the crowd.

Stanislavski had no agenda, hidden or otherwise, but he, too, needed more solid support for his schemes. No one in his immediate circle, for all their goodwill, possessed the expertise to help him launch a professional company. There had been talk, a great deal of it, but nothing concrete had materialized. Stanislavski later acknowledged that without Nemirovich he would have had a far greater struggle, for, quite apart from his literary gifts, Nemirovich had a firm sense of theatrical management. He understood budgets, schedules and deadlines – some said he was obsessed by them. Stanislavski had never been obliged to apply his own industrial management disciplines to his artistic life. He had only been concerned to get the production right, whatever the time-scale, and had financed his indulgences out of his pocket. A commercial theatre would require tighter control.

The two men met, therefore, on the best possible basis: common need. They possessed complementary skills; they shared the common views and aspirations of the intelligentsia, yet these factors alone cannot explain the extraordinary chemistry of that meeting which, having almost failed to happen, became one of the great legends of theatrical history.

They lunched in a private room so as not to be disturbed. The vast cavern of the main dining-room of the Slavianski Bazar is not the ideal place for a serious conversation. Their talk began at 2 o'clock on June 22 and ended at 8 o'clock on the morning of the 23rd over breakfast at Liubimovka. In those eighteen hours they agreed to found an Art Theatre with seats at popular prices; they agreed to create an ensemble which would place artistic aims above individual vanity. They went through the list of members of the Society and of Nemirovich's pupils at the Philharmonic School and selected those they considered capable of meeting the high ideals they had set. More importantly, they agreed a fundamental division of authority. Nemirovich was to have the last word in all matters concerning repertoire, Stanislavski was to have final control over all matters relating to actual staging. Each had a veto. This arrangement seemed to put each man's particular gifts to their best use. Before parting they agreed that it would take a year to set up the new company adequately. The euphoria of this first meeting left essential questions unresolved. Each man left Moscow for the summer –

Nemirovich for Yalta, Stanislavski for Liubimovka – assuming that the new company would be set up on his terms, but serious divergences of opinion on basic issues surfaced almost immediately and had to be resolved by letter across the length of Russia.

On July 12, Nemirovich sent a relaxed letter, written in pencil for speed and convenience, giving an account of meetings he had held, many of them encouraging, and of actors, seasoned professionals, he thought they could attract. Practical as ever, he gave an outline of possible takings and of the salaries they might have to offer. He wanted a provincial launch. His feeling was that a tour in the provinces would weld the new company together and bring it to a point where it could confront a Moscow audience by the 1899–1900 season. His assumption was that the theatre, in the initial stages at least, would be financed and owned by Stanislavski personally. It was important to Nemirovich that it should be kept private, with Stanislavski as the only shareholder. Stanislavski would control the company and, by implication, he would control Stanislavski. If extra finance was needed shareholders could be brought in at a later stage, say after three years, when policy was firmly fixed. It was natural for Nemirovich to assume that given the Alekseiev family assets, some 8,000,000 roubles, Stanislavski would, like his cousin Mamontov, want to create his own private company.

Stanislavski had his own ideas and, in his reply of the 19th, said no to both proposals. Success in the provinces, he assured Nemirovich, would cut no ice in Moscow. His plan was to expand the Society bringing in new blood. He had reached a tentative agreement with Vladimir Schulz, who arranged tours by foreign artists, to share the use of the Paradiz theatre, which had recently been renovated and modernized. Any productions he mounted would alternate with seasons by Réjane, Coquelin and the Lessing Theatre. It would thus be possible to demonstrate the potential quality of the projected new theatre to a sceptical Moscow public in a prestigious context.

He made it clear that the one thing he would not or could not do was create a privately owned theatre. His reasons were twofold. First, the Alekseiev fortune was not his to dispose of as he wished. He only had 300,000 roubles of his own. (Much of this was in fact tied up in trust funds.) He did not, he told Nemirovich, have the right to speculate with his family's future. It may be, although it is impossible to prove, that the family, particularly Lilina's parents, having seen vast sums poured into the loss-making Society of Art and Literature, made it a condition of their agreement to his turning professional that only a strictly limited portion of the Alekseiev capital be involved. Secondly, he could all too easily anticipate the criticisms that would be levelled against him if he did set up a private company; it would immediately be labelled as a money-grubbing exercise, the establishment of yet another Alekseiev monopoly. A public company, on the other hand, would be seen as a philanthropic, educational undertaking. In fact, apart from his initial investment of 10,000 roubles, Stanislavski never put any extra money into the theatre or attempted to rescue it from its financial difficulties.

Nemirovich was not to be put off. Replying on August 2, he expressed the fear that a limited company could all too easily degenerate into a purely commercial affair; shares could change hands and shareholders with an eye only to profit could start dictating artistic policy; a company controlled by Stanislavski would remain faithful to its original, educational ideas. 'The more I think about it,' Nemirovich wrote, 'the more I incline to an open and not just simply an art theatre.'

Stanislavski, in his next letter, spelled out the facts of bourgeois life more clearly:

'... Moscow society will neither trust in a private undertaking nor take it seriously, or if it does, it will be too late, when our pockets are empty and the doors of the theatre have been boarded up. Moscow will label my participation in a private scheme – look at the attitude to Mamontov – as petty commercial tyranny. But the creation of a limited company, and what is more a popular-price theatre, will endow me with the merit – that is what they'll call it – of being an educator, of serving an artistic and educational charity. I know the businessmen of Moscow. In the first instance they won't go to the theatre *on principle* and in the second, *on pure principle*, they will stump up a pile of money to support *something they have created*.

I learned recently that Mamontov has drawn up statutes for a popular-price opera-dramatic theatre and wants to submit them to the Ministry. Needless to say I lost no time in engineering an apparently chance meeting with him. He has promised to send the statutes to me in the next few days. It would seem that a public company is the latest thing.' (*MATL*, No. 6.)

Stanislavski was wise to be cautious. Within a year Mamontov, who had excited both envy and enmity by his success, was jailed on trumped-up charges of fraudulent share dealing and lost his entire fortune. As to a provincial launch the answer was still negative. He had spent ten years creating a company and his intention was to build on it. It would, in any case be impossible for him to abandon his business for the whole of the winter; he might just manage it for a public company but certainly not for a private one, with all the financial risks that involved.

Stanislavski's polite but firm ultimatum settled the matter. Nemirovich knew that without Stanislavski the new theatre was doomed before it started. But his anxieties ran deep and were never really assuaged. He could never rid himself of the fear that Stanislavski would be won over to the commercial ideas and values of his class, and became inordinately suspicious of anyone, however good their motives, who appeared to be gaining too much financial control. Thus, while having to accept the company Stanislavski had created, his entire strategy, over twenty years or more, was based on the necessity to acquire management control to protect his ideas.

On their return to Moscow both men canvassed support from potential investors. Even Stanislavski had underestimated the hostility of the possible reaction from the business community. The Society was one thing – it was part of respectable Moscow life – a new professional theatre, quite another. Attitudes were either frigid, ironic or openly hostile. The alternative was to apply for government money. On December 31 Stanislavski went to see Prince Golitsin, Chairman of the City Council, with a request for an annual grant of 15,000 roubles. Nemirovich made a follow-up visit on January 5, 1898. Since the notion was to provide good theatre at popular prices people could afford, the matter was referred to the Welfare Committee.

If the mills of God grind slow, the mills of the Moscow City Council ground still slower and by the time the inevitable refusal was received the 'Art Theatre' had been open for a year. Nemirovich used his connections in the Philharmonic Society to persuade a number of its directors to put up money, mainly small sums of 1000 or 2000 roubles. Similar sums were provided by members of the board of the Society of Art and Literature. The largest single investor was Savva Timofeievich Morozov who subscribed 10,000 roubles. The Morozov family, whose rags-to-riches story rivalled the Alekseievs', had interests in textiles, railways and banking. Savva Morozov had taken a degree in chemistry and followed this by a period of studies in England. Despite his thickset, rough, Tartar appearance, he was a man of great sensitivity and understanding. Few, meeting him, would have guessed that he was a depressive. His one condition for investing such a large sum was that he should always be the principal shareholder. This aroused Nemirovich's hostility. It seemed to confirm his earlier fears of an eventual surrender to commercial values, but he had no choice but to accept since Morozov was offering one third of the total launch capital of 28,000 roubles, slightly less than Stanislavski had personally invested in the Society of Art and Literature.

On April 19, 1898 Stanislavski assumed his role as Principal Director of the Association for the Establishment of the Moscow Open Theatre. On April 23, the *Russkie Vedomosti* published the names of the eleven shareholders. Stanislavski also signed a lease for the Hermitage Theatre on Carriage Row. His intention was also to present plays at the Sporting Club, thus preserving the connection with the Society.

The repertoire had yet to be decided and here again there was a wide divergence of views. Stanislavski was, on the whole, drawn to the classical or traditional repertoire. His instinct was to hand on the legacy of the past to the broad mass of the people and he tended to select plays which he had either seen in Moscow or on his travels. The list he put forward consisted either of works in the Society's current repertoire – *The Fruits of Enlightenment, Foma, Uriel Acosta, Much Ado About Nothing, The Bells, The Inspector General* – or which had been considered for future presentation – Aleksei Tolstoi's *Tsar Fiodor Ioannovich*, Goldoni's *La Locandiera*, Pushkin's *Boris Godunov*, Gogol's *Marriage* and Shakespeare's *The Taming of the Shrew*. He was to put on Lev Tolstoi's *The Power of Darkness*. Nemirovich, on the other hand, was much more drawn to the contemporary repertoire. If it were possible, he wrote to Stanislavski on June 21, 1898, he would only do modern plays. Unfortunately there were not enough good ones to fill a season. What did not interest him was what he called 'great men's trivia'. These included *Much Ado About Nothing, Twelfth Night, Taming of the Shrew* and the plays of Molière. What he wanted was a mixture of classic plays of evident artistic merit. The light comedies and vaudevilles Stanislavski wanted to introduce would, to his mind, do nothing to enhance the reputation of a theatre dedicated to serious drama. He also took the opportunity to make it quite clear when and where he would tolerate directorial licence. Stanislavski could do what he liked with the 'trivia', let his imagination run riot, as he showed every intention of doing, but:

'. . . it is essential from my point of view that it be taken as read that for a modern theatre with pretentions to any sort of significance, the plays of Hauptmann and even the less talented Ibsen are more serious and profound than the trivia by poets of genius like Shakespeare and Molière. For that reason I very much want to include in the repertoire *The Sunken Bell, Hannele,* and even *Lady from the Sea, Ghosts, Doll's House,* etc. . . .' (Nemirovich-Danchenko, *Iz., Pis.,* I, Moscow, 1979, p. 120.)

There was to be no nonsense here.

The long list of suggestions the two men threw at each other were whittled down gradually to a reasonable-sized repertoire. Nemirovich managed to scotch the idea of using the Sporting Club when, in June, he worked out the performance schedules and decided it was impractical to try and run two theatres simultaneously. It was no great loss to him. The Sporting Club meant a backward look to the Society of Art and Literature and he wanted Stanislavski to sever all his earlier connections in favour of their new partnership. In any case, as far as the members of the Society of Art and Literature were concerned, he had no high opinion of their talents. It was Stanislavski and Stanislavski alone that he wanted. As he wrote, 'You *are* the Society.'

Nonetheless, the Society served its purpose. Stanislavski amply justified his stand over staying in Moscow and using the Society as a springboard. The final season provided an attractive foretaste of what the Art Theatre would be able to offer. Two major new productions were presented, *Twelfth Night* and *The Sunken Bell*.

Twelfth Night opened on December 17, 1897. The production was well received. It seemed to the critic of the *Russkoe Slovo* that the cast played like a full orchestra under a great conductor. There was not one false note, not one harsh sound. It was neither too fast nor too slow. Stanislavski's Malvolio, on the other hand, ran contrary to the traditional view, and was less well received. Like many twentieth-century interpreters he saw the dark side of the character. The same critic found that:

'. . . he made the audience pay attention to him rather longer than they should, endowing him with strong feelings. The pleasure Malvolio took in the letters he received and then his indignation and rage were too strong, too tempestuous for this insignificant pedant and so, instead of drawing laughter, Malvolio drew pity.' (*Russkoe Slovo*, January 6, 1898.)

His next interpretation, Heinrich in Hauptmann's *The Sunken Bell*, again split critical opinion. For some the interpretation was too down to earth, too 'unheroic' and cluttered with 'superfluous realism'. For others it was a performance of true poetry, of 'titanic character'. Nemirovich was unreserved in his praise.

On January 31, 1898, the *Moskovskii Vestnik* speculated on the pleasure Moscow audiences would receive if Stanislavski and Nemirovich were to succeed in launching their new enterprise. A foretaste of that pleasure came from the Princess Elizaveta Fedorovna, who came to see the play three times. Support like this was important since the government had yet to make up its mind whether to permit the new theatre to open.

CHAPTER SIX

PUSHKINO

Five months were all that remained to pull the first season into shape. As the new theatre was to play in repertoire this meant working on four or five plays simultaneously – *The Merchant of Venice, Antigone, Hannele,* Aleksei Tolstoi's *Tsar Fiodor Ioannovich* and *The Seagull*. This in turn meant tightly interlocking rehearsal schedules, starting one play, going on to the second and the third and thereafter keeping them all going. There were designs to be prepared, materials to be bought and sets to be constructed. Stanislavski had engaged Viktor Andreievich Simov as his principal designer. Simov had learned his craft as a scenic artist in Mamontov's Private Opera Theatre. He had met Stanislavski in the autumn of 1896 and had thereafter been a visitor to Red Gates where he had seen and admired Stanislavski's own set models. He officially entered the theatre's employ on May 1.

Stanislavski attempted to solve as many problems as he could during the pre-production period. He had decided to open the season not with the best or most original play from the list but with *Tsar Fiodor Ioannovich*, a spectacular director's piece. In mid-May he set out for Rostov, to visit museums and collect material, determined not to present the conventionalized Russia which could be seen on the Mali stage. At the end of June he took Simov and members of the company on a tour of Rostov, Yaroslavl and other towns along the Volga to try and soak up the atmosphere of Old Rus. Simultaneously he briefed Simov on the designs he wanted for *Merchant*.

Members of the company read for parts in *Fiodor, Merchant* and *Antigone* but basic casting was kept fluid until Stanislavski had tested the capacities of actors whom he did not know. He had not yet decided what he himself would play in *Fiodor*, Boris Godunov or Prince Shuiski. Nemirovich's view was that it would help the play if he were to play Boris but he settled finally for Shuiski.

He was working under great pressure and alone. Nemirovich had a novel to finish and was away from late spring to the summer, at his wife's estate and then in the Crimea. The two men kept up a voluminous correspondence settling details of casting and repertoire. They agreed that Stanislavski would write the production plans, do preparatory work with the company and then hand over to Nemirovich who would start detailed work with individual members of the cast, while Stanislavski went on to the next production. This suited Stanislavski. Writing to Nemirovich on June 12 he said:

'I would be very happy if in *Tsar Fiodor* and indeed in other plays you would take the individual actors through their roles initially. I don't like it and can't do it. But you are a master at it.' (*MATL*, No. 13.)

The same letter, however, contains a gentle warning to Nemirovich not to interfere in the process of writing the production plan or to press for quick results:

'Let me pour out, sketch the play as I see it . . . independently . . . then you can correct it if I have done something stupid . . . I am always wary of falling under any kind of influence . . . Then my work becomes uninteresting and hackneyed. Sometimes I can't put down what I dimly perceive . . . And often these passages are better than all the rest. If unconsciously, instinctively I stick at these places be patient with me, give me time to clarify my ideas and put them into comprehensible form. You know, these details, prompted by instinct, give a play its flavour. I feel there will be very many of them in *Fiodor* so that we can get rid of the usual things we are accustomed to see in so-called Russian plays. To play them in that manner is absolutely unacceptable . . . We must get away from it as soon as possible.' (Ibid.)

On June 14, the new company assembled for the first time in Pushkino, some fifty miles from Moscow. They were a mixed bunch, former pupils of the Philharmonic School, ex-members of the Society, Darski, an experienced provincial actor, brought in to add weight, even Boris Alekseiev's fiancée, Olga Pavlovna Polianska, who had been a pupil at the Society's school.

The decision to rehearse outside Moscow had more or less been forced on Stanislavski. There was simply no convenient space in the city. The rehearsal rooms he had in mind had been taken over by Lenski who had also just launched a new company and the Hermitage would not be ready until the autumn. Nikolai Arkhipov, a former member of the Society, came to the rescue, offering a small theatre on his country estate. Pushkino was only a short distance from Liubimovka so while the company found accommodation locally, Stanislavski was able to live at home, coming over for rehearsals every day, often on horseback.

On the first day there was a short religious opening ceremony, after which Stanislavski made a speech which Meierhold described as being of 'great warmth and beauty'. To our more cynical age it sounds idealistic and romantic in tone but it left no one in any doubt as to why they were there and what was expected of them:

'Let us prize what has fallen to us, for fear that we should weep later, as a child weeps when a favourite toy has been broken. If we do not come to this enterprise with clean hands we will dirty and degrade it and go our separate ways across the face of Russia, some of us returning to our mundane, everyday tasks, others profaning the name of art in paltry little provincial playhouses and side-shows, just for a crust of bread. And remember this, should this happen we shall deserve to be ridiculed and abused, for the task we have undertaken is not just a simple, private affair, its nature is social.' (*SS*, V, p. 175.)

In his application to the Moscow City Council Nemirovich had been careful to state that they were aiming at middle- or lower-middle-class audiences. Stanislavski could afford to be more open in private.

'Remember, we are attempting to bring light into the lives of the poorer classes, to give them a few moments of beauty in the darkness that surrounds them. We are trying to create the first rational, moral public theatre and it is to this lofty aim we dedicate our lives.

It is for this aim we must leave our petty quarrels at home. Let us assemble here to work together, not to settle personal differences and squabbles.' (Ibid.)

Working in the comparative isolation of Pushkino proved beneficial. The new company lived as a community. As there were no servants, they had to keep the place clean and fend for themselves. The general handyman who had been engaged failed to turn up. Stanislavski insisted on participating on the domestic side and to set an example to others he was first on the duty rota. He believed that a theatre should be orderly, that actors should have working conditions which were clean and comfortable. It was a sign of respect for the art. Years previously, when he directed his first professional production, he had staged an angry walk-out on a drunken impresario in protest against the squalor in which he and his cast were expected to work. By the next day the theatre had been scrubbed clean. Working now, with his own company, he intended to remain true to his principles. Unfortunately, conscientious though he might be, he was not very efficient. This was hardly surprising as it is highly improbable that he had ever swept a floor or filled a samovar in his life, but efficiency was not the main issue. Attitude was what counted. Application to domestic chores was part of a broader concept of the way an artist, an actor should behave, a concept of discipline and dedication which Stanislavski called his Ethic and which was the essential companion to talent.

The workload was extremely heavy and discipline a practical as well as a moral necessity. Stanislavski introduced a daybook, in which a record of work, attendance, lateness and reasons for lateness was carefully noted. Critical comments could also be added. Rehearsals began at midday and went on until four. There was then a break for about three hours after which work was resumed, often going on until midnight. In addition to preparing *Merchant, Antigone* and *Hannele*, the company looked at Ostrovski's *We'll do it Ourselves* and Diachenko's *The Governor*, which was planned for a special performance at Pushkino itself but which never took place.

The company were slowly introduced to Stanislavski's working method, reading, research and extensive, detailed rehearsals 'at the table'. The action was defined before the play was actually moved or blocked. The general opinion, Stanislavski wrote to Nemirovich, was that the atmosphere was more like a university than a theatre. Some were disconcerted by this unfamiliar approach but Vladimir Lanskoi, a young actor recently graduated from the St Petersburg academy, described by Stanislavski as 'stupid but nice', declared that he had learned more in one rehearsal than in three years' study. That, Stanislavski commented, did not say much for the school.

During those few weeks at Pushkino Stanislavski and Meierhold forged life-long bonds of affection and respect. Meierhold was already a mature mind. Nemirovich later wrote that he arrived at the Philharmonic school fully fledged. In a series of letters to his wife, Olga, Meierhold set out his reactions to Stanislavski both as a man and as a director. On June 22 he told her:

'He just captures your imagination with the way he explains thing, creates the mood, the way he demonstrates things and gets carried away himself too! What artistic flair, what imagination!' (*MATL*, No. 18.)

Six days later he wrote:

'Alekseiev isn't talented, no, he's a genius, this director-teacher. What a wealth of erudition, what imagination . . .' (*MATL*, No. 20.)

Stanislavski returned this affection. On June 25, while giving Nemirovich an individual comment on every member of the company, he wrote, 'Meierhold is my darling'.

Everyone was learning – and not merely the young and inexperienced. Darski, who was to alternate the role of Shylock with Stanislavski, was treated no differently from the rest.

'And how, you will ask, is Darski behaving himself . . .? Is it possible for him to knuckle under to unaccustomed discipline? The fact is that not only does he submit to external discipline, he is completely reworking the role of Shylock, which he has been playing for such a long time. Alekseiev's understanding of Shylock is so free from clichés, so original that Darski hasn't dared protest once, but dutifully, though not slavishly (he's a clever man) is relearning the whole part, getting rid of the conventional and overblown. He has played this part for eight years and several times a year. . . .

Alekseiev plays the part better, of course. He has been perfecting it for years.' (Meierhold, *Perepiska*, pp. 18–19.)

The company were also being introduced to a new world of design. They saw the set models for *Merchant* on June 15. Meierhold wrote to his wife:

'*The Merchant of Venice* will be done à la Meininger, respecting historical and national accuracy. Old Venice will rise as a living thing before the audience. . . . On one side the old Jewish quarter, dark and dirty, on the other the square in front of Portia's palace, poetic, beautiful with a view over the sea. . . . There, darkness, here light; there despair and oppression, here gaiety and light. The set outlines the idea of the play all by itself.' (*MATL*, No. 18.)

The sets for *Fiodor*, eleven of them, caused an even greater stir when Stanislavski read the play on July 7. They had been much more troublesome to produce. Stanislavski worked with Simov throughout June and July. He was extremely demanding, posing what seemed like, and sometimes were, impossible problems. But, as Simov noted in his *Memoir*, the man was so charming you could refuse him nothing. It was the set for Act Three, Prince Shuiski's Garden, that proved the most original. Stanislavski wanted the Kremlin in the background. Unfortunately, the view of the Kremlin with which all Muscovites were familiar contained the church of Ivan the Great, which did not exist at the time of the play. Complete authenticity would simply upset the audience. Stanislavski suggested hiding the church behind a convenient clump of trees. Simov, or so he claimed, took this idea and extended it, filling the whole stage with trees and introducing a cut-out front-drop of birches right across the footlights. Writing to his friend Ekaterina Munt, however, Meierhold credited Stanislavski alone with such a revolutionary idea:

'The Shuiski Garden . . . is Alekseiev's idea. And do you know what's original about it? Trees stretch right across the stage parallel to the footlights. The characters will move beyond these trees. You can imagine the effect. Through the trees you can see the porch of Shuiski's house. The stage is moonlit.' (In N. D. Volkov, *V. E. Meierhold*, I, p. 107.)

In his history of the Art Theatre Nikolai Efros stated:

'To [the company] this innovation appeared a complete revolution, delighting them by its truth and boldness. . . . In the other models for *Fiodor* the director and his young army were delighted by the historical accuracy, the break with cliché in the treatment on stage of the ancient Russia of the Boyars.' (*MXAT 1898–1923*, p. 127.)

It was soon made clear to the cast that the reality of their acting was expected to match the reality of the sets. There were to be no actors' tricks, no 'peasant' acting of the traditional kind. A truthful presentation of the people was essential to the meaning of the production. Stanislavski took the view that although the play might be called *Tsar Fiodor* the real centre of the piece was the Russian people themselves. The failure of the Tsar, good and kind but unable to live up to the people's needs, provided the dominant theme. The crowd scenes, non-existent in the spoken text, became central to the action. Stanislavski went to greater pains than ever to give each walk-on an individual character. Nowhere is this more evident than in the final act's scene on the Yauza bridge. The stage direction, 'Across the bridge pass people of different condition', is the cue for fourteen paragraphs of detailed character descriptions in the production plan. In some cases they are almost minor dramas in themselves:

> '3. At curtain rise a German (in foreign costume) approaches a barge and meets a stevedore, asks him something. The stevedore not wishing to answer starts to go, the German stops him afresh with his hand and questions him again. It is obvious they don't understand one another. (Scene lasts 15 seconds.) Having examined the sacks lying about he undoes one of them, takes some flour in the palm of his hand, examines it, tastes it. Then he crosses the plank on to the barge and only returns when the fight begins. Then he and his wife rescue their goods.
> 4. The German's wife, heavily built, stout, with a kerchief, humbly follows him. She patiently waits until her husband has finished speaking to the stevedore. When her husband is examining the flour she notes down the number of the quantity. For this purpose she has an inkwell round her neck and paper and a goose-quill in her hands. When her husband goes on to the barge, she sits on a log and patiently awaits his return.' (*Rezhissiorskie Eksempliari, K. S. Stanislavskovo,* I, pp. 210–12.)

With *Fiodor* launched, there was a read-through, on July 21, of Hauptmann's *The Assumption of Hannele* which reduced everyone, except a sceptical Meierhold, to tears. However, he found the whole occasion too self-indulgent, with too much talk about form and 'beauty'. He wondered what had happened to the content of the play.

Although company morale was high and work was progressing well, Stanislavski was beginning to feel the strain. He had written to Nemirovich a month earlier to complain about the overload. He could not manage the business side and rehearse as well. He could see the money running out. Certain essential repairs at Pushkino had gone over budget although the company had taken to do-it-yourself rather than employ outside labour. Money was being spent on sets and costumes despite the fact that not a single play had been passed by the censor. The most vulnerable was *Tsar Fiodor* which was just the kind of historical subject which aroused the authorities' suspicions. Would any of the ecclesiastical characters be cut? If they were, it meant changing the cast-list and that would have a knock-on effect on the casting of all plays.

Nemirovich kept a level head throughout. By his calculation income would cover expenditure and at most a further 10,000 roubles would be needed in the late autumn. He would raise a loan himself rather than bring in another shareholder. He arrived finally on July 24, much to Stanislavski's relief, and stayed at Liubimovka, spending most of August coaching his former pupils from the Philharmonic School. Stanislavski took the opportunity, on August 5 and 6, to make a shopping expedition to Nizhni-Novgorod to buy materials for *Fiodor* – head-dresses, boots, skirts, kerchiefs, Persian silks, necklaces, aprons and plates, any kind of bric-à-brac that might seem useful. On his return he began work on the difficult task of preparing the production plan for *The Seagull*. Chekhov's play had been included in the repertoire at Nemirovich's insistence; he was determined to stage it and had fought hard to overcome Chekhov's absolute refusal to let it be seen in Moscow. The play's first run at the Aleksandrinski theatre in 1896 had not been quite the total disaster that subsequent legend has painted. It was under-rehearsed but had a strong cast which included Vera Komissarzhevskaia as Nina. It was the first night that had proved catastrophic. The audience had come expecting to see their favourite comedienne, Elizaveta Levkeieva, in a benefit performance of a light comedy. They were not prepared for the half-tones and subtleties of Chekhov's text. By the time Komissarzhevskaia got to the opening of the speech, 'Men, lions, eagles' they had had enough and erupted into jeers, catcalls and insults. Chekhov took refuge in a dressing-room and then roamed the streets half the night. None of the subsequent favourable comments, either from friends or in the press, could erase the memory of that dreadful evening. He vowed that if he lived for seven hundred years he would never write for the theatre again.

The memory of that humiliation lay at the root of Chekhov's attitude to Stanislavski's productions. He loved the theatre and was fascinated by it but feared nothing so much as ridicule. The dread that uncompre-hending actors and directors would expose him once again to the derision of an audience made him prickly and suspicious. *The Seagull* was performed in provincial cities but he had resisted all efforts to stage it in Moscow, although the Mali appeared to hold an option. Their intention was to present it at a benefit performance. When Nemirovich tried to put on the play at the Philharmonic School the Mali management had blocked him but had done nothing about the play since.

Nemirovich and Chekhov were friends. They used the familiar second person singular form of address in a way that Stanislavski and

Nemirovich never did in forty years of collaboration. Nemirovich decided to use their friendship. On April 25, 1898, he wrote to Chekhov asking for permission to do *The Seagull*. In this and in subsequent letters he spoke of the production as his own, not Stanislavski's. He advanced his own superior claims to understand the play better than any other director. Chekhov refused. It took three more letters, two written on May 12 and one written on May 16, before he finally obtained Chekhov's consent. In his reply of May 31, he clearly stated 'So I am to direct *The Seagull*!'

Stanislavski is mentioned only once in Nemirovich's correspondence. On August 21 he wrote to Chekhov:

'Alekseiev and I spent 48 hours going over *The Seagull* and many ideas took shape as to how to create the *mood* (and that's so important in the play).' (*Iz. Pis.*, I, pp. 143–4.)

It may be that Nemirovich emphasized his own role as a stratagem, on the assumption that an already nervous Chekhov would not confide his play to someone he did not know. However, for Nemirovich to regard himself as the prime force behind the production would have been entirely in keeping with his view of the partnership. The interpretation of the play was his. Stanislavski would translate what he wanted into stage terms and he would then take rehearsals.

Over the years Nemirovich would continue to construct an ever more personalized account of the rehearsal and staging of *The Seagull*, emphasizing the centrality of his own role. More and more he stressed Stanislavski's bewilderment at the text, his lack of knowledge of the milieu in which the play was set, his failure to appreciate Chekhov's lyricism. It is Nemirovich's version of events which has by and large prevailed since he was able to write it into Stanislavski's autobiography *My Life in Art*. The 1926 Russian edition of *My Life in Art* contains passages actually written by Nemirovich using Stanislavski's voice (see chapter twenty-four). In it we find:

'We both . . . approached Chekhov and the essence of his work in our individual ways: Vladimir Ivanovich as a man of letters and I through my own imaginative, artistic specialism, movement and images.' (*SS*, I, Moscow, 1988, p. 293.)

In Mrs Gurevich's copy of the typescript Stanislavski added a sentence which had originally appeared in the 1924 American edition:

'Vladimir Ivanovich *spoke* about the feelings he discovered or sensed in the work but I could not talk about them. I preferred to *illustrate* them. When we argued using words he did not understand me, I was not convincing. When I went up on stage and showed what I meant, I was comprehensible and eloquent.'

The Russian text then continues:

'At first these differing approaches to the play proved an obstacle. We had long arguments, going from the particular to the general, from individual roles to the play and art in general. We even had quarrels, but they were artistic quarrels and so not dangerous. On the contrary, they were useful since they taught us how we could dig consciously into the essence of art. As for the divergence of our approaches and the division of our talents in working on the characters, the literary and the directorial, that quickly became irrelevant. We were convinced that we could not separate *form from content*, the literary, psychological or social side of the work from the images, staging and material shaping that combined create an artistic production.' (*SS*, I, Moscow, 1988, p. 294.)

In the American edition Stanislavski referred much more graphically to them both tunnelling from opposite ends. The end of this section of *My Life in Art* was written by Nemirovich and incorporated unaltered by Stanislavski:

'... It was clear that for our work on Chekhov to achieve artistic results a clear combination of our talents was required: 1) of a man of letters and a teacher of the young like Vladimir Ivanovich, 2) of a director who was free from theatrical conventions, and capable of giving theatrical expression to the writer's moods, of revealing the life of the human spirit in his works, using his staging, acting style and new discoveries in lighting and sound.' (*SS*, I, Moscow, 1988, pp. 293–4.)

Nemirovich is entirely accurate in saying that the two men approached a play from opposite angles and this basic difference was to determine their relationship for the next thirty years. What is not accurate is the picture of a naive Stanislavski being guided and tutored into a great production, putting his skill for staging at the service of a superior 'literary' mind. For Nemirovich a well-spoken text was almost sufficient. The words, as literature, would carry the meaning. For Stanislavski it was the circumstances that gave rise to the words that were paramount. The words were part of the action and if they were not adequate to the events, he was quite prepared to change them.

When in early August 1898 Nemirovich gave his forty-eight-hour analysis of the play, he approached it as a work of literature, to be placed within the corpus of Chekhov's work, including the short stories. Stanislavski was deeply impressed, not to say over-awed by Nemirovich's considerable intellect. It was the first time he had encountered this kind of dramaturgical thinking, this coming to grips with a play's essential ideas. Nemirovich's analysis in the event proved an obstacle and Stanislavski was still confused when he went to Kharkov on August 10 or 11, to stay at his brother's estate.

Once there, he appears to have forgotten Nemirovich's analysis, allowing the play slowly to take him over, working instinctively, in his own way. He was in the heart of the Russian countryside. The sounds, the colours, the atmosphere, all found their way into the production plan. Stanislavski worked hard. By the end of August he had completed the first three acts. On the 30th he sent them off to Pushkino, though still full of doubts as he still could not see any real connection between Nemirovich's elaborate analysis and his own efforts. In an unpublished variant for *My Life in Art* he stated:

> 'What I wrote was so simple no one could convince me it was at all interesting or any use on stage. "If you want I will write it, but I don't understand who needs it" – that was what I said to myself. To my amazement I got great praise from Pushkino for my work.' (Quoted by Radishcheva, *Istoria Teatralnikh Otnoshenii*, p. 77.)

To Nemirovich he wrote:

> '. . . as I am not steeped in Chekhov the plans I am sending you may be completely unusable. I drafted them at random. . . . I got down to the last act. Nothing went through my head and I wouldn't dream of forcing it out. I am reading the whole play again in the hope that the three acts I have already sent (by registered post) will keep you busy for some time.' (*SS*, VII, p. 142.)

Just as Nemirovich had explained his 'literary' concept of the play, Stanislavski felt the need to explain and to a certain extent excuse his theatrical methods. At one point in his plan he notes: 'a cheap trick but it will work with an audience'. Frequently in their subsequent exchanges Stanislavski spells out the theatrical reasons for his staging, the use of theatre language itself. In many instances Nemirovich did not fully understand what Stanislavski was doing until after the first night.

Stanislavski adopted the same basic approach in creating the production plan, the 'score' as he came to call it, as he had with *Fiodor*. He simply moved in closer. He gave each character an individual rhythm, a way of walking and moving, mannerisms: Sorin's laugh is 'startling and unexpected'; Arkadina 'habitually folds her arms behind her back when she is angry or excited'; Konstantin is, in general, 'tense'; Masha takes snuff; Medvedenko smokes a lot. The production copy sets down every move, every gesture, exact facial expressions in almost cinematic detail. Small drawings show the physical position and relationships of the characters at key moments as in a story-board.

The detail is not present simply from a desire to reproduce the surface of life, or an adherence to what Stanislavski called 'vulgar naturalism'. The detailed physical action is intended to reveal personality, the inner state of thought and emotion. Writing in 1923, Efros recalled the impact of moments of silent action, citing a passage in Act Four where Chekhov asks for the sound of a piano two rooms away, playing a waltz. The text runs:

> 'MASHA (*dances a few silent waltz-steps*). The important thing, mother, is to avoid seeing him. I just wish they'd give Simon his transfer and then, you'd see, I'd be over it in a month. All this is so stupid.'

This Stanislavski expands into:

> 'MASHA (20 – MASHA *sighs, takes a pinch of snuff. Snaps the lid shut vehemently.*) . . . [DIALOGUE] . . . (21 – MASHA *sighs again, waltzes over to the window, stops beside it, looks out into the night, takes out a handkerchief and unbeknown to her mother, wipes away one or two tears which are rolling down her cheeks.*)' (*Rezhissiorskie Eksempliari K. S. Stanislavskovo*, II, Moscow, 1981, pp. 138–9.)

Efros commented:

> 'Once you had seen it you would never forget it, the profound sorrow, the feeling of shock, almost of doom in your heart, that resulted from those silent, almost mechanical waltz-turns Masha performed, the complete hopelessness, as she heard the distant music coming from Kostia's room. She simply heard it and made a few turns to the rhythm . . . that's all . . . but you never felt more pain for her blighted existence than in those few silent moments.' (*Ezhegodnik* MXAT, 1944, p. 290.)

These silent moments acquired ever increasing stylistic importance. Chekhov stipulates a considerable number of pauses. Stanislavski added to them, although it did not prevent him from contradicting Chekhov at one point with a peremptory, 'No pause here under any circumstances.'

The use of sound is also developed: natural on-stage noise – a window shutting, the clatter of plates – to heighten the moment, to define it more closely; off-stage noise – frogs, crickets, barking dogs – to create 'mood', 'atmosphere'.

> 'ACT ONE
> *The play opens in darkness. An (August) evening. A dim artificial lamp. Distant sounds of a drunken song, distant howling of a dog, croaking of frogs, the cry of a corncrake – help the audience to enter into the sad, monotonous life of the characters.*' (*Rezhissiorskie Eksempliari K. S. Stanislavskovo*, II, p. 55.)

Stanislavski stipulated August because he calculated that the moon would have been at the right angle at that time for the performance of Konstantin's play. Meierhold, the original Konstantin, was in no doubt as to the essentially *poetic* nature of Stanislavski's intentions. Speaking nearly forty years later he stated:

'You ask me if there were [elements of] naturalism in *The Seagull* at the Art Theatre and you think you are putting a trick question . . . Probably there were individual elements of naturalism but that's not important. The important thing is that it contained the poetic nerve-centre, the hidden poetry of Chekhov's prose which was there because of Stanislavski's genius as a director. Up to Stanislavski people had only played the theme in Chekhov and forgot that in his plays the sound of the rain outside the windows, the noise of a falling tub, early morning light through the shutters, mist on the lake were indissolubly linked (as previously only in prose) with people's actions. At that time this was a discovery; naturalism only came into being when it became a cliché . . .' (In 'Meierhold Speaks', *Novi Mir*, 1961, No. 8, p. 221.)

Nemirovich received the first three acts on September 1 or 2. On September 4 he sent his first reactions which were almost entirely favourable. There was only one serious disagreement and that concerned the play at the end of Act One. Pursuing his own highly personal view of the 'lyrical' Chekhov, Nemirovich insisted that Nina's opening speech represented poetry breaking through the mundane prose of life. He saw the young Konstantin as a symbolist poet and wanted Nina to be played with a kind of lyrical fervour. This placed the play firmly within the contemporary situation but had more to do with his view of literature than with Chekhov. Stanislavski saw the play not in terms of new literary forms but as the moment when the hidden conflicts among the characters came to light. Chekhov does not appear to have shared Nemirovich's 'lyrical' interpretation. During the rehearsals for the St Petersburg première he described Nina as a country miss shaking with fright on making her first stage appearance. Stanislavski applied his veto for the first time and Nemirovich had to give way. Nemirovich, although bowing to Stanislavski's decision, continued to foster the legend of a Stanislavski insensitive to Chekhov's lyrical qualities. His final account of *The Seagull* in his autobiography shows how far his imagination had taken him and is full of factual inaccuracies.

Other disagreements were a matter of detail. Nemirovich's own innate conservatism as a director made him cautious about some aspects of Stanislavski's plan. Wasn't he overworking the effect of actors turning their backs to the audience, particularly Sorin? Just as Stanislavski had put a line of trees across the front of the stage in *Fiodor*, so, in Act One of *The Seagull* he put a line of actors with their backs to the audience. The effect, which Nemirovich seems to have missed, was to link the real audience with the stage audience as they all watched Konstantin's play. Nemirovich was also concerned about the amount of attention paid to minor characters, he was afraid they might overshadow the leading roles.

On September 10 Stanislavski despatched the plan for Act Four with his reply to Nemirovich's comments:

'I repeat, personally I can't tell whether the plan for *The Seagull* is good or bad. I only know it is a talented and fascinating play but I don't know which end to start. I've come at it haphazard so do what you like with the plan. . . .

I fully understand and am in agreement with your remarks that when Treplev's play is being performed the minor characters should not kill the major. It's a question of method. . . . As is my wont, I provided a comprehensive sketch of each character. When the actors are on top of things I start taking away what is superfluous and select what is important. I go about it this way because I have always been afraid that actors will only come up with superficial, uninteresting ideas out of which you get nothing but commonplace puppets.' (*SS*, VII, p. 145.)

As to the number and variety of sound effects:

'Consider this, I put in the frogs during the play scene solely to create total quiet. Quiet is conveyed in the theatre not by silence but by noise. If you don't fill the silence with noise you can't create the illusion.' (Ibid.)

Continuous noise backstage and in the auditorium destroys the mood of a scene. Attention needs to be focused on deliberately created sound on-stage.

In 1938, when the production plan for *The Seagull* was published for the first time, Nemirovich paid homage to the greatness of Stanislavski's achievement:

'This is a supreme example of Stanislavski's *creative instinct* as a director. Stanislavski who was still indifferent to Chekhov sent me such rich, interesting, original, profound material for the production of *The Seagull* that it was impossible not to admire this blazing, masterly imagination.' (Quoted in Introductory Essay to production plan for *The Seagull*, Iskusstvo, Moscow, 1938, pp. 47–8.)

Chekhov, finally responding to repeated invitations to stay at Pushkino or Liubimovka, attended rehearsals on September 9 and 11 in Stanislavski's absence. He was put on the defensive before he had heard a line. When one of the cast informed him of the 'real' croaking frogs and barking dogs that were to accompany the action he commented sharply:

'Real . . . The stage is art. There's a genre picture by Kramsloi in which the faces are painted marvellously. What if you were to cut out the painted nose from one of them and put in a living one? The nose would be "real" but the picture would be a mess.' (Meierhold, *Teatr, Kniga O Novom Teatre*, St Petersburg, 1908.)

Nor was he pleased when he heard of Stanislavski's notion of bringing on a number of servants at the end of Act Three, where the script leaves most of the confusion of departure off-stage.

'. . . the stage demands a certain artifice. You don't have a fourth wall. Above all the stage is art, the stage mirrors the quintessence of life, you need not bring anything superfluous on to it.' (Ibid.)

When he finally got to see what was actually being done most of his anxieties disappeared. Writing to Stanislavski on September 12, Nemirovich was able to report:

'Your *mise-en-scène* proved a delight. Chekhov was in raptures about it. We just altered one or two details in the interpretation of Treplev – Chekhov did, not me. . . . He soon understood how your *mise-en-scène* strengthens the overall impression.' (*Iz., Pis.*, I, p. 154.)

On September 21 Chekhov, in typically oblique manner, wrote to P. F. Iordanov:

'If you happen to be in Moscow, go to the Hermitage Theatre, where Stanislavski and Vl. Nemirovich-Danchenko are staging plays. The *mises-en-scène* are amazing, the like of which have never been seen in Russia. By the way, my ill-fated *Seagull* is being done.' (*Pisma*, VII, p. 272.)

Chekhov also managed to see a rehearsal of *Fiodor* and was impressed, as he wrote to Suvorin on October 8, by the intelligence and genuine feeling of art the company conveyed, even if there were no outstanding actors. According to Nemirovich it was at this rehearsal that Chekhov first noticed Olga Knipper.

Apart from problems of staging, Stanislavski was preoccupied with his own performance as Dorn. He had always wanted to play Trigorin and had only reluctantly bowed to Nemirovich's insistence that he should play the doctor. Nemirovich felt, as he wrote to Chekhov, that it was a role which required an experienced actor with a first-class technique. Stanislavski struggled to find some way into the role but in late August he wrote:

'I am beginning to read through the part of Dorn but for the moment I don't understand it entirely and am sorry to have missed the discussion on *The Seagull*. . . . The part interests me, if only because it's a long time since I played a character part but, you see, I don't understand, or better, feel why I, rather than Kaluzhski, for example, should be Dorn, why all the people you say think I am right for the part. I am irritated by the fact that I do not understand what people expect of me in the part. I am afraid I will just be worthy in it and no more . . . I can see myself, for example, as Shamraev, or Sorin, or even Trigorin, i.e., I

can feel how I would transform myself into these characters but I can
only play Dorn tolerably, rather flatly, and nothing else. Initially one
always has the impression one can do well in any part except the part
one has been given. That is always the way with me at first. I will do
some reading. You have no time but someone else, Meierhold maybe,
who, as you say, is steeped in *The Seagull*, can give me a summary of
what was said about Dorn during the discussions and how he imagines
the character, what he looks like.' (*MATL*, No. 28.)

The statement 'or even Trigorin' is deceptively casual. His assumption
that this is the role he should really be playing comes through in his
production plan. Everywhere else his directions are highly detailed but
there is nothing as to how Trigorin's long speech to Nina, 'What's
wonderful about it?' in Act Two is to be delivered. It is as though
Stanislavski thought direction superfluous since he himself would be
playing the role. However, he struggled to find a line on the character of
Dorn, although his first solution did not please Nemirovich. Stanislavski
decided that Dorn was 'a lumpish, ageing, provincial Don Juan' and a
cynic. Faced with Nemirovich's disapproval, he abandoned the idea. He
was still searching for a new approach when Chekhov settled the
problem for him.

Although the overall shape of the production was satisfactory,
Nemirovich, and possibly Chekhov, felt that the Trigorin was weak. A
critical suggestion was then made:

'I asked whether Trigorin wouldn't benefit from having you
[Stanislavski] in the part.

"Much better," Chekhov answered.

'So you see, I owe you an apology for having kept this role from
you. The whole company, I gather, was expecting you to do it.' (*Iz.*,
Pis., I, p. 154.)

Stanislavski set out from his brother's estate somewhere around
September 15. Writing to Lilina he expressed his satisfaction at the
change of casting:

'. . . I've been through Trigorin – the part is dearer to my heart than
Dorn. At least there's something in it but in the other, nothing – and
they expect God knows what.' (*SS*, VII, p. 149.)

It was the rehearsals of *Fiodor*, however, that demanded his immediate
attention. The censor had finally licensed the play towards the end of
August. Nemirovich had written on the 24th to announce the news and
pass on the inevitable cuts. Stanislavski was irritated by the pettiness of
the changes and set about trying to repair some of the damage to the
verse, which the censor had succeeded in mangling.

He arrived in Moscow on September 18 and went straight to the theatre to see what progress had been made in his absence. The first scene depressed him considerably but matters improved in the second and went better after that.

The role of Tsar Fiodor had still not been cast although the opening was less than a month away. Stanislavski could not make up his mind. He found Moskvin's playing extremely moving but Meierhold was a main contender and one cast list, written in Stanislavski's hand, ascribes the part to him. Meierhold himself was under the impression that he, Moskvin, and another young actor, Aleksandr Platonov, would play Fiodor, Shuiski and Starkov turn and turn about. The rehearsal with Moskvin finally settled matters:

> 'Konstantin Sergeievich summoned me to the director's table and, much moved, with tears in his eyes, told me that I would play Tsar Fiodor and that we would start rehearsing the rest of the play the very next day.' (Moskvin, 'My First Role', *Sovietskoe Iskusstvo*, October 26, 1938.)

Nemirovich later took credit for this final casting, maintaining that Stanislavski had originally intended Moskvin for the role but had mishandled the young actor during early rehearsals and then lost confidence in him. It was thanks to his own coaching that Moskvin was able to develop his performance and so finally land the role.

Stanislavski now set about polishing and tightening up *Fiodor* and *Merchant of Venice*. Any idea of his playing Shuiski was now quite impractical. He had no time to prepare his own performance. Everything inevitably was behind schedule. Between rehearsals Lilina used her skills as a seamstress to sew the elaborately embroidered costumes for *Fiodor*. Even Stanislavski's mother joined the common effort, dipping lengths of braid in coffee to give them the right period look.

Elizaveta Vasilievna's willing cooperation symbolized the end of any opposition inside the Alekseiev family to Stanislavski's ambitions. He had succeeded in opening the door to professional life not only for himself but also for his brothers and sisters. Anna joined the company in 1899 and remained with it until 1903. Boris spent the season of 1900–1 with it, acting under the name of Polianski while, in 1903, Georgi took over the direction of the theatre in Kharkov, where he lived.

CHAPTER SEVEN

THE MOSCOW ART THEATRE

Moscow society awaited the opening of the new theatre and *Tsar Fiodor* with great excitement and not a little malice. They admired Stanislavski, he had been their idol, but they were also quite prepared to see him fall flat on his face. A failure would prove how stupid it was to transgress the code of one's class. On the other side there were those, the young, the intellectuals, who pinned their hopes on the new company. Stanislavski and Nemirovich knew there was only one answer – *épater les bourgeois*. They needed an unqualified success, a smash.

The audience on the first night, October 14, 1898, was a stiff one, with a large number of professional actors from the imperial theatres. Lenski and the young company at the rival New Theatre sent telegrams as did the pupils of the Philharmonic School. Stanislavski, who was not performing, was so nervous backstage that he upset the cast and had to be sent away before he produced complete hysteria.

The Art Theatre had not yet dispensed with the custom of taking curtain calls after each act. It was therefore possible to judge the way a performance was going as the evening progressed. The audience only thawed out slowly. There were not enough members in the company to make the opening scene really effective; the set for Shuiski's garden had a mixed reception, but after scene three the originality of the production, the combination of historical accuracy and theatrical splendour gradually won through and the penultimate scene, at the Yauza Bridge, was a triumph.

Ermolova, who was present either at the final dress rehearsal or the first night – the young medical student who accompanied her could not later in life remember which –

'. . . threw off a string of observations which brooked no objection. "That's acting! That's directing! Those are costumes! We put a padded jacket over our corsets and a fur coat and a peasant's headdress and think we're boyars' wives. All we've done is dress up! We've got a lot to learn from Stanislavski."' (Letter from G. Kurochkin to Stanislavski, January 26, 1938.)

The press on the whole was favourable. There was admiration for the audacity of the young company in tackling such a difficult play. The combination of realism and theatricality was praised. Efros devoted two articles to the production in *Novosti Dnia* on the 18th and 20th, concluding:

'There were two heroes at the first production of the Art-Open Theatre: the *mise-en-scène* and Mr Moskvin.'

The first hurdle had been passed but the theatre had to prove itself as a going concern – an almost impossible task. To present a season of plays, all of which needed to be more or less successful, with an inexperienced cast, and at the same time to break new ground, was to invite disaster. And so it proved.

After *Fiodor* Stanislavski put all his energies into *The Sunken Bell* and *The Merchant of Venice* to the detriment of his personal affairs. He did not go near his factory. His efforts were not rewarded. *The Sunken Bell*, which opened on the 19th, was a revival and made no impact. Stanislavski's interpretation of Heinrich was once again criticized for being too prosaic. *The Merchant of Venice*, which opened on the 21st, was no better received. The audience was disconcerted by the fact that Darski, on Stanislavski's instructions, played Shylock with a Jewish accent. This was considered inappropriate for a 'tragic' role. The press, not understanding that it had always been Stanislavski's intention to alternate the role with Darski, announced that he would take over in order to justify his interpretation. In fact Stanislavski never played the role. Some critics had condemned the production as anti-semitic and he was afraid that if he lent the weight of his reputation to Shylock he would only aggravate the problem. The play had many fine moments but it was 'caviare to the general'. This prompted Nemirovich to quote Tolstoi: 'In art, subtlety and the power to influence are almost always diametrically opposed.'

A further blow came when, on October 27, *The Assumption of Hannele*, the next production, was banned after protests by the church. A visit to the Metropolitan Vladimir of Moscow proved abortive. It was useless to explain that the translation the Metropolitan angrily waved at them was not the translation, duly passed by the censor, which was being used. The ban stayed. This was the first of many brushes with the authorities, frequently in the person of the Chief of Police, General Dmitri Fedorovich Trepov, a ruthless organizer of anti-revolutionary pogroms and later governor of the Winter Palace in St Petersburg.

Pisemski's *A Law unto Themselves*, which opened on November 4, failed to arouse any interest. Audiences simply stayed away. This was critical. The launch capital of 28,000 roubles, barely adequate in any case, had been used up. Box-office receipts, the only source of income, could not cover costs. On November 30, Stanislavski received a demand for 3000 roubles in rent from the theatre's landlords. If payment was not made by noon on December 1 the contract would be considered null and void and legal action would be taken.

On December 2 Goldoni's *La Locandiera* opened together with a short Viennese piece, *Greta's Joy*. As the *Moskovski Listok* commented, the theatre was half empty. The run of failures had destroyed its prestige. The Goldoni did nothing to stop the run of bad luck. Stanislavski received mixed notices as Ripafratta. Many critics found him too 'passive'. It began to look as though the theatre which had opened so successfully in October might well be forced to close its doors by Christmas. Everything now depended on *The Seagull* which was scheduled to open on December 17.

Stanislavski and Nemirovich marshalled all their combined talent and energy to ensure a success. Nemirovich made a number of changes to the blocking, which are noted in his hand on the production plan, and a number of alterations to the décor. The play had twenty-four rehearsals, nine of them taken by Stanislavski and fifteen by Nemirovich. This added up to some eighty hours' work, a great deal in contemporary terms. There were three dress rehearsals during which Stanislavski and Nemirovich examined every inch of the sets and checked and double-checked every lamp to make sure none of the effects would misfire. Stanislavski, nonetheless, considered the play under-rehearsed and insisted that the opening be postponed for a week. Nemirovich knew this would be a mistake and refused. Stanislavski then threatened to have his name taken off the posters but Nemirovich managed to talk him round although in later years he could not remember quite how he did it.

When opening night came a sense of crisis pervaded both stage and auditorium, which was by no means full. Maria Chekhova was so afraid of a failure, which she was convinced would be a death-blow to her brother, that she stayed away. Most of the cast were taking refuge in the contemporary equivalent of tranquillisers, Valerian drops.

'The house was poor. I don't know how the first act went. I only remember that all the actors reeked of Valerian drops. I remember how awful it was for me to sit in the dark with my back to the audience during [Nina's] monologue and that I unconsciously grabbed hold of my foot which had developed a nervous twitch.' (*SS*, V, p. 332.)

Nina's monologue, which had provoked catcalls in St Petersburg, was listened to attentively and throughout the rest of the act the audience appeared to be concentrating. Dorn's final speech came, with Stanislavski's 'atmospheric' effects.

'DORN: How tense they all are! How tense! And so much love. . . . Oh that lake's an enchantress! (*Gently.*) [114. MASHA *Bursts into tears, kneels, buries her face against* DORN'S *knees. 15-second pause. The wild waltz grows louder, a church bell tolls, a peasant's song, frogs, a corncrake, the knocking of the night-watchman and other nocturnal*

sound effects] But what can I do, my dear child? Tell me, what?' [115.
Curtain]'

After the curtain there was a silence which seemed to go on forever. They
had failed. But there are silences in the theatre which are more profound
than instant frenzied reaction. When the clapping began, it was, in
Nemirovich's words, like a damn bursting. He did not believe in
grabbing curtain calls. He insisted that they be properly spaced so that it
was possible to gauge the reaction more accurately. Three or four curtain
calls taken slowly meant success. Act One got six.

For the audience the evening was a unique experience. The writer A.
S. Lazariov wrote to Chekhov on January 19, 1899:

'I attended the first performance. In the first act something special
started, if you can so describe a mood of excitement in the audience
that seemed to grow and grow. Most people walked through the
auditorium and corridors with strange faces, looking as if it were their
birthday and, indeed, (dear God, I'm not joking) it was perfectly
possible to go up to some completely strange woman and say: "What
a play? Eh?" At all events, N. E. Efros, always so reserved and
"respectable", rushed up to me in the stalls, as I was going back to my
seat after the second act, stopped me at the entrance to the parterre and
exclaimed so that practically the whole theatre could hear: "Ah, what
a play, A.S.! What acting! What passion!"' (Quoted in Introduction by
S. D. Baluzhati to *The Seagull* Production Plan, Iskusstvo, 1938.)

By the end of Act Three the actors were weeping with excitement and
embracing one another. Nemirovich informed the audience that the
author was not present and suggested that a telegram of congratulation be
sent to Chekhov in Yalta. The suggestion was greeted with prolonged
applause. There was still Act Four to go. That, too, was a triumph.

The press was unanimous in its praise.

'The directors completely understood what the author wanted; the
actors completely understood the director's ideas and created a
performance which emerged not simply as an interpretation of the play
but as its very embodiment.' (*Teatr i Iskusstvo*, January 10, 1899.)

There were reservations, however, about some of the performances,
including Stanislavski's:

'The success of *The Seagull* was an extraordinary phenomenon. It
explained much to us, it opened our eyes to many things. The
performances of the actors of the Art Theatre in this comedy were far
from being irreproachable. One of the play's leading roles, the author,
Trigorin, was misunderstood and misinterpreted and the part of the
heroine of *The Seagull* was simply distorted but nonetheless we
forgave the artists their shortcomings. . . .' (*Russkaia Misl*, X, 1899.)

These criticisms were echoed by Maria Chekhova, who found Stanislavski 'limp' and Roksanova, who played Nina, 'very bad'. When she attended the play for the third time, however, the following February, she was able to report to her brother that both were now good.

An article in *Russkaia Misl* in January 1899 drew attention to the social, the critical implications of the production:

'. . . you cannot "do" a play like this. You can only experience it with sadness of heart and extreme sensitivity towards the sickness and suffering which is destroying certain circles in our society.'

It was important to follow *The Seagull* with another success but this was not to be. *Hedda Gabler*, which opened on February 19, failed to excite. Two other blows, considerably more serious, followed. On January 10 the theatre had given a special performance of *Locandiera* for factory workers, as a result of which Nemirovich was summoned by the Chief of Police, Trepov. It was explained to him that such performances needed special clearance by a fourth censor whose task it was to vet material intended for working-class audiences. The theatre had omitted this formality and could be in serious trouble. Nemirovich's attempts to talk himself out of it were brushed aside. It became quite obvious that the alternatives were conformity or prison. The notion of an 'open' theatre was being strangled by red tape. In a very short space of time the word was dropped from the title and the theatre became simply, at Chekhov's suggestion, the Moscow Art Theatre.

All was not lost, however, in the battle to bring drama to popular audiences. At the same moment that he was launching the Art Theatre, Stanislavski decided to build a fully equipped theatre at his factory for the workers. It took six years to raise the money for the building and to overcome the hostility of the authorities, but the theatre finally opened in 1904 and quickly became known as the Little Art Theatre. When he could Stanislavski attended rehearsals and gave notes.

As far as the big Moscow Art Theatre was concerned, ironically the worst blow came from Chekhov himself. The Art Theatre production of *The Seagull* had finally established him not only as *a* dramatist but probably *the* dramatist. He could be in no doubt of his success. His sister, who lived near the Hermitage Theatre, could hear people talking excitedly in the streets after the performance. Levitan, Russia's leading painter, wrote to him on January 8, explaining that when he read the play he had not understood it. The Art Theatre production had revealed all. He had seen Lenski, who 'is in raptures both about the play and the production'. On January 9 Chaliapin sent a telegram of congratulation, again both for the play and the production.

Chekhov was evidently pleased. On January 25 he wrote to a medical colleague, P. F. Iordanov:

'My *Seagull* is playing in Moscow to packed houses. It's a sell-out. They say the production is exceptional.' (Chekhov, *Pisma*, VIII, p. 47.)

It was natural, therefore, for the theatre to expect to be given his next play. It was obvious to everyone in the company that another Chekhov play was essential to bring in audiences. When Nemirovich was informed that *Uncle Vania* had been given to the Mali, he felt betrayed.

Chekhov never explained or excused his behaviour. Stanislavski's own explanation was that Chekhov played the two theatres off against each other, not wishing the play, which had a chequered history, to be performed. He told the Mali that he needed to rewrite and the Art Theatre that he needed actually to see their work before committing himself further. This does not fit the facts.

Having failed to exercise their option on *The Seagull*, the Imperial Theatres realized that the Art Theatre was a serious threat. In his diary, on February 4, the chief administrator, Teliakovski, noted that serious attention should be paid to the production methods of the new theatre and that whatever was useful should be taken over. It was a short step from there to luring away their most successful author. A few days later the principal director of the Mali, A. M. Kondratev, asked Chekhov if he could do *Uncle Vania*. Chekhov agreed. He was undoubtedly flattered by the offer. The Mali, after all, whatever its shortcomings, did represent official recognition, a success there would do something to compensate for the humiliation he had suffered in St Petersburg. It is doubtful whether he was aware how important another sure-fire success was to the Art Theatre. There was also a simpler reason for letting the Mali do the play: money. On February 22, Chekhov wrote from Yalta to Ivan Orlov, a doctor friend:

'. . . Next season my play [*Vania*] . . . will be done at the Mali. Lucrative, that, you see.' (Chekhov, *Pisma*, VIII, p. 100.)

In the event the Mali ruined its own chances. Chekhov and Kondratev had reckoned without the stupidity of the Repertoire Committee. On March 1 the company had read through the new plays, including *Uncle Vania*, which had been accepted by Kondratev and recommended it for inclusion in the coming season. However, some members of the Repertoire Committee took exception to Act Three, especially the attempted shooting of the Professor, which they considered somehow an affront to academic dignity. They insisted it should be rewritten. Nemirovich, who was a member of the committee, although he no longer attended its meetings, got wind of what was happening and on March 26 went to see Maria Chekhova. He explained that Chekhov would be required to revise the play and then resubmit it but that it would be some time before he would be officially informed of the decision. He then offered to stage the play as it stood. Could Chekhov telegraph his permission so that they could finalize their repertoire and start casting? Maria Chekhova was sufficiently concerned to write to her brother for the second time that day, suggesting that he contact the Mali to find out what was happening. Chekhov refused to contact anybody. On April 8 the Repertoire Committee made its expected demand for revisions. Chekhov, who arrived in Moscow on April 10, was sent a copy of the relevant minute and on April 13 or 14 went to see Teliakovski, in charge of the Moscow office of the Imperial Theatres. He remained calm and withdrew his play. He left Moscow on the 15th, handing the play over to the Art Theatre. The widespread notion that Chekhov refused to give *Uncle Vania* to the theatre because he hated Stanislavski's performance as Trigorin is therefore not borne out by the facts.

Chekhov did not see *The Seagull* until May 1 when a special performance, in make-up and costume but without sets, was arranged at the Paradiz Theatre. His reaction was mixed but on the whole followed informed opinion: he agreed with his sister and the critic of *Russkaia Misl* that Stanislavski and Roksanova were not good but endorsed the general view that the production was outstanding. Chekhov was a man of widely fluctuating moods – an effect of his tuberculosis. Gorki records that on a bad day Chekhov hated everyone. He therefore expressed various views in various ways to various people, depending on the moment. This has provided more than ample opportunity for selective quotation. To Stanislavski he said:

> '– You act splendidly, but that's not my character. That's not what I wrote.
> – What's wrong? I asked.
> – He wears checked trousers and has cracked shoes.
> That was all the explanation A[nton] P[avlovich] gave me, for all my persistence. . . . I only solved this riddle six years later when *The Seagull* was revived.' (*SS*, V, p. 336.)

Writing to Gorki on the 9th Chekhov was more brutal:

> 'I saw *The Seagull* without sets. I can't judge the play dispassionately since the Seagull herself was so awful, sobbing out loud all the time and Trigorin (the bellelettrist) wandered about the stage and spoke like some paralytic; "he has no will of his own", which the actor interpreted in such a way it made me sick to look at it. Still, on the whole, all right, thrilling. In places I couldn't quite believe I had actually written it.' (Chekhov, *Pisma*, VIII, p. 170.)

Chekhov's dominant impression of the overall production remained, nonetheless, positive. On the 15th he wrote again to Iordanov:

> 'In Moscow they performed my *Seagull* for me at the Art Theatre. The

production is amazing . . . the Mali theatre pales in comparison, as far as *mise-en-scène* and production are concerned, as inferior to the Meininger as to the new Art Theatre, which is performing at the moment in very poor conditions.'

He confirmed his judgement when he wrote to Stanislavski on June 24:

'I learned from Luzhski, dear Konstantin Sergeievich, that you are in Moscow. I, too, am in Moscow. Could we see each other? The fact is I was in Petersburg and talked to Marks [his publisher] about bringing out the play with your *mise-en-scène*. He liked my suggestion – and now the rest is up to you . . . Perhaps we can have lunch at the Slav Bazaar, if that suits you. I warmly shake your hand. Yours, A. Chekhov.' (Chekhov, *Pisma*, VIII, p. 208.)

From Stanislavski's point of view the first season had been only a partial success. The director had to an extent obscured the actor. There had been no major acting triumphs. Trigorin had been a great disappointment. It must be said, however, that if *he* had taken the wrong line on the character then so had Nemirovich, the 'expert', who had written to Chekhov after the first night to say that Stanislavski had 'successfully captured the soft, weak-willed tone' – precisely the quality to which Chekhov took exception. Nowhere is there recorded any disagreement about the interpretation of the role. Stanislavski himself attributed his failure to his lack of knowledge of the literary world and the fact that he had no living model on which to base his interpretation.

Yet where, in the script was he, or Nemirovich, to find the 'cracked shoes'? How were they to infer that Trigorin is shabby? Nemirovich had jokingly remarked in early rehearsals that he could serve as a model for the character, yet he was never less than elegantly turned out. Chekhov, too, had been smartly dressed as a young man. Tall, blue-eyed and athletic, he had looked very dashing. His dress sense declined as his body decayed. The key to the character was the older Chekhov himself, with his unkempt appearance, his notebooks and his passion for fishing. But that was not in the text Nemirovich had analysed so minutely.

Stanislavski's one real achievement, Lövborg in *Hedda Gabler*, went comparatively unnoticed, although it was appreciated by the more discriminating:

'An aura of genius surrounded Lövborg. This rarely happens in the theatre. Genius is talked about but not experienced. He made the audience feel it and not just take it for granted. And this to my mind was the most valuable aspect of the interpretation of Ibsen's character. Lövborg was a volcano of passion, he was all storm and whirlwind, he was all thunderstorm. And the actor was able to convey this element literally bursting out of its shell, tearing it apart.' (Efros, *MXAT 1898–1923*, p. 56.)

An eye-witness at the final dress rehearsal described the effect on the audience:

> 'At the final rehearsal, Stanislavski, as the wild genius Lövborg, who had just lost his manuscript, rushed on to the stage like a thing possessed – "all storm and fury". It was such a shock that there was a stir in the auditorium. Several people leapt to their feet.' (Quoted by E. Poliakova in *Stanislavski*, Moscow, 1977, p. 154.)

All this was achieved without any obvious external characteristics, no conventional signs of 'genius', and almost without make-up. It was achieved by inner transformation:

> 'It was Stanislavski's face and yet also the face of the extravagant genius, Lövborg. As if the "make-up" came from within, was there under the skin of the face and so transformed it. The only make-up here was the soul.' (Efros, *K. S. Stanislavski*, pp. 88–9.)

Lenski could not have asked for more.

It is difficult to locate precise turning-points in an actor's career but it is worth noting that this performance follows immediately on the encounter with Chekhov and the demands his plays made on the actor's inner life. In subsequent seasons Stanislavski gave performances in which the psychological is emphasized rather than external appearance and technique. The accumulated lessons of the past were beginning to bear fruit.

As far as the theatre was concerned the outside world was not to know in what dire financial straits the company found itself. The losing battle to capture audiences was forgotten. The Moscow Art Theatre was pronounced a 'success'. Thus the *Novosti Dnia* confidently stated that Stanislavski and Nemirovich had:

> 'established their audience and achieved something unparalleled in the history of Russian theatre, a continuous series of full houses throughout a complete season, with three or four plays. Needless to say the Open Art Theatre achieved its position under a barrage of criticism from all those who stand for the hackneyed, the *status quo* in the theatre.' (*Novosti Dnia*, March 1, 1899.)

The foundations of the Moscow Art legend had been laid.

CHAPTER EIGHT

UNCLE VANIA

The first season had not brought Stanislavski the actor the critical recognition he might have expected. He had felt obliged to abandon Shylock, Trigorin had been only a moderate success while his one major achievement, as Lövborg in *Hedda Gabler*, had gone almost unnoticed. It was Stanislavski the director who had triumphed.

The future was by no means certain but the shareholders approached it boldly. Given the losses there might have been a temptation to cut back. But they were determined to maintain standards and were not prepared to compromise on sets, production values or the rehearsal period; on the contrary, they planned to build a new theatre and provide it with all the latest equipment. As the first season ended preparations for the second began.

The repertoire was much as before. The first production would be another historic drama by Aleksei Tolstoi, *The Death of Ivan the Terrible*. This would be followed by *Uncle Vania*, a revival of *Twelfth Night* from the Society of Art and Literature and Hauptmann's *Drayman Henschel*. In later July, Nemirovich suggested the inclusion of another Hauptmann play, *Lonely People*. Chekhov, who was now following the theatre's activities with great interest from his 'exile' in Yalta, approved. He found the play 'intelligent and theatrical'. *The Seagull*, *Antigone* and *Fiodor* remained in the repertoire.

The full burden of creative planning fell once more to Stanislavski. It was a well-nigh impossible task, demanding total concentration of energy. The family business took second place. Always scrupulous in his affairs, at a shareholders' meeting on March 10, he proposed that since he was not providing a full service his salary be reduced from 5000 to 4000 roubles. Later that same month he took a so-called holiday with Lilina, actually spending the time working on the production plan for *Drayman Henschel*. As Lilina wrote to their daughter, Kira: 'Papa writes all day and thinks about his plan. I read.' Returning to Moscow in early April he began work on *Henschel* and *Ivan*. The first readings of *Vania* took place at the beginning of May. This time round there was no question of preparing a production plan well in advance. It was written during rehearsals. This had the advantage of bringing Stanislavski and Nemirovich closer together in the early stages but it also increased the pressure. The casting of *Vania* brought Stanislavski a great disappointment. During his visit to Moscow in May 1899, Chekhov had preliminary discussions with Nemirovich and Stanislavski about *Uncle Vania* which again revealed the difficulty of deciphering his texts. It was the 'checked trousers' problem all over again. Both Nemirovich and Stanislavski had decided that Vania would wear knee-boots, a cap and carry a horse whip, the normal costume for country gentlemen in the theatre. Chekhov would have none of it. He told them they had simply not read the play. Everything they needed to know about Vania's appearance was there:

> 'We looked at the original but all we could find was a reference to a silk tie Uncle Vania wore.
> "Yes! It's all in the script," Chekhov assured us.
> "Where in the script?" we asked in amazement. "A silk tie?"
> "Of course. He is an elegant, cultured man. It's not true that our landowners wear greasy boots. They are educated people, they dress well, with clothes from Paris. I put it all in the script."' (*SS*, I, Moscow, 1988, p. 300.)

Stanislavski had decided to play the title role and after these discussions about the tie came to the conclusion that Vania looked like Tchaikovski. He thought of him as a gentle, poetic soul. Nemirovich, however, had other ideas. For him, Vania was much more volatile, not a quality he found in Stanislavski. But he did find it in Vishnievski, who was originally cast as Astrov. He eventually persuaded Stanislavski to exchange roles and wrote to Chekhov assuring him he would make an excellent Astrov.

For his part, Stanislavski was more than a little worried. To have to struggle with a difficult role like Astrov, which he did not find at all sympathetic, while preparing three other productions, was an almost intolerable burden. Preliminary work continued and on May 24 Chekhov was able to see what had been done with the first two acts which he thought 'went splendidly'. Stanislavski decided to spend the summer in Moscow. Lilina and the children were sent to Liubimovka while he finished the production plan for *Vania*, rehearsed *Ivan*, sketched in the broad outlines of the production plan for *Henschel* and discussed the sets of *Vania* and *Ivan* with Simov. In mid-June he made a short trip to the Volga, with Lilina, buying materials for *Ivan* in Kazan. Finally, on June 29, he made what was now a regular visit to Vichy to take the waters, although this did not prevent him from continuing to work. Pressure was now so great that he was obliged to appoint assistant directors and supervise preliminary rehearsals. The first of these was Aleksandr Sanin who had been his close collaborator at the Society. On July 21 he sent Sanin the production plans for the crowd scenes in *Ivan*. In that same letter he announced his final disillusion with French theatre after seeing a poor performance of Feydeau's *La Dame de Chez Maxime* – 'routine, routine'. Two days later he wrote again:

> 'I have once more experienced the negative side of theatre. I am returning with the firm intention to strive for truth and the most realistic action both in tragedy and in the emptiest farce. Only then can theatre make a serious statement. Otherwise it is a toy (as in France) and a very boring toy.' (*SS*, VII, p. 163.)

He had written to his mother in even stronger terms.

> 'I impatiently await my return to Moscow as the West, with its bogus culture, its posturings and affectation, with all its marks of decadence, grates on my nerves appallingly.' (Letter to E. V. Alexeieva, July 20, 1899, ibid., p. 160.)

He left Vichy at the end of July, stopping over in Berlin on his way to Sevastopol where he was to join Lilina and the children. Once there he was again on the look-out for any genuine objects or materials or clothing which might be useful for *Ivan*. Although he was probably not aware of it, by the summer break of 1899 his relationship with the company had undergone a significant change. His genius as an artist was not in question but he seemed to have no real notion of the disciplines of running a professional and, whatever its high ideals, commercial theatre. Although he managed the Alekseiev family business with great efficiency, he applied none of his managerial skills to the theatre he had created. He thus gained the reputation, which he was never quite to lose, of a chaotic genius. He had always in the past worked to his own time-table, staging a production when it was ready, paying for it out of his own pocket with no concern for the box office. Now the context of his work had changed but he had not adapted to it. He was felt by the company to be someone apart, not quite 'one of us' and, indeed, there were two people – Stanislavski the actor and Alekseiev, the industrialist, who could shut the elaborately carved door to his private apartments at Red Gates and live a private life that did not depend financially or materially on the Art Theatre. His production assistants, Sanin and Luzhski, had also written to Nemirovich to complain about the relentless work schedule. It was time for a break.

Nemirovich defended Stanislavski against all charges. Great men, he explained to his colleagues, have great faults. Nonetheless he realized that he must take things in hand. He himself was exhausted and frustrated. Almost the entire burden of administration had fallen on him, leaving him no time to write. He decided for everyone's sake to draw up a work-plan for Stanislavski to cover the whole of September, dividing his time between planning productions and preparing his own roles. On July 23 he wrote frankly, 'You can't go on working the way you have been. You can't and that's an end of it.' He suggested that they should

meet in Sevastopol once he had joined his family, and discuss the new
season.

The meeting took place on August 9 and 10. Nemirovich found
Stanislavski in much better health, relaxed, open to suggestions and full
of creative ideas. He then suggested that they travel back to Moscow at
the end of the month. They took a private carriage and were thus able to
spend two more days in discussion. These days of intimate talk gave
Nemirovich immense satisfaction. He saw himself as the wiser, older
brother, the professional, guiding and schooling his younger brother, the
amateur. There was nonetheless a major disagreement between them.
Nemirovich was fully aware that for the Art Theatre to survive
commercially the season had to be tightly planned, and there had to be
two or three new productions, with dates fixed for the opening nights.
Stanislavski as an actor needed long rehearsal periods. He resisted the
notion of quick answers, what he was later to call the 'in general'. The
kind of detailed performance he conceived took time to put together and
to run in. He was rarely fully ready on the first night. Nemirovich was of
course, from an administrative point of view, right but his tight schedule
was to create problems during the coming season.

After their return to Moscow, with unconscious irony, he wrote:

'So, our work comes down to five plays. You've got to rehearse the
role of Ivan to perfection, get Astrov absolutely right, direct the whole
of *Ivan*, tighten up *Henschel*, bolster up *Twelfth Night* and run through
Antigone and *Fiodor*.' (*Iz., Pis.*, I, p. 188.)

As if that were not enough, he had also asked Stanislavski's help in
preparing *Lonely People*. He needed Stanislavski's capacity to visualize:

'One hint from you and I get a whole scene . . . Just take few scraps of
paper and write down the first thing that comes into your head – some
salad on a broken plate, physical attitudes, shouts, a departure by
steamer . . .' (N-D Archive, no. 1558.)

Nemirovich did make one concession. Stanislavski would only play the
opening performances of *Ivan*, then the title role would be taken over by
someone else – in the event, Meierhold – while he rehearsed Astrov.

On August 29 Stanislavski saw what his assistant had done on *Ivan*.
According to Knipper, Sanin was so nervous he practically bit his fingers
down to the knuckle. Stanislavski took over and rehearsed for the next
month, managing in the interim to provide Nemirovich with detailed
plans for the first two acts of *Lonely People*. On September 8 there was
a costume and make-up parade. The first dress rehearsals followed on
September 10 and 11. The final dress rehearsal was scheduled for the
27th and the play opened two nights later.

Stanislavski had taken a strong line with Aleksei Tolstoi's play,
expanding it into an epic, filling it with spectacle. Once again he insisted

on the crucial role of the people. This meant, as before, expanding the crowd scenes, making them central to the action. But it was a very different crowd from *Fiodor*. As he had written to Sanin on July 21:

> 'In rehearsal concentrate primarily on keeping the voices down, emphasize the subjugation, the signs of starvation, famished people shaking with cold. In short the two dominant moods are cold and hunger. In two or three places the crowd rises to a pitch which demands a terrifying flash of power which immediately subsides into total nervous exhaustion.' (*SS*, VII, p. 161.)

In his own interpretation of the leading role he once more pursued the psychological. This was a many-sided Ivan which Stanislavski created single-handed. Nemirovich, who was directing, simply let him get on with it:

> 'You managed to capture the most profound aspect of Ivan – his retribution for his whole life, for his tyranny, for all the vileness which filled his life and his character. You succeeded in painting a portrait that filled everything about it with horror yet also conveyed the human qualities in him that lead to destruction and inexpressible suffering. What must the sufferings be of a man who in his time condemned tens and hundreds of thousands of people to suffer for them to reconcile me, the audience, to him? How heavy the torment and the torture, of the most sincere and profound kind, that passes through me so that I can say to this fanatic: "God forgive you!"
> ... from the very first speech at the very first rehearsal I saw I was immediately satisfied with your interpretation. . . . This is why I reserved my notes until the final rehearsals. . . .' (*Iz., Pis.*, I, pp. 190–1.)

These notes were confined to warnings about excessive pausing and against overdoing an old man's cough.

Stanislavski asked for the opening night to be postponed. Hardly surprisingly, he felt under-rehearsed and unprepared. Nemirovich's rigidly tight work-plan, efficient as it looked on paper, remained precisely that, a paper plan. It made genuine creative work in Stanislavski's sense impossible. For Nemirovich there was a straight progression in mounting a play – analyse, plan, implement, polish. But that took no account of the hesitations, the doubts, the blocks an actor encounters in the creative process. It was the thinking of a man who had never genuinely created a role. Stanislavski fell ill just before the first night and though he agreed to go on, insisted, against the wishes of the company, that Nemirovich should make an announcement before curtain up stating he was unwell. Was he genuinely ill? Nemirovich thought at the time that he was being wilful and manipulative. His condition may have been a psychosomatic response to stress, above all a fear of failure. An illness would provide an excuse. Whatever Stanislavski's intention, the announcement sent a chill through the audience.

The production divided opinion. Chaliapin, who attended a rehearsal on the 25th, according to Knipper 'banged the walls with delight'. Efros, too, saluted Stanislavski's achievement in combining the Ivan of history, the myth-figure, and a real human being, in encompassing the heights of heroic tragedy and ordinary human drama. But the favourable judgements of the professionals were not shared by the public. Stanislavski's illness on opening night cannot alone account for the overall failure of the production.

Stanislavski's performance evoked the now familiar criticism that he had reduced a 'heroic' character to something commonplace. The public was simply not ready for his three-dimensional portrait although it was endorsed by Aleksei Tolstoi himself, who ascribed the generally adverse reaction to the fact that audiences and critics alike insisted on clinging to their outdated notions of what the theatre should be. Perhaps nowhere was Stanislavski more modern as an actor than in his continued attempts to destroy the conventional, two-dimensional image of historic or heroic figures in order to reveal the difficulty of actually living history and the human cost involved. Stanislavski's Ivan was not the towering monster made famous later by Eisenstein but a decrepit shambles of a man, impotent where he had once been strong, guilt-ridden where he had once been ruthless. That was what the audience disliked. But Stanislavski the director had also overloaded the play, attempting to endow it with meanings it could not bear. He had stretched the material beyond its endurance, trying to transform a minor play into an epic drama. That, combined with his own provocative interpretation, made it almost impossible for the production to succeed.

He was very depressed. Nemirovich wrote to Chekhov:

'. . . The actor [in him] is aware that he has *lost* his audience but he still has to go on performing. He spends an enormous amount of nervous energy but it doesn't get across, the audience does not like his *conception*. I don't know whether the audience is right or not. I'm so used to Alekseiev's interpretation which I find absolutely satisfying . . . What is exhausting for an actor is not so much the part as lack of success in it. And Konstantin Sergeievich is so worn out that he was not fit for work on the day of *Ivan* or the day after. That's why so far he has not been near *Vania*.' (*Ezhegodnik MXAT*, 1944, p. 119.)

One long-term consequence of this failure was the conclusion that Stanislavski was simply not a tragic actor, a judgement that has been repeated ever since. Chekhov, who had only seen Stanislavski in *The Seagull*, in one of his typically extreme snap judgements concluded that Stanislavski was a fine director, but as an actor he was no more than a rich dilettante, dabbling in art – an opinion he soon revised.

This latest failure was just one more disappointment to add to the comparative lack of success of the first season.

The opening of *Vania* was less than four weeks away. *The Seagull* was back in the repertoire; a matinée of *Twelfth Night* on October 3 was well reviewed and *Drayman Henschel* opened on the 5th to good notices but went on to play to poor houses. Stanislavski was still dogged by illness. He put himself entirely in Nemirovich's hands as far as Astrov was concerned – at least that is what Nemirovich claimed when writing to Chekhov after the opening. The production plan represented an advance over *The Seagull*. The sets Stanislavski had created with Simov looked as though they had been lived in; the props looked as though they had been used over many years and the costumes looked as though they had been worn. The action was full of the trivia of life, the deadening trivia against which the characters try to struggle in their attempt to remain spiritually and mentally alive. The detail of daily life was an essential agent in the drama.

Stanislavski found his way into the character of Astrov with difficulty. His method was still to work from the outside in, to establish a sequence of actions in the hope that they would stimulate the right mood and emotion. His insecurity in the early stages of rehearsal was indicated by his restlessness, his inability to keep still. When actors are uncertain or do not feel at one with their characters they become overactive, hoping that continuous movement will disguise the absence of genuine thought or feeling. Thus he wandered around the house and garden, noting everything, examining the plants, picking the heads off dead flowers. Above all, he swatted mosquitoes. He remembered how family and friends were tormented by these creatures during the summer at Liubimovka. The production plan contains instructions to everyone to swat them and even, as an added protection, to put handkerchiefs over their faces. Nemirovich was not at all happy with this particular piece of local colour.

> 'I don't want handkerchiefs on faces to keep off mosquitoes, it's a detail I simply can't take. And I can tell you for certain that Chekhov won't like it; I know his tastes and creative nature extremely well. I can tell you for certain that this particular detail doesn't introduce anything new. I'll wager that it will merely be numbered among those "excesses" which just irritate and do not bring any advantage to the theatre or to the work you are doing. It is even far-fetched from a real-life point of view. In short I cannot find any convincing argument for it, not one serious argument of any kind. And since there really is no argument for it, I cannot see why you won't give it up when I ask you.' (*MATL*, No. 57.)

It is clear from Stanislavski's *Notebooks*, however, that the by-play with the handkerchiefs, which so exercised Nemirovich was a rehearsal exercise, a very early example of Stanislavski's use of precise physical actions to create the kind of belief in a dramatic situation that leads to genuine characterization and away from the cliché.

The letter also contained another complaint. Stanislavski, hardly surprisingly perhaps, was not sure of his lines. What's the point, Nemirovich asks, of his trying to discipline other members of the cast when the company's leading director and producer is setting a bad example? Stanislavski remained obdurate. He could snap back when he felt artistically in a corner. So, for the time being, the handkerchiefs and the mosquitoes remained. Only gradually, as rehearsals progressed and confidence grew, did the welter of detail disappear. There were, however, more important problems of interpretation to be resolved, in particular the relationship between Vania and Elena, the professor's wife. Stanislavski's original intention was for her to play at a high level of intensity. Nemirovich did not agree.

> 'You interpret the little scene between Vania and Elena (Act Two) as though she was genuinely afraid about his drinking. That's not in the play, on the contrary, for Elena to be afraid in these circumstances is *not at all in keeping* with her character.
> – You've been drinking again today. What's the point?
> The very structure of the sentence gives a much quieter tone, the languid tone which marks Elena's attitude to everything going on around her.' (Ibid., p. 199.)

Nemirovich was also worried about the final scenes in Act Four between Astrov and Elena. So was Knipper. Stanislavski, she wrote to Chekhov, was playing the scene like a passionate lover, clutching at feeling like a drowning man at a straw. Chekhov, who resolutely refused to give explanations to actors when they met him, was willing to be categorical on paper:

> 'But that's wrong, absolutely wrong. Astrov finds Elena attractive, she captivates him with her beauty but in the last act he already knows that she is lost to him forever – and he speaks of her in this scene in exactly the same tone as he speaks of the heat in Africa and he kisses her simply because there doesn't seem anything else to do. If Astrov plays this scene vehemently it will ruin the mood of the whole fourth act, which is quiet and muted.' (Chekhov, *Pisma*, VIII, p. 272.)

When Chekhov finally saw the full production of *Vania* in Sevastopol in April 1900, he offered only one comment on Stanislavski's performance, which again related to the problematic Act Four:

> 'Listen, he whistles. Uncle Vania moans and groans but *he* whistles. (*SS*, VI, p. 342.)

Stanislavski found this difficult but gradually began to introduce a greater degree of apparent cynicism into the role. Once again, the key was Chekhov himself. Chekhov was a doctor, like Astrov; Chekhov spent his last years creating a garden in Yalta, bringing plants, trees and shrubs from all over Russia, Astrov plants forests. Chekhov, although deeply sensitive and vulnerable, constantly hid his feelings behind a flow of banter and irony. It was that feature that Stanislavski's Astrov initially lacked.

Even if Stanislavski the actor had not yet found the right tone, Stanislavski the director realized that Act Four as a whole was a problem. He confided his anxieties to Efros:

> 'The basic idea is in "they've gone". The director must make the audience feel clearly what their departure means – so everyone goes home depressed, as though the lid had been nailed down on the coffin and everything was dead for ever. Without that the act doesn't exist, without that there's no end to the play. . . . What would happen if the audience didn't feel they were really "going" but merely that the actors were wandering back to the dressing-room to take off their make-up? Can an actor convey everything he has to with just one exit?
>
> I'm told there are actors who can do this. I haven't seen them. I don't know them. During one rather tedious break in rehearsal while we were trying to work out an answer as it were, one of the crew, who was tinkering with the set, started banging with a stick. And we . . . suddenly detected in that banging the clatter of hoofs going over a bridge. Why not make use of it, providing it conveyed the author's intention truthfully and expressively and gave us what we needed to achieve the aim of the production?' (Reported by Efros in *MXAT 1898–1923*, pp. 232–3.)

The same, he added, was also true of many other details in the production. This statement again stresses the organic, functional nature of Stanislavski's production effects. They are there to illuminate the play and if necessary cover the deficiencies of the actors.

By opening night the problems had been ironed out. Stanislavski and Nemirovich could congratulate themselves on another effective and creative collaboration. On October 23 Meierhold wrote to Chekhov:

> 'The play is exceptionally well directed. What I note above all is the artistic restraint which is sustained throughout the entire production. For the first time the two directors fully complement each other; one, a director-actor, has a great deal of imagination but is inclined to go over the top; the other, a director-author, protects the writer's interests. And it's well for the latter to have the upper hand.' (Meierhold, *Perepiska*, Moscow, 1976, p. 23.)

As to Stanislavski's Astrov, it was considered by many to be his finest role in any Chekhov play, not excepting Vershinin in *Three Sisters* which

he was to play a year later. Writing to Chekhov, Nemirovich described
the line they had taken on the part:

> 'We present Astrov as a materialist in the best sense of the term,
> incapable of loving, relating to women with elegant cynicism, scarcely
> perceptible cynicism. There is sensitivity but no passion there. And all
> this in that half-joking form women find so attractive.' (*Iz., Pis.*, I, pp.
> 195–6.)

But there was more to Stanislavski's interpretation than that. His
performance as Astrov revealed an inner tension born of struggle. The
word 'tense', 'tensely', occurs frequently in Stanislavski's production
notes. Astrov is a man of strong convictions, if not of strong passions, but
a man who undercuts himself with a deprecating remark as soon as he
feels he has revealed too much about himself. He drinks to deaden the
pain and if he drinks too much it is because there is too much pain. Late
in life Knipper maintained that Stanislavski's insight into the character
sprang from an identification of his own attempts to create a new kind of
theatre with Astrov's attempts to plant new forests. Astrov's frustrations
were his frustrations. She also recalled the depth and feeling with which
he played his last scene with her incidentally revealing the measure to
which he had brought together into a complex being the intense lover he
had originally conceived and the cynic Chekhov had described:

> '. . . what a wonderfully poetic and courageous person he created in
> Astrov and with such lightness of touch. And in the last act when he
> went over to the map of Africa and looked at it: "Ah, the heat in Africa
> – it must be dreadful". How much sorrow was packed into the
> experience of that bitter phrase.' (Olga Knipper Chekhova, *O
> Stanislavskom*, p. 266.)

The audience found a broader social meaning in the performance. For
them Astrov's struggle and suffering went beyond the personal to the
state of Russia itself. Efros placed Astrov in the line of the 'superfluous
men', that peculiarly Russian phenomenon – men of talent and ability
who for one reason or another never fulfil their promise and make no
mark on their age, effect no change and finally succumb beneath the
dead-weight of history. Astrov is on his way to join their ranks:

> 'All Astrov's traits emerged clearly defined and life-like in
> Stanislavski's performance, all the elements of the image equally – the
> typical and the individual. He plays the social and the psychological
> aspects clearly. He revealed this man in his entirety. You could clearly
> feel the "wood-demon" already running to seed, coarsening, yielding
> to the pressure of "a way of life" but with brave hopes and thoughts
> still glowing under the embers. You could feel the soul of a gifted poet,
> flying across the centuries, dedicated to the most far-distant dreams.

You could see the broad sweep of this soul, in which there was a great thirst for beauty. . . . His interpretation excited, delighted the audience, saddened them, evoked in them fierce protest against that form of Russian life which turns Astrov into a mere "crank", a new variation of "superfluous men", and little by little transforms great strength, great power of soul into everyday triviality.

Stanislavski's Astrov was fully realistic but it was also romantic. And with all that it was beautiful as a piece of theatre.' (Efros, *MXAT 1898–1923*, pp. 237–8.)

As for Stanislavski himself, he was astonished at his own success. 'I do nothing and the public loves it,' he remarked to Knipper, showing he had yet to learn the supreme actor's art: 'doing nothing' to maximum effect.

The production did not enjoy the immediate success *The Seagull* had obtained. It took hold only slowly but established a permanent place in the repertoire which *The Seagull* did not. It was the capacity of the Moscow Art Theatre, through productions like *Vania*, to speak to its age, as, in the past, only great literature had done, that made it a focal point for advanced opinion.

In January 1900, Gorki saw a performance of *Vania* after which he confessed to Chekhov that although he was not exactly the sensitive type he had cried like a schoolgirl. The play, he wrote to Chekhov, tore him apart like a rough-edged saw. He went back for a second visit, arriving for Act Three, and wrote to Chekhov again. His praise for the production was high but not unconditional:

'Pity that Vishnievski doesn't understand Uncle but on the other hand the rest are a wonder. Stanislavski's Astrov in minor respects is not what it should be. Still, they all play marvellously! The Mali theatre is unbelievably crude in comparison with this company. How aware and intelligent these people are, how much artistic flair they have! . . . All in all this theatre gave me the impression of being solid, serious and important. I'm sorry that I don't live in Moscow otherwise I would go to this marvel of a theatre.' (Gorki, *SS*, XXVIII, p. 117.)

Chekhov's response was to invite him to Yalta in April, when the company would be on tour:

'You need to get nearer this theatre and observe it so you can write plays.' (Chekhov, *Pisma*, IX, p. 67.)

Of his own experience, in November 1899 he had written:

'. . . I thank heaven that, sailing through the ups and downs of life, I finally came on such a wonderful island as the Moscow Art Theatre.' (Chekhov, *Pisma*, VIII, p. 297.)

If the young Gorki was a visitor to the theatre so was the elderly and now

immensely venerable Lev Tolstoi. He saw *Vania* on January 24 and was
pleased with Stanislavski's performance and with the production as a
whole. On February 18 Lenin paid his first known visit to the theatre to
see *Drayman Henschel*. His endorsement of the theatre's policy and his
approval of its artistic practice were later to assure the company's
survival. Even Ermolova, who had spent her life at the Mali, talked of
leaving and joining the new company.

In the meantime, Hauptmann's *Lonely People*, with Meierhold in the
lead, had opened on December 16 to a huge success, although most of the
company were prepared either for a total flop or, at best, a lukewarm
reception. But, here again, a skilfully orchestrated portrayal of domestic
life, presented in what was now the company's 'Chekhovian' manner,
found an echo in the public mind. Although the debts were mounting, the
future seemed bright.

CHAPTER NINE

THREE SISTERS

By the time the season ended on February 20 Stanislavski was almost at breaking-point. He had pushed himself hard, performing even when not in the best of health. He was exhausted yet could not sleep. Tension had been increased by his first serious disagreement over management with Nemirovich. Its subject was Savva Morozov.

Without Morozov the theatre would have gone under. Apart from his original investment, he had put up 21,000 roubles at the end of 1899 in order to extend the lease on the Hermitage theatre. He later subsidized the 1900–1 season to the tune of 120,000 roubles. From time to time he would give money to actresses to buy the costumes they needed for modern roles. He was now a constant visitor to the theatre, attending rehearsals and generally taking an interest in the day-to-day running of the company. There was nothing malicious in this, no sense that Morozov was protecting his investment. He was simply passionately devoted to the Moscow Art Theatre and what it stood for. But Nemirovich suspected a take-over in which he would be the loser. The resentment he had felt against Morozov from the very beginning, and which he had found it increasingly difficult to keep hidden, burst out in an angry letter which he wrote to Stanislavski just before the end of the season:

> 'Did I start this business with you for some capitalist to come along and try to turn me into – how shall I put it? – a kind of secretary?' (N-D Archive No. 1571.)

Stanislavski, normally reticent in all personal matters, sent back a letter which was equally exasperated in tone. He had been here before. He had seen the Society of Art and Literature founder in a welter of pettiness and selfishness, just the sort of destructive emotions displayed in Nemirovich's letter. He had tiptoed a path through the rampant egos of colleagues, filling in the cracks, discreetly, where he could, often made himself look ridiculous in the process – for Nemirovich's sake. He had made financial sacrifices, denying his family essentials, and reducing his own personal budget. As to any artistic satisfaction, there was not much of that left:

> 'I have reconciled myself to the fact that (often) I neither play in nor

direct things I long to do but act what I have to, not what I want to. In a word I am ruining myself financially and morally, without complaint as long as my nerves are not stretched to breaking-point. That's the stage we have obviously now reached and, as you can see, I have started to kick. . . . In fact I'm sick and tired that everyone else seems to have the right to talk about themselves but *I'm* not . . . and that's unfair. . . .

I will not remain in the theatre without you. We started it together and should lead it together. I recognize in you, of course, as in any human being, certain deficiencies but at the same time *I value your many good qualities highly* and especially the good relationship you have with me and my work. Without Morozov I cannot remain in the theatre *under any circumstances*. Why? Because I value Morozov's good qualities. . . . Remember, I have no money, I have a family and moreover *have no right* to take risks with that part of my property. I believe . . . in Morozov's honesty blindly. My confidence in him is so rock-solid that I have no written agreement with him. It's superfluous. . . . In the future I'm not going to play a double game, trying, privately, to reconcile Morozov with Nemirovich and vice versa. If conflict is unavoidable then let it happen quickly and our enterprise be wrecked while it will still be missed, let us Russians prove once more that we are rotten to the core and that personal egoism and petty ambition will destroy anything worthwhile . . .' (*MATL*, No. 74.)

This exchange was the first of many similar arguments over the next few years. It marked perhaps the end of the pioneer days when everything was sacrificed to the common goal. Success was to bring its own problems. For the moment, however, Stanislavski's uncompromising tone put an end to discussion.

He took a short rest with Lilina although it was not long before he made an expedition to the Archangel area to study the northern landscape and collect material for Ostrovski's *Snow Maiden*, the by-now almost regulation 'spectacular' which was to open the 1900–1 season. Rehearsals began in March but were interrupted the following month by a tour which had been arranged for Chekhov's benefit. His health did not allow him to come to Moscow and he had not yet seen *Vania*. The company therefore decided to take four productions – *Seagull, Vania, Lonely People* and *Hedda Gabler* – to Sevastopol and Yalta on the principle 'if the mountain won't come to Mahomet, Mahomet will come to the mountain'. The company were a little disconcerted to learn that many figures from the Russian literary establishment were to be present but set off on the two-day train journey with determination.

It was an idyllic 'month in the country' for all. Chekhov was pleased with the production of *Vania* and impressed with Hauptmann's gifts as a dramatist, as opposed to Ibsen whom he did not rate at all highly – 'not a

playwright'. According to his sister, Maria, it was the happiest time he
ever spent in all his years of enforced exile in Yalta. He was constantly
at the theatre and even, one day, tried to teach the stage carpenter how to
imitate a cricket. Stanislavski, for his part, was fascinated by the
conversation of the literary men present at the many lunch parties.
Chekhov, in particular, brought books and literature alive to him in a way
his schoolmasters had never succeeded in doing. He also came to know
two men who were to become life-long friends, Sergei Rachmaninov and
Maxim Gorki. He found Gorki fascinating:

> 'For me centre stage was held by Gorki who immediately excited me
> with his charm. In his unusual figure, face, [provincial] accent,
> extraordinary way of gesticulating, revealing the peasant in him at
> moments of high emotion, in his bright, childlike smile, in the at times
> tragically heartfelt expression of his face, in his colourful, expressive
> speech, whether light-hearted or intense, there appeared a certain
> gentleness of soul and grace and looking at his stooping body one saw
> a special kind of physical expressiveness and outward beauty. I often
> caught myself admiring his stance and his gestures.' (*SS*, V, p. 345.)

Gorki was equally taken with Stanislavski. On May 1, as the party was
breaking up, he gave him a photograph with the inscription:

> 'To Konstantin Sergeievich Alekseiev, a great and beautiful man, an
> artist and the creator of a new theatre. I wish, with all my heart, that
> every sensible man who meets you for the first time may love and
> respect you as I now love and respect you. . . .'

Rehearsals for *Snow Maiden* resumed in Moscow in May immediately
on the company's return and in the middle of the month work also began
on *An Enemy of the People*. There was a major casting problem in *Snow
Maiden*. Stanislavski could not find anybody he thought right for the role
of Tsar Berendei. It was finally offered to a young actor who was to
become one of the great stars of the Moscow Art Theatre, Vasili
Kachalov. Not that Kachalov had been enthusiastically welcomed into
the company. In March he had auditioned at Nemirovich's invitation, in
the roles both of Boris Godunov and Ivan the Terrible in *The Death of
Ivan the Terrible*. Stanislavski's reaction had been discouraging. He had
said, quite frankly, that he was not sure that he and Kachalov spoke the
same language or that they could use what he had to offer. On the other
hand they did not want to lose him because in time he might become a
Moscow Art kind of actor. What he was trying to tell Kachalov,
discreetly, was that he had too many bad habits as an actor. The
following day Nemirovich was rather more blunt. Kachalov nevertheless
elected to stay and for two months attended all the *Snow Maiden*
rehearsals, watching and learning. His application was rewarded. One
day Stanislavski came up to him, drew him to one side and explained that

as everyone else had failed as Berendei he could try. Three days later he showed what he could do. This time Stanislavski applauded:

'That was wonderful! You are one of us! You've understood it all! You've understood the most important thing. The very essence of our theatre. Hurrah!' (*V. I. Kachalov*, Iskusstvo, Moscow, 1954, p. 24.)

Stanislavski was rarely lavish with his praise but when he saw something of real quality he was open-hearted with his generosity. He had recognized Kachalov's obvious talent at their first encounter. He was tall, slender, elegant, well educated, with a naturally musical voice. Indeed reference to his 'velvet tones' became a critical cliché. But he had come to Moscow convinced that he had nothing to learn and it showed. He was, he told his friends, 'a proper actor'. When he had auditioned in St Petersburg he had turned up in a top hat and a vivid orange overcoat, very much the leading actor. Such an attitude did not suit Stanislavski. But now he had proved that he was both willing and able to learn. Hence Stanislavski's delight. He worshipped nothing so much as real, native talent but he would not tolerate conceit – 'Love the art in yourself, not yourself in art.' Kachalov had come through.

Work continued on *Snow Maiden* and *Enemy of the People* intensively throughout June, so much so that on July 10 Nemirovich wrote insisting that Stanislavski should rest for the remainder of the month and the whole of August. Rest, in reality, meant simply being out of Moscow. Stanislavski continued to plan *Snow Maiden* and learn the part of Dr Stockman. Disillusioned by his previous year's visit to Vichy he stayed in Russia, going first to Essentuki to take the cure, then to Novosibirsk, from there to Yalta where he joined up with the rest of his family and thence to Alupka. As always, when absent from the centre of things, he engaged in a voluminous correspondence.

Being so near to Chekhov's home Stanislavski was able to contact him and finally to report to Nemirovich on August 9 with exciting news:

'*I am writing in terms of the utmost secrecy.* Yesterday I managed to drag out of Chekhov the fact that tomorrow he is going to Gursuf to write. He will be back in Alupka in a week and will read what he has written. He hopes to be able to deliver the play on September 1 . . . He is writing a play about the life of military men with four roles for young women and 12 for men. I know that we can expect good parts for Meierhold, Knipper, Sheliabushskaia, Vishnievski and Kaluzhski [Luzhski] . . .' (*SS*, VII, p. 185.)

Great efforts had been made to persuade Chekhov to write another play. It was essential for the new season. This time it seemed, the play would really be their own. *The Seagull* had been rescued, as it were, from theatrical hacks; *Vania* was a revision of an earlier piece; the new play would be specifically tailored for the company. Chekhov had in fact indicated to Knipper, soon to be his wife, that he wanted to write something for her. But work for him was an increasing effort and it was by no means certain that he would be able to deliver on time.

Stanislavski returned to Moscow at the end of August and saw the work which had been done on the first three acts of *Snow Maiden*. He was pleased with what had been achieved and took over rehearsals on September 4. Gorki attended rehearsals and brought with him Leopold Sulerzhitski who was to become Stanislavski's most devoted assistant, disciple and friend.

Immense care, attention and money had been lavished on *Snow Maiden*. Stanislavski had insisted on visual authenticity as usual but out of that Simov had created a magical world. The sets and costumes were dazzling. The production was full of imaginative detail but when it opened on September 24 it was a flop. Critical opinion was sharply divided. Gorki wrote a glowing letter to Chekhov on the quality of the acting. Efros praised the production for its richness and brilliance of invention but others found it overloaded. Kachalov was badly mauled by one critic for his interpretation of Tsar Berendei. Stanislavski immediately sent him a letter of support, taking full responsibility for the line that had been taken on the role and begging the young actor not to lose faith in himself. As for the audiences, they simply stayed away or, as Meierhold put it, slavishly repeated the carping criticisms which had appeared in the popular press.

It was Meierhold, in a letter to Chekhov on October 1, who put his finger on the true reason for the play's failure.

'... *Snow Maiden* is simply old-fashioned. It's obvious that in troubled times like ours, when everything is falling apart around us, a simple appeal to beauty is not enough. ... Gorki considers, I don't know why, that the public and the press are ignorant. Our critics are ignorant, that's a fact. ... But the public? Credulous it might be but it hasn't lost its instinct. Isn't the play, surely, beautiful but thin?' (Meierhold, *Perepiska*, p. 28.)

Meierhold's analysis was proved correct by the phenomenal success of *An Enemy of the People* which opened a month later. Stanislavski's Stockman was one of his greatest performances. It was also one of his most instinctive. His remarkable attribute as an actor was his capacity for physical transformation from within. Astrov had been pudgy, running to seed; Stockman was thin, wiry, stooping, with a characteristic gesture of the hand. Where Astrov had been all circles Stockman was all angles. Stanislavski even succeeded in making his giant frame appear small. He slid into the character with an ease he had rarely, if ever, experienced before.

Stockman's body and physical patterns were put together, mostly unconsciously, from various sources. The basic shape was derived from

Rimski-Korsakov. The hands, Stanislavski realized much later, came from a German doctor he had seen in Vienna and the emphatic jabbing gesture from Maxim Gorki, whom he had observed in April of that same year. Yet if much came spontaneously, Stanislavski's artistic intentions in creating such an eccentric body were quite deliberate. Just as in *Acosta* he had replaced the conventional, idealized figure of a 'spiritual' man with a real person coming to grips with a concrete situation, so he now decided to play Stockman not as an intellectual with a gift for making clever speeches, but as a crank. He looked for physical characteristics which would express mental quirks. The two fingers became all important. He decided to pick everything up with two fingers only. He practised at home – his friends thought he had gone mad – and only when he could perform this action automatically, with dexterity, did he appear at rehearsals and only then did he deliver Ibsen's text. The physical characterization impressed everyone who saw it. The hands, with their characteristic shape, were photographed from many angles and a statuette was cast, fixing for ever the combative figure of Stanislavski-Stockman.

There was more to the performance, however, than a brilliant physical composition. Many friends and colleagues saw considerable affinities between Stanislavski's own personality and Stockman's – the passionate idealism, the same commitment to truth, the same lonely struggle against falsehood and corruption. Kachalov maintained that everything that was best in Stanislavski went into his performance. Certainly there is something of Stockman's Act Five naïveté and courage in Stanislavski's own character. And the decision at the end to bring in the poor off the streets and educate them was the kind of impulse he understood. This was not, of course, the first time that Stanislavski had played the part of an individual against the mob and the production notes for Act Four recall the mob scene in *Uriel Acosta*. As in *Acosta* Stanislavski insisted that the crowd should be individuated, real people in real circumstances, people with whom the audience could identify.

In this production the skills he had acquired came together, the intimacy he had learned to project for Chekhov's plays and his capacity to orchestrate a crowd. As for the 'message' of the play, that was left to Ibsen. It was not consciously played. All the effort went into making people and events as laid out in the script, the 'given circumstances', authentic. In terms of a Realist aesthetic a goal had been reached.

Letters poured in but intelligent public reaction was best summed up by Sulerzhitski who wrote to Stanislavski on October 21, after a dress rehearsal:

'You don't only work upon the senses but penetrate into the very soul, you enter life itself, to a man's very "holy of holies" in a way that only a close, understanding, sensitive friend can do. . . . Listening to

Stockman I found corroboration of the fact that there is not and cannot be any other outcome except the acknowledgement of truth no matter where or when, without regard to the consequences of that acknowledgement. I was always conscious of that truth, of course, but you shifted it from the realm of consciousness to the realm of feeling, i.e., you did what was necessary for that consciousness to give living results, expressed in deeds and actions.' (K.S. Archive.)

The enthusiasm, the passions which the production aroused were unprecedented. Stanislavski experienced in full measure that electric flow of energy which passes from stage to auditorium and back not only when the performance is exciting but when ideas, feelings and convictions are shared.

Chekhov arrived in Moscow on October 23, in time for the opening of *Enemy of the People*, bringing with him the first draft of the script of *Three Sisters*. Work on the play started immediately, three months behind schedule. This was to be the first Chekhov play Stanislavski directed without any initial help from Nemirovich who was preoccupied with the final stages of a rehearsal for *When We Dead Awaken*, his first venture as a solo director.

The first reading took place on the 29th. It was a failure.

'There was a stunned silence. Chekhov gave an embarrassed smile, coughed nervously and wandered among us . . . Snatches of remarks were heard: "This is an outline, not a play", "It's unactable, no real characters, just a few hints".' (*Dear Writer . . . Dear Actress*, p. 70.)

Nemirovich considered it inferior to both *Ivanov* and *The Seagull* which remained his favourite Chekhov plays. It was not 'lyrical'. It was perhaps for this reason that he decided to let Stanislavski work on it alone.

In the discussion which followed Chekhov heard his play qualified as a drama or a tragedy, while he insisted it was a comedy. When one of the more pretentious members of the company began a pseud-philosophical discourse he quietly slipped away. Stanislavski went round immediately to his flat, where he found him in an angry mood but managed to calm him down. Chekhov's reaction, apparently that of an author faced with a group of uncomprehending, not to say obtuse, actors would be understandable were it not for the fact that their response to his script coincided with his own privately expressed views. The play, as he wrote to Knipper, had started well but he became less and less satisfied with it as time went on. Whatever he had intended to write, it was coming out differently. He was worried about the structure; to have four leading female characters seemed both unreasonable and unmanageable. He found the play as it developed long and boring. In a letter to Vera Komissarzhevskaia he described it as 'gloom and doom'. He was convinced that it would be a flop and that he would suffer another humiliation. At the back of his mind was the fear that he would once more suffer the irksome accusation that he was a pessimist. The pseudo-philosophical discourse to which he had been subjected only served to confirm his worst suspicions. Hence his displeasure.

It was as though he hoped that, at the first reading, the cast would discover the comedy he had intended to write, and then blamed them for failing to do so. What, in any case, did he mean by 'comedy'? Turgenev had called A Month in the Country, with all its destructive elements, a comedy; Molière's Le Misanthrope, for all its black moments, is a comedy. In that sense Three Sisters is a comedy and, after much work, Stanislavski found sufficient positive elements to place it in that category. Chekhov apart, everyone, including his own family, found a deep well of sadness in the work, lacrimae rerum, and while the typescript gives no genre, the first published edition and all subsequent editions describe the play as a 'drama'.

Chekhov's nervousness and irritability had already expressed itself in his reaction to an article by Efros in September in which he had stated that the title Three Sisters was considered unsatisfactory and would be altered. Chekhov wrote an angry letter to Knipper denying any intention to change the name of the play, even if he did not himself like it. Nemirovich managed to smooth things over and Efros agreed that in future he would be more careful in checking his sources.

With these initial difficulties out of the way rehearsals proceeded. Chekhov remained in Moscow throughout November, meeting Stanislavski several times to discuss the production. He then returned to Yalta, his Devil's Island as he described it, but, feeling more and more restless, decided to go abroad to rewrite the script. This he did in Nice during December and sent off the revisions act by act. He relied on Knipper to keep him informed of the play's progress both in rehearsal and performance. Tense and anxious, as his letters demonstrate, he kept on the move, travelling to Pisa, Florence and Rome. He was, in consequence, difficult to contact, but nonetheless continuously complained that he was starved of news.

At first Stanislavski was hesitant about tackling Chekhov's revisions. He was already overstretched and now he suddenly found himself without Nemirovich, who had been obliged just before Christmas to take his ailing sister to Menton. He was tempted to delay rehearsing the changes until Nemirovich returned. In the event he decided to push on. Gorki described Stanislavski's Three Sisters as 'music, not acting', thus providing the key to the formal pattern of the production. Writing to Chekhov in January 1901, Stanislavski outlined a symphonic concept of the play's structure, virtually allegro, andante, scherzo and finale:

'Act One – joyous, lively,
Act Two – Chekhovian mood,

Act Three – terribly tense, works on speed and nerves. Towards the
end energy has run out and the tempo slackens,
Act Four – not sure yet.' (*SS*, VII, p. 205.)

The major theme of *Three Sisters* was once more the destructive effect
of the trivia of life. In this play, however, no one plants trees, there is no
positive reaction, no concrete investment in the future. There is only
hope and stoical endurance. The Prozorov family is invaded by vulgarity,
in the person of Natasha, that 'lower middle-class vulgarian'
(*meshchanka*) as Masha describes her, and its members suffer physical
and moral destruction (Andrei), the loss of loved ones (Masha and Irina)
or the demoralizing effect of unrewarding work (Olga). Stanislavski's
production plan clearly marked the progress of the action. The staging
was an expression of the human drama. Stanislavski's eye was
cinematic. He was aware of the effect of visual signals. He used the
langauge of the theatre – sound, lights, props, setting – to reveal
psychological states, shifts in relationships and social meaning.
Everything was in the action. All that was lacking were the camera
angles.

The setting for Acts One and Two, the drawing-room, was not an
enclosed box set. Chekhov indicates a drawing-room with pillars upstage
behind which is another large room. To this, in collaboration with his
designer, Simov, Stanislavski added a small room with five windows
downstage right, a 'Lantern', with three steps leading up to it, a hall
upstage right, a staircase upstage left and the door to Andrei's room,
downstage left. The life of the household went on all round. The
drawing-room was a place people passed through on their way *from*
somewhere *to* somewhere. And the house lay within a community,
whose presence was continuously felt.

In Act One, the most positive in tone, spring was in the air. The tops
of the trees, beginning to bud, could be seen through the windows of the
'Lantern'. The cooing of doves could be heard. By Act Two a
fundamental change had taken place. The house was in the grip of winter;
outside the roofs covered in snow, the windows frozen fast. The
'Lantern' was blocked off by the grand piano which had been moved in
front of the steps. The entrance to the dining-room was covered by a felt-
clad screen. The stove hummed. Later a mouse could be heard gnawing
in the wainscot. Toys were scattered everywhere, including a clown with
clashing cymbals. Natasha's influence was evident in all the changes.
Her opening dialogue is concerned with the lamps. This Stanislavski
carefully prepared. He also took the opportunity to make a statement
about the marriage before the act proper began.

'It is dark in the drawing-room, the fire is almost dead, there is only a
beam of light from the open door to Andrei's room. From time to time
Andrei's shadow flits across the beam of light. He is pacing his room,

1a Stanislavski's mother, Elisaveta Alekseieva, and father, Sergei Alekseiev.

1b The Alekseiev house at Red Gates where Stanislavski lived
from the age of a few months (1863) to 1903.

2a Stanislavski aged 10 years.

2b The theatre at the country estate in Liubimovka built when Stanislavski was 14 in 1877.

3a *The Mikado* 1887. Yum-
Yum – Anna Alekseieva.
Nanki Pu – Stanislavski.

3b Stanislavski as the
Knight in Pushkin's *The
Miserly Knight*, 1888.

4a Stanislavski as Ferdinand in the play *Kabale und Liebe* (Schiller). His wife, Lilina, as Louise.

4b *The Fruits of Enlightenment* (Tolstoi). Stanislavski, 1891.

5 *Foma* (Dostoievski/Stanislavski) Lilina, Stanislavski, 1893.

6a *Much Ado About Nothing* (Shakespeare)
Stanislavski as Benedick, 1897.

6b *The Last Sacrifice* (Ostrovski)
Stanislavski, 1893.

6c *Uriel Acosta*, 1895.

7a Chekhov with the
Art Theatre Company.

7b *Uncle Vania* (Chekhov)
Stanislavski as Astrov.
1899.

8a *Uncle Vania*
(Chekhov) Act III.
Stanislavski as Astrov,
Olga Knipper-Chekhova
as Elena.

8b Stanislavski as
Vershinin in Chekhov's
The Three Sisters.

going over his lectures. We hear Andrei's footsteps, the drone of his voice, sighs, nose-blowing, chairs being moved. Then nothing. He has stopped by the table and is leafing through some exercise books (rustling of pages). There could be the sound of something like weeping. Then nose-blowing again, footsteps, a droning voice and his shadow on stage.

In the dining-room the lamp (hanging over the table) is about to go out. It flickers then dies. The lamps in the hall cast patches of light (through the hall windows) on the floor. Beams of light in the dining-room from the half-open doors leading to the corridor. Municipal street-lighting (transparent) in the dining-room window. . . .' (*Rezhissiorskie Ekzempliari, K. S. Stanislavskovo*, III, p. 132.)

Into this comes Natasha, the obsessive 'good wife and mother', with her sense of what is 'right and proper', her unimaginative and insensitive conformity to what she imagines the 'rules' are. Within a few lines of dialogue the audience knows what has happened during the interval.

Later in the act Stanislavski used the children's toys to counterpoint the dialogue. Thus, when Irina dreams of going to Moscow, Vershinin plays with the clown and his cymbals. When Vershinin, on his side, suggests talking a little philosophy, Tusenbach plays with a music-box. The contrast between high seriousness and triviality was physically conveyed. Doubt is cast on the characters' capacity to achieve even part of their ambitions, without explicit comment. Inside and outside the house there is always distraction. Act Three is filled with noises coming from the town as the fire rages. It is in moments of high emotion, such as Masha's farewell to Vershinin in Act Four, that Stanislavski deliberately strips everything down.

However good the plan, the actual process of rehearsal proved hard going. The cast were enthusiastic and worked well but the pace was sluggish and the play would not come alive. Stanislavski came to the conclusion that only an overall increase in tempo would get them out of trouble. He insisted that Act Three move along quickly and instructed the actors not 'to overdo the pauses'. He also, as Knipper reported to Chekhov on December 16, introduced moments of more general movement, as in Act Two, where he elaborated upon Chekhov's stage directions:

'Tusenbach swoops down on Andrei, sings *"Seni, moi seni"*, everyone dances – Irina, Chebutykin. Then when Tusenbach plays a waltz Masha leaps out, first dancing alone, then she is caught by Fedotik but she pushes him away (he's no good) and Irina dances with Rodé and into all this racket walks Natasha.' (*MATL*, No. 99.)

By the time Nemirovich returned in January 1901 the company was very divided over Stanislavski's production. Nemirovich, with his decisive approach, always provided a sense of security which Stanislavski with his endless searching and changes could not. He was also very tired and locked in a bitter battle with Knipper of whom he was frequently very critical. So fundamental were their disagreements that it would seem he considered taking her out of the play altogether.

The problem was Act Three. Knipper, as Masha, wanted to play the scene in which she admits her love for Vershinin on a note of high, almost desperate emotion, as a 'confession'. In his production plan Stanislavski had made this an intimate moment. He insisted that by this point in the act exhaustion had set in. Throughout the play, whenever possible, he would group the three sisters together, to mark the closeness of their relationship. He placed Irina on the sofa, with Masha and Olga kneeling beside her. Masha 'speaks quietly, drawing Irina's and Olga's heads closer to her'. Knipper wanted to move away to give herself more dramatic freedom.

Nemirovich had to arbitrate. Despite his low opinion of the play, of which Chekhov became aware, he approached the production very carefully, saw two run-throughs of the first three acts – Act Four had yet to be rehearsed – and came to the overall conclusion that the direction was cluttered, overloaded with detail. He objected to effects such as the scratching mouse in Act Two. Stanislavski, he noted privately, was losing valuable time looking for effects that did not advance the action. He cleaned up the action to release the play's forward movement. It became clear that a scene could be dull even though there might be nothing obviously wrong with the direction; the problem lay in its rhythmic relationship to the one before. The question of flow also emerged as one of cardinal importance. There would be no abrupt changes once the action had started. Transitions had to be incorporated into a continuous whole like a sustained melodic line.

This provided the key to the problems of Act Three. Nemirovich agreed with Stanislavski. Masha's scene needed to be quiet. In order to enable Knipper to do that, it was necessary to modify what had gone before. The whole mood of the act needed changing. This Nemirovich achieved by placing a *physical* control on the scene – the state of the characters, just before dawn, after a sleepless and exhausting night. Each would respond according to his or her temperament and, while there might be a certain edginess, there would be no high passion. He also reduced the level of on-stage noise, to which Chekhov had also objected. Finally, Chekhov gave his own opinion. Writing to Knipper on January 21, he told her:

'My dearest, Masha's confession in Act Three just isn't a confession but simply a candid conversation. Do it tensely but not desperately, don't shout, even smile from time to time, mainly try and feel the weariness of the night.' (*MATL*, No. 119.)

With the whole mood of the scene now toned down, Knipper was able to play the scene as Stanislavski and Chekhov wanted.

The end of the play was also proving problematic. In the original version, Tusenbach's body is carried across the stage after Olga's final 'If only we knew.' Chekhov was not sure that this would work but Stanislavski persuaded him to leave it in. When he got into rehearsal he realized this was a mistake.

> 'Chekhov must be made to understand that if we follow his version we shall have to put in a crowd scene and also the noise made by the people carrying the body, otherwise it will just become a ballet. If we carry his body across such a narrow stage the set will wobble. The crowd would make a noise with their feet. This will create a deadly flat pause. And can the sisters be left to stand indifferent as Tusenbach's body is carried past? We would have to find some action for them. I'm afraid that if we try to hit too many targets at once we shall miss the main point, which is to present the author's final, optimistic conclusion, which counterbalances the many heavier passages in the play. Carrying the body across will either be boring, dispiriting and artificial or (even if we did manage to overcome all the difficulties) terribly ponderous, merely adding to the general impression of heaviness.' (*Rezhissiorskie Eksempliari, K. S. Stanislavskovo*, III, p. 289.)

Serious casting difficulties were now becoming apparent which threatened the careful balance which both directors had worked for and by and large achieved. Neither Meierhold as Tusenbach nor Sudbinin as Vershinin were adequate. Knipper had seen the problem earlier. She had written to Chekhov on January 7 that Meierhold lacked 'vitality, strength, life – he's dreary.' Stanislavski worked hard to bring Meierhold's performance to life, driving him almost mad in the process. His method was to provide actions which would induce a physical state out of which the words would emerge with the right emotional tone. On one occasion he went up on to the stage with a piece of paper and said, 'Go to the piano, say the first three words, see the paper, pick it up, open it as you are going to your seat and continue talking.' It worked. On another occasion he had Meierhold uncork a bottle during a long speech. Having to concentrate on the problems created by the cork he stopped 'saying lines'. But Meierhold's frustration and anger prevented him learning the lesson Stanislavski was providing and his performance still did not pull together. Everyone knew that the ideal actor for the part was Kachalov but nothing was done. A dull Tusenbach accompanied by a heavy-handed Vershinin meant that much of the play's humour was lost, and with it those optimistic elements which are essential to counter-balance the more negative moments. The only answer was for Stanislavski to take over. About a week before the opening he read the part through for Nemirovich, who told Chekhov that it was 'more than interesting', and started rehearsals proper on January 23. The play opened on January 31.

Stanislavski's Vershinin, born of unforeseen circumstances, proved one of his greatest performances. Knipper remembered it with affection and admiration all her life. It was, once again, his capacity to give genuine life to the dreams and ideals expressed in the script, to make them vital rather than rhetorical, which impressed audiences and critics alike. The social meaning of the play, the implicit criticism of the corrosive effect of Russian life, had been made clear. Thus it was possible for a teenage boy to write:

> 'I shook with rage all over when I saw *The Sisters*. I mean, what these people have been reduced to, so cowed, walled in. Decent people, the Vershinins and the Tusenbachs, those dear, lovely sisters, I mean, such noble creatures who could have been happy and made others happy too. On my way home from the theatre I clenched my fists so tight they hurt and in the shadows I seemed to see the monster to which we must deliver a shattering blow even if it costs us our lives.' (Quoted by Poliakova, *Stanislavski*, Iskusstvo, Moscow, 1977, p. 178.)

In Nemirovich's judgement nearly forty years later, the production was:

> '. . . the Art Theatre's best presentation both for the perfection of the ensemble and Stanislavski's direction.' (Nemirovich-Danchenko, *Iz Proshlovo*, p. 218.)

Sooner or later the Art Theatre had to confront a different audience, the critics and public of St Petersburg, the seat of government. Moscow, for all its past glories, was more or less 'the provinces'. As soon as the Moscow season had ended on February 11 with a performance of *Three Sisters*, the company moved to St Petersburg.

They were in no doubt as to the reception they could expect from the critics – prejudice and snobbery – and their expectations were fulfilled. The bulk of the company were written off as nonentities, good as an ensemble but lacking outstanding individual talent. In response to a distressed Knipper, Chekhov replied that he had never expected anything but muck from the St Petersburg press. Only Chekhov and Stanislavski emerged unscathed. The most grudging critics had to admit their overwhelming talent. By the end of the tour, Stanislavski was hailed as Russia's greatest actor.

Audiences were another matter. Their enthusiasm was more voluble than in Moscow. *An Enemy of the People* provoked the greatest excitement. At the second performance on February 26 the house went wild, applauding continuously during Act Four, the scene of the public meeting, and, finally, at the end of the play, rushed down to the front of the stage, trying to drag back the curtains so they could see the actors, with shouts of 'Thank you, Stanislavski' on all sides. A further and more significant display took place at the performance of March 13. Earlier in the day there had been a demonstration of students in Kazan Square protesting against the implementation of a law which enabled the government to expel 'uncooperative' students and force them into the army. The demonstration had been brutally broken up and many of the participants had been thrown in jail. In the evening they were released. It was a tradition after such events to go, en masse, to some congenial place, somewhere they would feel at home. They chose to go to people whom they considered soul-mates, the company of the Moscow Art Theatre.

'In the final interval there was a stir among the audiences, there were whispers of "Students, students" on all sides.

People were uneasy. . . . What was going on? Which students? Nobody understood anything.

Suddenly, indeed, all the aisles, especially in the "gods", were filled with students, young men and women. It transpired they were demonstrators who had just been let out of "jug".

Hungry, exhausted, but happy and excited at suddenly being set free, the whole crowd had come straight from jail to the theatre they loved. Stanislavski gave orders for them to be given tickets. And then, in the last act, Doctor Stockman, who has returned from a hostile meeting, where he has been more or less manhandled, looks at the tears in his new frock coat and says: "When you go out to fight for freedom and justice you don't put on new trousers." . . . There was nothing emphatic in the actor's delivery, not a glance towards the audience but that sentence full of expression and quiet simplicity and, at the same time, tragic humour caused a real electric discharge in an audience that was, in any case, already "charged up". In a single moment a contact had been established between actor and audience and the audience, without exception, immediately responded with a stormy, elemental explosion of feeling. . . . It wasn't applause but a genuine, stupefying and even frightening demonstration.

The character of Stockman had grown at an instant from an individual rebel into a figure of enormous political significance.

The manager and the box-office manager ran into the theatre. . . . The temperature suddenly rocketed.

'– Well, we'll all be arrested and the play will be stopped – that's what went through the minds of all us students, who were inured to catastrophes of that kind. But the performance just went on to the end. Some invisible but powerful "hand" prevented police interference and the inevitable "scandal".' (Recalled by O. Bogolioubova, K. S. Archives.)

Ten days later, as the tour finished, a group of students, a 'family' of friends, wrote to Stanislavski with their thanks:

> '. . . the tragic events of recent times have scattered that family. The brightest memories which our banished comrades took away with them to the darkness of the provinces were the artistic images and pictures which you created.' (Art Theatre Archives.)

It was responses such as these which further convinced Stanislavski, if, indeed, he needed further convincing, that the function of the theatre was, according to Tolstoi's principle, to make the content of art transparent, not to make overt ideological statements. He had spoken loud and clear to a new generation. What more did they need to be told, other than what they had seen on stage?

By the end of the tour even sections of the press were having to modify their attitude, although prejudice died hard. As for Stanislavski himself he had little time to enjoy his triumph. He immediately began work on Hauptmann's *Michael Kramer*. His mother was horrified. She felt he needed a rest, not all the nervous strain involved in this 'heavy and depressing play'.

CHAPTER TEN

THE LOWER DEPTHS

The theatre was now able to fulfil what Nemirovich regarded as one of its prime functions: the presentation of outstanding contemporary Russian plays or unfamiliar foreign plays dealing with important social issues. In addition to Hauptmann's *Michael Kramer*, the 1901–2 season included Ibsen's *The Wild Duck*. Over the next four years works by Chekhov, Ibsen, Tolstoi, Hauptmann were brought into the repertoire and Gorki, who had only published short stories, launched on his career as a dramatist. On October 30, 1900, during a performance of *Lonely People*, he suddenly announced his intention of writing a play. In the event, he started work on two simultaneously – *Small People* and *The Lower Depths*. In choosing to present works by a notorious rebel and former political prisoner, the Art Theatre was courting danger. The least it could expect were long battles with the censor.

The theatre was interested mainly in *The Lower Depths* but it proved the more troublesome to write. Gorki found that he could not control his material. His characters had taken over and, he said, simply would not stop talking. *Small People* was finished first and delivered in October 1901. Stanislavski sent his impressions and comments, which Gorki gratefully acknowledged.

The play is concerned with a small, petit-bourgeois family, its narrow-mindedness and meanness both material and spiritual. In ideological terms the central character is the adopted son, Nil, typical of the progressive 'new man' whom critics like Chernichevski had insisted was an integral part of revolutionary literature. Both Gorki and Chekhov were convinced that Stanislavski should play the role. They were in one sense right. Nil is the lead role. It requires an actor of strong personality able to dominate the play; on the other hand, Stanislavski, at thirty-eight, with his upper-middle-class background, realized that he could not play a rebellious working-class train driver of twenty-five. He was able to form strong personal and artistic relationships with turbulent young artists – Meierhold, Gorki, Sulerzhitski and, later, Vakhtangov – preferring to do battle with them rather than live in docile agreement with the less energetic and the less able – but it was quite another thing actually to try and play, or to embody this new generation, from which he was culturally and historically separated. He was convinced that you could not 'act' Nil.

It was not a character part and that was what it would become in his hands. You had to 'be' Nil. He was afraid, as he wrote to Chekhov, that the audience would get Stanislavski in costume and not the character. In the event, the production suffered greatly from the fact that there was no one of the right age and of outstanding talent to take on the role. New actors were needed for new plays. They had to be created.

There was insufficient time to include *Small People* in the Moscow season. Nemirovich had only read the play to the company at the end of December and with the St Petersburg tour due to open on February 19 there was insufficient time for adequate rehearsal. Nemirovich's own play, *In Dreams*, which was less demanding, was put in as a stop-gap. Gorki made no secret of his contempt for the piece which, while playing to full houses on the strength of Nemirovich's popularity, left audiences cold. *Small People*, it was decided, would be given a try-out during the St Petersburg tour while waiting for *The Lower Depths* which would, it was hoped, be ready by the autumn.

To stage Gorki in Moscow was bad enough, but to do it in St Petersburg under the nose of the imperial court and all its ministers was something else. Even the extensive cuts made by Stanislavski and Nemirovich did not satisfy the authorities, who not only made further substantial cuts but also insisted that a special dress rehearsal be given for a small group of officials so that they could assess the play. Knipper wrote to Chekhov that the cast were outraged at seeing the script reduced to nothing while she herself felt that Gorki had been betrayed. Yet the company found an unexpected ally in the snobbishness of St Petersburg society, confident of its own position and waiting to be shocked and titillated by 'progressive' ideas. Nowhere was the dichotomy of attitude more clearly displayed than in the behaviour of Prince Shakovskoi who showered the cast of *Enemy of the People* with gifts, then took umbrage at the word 'revolutionary' in the last act and insisted it be cut and himself participated in the butchery of Gorki's text.

The Art Theatre was 'in' thanks to a visit by the Tsar on March 13, and when news of the private dress rehearsal got round, a battle ensued among the great and fashionable for the remaining seats. The government decided, in response, that all the usual ushers should be replaced by uniformed police who would ensure that no undesirables gate-crashed the performance. This produced alarm among the audience. Nemirovich insisted that the police withdraw and leave the normal ushers to their task. During the course of the evening he was sent for first by the assistant chief of police, then the chief of police and finally by the governor of St Petersburg himself. He resolutely refused to leave the theatre during the performance. He presented himself the next morning and explained his position. The governor, anxious not to ruffle the feathers of his fashionable masters, agreed that the sight of uniforms would, perhaps, be disconcerting.

On the first night the police were present but in full evening dress. Mounted police patrolled the streets outside. Nemirovich had, however, taken the precaution of appealing to the students beforehand not to make any demonstrations as they had during *An Enemy of the People*. Gorki's play, he explained, was important to the survival of the theatre. They could not afford to have it banned. The students complied and it was only at the final performance that one solitary cry of 'Down with the Grand Duke' was heard. As for the audience, they were far less concerned with Gorki's politics than with the strapping young actor, Baranov, who had been taken from the Moscow Art Theatre School to play the part of Teterev, the cantor. They swooned with delight over this true son of the Russian soil. Here was another Chaliapin, they said. They praised him and lionized him. He stole all the notices. Success went to his head together with a not inconsiderable amount of alcohol, and he destroyed his own career.

By April, Gorki was able to show Stanislavski the first two acts of *The Lower Depths*. By July, it was complete and, during Stanislavski's absence abroad, sent to Chekhov and Knipper who were staying, at Stanislavski's invitation, in Liubimovka.

Knipper had fallen seriously ill during the St Petersburg tour and had needed surgery. Stanislavski, she wrote to Chekhov, fussed over her as if she were his own daughter. Shortly after Stanislavski and Lilina went down to the Crimea, Knipper had a relapse. Chekhov stayed constantly at his wife's bedside and on their return Stanislavski and Lilina took turns to sit with him. It was only at this stage in their relationship that Stanislavski felt at ease in his company. The crisis and the intimacy of the sick-room brought them close together.

'Up till then, even though I had known Anton Pavlovich for a long time, I could not feel at ease with him, I could not establish an easy relationship, I was always mindful of the fact that I had someone famous before me and tried to appear more intelligent than I really am. This unnatural behaviour truly inhibited Anton Pavlovich. He only liked open relationships. My wife, who established that kind of simple relationship from the very start, always felt more at ease with him than I. . . . It was only during those long days when I sat with Anton Pavlovich in the room next to the sick-room that I was for the first time able to discover that openness in our relationship. Those days brought us so close together that Anton Pavlovich would sometimes come to me with requests of an intimate nature about which he was very reserved. For example, having learned that I knew how to inject arsenic – I had boasted to him somewhat of my ability to perform that operation – he asked me to give him an injection. . . .' (*SS*, V, p. 359.)

The injections, given in the buttocks, formed part of Chekhov's treatment and had to be given regularly. It was agreed that, for the time

being, Stanislavski would do them. Unfortunately, he had only injected
with new needles before whereas the needle Chekhov gave him was
blunt from much use. Try as he may Stanislavski could not pierce the
skin and his efforts caused Chekhov considerable pain, although he
merely gave a short cough. Panic-stricken, Stanislavski pressed the end
of the syringe against the skin, moved it a little and pretended to give the
injection, emptying the contents on to a towel. Chekhov turned to face
him with a friendly smile and said 'marvellous', but Stanislavski was
never asked to repeat the operation.

Stanislavski suggested that as soon as she was sufficiently recovered,
Knipper and Chekhov should move into the house at Liubimovka where
Knipper could convalesce while he and Lilina were abroad. The offer
was gratefully accepted. Chekhov was already hinting at a new play and
it was at Liubimovka that *The Cherry Orchard* was conceived. In late
June Stanislavski joined Lilina and the children in Franzensbad and in
July visited Bayreuth where he was taken back-stage by Cosima Wagner.
There he had an opportunity to see how the wave effects were created for
the opening of *Der Fliegende Holländer*. The copious technical notes he
took on that occasion were later incorporated into the opening of his 1929
production plan for *Othello*. On August 19, the family returned to
Liubimovka, where Knipper was still recuperating, and on the following
day Stanislavski gave the first reading of *The Lower Depths*. On August
22 he discussed the plays with Nemirovich and the company.

At the beginning of 1902 the lease on the Hermitage ran out. The
Moscow Art Theatre Board signed a twelve-year lease on the Omon
Theatre in Kamergerski Lane, formerly used for operettas and cabarets.
The plan was to gut the interior and create a new auditorium, entirely
plain, without the usual plush gilt, or anything that might distract
attention from the stage itself. There was to be no orchestra pit, since
neither Stanislavski nor Nemirovich approved of the practice of playing
light musical interludes during the intervals. They were another
hindrance to proper concentration. The very latest lighting and technical
equipment was to be installed. The theatre would in every way be state-
of-the-art.

This ambitious scheme was launched at a moment when the theatre
was deeply in debt and when the existing shareholders were refusing to
put in any more money. The cost of the reconstruction, some 300,000
roubles, was borne by Morozov who not only supervised the work,
particularly the electrical installations, himself but, when necessary,
picked up a hammer and joined in. He leased the theatre to the company
for a modest 10,000 roubles a year and guaranteed an annual subsidy of
30,000 roubles.

The time had come to reorganize the theatre's finances and create a
new company on a new basis. In July 1897 Nemirovich had predicted
that by 1900 the theatre should be sufficiently well established for the

actors to share in the profits. Morozov now proposed that the actors should become shareholders and own their own company. He bought out the existing shareholders and then offered to lend any actor who needed it the money to acquire stock against a bill of hand. As none of the actors had private means they all borrowed from Morozov which meant that by the summer he was virtually the sole owner of the company.

It was strictly understood that shares could be acquired by invitation only and a list of potential shareholders was issued in January 1902. To everyone's delight, Chekhov agreed to invest 10,000 roubles, to be paid in instalments before the end of 1903. Some names were conspicuous by their absence: Sanin, Stanislavski's production assistant, and Meierhold. An uncomfortable meeting of the new shareholders in February decided who among the actors were to stay and who were to go. Meierhold, who was already feeling at odds with the theatre's policy, did not wait to be pushed out but resigned, taking a number of other members of the company, including his sister-in-law, Ekaterina Munt, and the hapless Roksanova – both of whom Chekhov disliked – with him to form a theatre in the provinces. On February 24 he published a letter in the *Kurior* denying any financial basis for his departure.

The cause of Meierhold's exclusion was a letter he had written to Chekhov, criticizing *In Dreams*. The contents of the letter became known. The most probable source was Knipper. Ironically she disliked the play, too, she thought it emotionally sterile and had only agreed to appear in it after being morally blackmailed by Nemirovich. There had been some booing on the first night, which, it was now concluded, Meierhold had organized. This was the story that was told to Stanislavski who swallowed it whole, possibly because he was aware of the tensions between Meierhold and Nemirovich. He could be, as Nemirovich once reminded him, very fierce when he had been 'got at'. He angrily refused to speak to Meierhold, who begged to be allowed to come and see him. An acrimonious correspondence ensued. (*MATL*, Nos. 155, 163, 164, 165.) Meierhold later referred to the whole period as one of the worst in his life, while Stanislavski, once he learned the truth, was deeply remorseful.

There was a great deal of bitterness in the air. Knipper described the whole affair as 'disgusting' while Chekhov wrote a letter of protest to Nemirovich. He was particularly outraged by the departure of Meierhold, whom he respected not so much, as he admitted, for his talents as an actor, which had proved disappointing, but for the intelligence which came through in his performances.

Stanislavski, by a serious error of judgement, kept his distance from the whole process of reorganization, maintaining his original investment and no more. He made no comment in public but later in the year, in a letter to the St Petersburg actress, Kotliarevskaia, expressed his relief that what he called the 'disruptive element' had gone. He did, however, regret the loss of Sanin.

New articles of association were drawn up giving Morozov almost absolute power over the members of the board and the administration. Current policy on repertoire was endorsed and a resolution was incorporated into the statutes giving priority to plays of significant social content, irrespective of box-office appeal.

This decision produced immediate conflict. Nemirovich, jealous of his control over repertoire, clashed violently with Morozov at a board meeting when Morozov tried to give pride of place not only to Gorki, of whom Nemirovich was suspicious, but to the circle of writers around him. Nemirovich considered these writers inferior and he refused absolutely to allow the theatre to be identified politically or artistically with any one school or tendency. A spectacular shouting-match ended with Nemirovich storming out, slamming the door behind him. Nemirovich might have spared himself the dramatic gesture. The new statutes fully confirmed his power over the repertoire, even the right to stage plays of his own choosing against the wishes of the board, that is, Morozov. He could also exclude, if he wished, those plays Stanislavski wanted to present in his aim to develop the art of the theatre and of the actor. There had in fact been a significant shift of power in Nemirovich's favour, although Stanislavski did not realize it at the time. His artistic veto meant much less now than it had before.

After the turmoil of the preceding months, during the summer of 1902 Stanislavski took stock of his position, further defining his concept of the theatre as an art in itself. He confided his reflexions as ever to his notebook:

'. . . the author writes on paper. The actor writes with his body on stage.'

'The score of an opera is not the opera itself and the script of a play is not drama until both are made flesh and blood on stage.'

'The theatre is a synthesis of literature, music, the living word, living characters, living movement and dance against a life-size artistic background.' (K.S. Archive, No. 757.)

He then made the first tentative notes on a 'grammar' of acting that ultimately became *An Actor's Work on Himself.*

The development of these ideas inevitably set him on a collision course with Nemirovich, who had also spent the summer thinking about the future. In July Nemirovich wrote to Knipper at Liubimovka telling her that he would fight anything that consciously or unconsciously tried to deflect the theatre from its true path. He would wage a campaign but for the moment did not intend to show his hand. (*MATL,* No. 180.) The central question was one of control, *his* control. Stanislavski and the rest of the company must be brought into line. He drafted a letter to Stanislavski which he did not send, finding it too explicit. In a toned-down version sent at the end of July, he reverted to a familiar theme:

Stanislavski the wayward amateur. Some kind of order must be introduced into his relationship to his assistant directors. Time was being wasted because he either was not explicit or did not stick to his production plan. The result was frustration.

'This is what happens. The director was anxious to do the best he could according to your production plan so you would think the act was ready. He worked intensely; at first the actors were half-hearted, then he got them going. The act is set. You arrive. You whisper to me that none of it is any good but that we must be supportive to the director and the cast. You then go into your act . . . i.e., you praise them loudly for all their hard work. Then you arrange rehearsals and start to alter everything . . . After two rehearsals nothing is left of all the hard work that has been put in. Revolt wells up in the hearts of Sanin and the actors . . .

If he starts to justify himself by reference to your own production plan, you answer, "Yes, yes, yes. It's my fault. Don't let's argue about it. But this isn't right, we must rework it." Or, "Ah, dear God! What rubbish I wrote in the production plan. It's clear when you see it in rehearsal."

But it wasn't rubbish – and that is where the disaster lies. It comes out as *rubbish* because the ideas you wrote in the production plan have been wrongly understood.

And so we must decide once and for all that immediately after the blocking, until the roles have been learned, rehearsals must take place with *you there*. Then, once an act has been set, the second director can go over it.' (*MATL*, No. 181.)

At the same time Nemirovich also sent a letter to all the members of the company in which he set out his views on policy, stating, 'The theatre exists for dramatic literature'. (*MATL*, No. 182.)

Stanislavski's reply to Nemirovich's letter has been lost but on August 7 Nemirovich continued his 'campaign' in a letter (*MATL*, No. 183) in which he dealt in much greater detail with the policy matters he had referred to in his letter to the company. It is a comprehensive review of the first four years of the theatre's life and a list of everything that, in his view, had gone wrong. His main thesis is that their partnership, by which he actually meant his own control, had been undermined by well-meaning but essentially harmful friends. There were two dangers, one that the theatre, under the influence of Gorki and Morozov, would be seen to take a specific political line, the second that it would become a social meeting placed for Moscow's idle rich. When these two trends came together, the danger was all the greater. 'I am not,' he stated, 'blaming anyone, you understand . . .', yet it is significant that all the bad influences he detected were Stanislavski's intimates or colleagues.

It was in this atmosphere of burgeoning dissension that in October the

Art Theatre finally moved into the premises it was to occupy for the next seventy years. Within a few months Stanislavski, too, had moved, selling Red Gates and acquiring a house on Carriage Row (Karetni Riad) opposite the Hermitage Theatre.

He had a new theatre, a new home, but no new burst of creative energy. The theatre was in danger artistically. It was beginning to lose sight of the distinction between realism, which was its stated goal, and naturalism which it ostensibly rejected. Passion for detail was beginning to take over and *Small People* was its first victim. With some eighty cuts imposed by the censor, the play opened on October 25 to a lukewarm reception. Watching the play in rehearsal, Gorki himself had found it 'staggeringly boring . . . long, boring and stupid.' Efros blamed the production:

> 'The dramatic essence of Gorki's play was lost in these trifles, the energy of the actors was stifled under the weight of contrived character traits, voices, grimaces and the audience's attention was diverted from what was essential and important to the incidental and the quaint.'
> (*Novosti Dnia*, October 27, 1902.)

The next production, Tolstoi's *The Power of Darkness*, suffered a similar fate. Stanislavski had wanted to do the play in 1895. He had visited Tolstoi to discuss changes to Act Four. Tolstoi had agreed to rewrite it on the lines Stanislavski suggested to him. The production never materialized. Stanislavski had now reworked Act Four himself, combining two earlier versions, and in early May asked Chekhov, who was living in the Crimea, near Tolstoi, to act as his intermediary and get approval for the revisions. Tolstoi's son, Sergei, approved the changes when he attended rehearsals towards the end of the month. Stanislavski made one of his customary trips with the wardrobe mistress, Grigorieva, to the Tulska district in search of materials and local colour. Sketchbooks were filled. They returned laden with shirts, coats, pots and pans, and they brought in a peasant couple to advise on manners and customs. The woman proved to have genuine dramatic gifts, and after she had filled in at one rehearsal for the actress playing Matriona who was ill, Sergei Tolstoi, carried away by the reality of her performance, suggested she take over the part. This was agreed. She was dropped, finally, because in moments of high feeling she abandoned Lev Tolstoi's text and insisted on improvising her own dialogue using language so foul no censor would possibly pass it. Stanislavski was loath to lose her entirely and put her first in the crowd, then gave her a moment on her own when she crossed the stage, humming a song. Even that destroyed the credibility of what came after; even when singing off-stage she eclipsed the rest of the cast. Anything and everything she did merely served to highlight the superficiality of the rest of the acting. In the end they recorded her singing a song and used it as background.

Writing to Sulerzhitski on November 28, Sergei Tolstoi commented:

'[The actors] worked very hard but nonetheless it is evident what a gulf there is between them and the peasants. At bottom only actors from the peasantry itself could play *The Power of Darkness* really well.' (V. V. Luzhski, Archive No. 6396.)

The whole episode marked a giant step backward. Stanislavski had known ever since his experiments at Liubimovka, twenty years earlier, that 'real' truth and theatrical truth are of a different order. He had written in his notebook of the 'essential laws of the stage'. All that had been forgotten. Had he been able to draw less superficial performances from his cast, and from himself, he might have been less carried away.

Chekhov found the production, which opened on December 5, had 'a great many good intentions and affection for the task in hand', but nothing could hide the fact that it was all local colour and little else. The poetic insight of *The Seagull* had degenerated into mere stylistic mannerism. Stanislavski's own judgement in *My Life in Art* was categorical:

'Realism only becomes naturalism when it is not justified by the artist from within.

. . . the external realism of the production of *The Power of Darkness* revealed the absence of inner justification in those of us who were acting in it. The stage was taken over by things, objects, banal outward *events* . . . which crushed the inner meaning of the play and characters.' (*SS*, I, p. 261.)

The play, nonetheless, enjoyed some success although Stanislavski's own performance at Mitrich was a disaster. He applied mountains of make-up and putty, bumps and protruberances but it remained a soulless, mechanical exercise. He gave only three performances.

The Lower Depths was given the same careful preparation. Gorki provided Stanislavski, who, as he had wished, was playing Satin, and Kachalov, playing the Baron, with biographical sketches filling in the background. Stanislavski felt that the usual analytical discussions were not enough. He needed living models to stimulate his imagination. On the evening of August 22 therefore, the company, together with Simov, paid a visit to the Khitrov Market. The assembled tramps and thieves were flattered to be visited by a group of actors and impressed by the name of Gorki. Much drink flowed and personal secrets were revealed. Stanislavski found what he was looking for, an ex-officer who had gambled away a fortune. His manners were perfect and Stanislavski noted that despite his ragged clothes, his beard and moustache were neatly trimmed. Simov made innumerable sketches. Later he took a number of photographs of locations which would serve as a basis for his sets.

The visit served its purpose. When rehearsals began in the autumn Stanislavski had a total picture both of the characters and of their environment. The production plan is filled, as usual, with details of moves and objects, all exactly and perfectly true to life. At one session he gave a virtuoso display, demonstrating a string of characters, one after the other, almost without a break between, to the students who were to play the small parts. Above all, he insisted, there was to be no sentimentalization, no display of pity or condescension to these people. They were what they were. Gorki's intention was not to make the audience feel sorry for them but to provoke the kinds of social change which would make their condition impossible.

The play badly needed an outside eye. The individual elements of the staging, good in themselves, accurate, truthful, were not adding up to a performance. There were many trees but no wood. Stanislavski himself needed a director. Nemirovich once again stepped in and pulled the production together, giving it some much-needed pace. He more or less told Stanislavski to start again. A letter written during the autumn of 1902 begins gently but finishes on a much more hard-hitting note. Perhaps, he suggested, it was time for Stanislavski to do something different as an actor? Everyone in the company was all too familiar with his ways, the irritability and tension that reduced him to a state of exhaustion. Satin offered him an opportunity to be a slightly different actor from the one they knew. Why couldn't he relax a little?

'. . . you have great difficulty in just surrendering to a role and that is because you have no faith in the audience's intelligence, because you think you have to hit them on the head all the time. You want to make something out of practically every sentence and it becomes difficult to listen to you because as the dialogue proceeds I, the audience, have long since understood from your facial expression and gestures what you want to say or act but you continue to play some detail at me which is not going to interest me overmuch by being prolonged. This happens not only with individual lines but even in the middle of speeches and lines.' (*MATL*, No. 186.)

The answer was to play against the tragic nature of the script. *The Lower Depths* would be played like Act One of *Three Sisters*. Not one tragic note would be allowed to creep in. This would bring something new to the stage.

In practical terms he offered the following advice:

'1.   Don't thrust the part and yourself on the audience. It understands both it and you;

2.   Don't be afraid the role won't exist in those places where a great deal of acting is not appropriate to the situation. If there's nothing to play it's almost a mistake to do anything and easy to wear

yourself out prematurely; . . .
3.   Learn the lines by heart;
4.   Avoid excess of movement;
5.   Keep the tone vigorous, light and vital, i.e. with vitality, *carefree and vital*.

For example, I can easily imagine Satin at the beginning of the fourth act like this: he is sitting, he does not collapse in a chair as you are doing but leans against the stove, his head clutched in both hands looking out into the audience to the dress-circle boxes. He sits like that a long time, immobile, throwing off his words, not once turning to look at the people who answer him. He gazes at a fixed spot, obstinately thinking about something but hearing what is being said around him and answering quickly. . . .' (*MATL*, No. 186.)

Whatever the merits of his criticisms, this would seem to be another stage in Nemirovich's 'campaign' to assert his authority. He had questioned Stanislavski's management skill, his rehearsal methods, his friends and associates, now it was his acting technique. But, as Stanislavski wrote to Chekhov, if all he had to do was just say lines with lightness and pace, where was the characterization? How did he prevent everything coming out the same? How could he point the really good lines?

Behind this disagreement about delivery, however, lay a deeper disappointment about the character itself. In his production plan, Stanislavski had described Satin as corrupt, a swindler, yet still capable of some decency of feeling and of change for the better. He had been deeply impressed by his visit to the down-and-outs and had been shocked by the total destitution in which they lived, the utter lack of personal possessions or comforts. He wanted to confront the audience with the starkness of reality. For him the central question was how did Satin end up in a doss-house like this?

Nemirovich considered Stanislavski had allowed his personal reactions to distort the true meaning of the play. He did not want the play turned into a social tract. He systematically toned down all the excesses of the drinking scenes and the violence of the fights. Fights with shoes replaced fights with bottles. Above all he insisted, with Gorki's approval, that Satin should be played as a much more 'romantic' figure. They wanted someone like Don César de Bazan in Victor Hugo's *Ruy Blas*, a dashing nobleman, who in Hugo's words 'wears his rags majestically'. Don César was a character of whom Gorki was particularly fond and he is mentioned in *Small People*.

Stanislavski considered the whole Don César idea tasteless but bowed to Nemirovich's judgement and did his best to reconcile the conflicting advice he had been given, to say the lines simply but be dashing at the same time. The production photographs show him sitting in the position

Nemirovich had indicated for Act Four at one moment, and standing jauntily, a cigarette butt in his mouth, at another.

The play, which opened on December 18, had a huge success, equal to that of *The Seagull* and *An Enemy of the People*. It made Kachalov a star and brought Stanislavski further accolades. Gorki was overwhelmed. He wrote:

> 'It was only at the first performance that I saw and understood the amazing leap forward that all these people, who were used to creating characters by Chekhov and Ibsen, had made. Something of themselves had been released.' (Gorki, *Perepiska*, Moscow, 1986, p. 225.)

Stanislavski himself was not so happy. Writing to Chekhov after the first night, he was extremely diplomatic in his presentation of the problems the production had encountered. He loyally praised Nemirovich for having found the right tone for the play and blamed any dissatisfaction he felt with his own performance on himself. He had not been able to find the right balance, as he had in *An Enemy of the People*, between his awareness of the character and his awareness of the play's social message. He expressed his true feelings to others. To Efros he confided that he found there was something false in his performance of Act Four but he also thought the writing was flawed, the character of Satin was contrived and theatrical. He confided to Knipper that he felt he had created nothing, just gone on and said lines, and whatever the success of the play, both it and the production were lies and nonsense.

The only public sign of disagreement was the absence of both Stanislavski's and Nemirovich's names as directors on the posters. Stanislavski had gone along with Nemirovich's decisions but he would not artistically endorse them by putting his name to the production. But either both directors' names had to appear, or neither. There was none. And it was neither each time in the future when Stanislavski and Nemirovich had a serious disagreement about interpretation.

Nemirovich took all the credit for the production, which he considered a high point in the history of the Art Theatre. For Stanislavski it was no such thing. It did not represent any kind of advance, certainly not in acting technique. In general, he found his own performance external and mechanical.

The remainder of the season brought Stanislavski little consolation. Nemirovich had decided to stage Ibsen's *The Pillars of Society*, which he disliked intensely and he was also saddled with the role of Bernick which he considered 'heavy-going and unrewarding'. The rehearsal period was not happy. Everyone was depressed. Stanislavski found the production unimaginative and the set, which he had approved, a mistake. His disagreement with Nemirovich also extended to individual characterizations. Knipper reported that he and Nemirovich were fighting like cat and dog over her performance as Lona. He was uncharacteristically uncooperative in rehearsal, often insisting on working in French. Nemirovich kept a brave face on it, writing to Chekhov on February 16:

'The more I fight with Alekseiev the closer I get to him, since we are both united by a fine and healthy love for the same things.' (*Iz., Pis.*, Moscow, 1979, p. 319.)

The play opened on February 24, 1903, to good reviews and, as Knipper remarked, 'even Efros for once did not nit-pick'. Disagreements continued into the autumn.

The production of *Julius Caesar*, which was scheduled to open the 1903–4 season, brought the differences between the two men into sharp focus. Stanislavski had not wanted to include the play but Nemirovich had insisted for two reasons: first, because he, too, thought the theatre was in a rut, playing safe, choosing to do *The Pillars of Society* rather than one of Ibsen's later, more difficult plays, putting on comfortable plays for comfortable bourgeois audiences; second, because he wanted to establish his reputation as a director equal in stature to his partner. The most effective way to do so was through a successful production of a major classic.

On May 31, Nemirovich left for Rome with Simov to prepare the sets. In his absence Stanislavski began making notes for the production. He gave his broad views on an approach to the play but provided much more detailed suggestions for the crowd scenes. The two men kept up a regular correspondence. By June it became obvious that Nemirovich was going his own way. Rome had had an enormous impact on him: the scale, the spaciousness of the ancient Forum, that was what he wanted to reproduce. Stanislavski pointed out that it would be difficult to create the impression of a mob with a handful of actors if the set had a large open space in the middle. Nemirovich nonetheless insisted on his own way. He was equally insistent over the interpretation of Act Two, in particular the scenes between Brutus and Portia and Brutus and Ligarius.

Once rehearsals began on August 7 there was no respite for anybody. Nemirovich poured all his energy into the production. According to Knipper the endless rehearsals, day and evening, the costume fittings, the make-up sessions, the crowd scenes, were 'hell'. Nemirovich emphasized the broad political themes. What interested him was not individuals but the total situation, the death of a republic. This gave Stanislavski, as Brutus, little scope for psychological exploration. The result was a mis-match between actor and director. Stanislavski, realizing how difficult he had been during *The Pillars of Society*, which with his sense of discipline he truly regretted, buckled down and did his best to conform to the over-all production concept. He also collaborated in the staging of the crowd scenes, which proved the high points of the evening. But he disapproved of the production style which he found picturesque. His own instinct would have been to dirty the costumes and put patches on them rather than have a display of pristine whiteness. Nemirovich was aware of this, aware, too, that he was going against their agreed policy of 'artistic realism' but at the same time he was convinced that it was right for this particular play.

Nemirovich's slave-driving paid off. The play opened on October 2 to a generally warm reception. The production was much admired, not least for its historical accuracy. Parties of schoolchildren were brought to see the production to get an idea of life in ancient Rome. For Stanislavski, however, it merely confirmed all his worst fears concerning the artistic sterility of the theatre. His own performance as Brutus found little general favour and, once again, he was accused of being insufficiently 'heroic'. 'Nobody likes it,' Knipper wrote. Even the usually sympathetic Efros wrote:

> '. . . there was neither a Brutus who was Hamlet-like, nor the Brutus as the artist apparently conceived him. The central bone-structure, the spine of the tragedy was approached coldly.' (N. Efros, *Teatr i Iskusstvo*, No. 41, p. 754.)

Sulerzhitski, however, took an entirely different view. He wrote to Stanislavski:

> 'Up till now I "knew" what Brutus was, I respected his "type", if I can so express it, but for me he was distant, alien and cold. He existed only in the mind, in the realm of abstract ideas. You, your performance, transformed that beautiful but cold classical statue into a living being, you clothed him in flesh and blood, you warmed him with tribulation and brought him down from his inaccessible marble pedestal and into men's hearts. . . .
>
> I do not write to Alekseiev, whom I do not know at all; I write, not as an acquaintance, but as a member of the audience, wishing to join the actor in sympathy for Brutus who died as all fine things must die in this life, where only lies can triumph. . . .
>
> I write to Stanislavski, who more than once already had upheld and strengthened people in their believe in "man".' (Sulerzhitski, Moscow, 1970, p. 433.)

Another commentator, doubtless with the contemporary political situation in mind, noted:

> 'Shakespeare's Brutus is an abstract, ideal man, who in given historical circumstances, quite uninvited, like all useless dreamers, foists his freedom-loving dreams on the people, but Stanislavski tried to speak in the name of the people, as if those people had no other dream save democratic freedom.' (L. V. Goldenweiser Archive, MXAT Museum.)

Ermolova declared the performance 'beautiful'. Maria Chekhova, who

apparently was present on one of Stanislavski's good evenings, thought
he played better than anyone. Diaghilev admired him, too, in the Forum
scene. Kotliarevskaia, writing to Stanislavski on October 27, summed up
the whole debate:

> 'On all sides I read and hear contradictory opinions: some condemn
> [his] Brutus, others praise it . . . I know your creative work and
> understand why 50% of the public condemn you, 40% don't
> understand you and only 10% understand and are delighted by you.
> It's very clear to me: you play in a tone and manner in which people
> *will* play but in which for the moment only you, the first, play. In
> twenty years they'll all be doing it your way but right now it's new,
> alien and incomprehensible.' (K.S. Archive.)

As for Nemirovich, he gave Stanislavski's final performance his full
support. It matched his political view of the play:

> 'His performance as Brutus, conceived as an ardent republican, was
> bold, interesting, beautiful and physically expressive. But it was
> totally removed from the Brutus established in the public's mind. And
> at that time, when the other actors became more and more mechanical
> from performance to performance, confining themselves within their
> own acquired technique, he, Konstantin Sergeievich, on the contrary,
> as it were, tried to surmount his lack of success and continued to
> work.' (N-D Archive, No. 127.)

It was, nonetheless, torture, made worse because being, technically, a
heavy production, *Julius Caesar* had to be played in blocks and not in
repertoire. There was, therefore, no respite, no time to recover lost
energy. Stanislavski had to go on night after night, struggling through a
performance he knew most of the audience did not want to see. The
interpretation which had refused to come alive for him during rehearsal
did not come alive in the actual playing. It was only in the following year,
during the St Petersburg tour, that there was some glimmer of light. For
the moment it seemed to him that the very scenery was drenched in the
sweat of his own useless endeavours.

It was not until three weeks into the run that he confided his
unhappiness to Nemirovich. His comments, which appear mainly to have
consisted of self-criticism, produced a violent reaction which threatened
to destroy the theatre altogether. He voiced them in Morozov's presence
and Nemirovich jumped to the conclusion that there was a conspiracy
against him. He drafted a letter (*MATL*, No. 212) full of bitterness and
anger, which he read to Luzhski, Vishnievski and Knipper on the day of
the first meeting to discuss the casting of *The Cherry Orchard*. He was
outraged to think that a production in which he had put the best of himself
and which had achieved critical success could be dismissed as inartistic
by the two other senior members of the management. Stanislavski had

been equally negative about *The Lower Depths* which had been a huge success and had offered not one word of praise for *Pillars of Society*. His whole view of Nemirovich's work was negative. What rankled Nemirovich most was that while his own successes were passed over, Stanislavski's failures, like *Snow Maiden*, were cited as conclusive proof of his brilliance. All he got from Stanislavski were constant jeremiads that the theatre was going into a decline, that it was sliding downhill and would end up like the Mali – the ultimate term of abuse in Stanislavski's critical vocabulary. It was a short step from defending his own qualities as an artist and reaffirming his own aesthetic beliefs to attacking his colleague's abilities as a director. Nemirovich now reduced Stanislavski's ability to visualize scenes in concrete terms, so effusively praised in happier days, to a mere capacity to create incidental detail while the main thrust of the play was lost. In *Caesar*, he argued, Stanislavski had failed to appreciate the overall meaning, the *concept*, and had been principally concerned with the design and cut of a particular toga. The trouble once more was Stanislavski's fashionable friends who wanted something more 'spicy' and 'original'. With such major differences between them, Nemirovich ended, what was the future of the theatre to be?

Knipper was alarmed at the turn of events. On October 28, immediately after Nemirovich had read his letter, she reported the situation to Chekhov, giving full support to Nemirovich and his view of himself as the injured party:

> 'All this is not good. There must be fairness, openness and trust between K.S. and V.I., otherwise it will be impossible to work. Please God things will be smoothed over very quickly. But if Nemirovich goes I won't stay in the theatre. K.S. cannot be at the head of things. He's a hopeless mess.' (*MATL*, No. 214.)

Stanislavski, in his equally emotional reply, called Nemirovich's letter 'a bolt from the blue'.

> 'In God's name what are you accusing me of, duplicity, conspiracy or just plain stupidity? . . . Calm down and try to understand what it really was I said. If I criticized anybody it was myself . . . I spoke so frankly because your role as a director is clear, well-established, acknowledged by everyone.' (K.S. Archive.)

He then drew attention to his own sacrifices and his genuine efforts to work in collaboration with someone else when for fifteen years he had been totally independent. Against all his principles, he had turned a blind eye to the bad behaviour that was now prevalent in the theatre. He felt his own position had been seriously undermined. He, too, was at breaking point:

> 'Do you think I don't realize the extent to which my importance in the

theatre has declined? Do you think I don't see that in a short while it will be reduced to nil? . . . One thing I prize greatly: the right to express my artistic "credo" openly. I am beginning to lose that right. Haven't you noticed how obvious this has become recently? I speak to Tikhomirov [the director of the Art Theatre School] *purely privately* about the new things he is doing (Tikhomirov knows my position in the school – precisely nil) and they all declare that I am creating confusion and that students have left because of me. If I give any kind of advice or instructions they all shout "he's creating confusion!" and no one takes the least trouble to examine my ideas more closely. If I ask for someone to be fined – for blatant misconduct about which I would have created a scandal five years ago and had the theatre up in arms – now my words are quietly passed over in silence and nothing happens. If I give any kind of artistic advice "crank" is written over everyone's face.

My ideas have produced a worthless harvest and actors are praised for it and I suffer, witnessing the desecration of that which is sacred and precious to me. But I say nothing. . . . I will not lift a finger to create a new position for myself at the theatre. If I am on the slippery slope then the sooner I hit bottom the better. I am a very reserved man and say much less than I think. I hand over the theatre without a struggle. If I am needed then let me be treated with care and tact. If not, then get rid of me and (if it is inevitable) the sooner the better. . . .

Affectionately and devotedly yours, K. Alekseiev. If I have in any way offended you I am sorry. It was quite unintentional.' (*MATL*, No. 213.)

Allowing for a degree of exaggeration, or even self-dramatization, the letter confirms the extent to which Stanislavski was separated, and remained separated, from the daily life of most of the company. He might be called familiarly Kostia behind his back but no one said it to his face. He remained Mr Stanislavski – Konstantin Sergeievich. He was, of course, unlike the rest of the company, including Nemirovich, in that he had a complete life outside the theatre. There was the Alekseiev business and all the Alekseiev connections. He commuted between two worlds. His determination to create good theatre was matched by no one but he was not economically dependent on it and that made a difference. In personal habits he was perhaps rather more restrained than his colleagues. He smoked heavily but did not drink. He detested drink in the theatre and on one occasion was found weeping because he had seen a member of his cast very much the worse for wear. He was entirely faithful to Lilina and his attitude to relationships outside marriage tended towards the puritanical. He relaxed little. Possibly, too, he distanced himself from the rest by his increasingly frequent assertions, at the moment when the theatre appeared to be doing well, that things, in fact, were going very wrong.

Nemirovich was deeply touched by this letter and regretted ever having sent his own. He had been reduced to tears. The villain of the piece was Morozov and his influence.

> '*I am very fond of you and value you highly* and it is good for me to work with you but when it *seems* that you are falling under influences which are hostile to my very soul then I become suspicious and everything I hold dear within me takes offence. . . . But everything you wrote about your own position is exaggerated *in the highest degree.*' (*MATL*, No. 215.)

The air, for the moment at least, had been cleared and attention could now be devoted to the production of *The Cherry Orchard* which had to be prepared in two months if it was to be included in the current season.

CHAPTER ELEVEN

THE CHERRY ORCHARD

It was the thought of *The Cherry Orchard* that kept Stanislavski going during the long misery of *Julius Caesar*. After three unhappy productions in a row he could only think what a blessed relief it would be to get back to Chekhov. Even one of his favourite roles had been temporarily denied him. It was not until mid-October that he was able to play Vershinin again. He wrote to Chekhov expressing his pleasure at being back once more on congenial ground, openly confessing his dislike of *Caesar*, and begging for the new play as soon as possible. When he went to collect it on October 18, although the most courteous of men, he did not even greet Knipper but simply put out his hand for the manuscript. He read the play at home on the following day and immediately sent Chekhov a telegram:

'. . . I think this is the best play you have written. . . . I feel and value every word.'

In a letter to her husband on October 20, Knipper confirmed:

'Konst. Serg., it can be said, has gone mad about the play. The first act, he says, he read as a comedy, the second he found thrilling, in the third act he was in a sweat and in the fourth he cried the whole time.' (*Olga Leonardovna Knipper-Chekhova*, I, Moscow, 1972, p. 307.)

Stanislavski had personal reasons for being attached to this particular Chekhov play which did not excite the same enthusiasm from Nemirovich. It had been conceived at Liubimovka. Two of the characters were based on people he knew. Charlotta was inspired by a local English governess and Epikhodov had many of the characteristics of the family servant who had looked after Chekhov during his stay. Trofimov also had a local model. Even the Act One set recalled the Alekseiev home:

'I drink coffee on the old sofa No. 1 [on the ground plan]; the sofa is placed just where it was at Liubimovka, in the connecting room, just by our dining-room. Remember?' (Ibid., p. 334.)

Yet, for all the enthusiasm with which the script was greeted the whole production was marked by disagreements of the most fundamental kind. A major problem to arise was casting. Chekhov was writing specifically for the company and had his own ideas. On October 14 he wrote to Knipper:

> 'Read this through when you've finished the play
> 1. Liubov Andreievna [Ranevskaia] will be played by you, there's no one else . . .
> 2. Ania can be played by any young actress;
> 3. Varia, perhaps Maria Petrovna [Lilina] could take this role.
> 4. Gaev is for Vishnievski . . .;
> 5. Lopakhin, Stanislavski;
> 6. Trofimov the student, Kachalov;
> 7. Simeonov-Pishchik, Gribunin;
> 8. Charlotta – difficult question . . .;
> 9. Epikhodov, perhaps Luzhski would not turn it down;
> 10. Firs, Artiom;
> 11. Yasha, Moskvin . . .' (Chekhov, *Pisma*, XI, pp. 273–4.)

The first casting meeting took place on October 28, in the middle of the emotional exchange of correspondence between Stanislavski and Nemirovich. Whatever Chekhov might think, members of the company had their own ideas. Stanislavski was reluctant to play Lopakhin, although it had been written for him. Lilina was resolutely against his taking on the part. Also, quite inappropriately, she wanted to play the seventeen-year-old Ania, a part for which, in her mid-thirties, for all her talent, she was far too old, as Stanislavski later recognized. An exchange of letters followed, Chekhov urging Stanislavski to play the part he had written for him, Stanislavski indicating as tactfully as he could that he would rather play Gaev. Writing to Chekhov on November 3 and 4, he offered to look at both roles:

> 'I can't say which part I want more . . . To tell the truth I am afraid of Lopakhin. It's said my merchants don't come across, or, rather seem theatrical and false. . . . Lopakhin is good, small – sweet-natured but strong. . . .
>
> I like Lopakhin and will play him with pleasure but I can't yet find the right tone in myself. I'm trying hard and with great interest nonetheless. The trouble is that Lopakhin is not just a simple merchant, with their characteristically pushy manner. I see him exactly as you describe him in your letter. It needs great control over the tone so as to touch in the mundane elements of the character. All I'm managing to produce so far is Konstantin Sergeievich trying to be nice.' (*SS*, VII, pp. 269–70.)

The arguments are reasonable but unconvincing. There is an inner resistance behind the words. Stanislavski may not have wanted to be identified in the public mind with a class which, on the whole, he despised and from which, with a few exceptions, he had distanced himself. This would perhaps explain Lilina's attitude. But Stanislavski knew by now those characters with whom he could easily identify. In the space of a year he turned down Nil in *Small People* and now Lopakhin, both a new breed. This had nothing to do with any political views he may have held. It may have had a great deal to do with an instinctive recognition that he belonged to a certain milieu and period, a certain historical moment, which prevented him from identifying *internally* with certain parts. He could produce an external characterization any time but that did not satisfy him. He could play middle-class and professional idealists (Astrov, Stockman, Vershinin), gentlemen on the skids (Satin), but not the young and rebellious (Nil) nor the upwardly mobile (Lopakhin). In the end, therefore, as everyone expected, he played Gaev.

There was another significant departure from Chekhov's casting, that of Epikhodov. When he came to write *My Life in Art* twenty years later Stanislavski stated that there was no role for Moskvin and that, since they could not waste a good actor, the part was assigned to him. He seems to have forgotten that Chekhov had suggested Yasha. The problem was that whereas Chekhov had described Epikhodov as fat and breathless, Moskvin was small and skinny. In the event Moskvin, who was brilliantly inventive, pulled off a *tour de force*, adapting the role to his own physique and personality, so well indeed that when a somewhat nervous company showed Chekhov the results he declared:

'That's just what I meant to write. It's tremendous, I tell you!' (*SS*, I, p. 267.)

Nemirovich announced the final casting on November 5. Rehearsals, that is preliminary discussions on the characters and their relationships, began on the 9th. Yet even as the problems of casting were being sorted out, a much more serious disagreement emerged, concerning, once more, the basic nature of the play. Having called *Three Sisters* a drama, Chekhov had then insisted it was a comedy. Now, having designated *The Cherry Orchard* a comedy, he insisted it was a farce. He had undoubtedly wanted to write a farce. In a letter to Knipper, written on April 22, 1901, he had spoken of writing a 'four-act vaudeville or comedy for the Art Theatre' which he would deliver at the end of 1903. He obviously convinced himself that he had done just that. Writing to Lilina on September 15, 1903, he told her:

'What came out was not a drama but a comedy, almost in places a farce and I'm afraid I'm going to catch it from Vladimir Ivanovich [Nemirovich].' (Chekhov, *Pisma*, XI, p. 243.)

Stanislavski was categorical in his disagreement:

'This is not a comedy, nor a farce you have written. It is a tragedy whatever prospect of a better life you hold out in the last act.' (*SS*, VII, p. 265.)

Nemirovich took substantially the same view. In a telegram sent to Chekhov on October 18, he referred to the play as a 'real drama', but also expressed mild objections to an 'over-indulgence in tears'. This, combined with his statement that Ania was like Irina in *Three Sisters*, brought a rebuttal from Chekhov. Only Varia, he maintained, weeps and she is a cry-baby anyway. Ania never cries. What he asks for is people to speak 'through their tears'; which is an indication of mood, not of actual weeping.

Chekhov appears to have forgotten his own script, which contains gradations of weeping. Within a few lines of Trofimov's entrance in Act One Varia first speaks 'through her tears' then 'weeps', Trofimov speaks 'through his tears' while Ranevskaia 'weeps quietly'. In Act Three, after the announcement of the sale of the cherry orchard, Ranevskaia is twice instructed to weep *bitterly*. As Nemirovich remarked cryptically 'in a vaudeville you don't weep'.

Chekhov had to bow to the concerted view of the company, his frustration increased by the fact that there was no prospect, as far as he could see, of his being able to attend early rehearsals. He was coughing badly and his digestive system was giving him trouble.

Nemirovich, although listed as co-director, kept a discreet distance, doubtless in an attempt to improve relations with Stanislavski. None the less he did not renounce his role as watch-dog. Explaining his position to Chekhov, he wrote:

'Konstantin Sergeievich must be given his head as the director. First, he has staged nothing for the best part of a year and, in consequence, has built up a great store of energy and imagination; secondly, he understands you completely; thirdly he has left his whims a long way behind. But, of course, I shall keep a sharp eye on him.' (*Iz., Pis.*, I, pp. 351-2.)

In Chekhov's eyes, therefore, the full responsibility for staging and interpretation lay with Stanislavski. In an attempt doubtless to indicate to Chekhov that his views had registered, Stanislavski wrote on November 23 indicating that he was seeking something a little less 'heavy' than past productions:

'What can I say about rehearsals? The general tone has yet to be found. . . . With every play we are finding it more and more difficult to transform ourselves and be something different. It may well be that the whole play will be done in a completely different way from earlier ones. Everything will be lighter, brighter . . . In short we want to paint everything in watercolours.' (*SS*, VII, p. 276.)

Stanislavski, Simov and Nemirovich spent a long time over the sets. On November 5 Stanislavski wrote to Chekhov saying he would like to play Acts Three and Four in the same set – the ballroom. Chekhov agreed.

Stanislavski worked fast. The production plan for Act One was written in a single day, November 12, with a first rehearsal two days later. Act Two was ready by the 18th and in rehearsal by the 21st. On December 4, in spite of ill health, Chekhov arrived in Moscow and stayed until the play opened the following January. He was in an aggressive mood, more sensitive than ever to possible misinterpretations of his play. There had been yet another brush with Efros, who had published an outline of the plot in which it was stated that Act Three took place in a hotel (*gostinitsa*) rather than in a drawing-room (*gostina*). Chekhov reacted angrily, calling the article 'a crude hoax that bears no relation to reality'. Nemirovich hurriedly wrote an article setting the record straight and taking the blame on himself. It was he who had briefed Efros, although he pointed out that he had, in fact, found *gostinitsa* in the original manuscript. Chekhov brushed the whole incident aside but still refused to speak to Efros for some considerable time.

It was with Chekhov in this frame of mind that work on *The Cherry Orchard* began. Chekhov attended only five or six rehearsals but they were increasingly uncomfortable. He took against almost everything. Sometimes his comments were mildly ironic. Faced with Stanislavski's usual battery of sound effects he did, however, on one occasion, allow himself the remark:

> 'Listen, I shall write a new play which will open like this: "How wonderful, how quiet! Not a bird, a dog, a cuckoo, an owl, a nightingale, or clocks, or jingling bells, not even one cricket to be heard."' (*SS*, I, p. 270.)

This remark was pitched deliberately loud enough for Stanislavski to hear. The words registered but Stanislavski knew that he needed atmospheric devices to get his actors off the ground. Chekhov had, on the other hand, been delighted to learn in July that Stanislavski had recorded the sound of a shepherd's pipe at Liubimovka. It was a sound he had heard and liked. Not so acceptable was the idea of introducing a passing train in Act Two – an idea that was quickly dropped. But Chekhov's comments and objections became increasingly radical. One time it was the cast that was wrong – and he wrote some savage letters on the subject – another time it was Stanislavski's direction that was wrong, another time it was the interpretation of the lines that was wrong. Eventually he stopped attending rehearsals altogether. The exact cause is not clear. Knipper claimed that Stanislavski and Nemirovich asked her to keep him away. Nemirovich claimed that he had told Chekhov to go home because he was merely being a nuisance. Simov, the designer, claimed that Chekhov walked out because Stanislavski ignored some objections he made to the way a scene was being directed.

One of Chekhov's main objections to the production as a whole was that it was over-elaborate. Things were not being done 'as in life'.

Nemirovich, who had so often in the past urged Stanislavski towards greater simplicity, on this occasion defended what he called Stanislavski's 'poetic' approach. The play needed it.

Chekhov thus found himself in conflict with the entire Art Theatre both as regards the nature of the play and its interpretation. Nonetheless he provided a considerable number of rewrites as work progressed. He even agreed to a major cut. Act Two originally ended with a scene between Charlotta and Firs in which they exchange reminiscences about their childhood, revealing their loneliness. Stanislavski found this ending too downbeat. It was difficult to pick the play up afterwards whereas if the act ended with the exit of Trofimov and Ania the tone was much more positive. Reluctantly they asked Chekhov to take it out and after a very short hesitation he agreed. The scene did not appear in the published edition. Stanislavski reproached himself bitterly afterwards. He felt that his own inability as a director to make a scene work had resulted in the loss of a fine piece of writing.

For the first time the production plan contained notes on the motivations of the characters as well as details of the blocking. There are explanations of the psychological and social mechanisms at work. Nowhere is this more apparent than in Act Three, where he charts Lopakhin's behaviour after he has announced that he has bought the cherry orchard.

Stanislavski's staging is as follows:

'RANEVSKAIA. Has the cherry orchard been sold?

LOPAKHIN. (*202. Guiltily, examining his handkerchief. Looks down. Doesn't answer at once.*) It has.

RANEVSKAIA. (*203. Pause, barely audible.*) Who bought it?

LOPAKHIN. (*204. Pause. Even quieter and more embarrassed.*) I bought it. (*205. Agonizing pause. Lopakhin feels badly and this arouses the beast in him. The awkwardness of his position starts to make him angry. He nervously pulls at his handkerchief. Ranevskaia just sinks down and remains in that position for some time. She takes nothing in, understands nothing. It is as if she has suddenly grown old. She sits still at the side of the table. For Varia, it is a huge drama. She is both depressed and outraged. Pishchik tugs at his beard, looking first at Ranevskaia then at Lopakhin. In the ballroom the guests are sitting round the walls listening to the recitation of the second verse by the Station Master (although he can't be seen). Varia breaks the pause. She steps forward, throws down her keys and goes downstairs. This exhausts Lopakhin's patience. He is irritated. His tone is bitter and insolent as he almost shouts.*) I bought it. (*206. Pause. Having shouted, Lopakhin tears his handkerchief in two and flings it away. He is still for a moment. He calms down. Then he gets up, covers his ears with his hands and crosses to the table. 207. On the cross.*) Excuse me a moment, ladies and gentlemen, my head is spinning, I can't say anything. (*208. Ranevskaia is motionless. She has shrunk even smaller. She looks vacantly at the floor. Lopakhin goes to the table. He wants to drink some seltzer. He up-ends two bottles – nothing. He pours some from a third bottle which Varia hasn't cleared and crosses, glass in hand, to the table with the semi-circular sofa, away from Ranevskaia. He sits. Pishchik closes the doors so that the guests can't hear what is going on. Having closed the doors Pishchik goes to Lopakhin and sits on the arm of the sofa. Now, at a distance from Ranevskaia, the feeling of pleasure and commercial pride leads them way over a proper sense of embarrass-ment and Lopakhin begins to boast as a businessman does faced with his brother-merchants or his assistants. 209. The account of the sale (not small-minded) with artistic enthusiasm over his skill and efficiency. It is essential in order to justify Lopakhin that there should precisely be this 'artistic enthusiasm'.*) We got to the auction. Deriganov was already there. Leonid Andreich [Gaev] only had fifteen thousand and Deriganov immediately bid thirty thousand over the arrears on the mortgage. I saw how things were going and pitched in with forty. He bid forty-five. I bid fifty-five. He was going up in fives, you see, and me in tens. So, it was all over. I bid ninety thousand over the arrears and it went to me. Now the cherry orchard is mine! Mine! (*210. Gross guffaw. He clowns, leaning his head on the table, ruffles his hair, butts Pishchik who is sitting next to him in the chest. Stands up, raises his arms and beats his chest. He continues his speech as he does so. All this clowning is explicable by the force of his character, his unbridled nature, his ecstasy.*) God Almighty, gentlemen, the cherry orchard is mine! Tell me I'm drunk, or out of my mind, or that I'm imagining all this. . . . (*211. Pause. He thumps the table and the sofa like a kulak. Laughs.*) Don't you laugh at me! Don't you laugh, don't you dare! (*212. Suddenly stops and changes tone. Now he is stern, imperious. The drink is coming into its own. 213. He moves forward. Now he knows no mercy. The drink has gone to his head. He cannot feel Ranevskaia's sorrow and misery. Darkening malice and resentment towards the humiliations and trials of his childhood have been aroused in him. All this will be accepted if the actor goes at it boldly, powerfully, like a warrior not a bruiser.*) If my father and grandfather were to rise from their graves and see what's gone on, how their Ermolai, their beaten, semi-literate Ermolai who ran barefoot in winter, this same Ermolai, bought the property where his grandfather and his father were slaves, where they weren't even allowed into the kitchen. (*214. He strides boldly about the room. Ranevskaia at this moment seems to have shrunk even more.*) I'm dreaming, this is just an illusion, lost in the mists of ignorance. (*215. Angrily steps on the keys and picks them*

*up. 216. For a moment there is a touch of remorse and if not love
then some kind of positive feeling for Varia*.) She threw away the
keys to show she's not mistress here any more. (*217. Pause. He
thinks for a moment. The question of marriage flashes through his
mind but it is gone in a moment and he jingles the keys more angrily
than ever*.) So what does it matter? (*218. Turns to the glass doors,
opens them and shouts all his dialogue into the ballroom, standing
on the threshold. There is a minor commotion in the ballroom. All
those sitting down prefer to go and sit a little further off from
Lopakhin*.) Hey, you in the band, play, I want to hear something!
Come and see, all of you, how Ermolai Lopakhin takes his axe to that
cherry orchard and the trees come crashing down. We'll put up villas
and our children and great grandchildren will see a new life! . . . Let's
have some music! (*219. The band strikes up a trite little polka and
Lopakhin dances backwards, bumping into Ranevskaia who has
sunk on to a chair next to the table and is weeping bitterly.
Lopakhin's mood suddenly drops – at the sight of those tears the
good and sincere man in him and his tender love for the whole family
and for her especially is aroused . . . 220. He drops to his knees,
kisses her hands and skirt like a little puppy dog (the fact that he is
drunk helps). He weeps. The more sincerely and tenderly the better.
Why then, if he is so tenderhearted, didn't he help Ranevskaia?
Because he is a slave to merchants' prejudices, because they would
have made him a laughing-stock. Les affaires sont les affaires*.)
Why, oh why didn't you listen to me? My poor, dear friend, you
can't go back now. (*221. Ranevskaia hugs him and both weep.
Pause*.) Oh if only all this could be over quickly. If only our
miserable mess of a life could somehow change soon. . . .
(*Rezhissiorskie Ekzempliari, K. S. Stanislavskovo*, III, pp. 422–5.)

By the end of the act, as if to mark the change, the trite little polka has
given way to a rough peasant dance.

The vision, as has been noted earlier, is cinematic; the psychology has
the detail of the novelist. The very heavy demands both in terms of
understanding and technique which Stanislavski placed on a still inexperienced company are evident. There is also just sufficient contempt in
his insight into Lopakhin's mechanisms to explain why he did not wish
to play the part himself.

When the play opened, on January 17, 1904, it was inevitably under-
rehearsed, just as Nemirovich had feared. The opening night was
combined with a ceremony to mark Chekhov's birthday. This took place
during one of the intervals. Chekhov detested ceremonies of this kind
and when one of the worthy professors began his address: 'Dear and
respected . . .' he gave Stanislavski a sideways glance. Both men thought
"book-case" – Gaev's speech. But the real words, "Anton Pavlovich"

came out. Chekhov's lips twitched and the moment was over.

It is difficult to see how the play, which demands concentrated attention, could have made its full impact, even if the production had been absolutely ready on an evening which was half performance, half celebration. Success was only moderate. Over the following weeks the production ran itself in but Chekhov was not there to see it. He never, in fact, saw the production in a finished state. He had to rely on second-hand reports. He was not happy with the opening night. He wrote to Leontiev on January 18:

'My play was on last night and that's why I am in a bad mood.' (Chekhov, *Pisma*, XII, p. 14.)

The day after he wrote to Batioushkov:

'It will be better if you come just before Lent. Because I don't think the actors will have come to their senses before then and play *The Cherry Orchard* with a little less confusion and vagueness than they are now.' (Ibid., p. 15.)

Faced with critical comment which, as he had feared, accused him of pessimism he grew more and more impatient with the production. He insisted again that the play was farcical. Much as Brecht was to complain later about the public's sympathetic attitude to Mother Courage, Chekhov insisted that Ranevskaia learned nothing, that she was incorrigible. The letters he received did not help. Members of Knipper's family reported, in March, that Act Four was appalling and that Stanislavski was dragging everything out. On March 29, in despondent mood, he wrote to Knipper:

'An act which should last twelve minutes *maximum* takes forty in your production. All I can say is, Stanislavski has ruined my play. Well, I leave him to God.' (Ibid., p. 74.)

Yet Chekhov had particularly praised Stanislavski's last exit in Act Four, during one of the final dress rehearsals and Knipper had written to her husband on the 18th that in everyone's opinion the production had achieved a better balance. What had happened? Probably, as so often in a production, unless the director keeps a tight rein on things, the performance had spread. As each actor discovers new depths in his role there is a temptation to linger, to play every moment to the full. Nemirovich had already criticized this tendency in Stanislavski's own work but it was, in fact, inherent in Stanislavski's total approach. The in-depth exploration of every moment was bound to slow, not to say bog things down. Writing to Efros in 1908, Nemirovich said that he had come to realize that at a certain point, when exploratory work had been done, a production had, as it were, to skim the surface. Even if the cast did indulge themselves, Chekhov's claims that the act should be played in twelve minutes *maximum* is nonetheless unrealistic. It would take more than twelve minutes merely to read the text aloud decently. Given the amount of action, Chekhov's own marked pauses (ten) and Ranevskaia's prevarications and delays, one should allow at least double the reading time. How seriously can Chekhov's remark be taken, given his admission to Stanislavski that he could not tell how a play would go merely from reading it? Stanislavski, certainly, was convinced that Chekhov misjudged his own works. In his *Notebook* for 1926, recalling the way, at a first reading, Chekhov warded off actors' questions with the reply, 'I have written all I know,' he stated.

> 'The fact is that he was unable critically to evaluate his own plays and listened to other people's views with great interest and even astonishment. The thing that surprised him most, and which he went to his grave without ever being able to reconcile himself to, was the fact that his *Three Sisters*, and subsequently his *Cherry Orchard*, was a serious drama of Russian life. He was absolutely convinced that this last was a light comedy, almost a vaudeville.' (*SS*, V, pp. 348–9.)

And, indeed, in April 1904, four months after the play had opened and two months before his death, the fact that the play had been described on the posters and in the press as a drama still rankled. He wrote to Knipper, 'Nemirovich and Alekseiev absolutely see in my play something I did not write,' and then went on, 'neither of them ever read my plays attentively.'

Yet it was not only Stanislavski and Nemirovich and their contemporaries who saw Chekhov's plays as drama. Vakhtangov, twenty years Stanislavski's junior, was also in no doubt that Chekhov's plays were essentially tragic in nature.

It was, perhaps, Gorki who came closest to a genuine understanding of Chekhov's tone of voice, that of a clinician. As a doctor, he noted, Chekhov was objective about his characters, noting signs and symptoms. His diagnoses were, however, to be read as a call to action not an excuse for hopeless resignation. A proper realization of the justice of this view only came slowly, with later generations, and even then with difficulty.

At the end of June, Chekhov died in Badenweiler. Sulerzhitski brought news to Stanislavski and Lilina at Liubimovka. On July 3 Stanislavski wrote to Knipper, describing their grief. They had, he told her, just kept talking to prevent themselves from breaking down.

Stanislavski and Lilina had little time to comfort one another. He was obliged to accompany his ailing mother to Contrexeville. On the journey he thought of Chekhov and nothing else – his ways, his voice, his gestures. From Contrexeville he wrote to Lilina:

> 'I never thought I would be so attached to him and that it would create such a yawning gap in my life.' (*SS*, VII, p. 293.)

An era had passed.

PART TWO

THE BIRTH OF THE 'SYSTEM'

CHAPTER TWELVE

MEIERHOLD

Chekhov's death was not the only reason Stanislavski had to be depressed in the summer of 1904. Nemirovich had precipitated a crisis as a result of which both Gorki and Morozov severed their connections with the theatre.

Gorki had read his new play *Summerfolk* to the company on April 18 without much success. Stanislavski was cautious, reserving his comments. Nemirovich, still smarting from Gorki's contemptuous dismissal of his own play, *In Dreams*, which had flopped so badly, wrote a letter so scathing in its criticism as to be insulting. He accused Gorki of lacking respect for the Russian intelligentsia. He told him the play was shapeless and formless, having no centre or plot, in short that it was little more than raw material. Gorki was incensed. No theatre of which Nemirovich was the head, he replied, would be allowed to stage his plays. The breach was total. Nothing Stanislavski could do or say would make him change his mind. Later in the year, on December 12, he sent a telegram refusing to allow his latest play to be put on:

'Notwithstanding my personal liking for you, Nemirovich's conduct towards me obliges me to refuse to allow the theatre to produce *Enemies* and further to decline any kind of connection with the Art Theatre.' (G. S. Burzhdalov Archive, No. 689.)

Morozov was so angered by Nemirovich's behaviour that he resigned from the board. Only in the autumn did he agree to maintain an investment of just under 15,000 roubles while making it clear no further help would be forthcoming in the future. Stanislavski had lost a valuable ally and the theatre its main source of financial security. Nemirovich shed no tears.

The company was generally unsettled. Kachalov threatened to quit but could not bring himself to do so. His emotional and artistic debt to Stanislavski was too great for him to leave at a moment of crisis; however, his final decision to remain was not taken until late July so that Stanislavski only received the welcome news on his return from France, having spent the summer wondering whether in addition to losing his closest business partner and his best new playwright he was also to lose his best actor.

He was frustrated, too, by his failure to achieve his broader objectives. He had not forgotten his aspirations of the 1890s, when he had dreamed of creating a network of provincial theatres. Now he could see the Moscow Art Theatre as a potential power-base for a complete reform of Russian theatre but, given the derision his more idealistic attitudes excited among his colleagues, he realized that his ambitions could only be achieved through a new generation. He needed the energy and enthusiasm of the young. He began to look for possible future leaders in the School. In the winter of 1903 Boris Pronin, a student, was surprised to receive a summons to Stanislavski's dressing-room after a performance of *Julius Caesar*. He was expecting to be disciplined for having laughed during the scene in the senate.

'With a heavy heart he knocked on the door of Konstantin Sergeievich's dressing-room. "Come in" came the voice. He stepped through the door and recoiled quite involuntarily: Stanislavski was completely naked. That was his way of relaxing after the strain of playing Brutus. Konstantin Sergeievich with gentle affability invited him once more to come in and sit down. According to Pronin, in that mentally complex giant there was a childlike simplicity as he stood there smoking. Thus, just as he could wear any kind of costume, he could wear his own naked flesh genuinely with the utmost Hellenic simplicity.' (Reminiscence of V. P. Verigina in *O Stanislavskom*, p. 357.)

Stanislavski, far from delivering the expected reprimand, asked Pronin home so that they could discuss plans for the future.

When Gorki set up a theatre in Nizhni-Novgorod early in 1904 Stanislavski saw it as the first of his projected network. He immediately provided it with the financial support he had always denied the Art Theatre and released Tikhomirov, who ran the Art Theatre School, and a small number of pupils to strengthen the company. Further financial support came from Morozov in April, once he had broken with the Art Theatre. It was a brave enterprise but everyone had reckoned without the hostility of the authorities, particularly the censor who managed to ban every play that was put forward. The project was abandoned in the early autumn.

Even had Gorki remained with the Art Theatre the problem of new repertoire would have remained. Tastes had changed. Realistic staging and, more particularly, the plethora of detail that had characterized the Art Theatre's recent productions was no longer acceptable. Progressives now demanded plays which dealt with more intangible aspects of human experience and which were more formally experimental.

The new avant-garde was represented by the Symbolists and their spokesman Valeri Briusov, who advanced his ideas first in an influential article, 'Unnecessary Truth', which appeared in the magazine *Mir*

Iskusstva in 1902 and later in his book *Teatr: Kniga O Novom Teatr* published in St Petersburg in 1908. The very notion of realistic staging was attacked. The more 'real' the sets, props and costumes the more 'conventional' they actually were. The 'real' actually was a convention. Why, Briusov asked, is night represented by an ingenious manipulation of light instead of a total blackout, which would indeed correspond to reality? The current compromise, elements of set, minimum of objects, does not solve the problem for against this conventionalized background all too palpable actors are moving and their attempts at physical and vocal artificiality are, at best, spasmodic. An extreme solution would be to replace actors by dummies with gramophones inside but that would remove the whole undertaking from the realm of art. It would put the theatre in the same relationship to the dramatist as typography is to the poet. The inescapable fact, Briusov maintained, was that realism and semi-realism limit the imagination of the audience and the creativity of the actor. The answer must lie in a return to Aristotle's definition of drama as the imitation of an action and to the actor as the creator and agent of that action. 'The art of the theatre and the art of the actor are one and the same thing.'

This was precisely the kind of radical challenge which Stanislavski needed. True to form he went from one extreme to the other, from the totally external to the totally internal. Even Chekhov, towards the end of his life, was moving in a new direction. He was interested in the Belgian dramatist, Maeterlinck, the most static and mystical of contemporary dramatists and, in the autumn of 1902, encouraged the Art Theatre to put on an evening of his one-act plays. The plot of Chekhov's projected last play, which he outlined to Stanislavski at their last meeting in May 1904, showed clear signs of this new influence.

> 'A husband and his friend are in love with the same woman. He went through the whole tragedy, the individual incidents of which were not yet clear, even to the author. The tragedy ends with first the husband, then the friend deciding to join a distant expedition. The last act, according to Chekhov, should take place at the North pole. Chekhov saw a ship lost in the ice, with the two heroes on it, the husband and the friend, who look into the far distance and see rushing by the ghost of the woman they both loved.' (Interview in *Rech*, July 2, 1914.)

Gorki had always recognized and respected the element of symbolism in Chekhov's work. It was logical therefore that in his search for change Stanislavski should accept the judgement of the two writers he knew best. He decided to act on Chekhov's suggestion and stage three short plays by Maeterlinck – *Les Aveugles*, *Intérieurs* and *L'Intruse*.

Finding a new style and a new method of approach was not easy. In May Konstantin Balmont, who had translated the three Maeterlinck plays into Russian, met the author to ask for his comments. As far as the dialogue was concerned Maeterlinck wanted neither romantic declamation, nor total realism but something in-between: expressive speech but understated. Stanislavski experienced enormous difficulty in getting a line on the production. How was he to 'make the untheatrical theatrical'? How was he to communicate the eternal, the intangible? Inevitably he exploited his skill as a producer, his capacity to manipulate effects, to fill the gaps. Maeterlinck's mysterious world was conveyed by a series of elaborate stage effects, which engulfed a largely static cast. He used a great deal of music – an excessive amount in Nemirovich's view – starting the evening with a five-minute overture by a hidden orchestra. But that did nothing for the actors. He realized that a new acting technique was necessary but his own experiments at home in front of a mirror, both vocal and physical, proved unsuccessful. In any case there was not time to retrain the company. He conveyed his anxieties to his cast, who struggled throughout August to come to terms with this unfamiliar material.

The final result was a hotch-potch of acting and production styles which, when it opened on October 2, pleased nobody. The critics felt that Stanislavski had failed to capture the essence of Maeterlinck's symbolism because of his production technique; the public was simply confused both by the material and the apparent change of direction the theatre had taken. One medical student wrote a letter of protest against the total absence of positive values in the plays. The unremitting doom and gloom of Maeterlinck's texts were unlikely, in any case, to appeal to an audience already depressed by the news of Russia's endless humiliations during the Russo-Japanese War.

Both Stanislavski and Nemirovich felt that the new season must contain a tribute to Chekhov. Nemirovich directed *Ivanov* with Stanislavski in the role of Shabelski. The opening, which was scheduled for October 12, had to be postponed because of the death of Stanislavski's mother. When the play opened a week later Stanislavski turned in what was considered one of his best performances. His own success, however, did not reconcile him to Nemirovich's production which once again he found pedestrian.

Stanislavski's own tribute to Chekhov took the form of three adaptations of short stories under the title *Miniatures*. There was an opportunity here to attempt more experimental staging. In 1899 he had conceived the notion of a sequence of short dialogues and sketches by Chekhov and others which would be presented on a specially constructed platform on the stage proper with elements of décor and props ready to hand. Scene was to follow scene without closing the curtain in a kind of cinematic rhythm. Unfortunately he did not follow the idea through. *Miniatures* was much more conventionally presented. The first night, on December 21, when the Chekhov pieces were accompanied by another one-act play, *At the Monastery*, which Nemirovich directed, was a total flop. Stanislavski said goodbye to 1904, which had been so disastrous in professional and personal terms, without regret.

The final production of the 1904–5 season, *Ghosts*, did little to raise his spirits. He and Nemirovich were to co-direct but they agreed on almost nothing. Stanislavski described Nemirovich's mood as 'sour, as it has been all winter'. The sets gave endless trouble. In addition to Simov, Stanislavski called in a second designer, Kolupaiev, and a design apprentice, Andreiev. Model followed model, some made by Stanislavski himself, and were rejected; furniture was continuously moved about to allow the actors freedom of movement. Nemirovich made no positive contribution at all to the discussions. Stanislavski admitted that he himself became thoroughly bad-tempered at his inability to give concrete form to the ideas that were running about in his head.

Building on his experience with the Maeterlinck plays, Stanislavski demanded a broader approach, less detail and more mood, in the early rehearsals. For the first time he publicly contradicted Nemirovich's basic method:

'We did a breakdown of the characters. [The cast] wanted to delve into every detail *à la Nemirovich* but I put a stop to it. What actors need initially is the general tone of their parts, the basic colour as it were. When an actor has discovered and feels at home with the overall outline, character and mood, then you can show him various details and nuances. I have noticed that when Nemirovich is directing and goes into minute detail at the outset the actors are confused by the complexity of the material and get bogged down and the characters, even when the feelings are simple and straightforward, are vague.' (*SS*, V, p. 268.)

When Nemirovich took over rehearsals using the hastily written production plan, Stanislavski sat on the sidelines providing more detailed explanations whenever he thought necessary. This, as so often, included graphic demonstration. Knipper, who was playing Regina, was having trouble establishing a definite speech pattern for the role. The character came and went all the time.

'Konstantin Sergeievich ran lightly on to the stage, stood in a corner and in silence in the space of about two minutes assumed the insolent coquettishness, the lust of life and the predatory essence of Regina's character. As Konstantin Sergeievich imagined himself as Regina, above all his eyes lit up in a special way, then a stream of fiery energy ran along his shoulders which were slightly hunched and raised. It ran down to his hands; his wrists came to life and the palm of his right hand, as though compressing the resistant air, landed in the palm of his left. The hands were tightly clenched, locking in the energy. The whole essence of Regina was contained there.' (Reminiscence of V. P. Verigina, *O Stanislavskom*, p. 350.)

Stanislavski had found a physical solution to a vocal problem. Rather than attempt to deal with speech patterns at a superficial level he saw the voice as part of a total physical characterization in which the body responded organically to inner impulses. His demonstration was the spontaneous reaction of an experienced professional, which he was not able as yet to analyse. He could not formulate in objective terms the principle which lay behind it. He insisted that the cast play against the tragic thrust of the play. He wanted firmness of tone and a good pace. By firm tone and good pace he did not mean superficial bravura and hack virtuosity but an actor's capacity, once he is confident in a part, to move swiftly from one extremity of mood to another. The key is in the notion of *tempo*. Tempo is not speed and rant but an ability 'to juggle easily with even the strongest emotions'. This is what audiences find exciting.

Stanislavski's dismissive attitude towards Nemirovich's working methods in this production was not an isolated phenomenon. He felt that the theatre had become too 'literary' and that his own creative development was being stifled by too great a subservience to the letter of the text.

This was clearly illustrated by his treatment of the opening of *Ghosts*. When he came to plan Act One, he considered, somewhat arbitrarily it must be admitted, that Regina's first line to Ekdal, 'What are you doing here?' and Ekdal's own entrance were unmotivated.

'In Ibsen the carpenter enters the living-room without rhyme or reason and stands there doing nothing while engaging in a long dialogue. But we are in the theatre. It had to be changed. I decided on this: at the beginning of the act he is busy with the lock on the French windows. A steamer passes during the pause. He starts to hammer and Regina runs in. The scene continues with him working and her tidying up. Then everything comes alive. Only to do this we shall have to change the author's opening words and move sentences around. What else can we do? It seems to me not to do it is just pedantry.' (*SS*, V, pp. 263–4.)

Nemirovich could only find such an attitude deeply offensive.

Stanislavski had started to build a new circle of collaborators. Liubov Gurevich, with whom he had been in correspondence since the first St Petersburg tour, became his literary adviser, a role she was to fulfil for some thirty years. More than any other single individual she influenced the shape and structure of his writing. He then engaged Leopold Sulerzhitski, ex-merchant seaman, revolutionary, devotee of Tolstoi, as his personal assistant and paid for his services out of his own pocket. Nemirovich resented him deeply, as he resented anyone who came between himself and Stanislavski, and Sulerzhitski was never allowed to hold any official position on the staff of the Moscow Art Theatre.

Undeterred by Gorki's negative experiences, Stanislavski returned to the question of a general reform of the Russian theatre. On February 13 he called a number of senior colleagues to a meeting at his flat and again proposed a chain of provincial theatres under the general control of the Art Theatre. Members of the main company would be seconded to the new theatres and Art Theatre productions sent out on tour. The first theatre in the chain would open in the 1905–6 season. He might be prepared to put in 100,000 roubles of his own money. Stanislavski was without doubt thinking of tying in with Gorki who was planning to start a theatre in St Petersburg with the former Art Theatre actress, Andreieva, and Vera Komissarzhevskaia, who had herself considered joining the Art Theatre in 1902. Stanislavski had already been invited to become a guest director.

The meeting agreed that in general the scheme was a good one although, as usual with Stanislavski's schemes, some found it naïve and badly thought-through. It was Nemirovich who dealt the death-blow by raising all manner of practical difficulties. How, he asked, was a small undertaking like the Art Theatre, which was still not financially viable, to assume such a heavy responsibility? Where were the actors to come from? What would happen to the main company and its productions if its members were being sent into the provinces? How were the tours to be financed? These were, on the face of it, perfectly reasonable questions. What worried Nemirovich, however, was his own implied loss of control. If there was to be reform it would have to be on his terms, not Stanislavski's and certainly not Gorki's.

It was during these abortive discussions that Meierhold returned to Moscow. He had been working with his own experimental group. He claimed that he had the solution to the problem that had defeated Stanislavski – how to convey the ineffable. He had absorbed Briusov's ideas and made them work. He had passion, he had energy; he was extreme, he was intransigent – 'The theatre must be a hermitage and the actor forever a dissident'. Stanislavski responded to this outpouring of ideas with the enthusiasm of a man dying of thirst. He was not sure he understood his young colleague, or could say whether he was good or bad, a genius or a charlatan; he only knew that he needed him. Meierhold could be the right person to extend and expand the work of the Art Theatre and provide a way out of an artistic impasse. Meierhold was a man after his own kind, an artist who created in and through the theatre itself, not through literature. There was an affinity between the two of them which purely theoretical or aesthetic disagreements could not destroy.

Meierhold felt that by the warmth of his welcome Stanislavski was somehow making amends for having treated him so badly three years earlier. He left Moscow again during the rehearsals for *Ghosts* but by April sent Stanislavski an outline scheme for a Theatre-Studio, a term which he invented himself. The scheme, based on discussions they had held earlier, embodies both Stanislavski's ideas for a wider social role for the Art Theatre and Meierhold's ideas on new theatrical forms. In May, Briusov agreed to give the venture his artistic support as literary adviser. The rest of the month was spent defining the artistic principles on which the Studio was to operate.

The company was composed of members of Meierhold's New Drama, members of the Art Theatre itself, pupils from the Art Theatre School, including Boris Pronin, and a number of actors from the Aleksandrinski Theatre in St Petersburg. Officially the Studio was attached to the Art Theatre; in reality it was subsidized almost entirely by Stanislavski. The main company were far from being sympathetic to the venture which many regarded as another piece of idealistic nonsense.

Stanislavski converted a barn at Mamontovka, not far from Pushkino, so that the company could rehearse during the summer. It seemed as though the Art Theatre, with all its early hopes and freshness, was starting all over again. He then lost his head, as he had when he created the Society of Art and Literature. He had intended to use the Hunting Club for performances, but instead he took on an empty theatre in Povarskaia Street, which Sergei Popov, a former associate in the Society, found for him. It was a 1200-seater, far too big for experimental work and in need of repair. He had the auditorium completely redecorated at his own expense. This cost him over 20,000 roubles. Having set the Studio up he did not interfere. Meierhold was given an absolutely free hand.

For his part, Stanislavski wanted to carry over the new artistic policy into the main company. He was due to direct Knut Hamsun's *The Drama of Life* in the coming season, an abstract, highly symbolic text. Discussing the play with Nemirovich he announced his intention to start rehearsals using improvisation, dispensing with all preliminary discussion and analysis, attempting to stimulate the actors' creativity through action. Nemirovich was outraged. He had concealed his dislike of the new Studio under a veil of politeness, sending a message of congratulations and encouragement to the new young company at its inauguration on June 3. But the sight of his colleague violating every artistic principle he held dear proved too much to take. Changing a few lines in *Ghosts* was one thing, now the whole supremacy of the text was in question. He attributed Stanislavski's behaviour to the malign influence of Meierhold whose interest it was to drive a wedge between them.

Between the 8th and 10th he wrote Stanislavski a huge twenty-eight page letter with an almost equally long postscript in which he poured out his feelings of anger and resentment. He analysed the entire season. He brought up every disagreement, every imagined slight or insult. He attempted to apportion blame or merit for every aspect of the new productions. Yet the basic message was clear: it is thanks to me that you have become an effective professional; be guided by me or you will revert to the self-indulgent, capricious amateur you were when I met you.

'. . . in the last four or five years you allowed a number of restraints to be placed on your artistic temperament. You trusted, as it were, my *reason* and allowed that *reason* to govern, so that our theatre could enjoy real success. You saw from your own experience that with no one to control your temperament you destroy the best pearls of your own talent. Left to yourself you create with one hand and destroy with the other. There is not one single production to date, including *Three Sisters*, that would not have come to nothing had it not been for my control, not only literary but artistic. . . .

Now suddenly you seem to think that real art only existed at the Sporting Club where there was nothing to restrict your ideas. . . . You suddenly decided to give full rein to your own will, not realizing that your temperament would take over and ruin everything we have built up over seven years. . . . Under the influence of Meierhold's absurd chatter on the necessity of rehearsing as the spirit moves, the desire rose in you to exploit a method you have obviously been "thinking of for some time". This revealed very clearly a yearning to throw off "the yoke of reason".

In your serious moments you emerge as a teacher of the ethical view of art. Then you are a great man. But not when, unbeknown to yourself – because you are tired, artistic energy is beginning to flag – you transform serious matters into a personal plaything. Then you are no more than a talented but naughty child busy with trifles.' (*MATL*, No. 265.)

Finally Nemirovich put a question almost too ridiculous to ask: was it possible that Stanislavski was jealous of him as a director?

In his brief reply Stanislavski, as in their earlier exchange, pointed to his own sacrifices and rebuked Nemirovich for his egotism, which was now doubly inappropriate, given the state of unrest in Russia. The country was still reeling from the shock of the massacre of innocent workers and peasants in St Petersburg in January, on Bloody Sunday. It had suffered a series of humiliating defeats in the war with the Japanese. It was time to think of work, not hurt feelings:

'Dear Vladimir Ivanovich,
I admire your many qualities, your talent, intelligence and so on. . . . And I am distressed at the deterioration in our relationship . . . I rack my brain over ways to improve it. . . . I don't think our relations can be improved by talking about them. . . . Instead of talk, work. That's your most powerful weapon against me. . . .

Let's say things are as you write. It's all my fault, my despotism, my whims, my obstinacy and the remnants of my amateurism. . . . I only ask one thing. Make life possible for me at the theatre. Grant me some kind of satisfaction, without which I cannot work. Don't let the time come when love and faith in our theatre will disappear *for ever.*

. . . at the moment, like everyone else, I am concerned for what is happening in Russia. Let us not talk of professional jealousy and pride. Dear God, I have finished with them forever. . . . I have never felt jealousy in my work as a director. *It is an activity I do not enjoy.* I do it out of necessity. In the realm of acting I have surrendered my pride, doggedly giving way to others and burying that side of me. From now on I shall only play so as not to lose the ability to demonstrate to others.

Try and appreciate the personal effort I have made. . . .

I do not value my success as a director but the theatre does. And that's the only reason I take pleasure in it. . . . Take my name off the posters once and for all. Think rather what it cost me to surrender my primacy of place as an actor to Kachalov and others . . . I have become . . . more demanding because of all that I have crushed in myself. I now have the right to demand full-scale, widespread theatrical activity throughout the whole of Russia. . . .

Perhaps I may come a cropper but I might also die in peace. . . . Let us work now as *at this moment* every *decent* man *must.* Do what I did. Kill your pride. Defeat me with the theatre and with work. . . .

Affectionately yours, K. Alekseiev.' (*MATL*, No. 266.)

On June 28 Nemirovich wrote a conciliatory letter (*MATL*, No. 267), backtracking on his pretensions as a director; there could be no comparison between himself and Stanislavski, but he could not help wondering if their collaboration had always been doomed to be transitory. Their paths had crossed briefly and there had been the illusion of unity. Then the momentum of their own artistic development had caused them to part. But a compromise was still essential for the good of the theatre and the people working in it. He would interfere less, although he reserved the right to express his opinion when it appeared absolutely essential. He appealed to Stanislavski to meet him half way, so that they could benefit from each other's gifts. Once again a truce was reached.

Stanislavski received the letter at the spa at Essentuki, where he was taking a much-needed rest while working on the plans for his production of *The Drama of Life* which he claimed would be 'revolutionary' in style.

Writing to Gorki on July 20 he shared his misgivings about the 1905–6 season. It was going to be 'difficult and dangerous'. He was to be proved right in more senses than one. For all its emphasis on art and aesthetic standards, the theatre was still a commercial enterprise. There was the lease to be paid and production costs had already pushed them over budget. The new productions had been carefully balanced. The 'revolutionary' *Drama of Life* and the experiments of the Theatre-Studio would be counter-balanced by the greatest of Russian classic comedies, Griboiedov's *Woe from Wit*, and Gorki's *Children of the Sun*. Gorki had agreed to set aside his resentment against Nemirovich and release the play when Stanislavski appealed to him, as a friend, for support. A Gorki play was a box-office certainty and as such was badly needed. Also included in the season was a revival of *The Seagull*, with Meierhold in his original role as Konstantin, and Stanislavski offering his new interpretation of Trigorin.

Stanislavski returned to Moscow in the first week in August with the production plan for *The Drama of Life* substantially complete. On the 7th, Gorki read *Children of the Sun*, for which Stanislavski was also to be responsible, to the company. Despite previous differences, Nemirovich was unreservedly cooperative. Apart from directing the Gorki and the Hamsun and playing in the *Seagull* revival, Stanislavski was scheduled to play Famusov in *Woe from Wit*.

On August 11 Stanislavski, accompanied by Knipper, Kachalov, Vishnievski and other members of the company went to Pushkino to see the work of the Theatre-Studio. During the course of the day they saw Hauptmann's *Schluck und Jau*, Maeterlinck's *La Mort de Tintagiles* and Ibsen's *Love's Comedy*. The Hauptmann was well received, and the Maeterlinck greeted with rapturous enthusiasm. The Ibsen was immature but nonetheless showed promise. Stanislavski returned to Moscow well content and confident that the risks he had taken, both artistic and financial, had been justified. In early September he took a two-week break in Sevastopol, leaving Nemirovich in charge of rehearsals.

The Drama of Life and *The Children of the Sun* were diametrically opposed in production style. The Hamsun was an essay in abstraction. The production plan was filled with sketches indicating physical attitudes. The body is the dominant medium of expression. The Gorki, on the other hand, was treated in the now familiar Art Theatre manner, with an excess of naturalistic detail. Yet Stanislavski saw the two leading figures, Kareno and Protassov, as essentially similar – naïve, quixotic, idealistic – but in this play, as in *Summerfolk*, Gorki was sharply critical of the intelligentsia. This Stanislavski failed to grasp. Gorki was by no means pleased with the overall approach. He successfully resisted Stanislavski's intention to bring on a real horse in Act Two but could not prevent the clarity of his intentions from being submerged beneath a welter of 'unnecessary truths'. Writing to a friend on September 25 he stated that the whole play had been distorted and would be a resounding failure.

The season started badly. *The Seagull*, which opened on September 30, failed to catch on. At the same time there was discontent among the young actors of the Theatre-Studio. They were worried about their future. They asked to be allowed to concentrate wholeheartedly on their work and their stated mission of creating new theatre. Back in Moscow, removed from the protective atmosphere and camaraderie of Pushkino, the latent hostility of many of the company had become apparent especially during Stanislavski's absence. It was to him they appealed for help.

From October 14 to 19 there was a general strike in which the Moscow Art company participated. Despite an imperial decree, guaranteeing civil liberty, issued on the 17th, the secret police openly murdered a leading revolutionary figure, Nikolai Bauman, on the 18th. There was further bloodshed at Bauman's funeral on the 20th, when Cossack regiments went into action. Apart from the troops, bands of right-wing extremists, the Black Hundreds, were also active, terrorizing, attacking and murdering known or suspected dissidents. Stanislavski put himself in danger. His signature – K. Alekseiev – appeared on the protest handed in to the Duma on the 21st.

Such was the political atmosphere when the public dress rehearsal of *Children of the Sun* took place on the 24th. Everyone was expecting an 'incident'. It duly occurred.

'The audience was extraordinarily tense throughout the performance, expecting every possible kind of excess. And then, when, towards the end of the play the crowd – members of the company – broke through the hedge of Protassov's house, appearing as provocateurs, agitators and an "angry mob" and Germanova, playing my wife Elena, fired at the crowd, and I, as required in the action, fell to the ground, something completely unexpected and unimaginable occurred. The audience, not knowing who had fired at whom and why, took the actors rushing in for members of the Black Hundreds, who were breaking into the theatre to kill us and concluded that I was the first victim. There was an unbelievable uproar. Some women had hysterics. Part of the audience launched themselves towards the footlights, evidently ready to defend us. The rest went to the exit doors to cut off the escape. Someone leapt to where his coat was hanging to get a revolver from its pocket. Someone shouted, "curtain".

Vl. I. Nemirovich-Danchenko appeared before the curtain, asking the audience to allow the performance to finish, trying to calm them by telling them that the end was a happy one. When the curtains opened the audience had still not settled down. There were shouts of "Kachalov, get up! Get up, Kachalov!" I got up, showed that I was still alive then lay down again.' (*Vassili Ivanovich Kachalov*, Iskusstvo, Moscow, 1954, pp. 39–40.)

One critic at least protested against being obliged to see on stage what he had already experienced in the streets.

At the same time the Theatre-Studio unveiled the final results of its work. Stanislavski needed the Studio to succeed and he had done everything he could to make success possible. Realizing that Meierhold was overworked he asked Nemirovich to replace him in *The Seagull*. He did not conceal the extent of his financial commitment and the consequences of failure. Nonetheless the Studio did fail and Stanislavski was too honest to pretend otherwise. Work which had seemed impressive in a converted barn proved inadequate in a fully equipped professional theatre. Stanislavski contributed in a minor way to the fiasco. *La Mort de Tintagiles* opened in semi-darkness, with the cast almost in silhouette. After a while Stanislavski insisted that the lights be brought up on the grounds that audiences needed to see the actors' faces. He ignored protests. The increased lighting revealed the painful truth, the inadequacy of the young cast, who wavered between an uncertain realism and equally uncertain stylization. The evening demonstrated nothing more than a clever young director exploiting a group of actors to illustrate his own ideas. There had not, in Stanislavski's or indeed Briusov's sense, been a genuine breakthrough. The performance was brought to an abrupt end. Stanislavski disposed of the lease, paid off the carpenters and other craftsmen and gave the technical staff a year's severance pay. He had lost at least 20,000 roubles at a time when, because of political unrest, his factories were selling less and profits were plummeting. Any artistic disappointment was almost exclusively his. Neither Nemirovich nor other members of the company were sorry to see the Studio fold or to witness, once more, the departure of Meierhold.

The experience had not, however, been entirely unprofitable. Meierhold and Briusov both concluded that there could be no compromise with the Moscow Art style. There had to be a new method of training actors. This Meierhold set out to discover. Nonetheless Briusov made a crucial distinction – as did Meierhold – between Stanislavski, whom he saw as an enquiring, probing artist, and the Moscow Art Theatre as an institution. Thus it was possible for Briusov to write some months later:

> '. . . I am ready with all my heart, as far as my strength and abilities allow, to assist you in any endeavours undertaken in the spirit of the former Studio. I ask you most earnestly, if there is a place for me in that work, to call on me.' (Briusov to Stanislavski, May 15, 1906, *SS*, VII, p. 711.)

Stanislavski, for his part, was left with a set of unanswered questions concerning his own art and his future. He could not return – much as Nemirovich would have welcomed it – to the methods now traditionally employed.

The political situation continued to deteriorate. In October there was another general strike followed by a Bolshevik-inspired revolution. Fighting broke out in the streets. Stanislavski insisted that rehearsals for *Woe from Wit* continue despite the gunfire outside. Nobody was sure how the cast could get home safely. In the end even Stanislavski's obstinacy had to give way and work was abandoned.

There was more than an artist's pride or pig-headedness involved in Stanislavski's persistence. True to his conviction that major classics were an instrument of progress, Stanislavski saw the production of Griboiedov's play as a contribution to the revolution:

> 'It occurred to me that the strike was a very good thing and even advantageous to the theatre. We had time to prepare *Woe from Wit* for without it the theatre could not continue to survive. In a word, I tried to demonstrate that *Woe from Wit* was the only play in tune with the revolution.' (K.S. Archive, No. 1093.)

The Drama of Life was shelved.

The revolution lasted one week before it was brutally and bloodily suppressed. The extreme right-wing terrorist groups, the Black Hundreds, set about exterminating revolutionary leaders and suspects; anti-Semitism reared its head. The concessions to democracy the Tsar had granted earlier in the year appeared to have been swept away in the blood-bath. It seemed that all hope of progress in Russia had disappeared. It was a moment of black despair. Stanislavski was overcome by a sense of futility. Had art, he asked himself, any real function, or any contribution to make, in such circumstances? Would he ever realize his dream of a popular, open theatre? He decided, with Nemirovich, to close the theatre and take the company on its first foreign tour.

CHAPTER THIRTEEN

FIRST FOREIGN TOUR

Stanislavski left for Berlin on January 24, 1906, in advance of the rest of the company. The tour had been so hastily agreed that arrangements were still incomplete. The repertoire – *Tsar Fiodor, Uncle Vania, Three Sisters, An Enemy of the People, The Lower Depths* – reflected none of the company's recent experiments but productions which were now solidly established. *Fiodor* was no longer in the repertoire and had to be re-rehearsed.

In Germany the tour was given wide but dignified publicity. August Schultz, the German translator of Chekhov and Gorki, gave a lecture in Berlin on February 1 and the *Nationalzeitung* published an interview with Stanislavski on the 8th.

The season opened on the 10th almost inevitably with *Fiodor*. In the first-night audience were Gerhart Hauptmann, Arthur Schnitzler, Eleanora Duse and the young Max Reinhardt. The performance was an immense success. The leading critic, Alfred Kerr, wrote some years later:

'What I saw in that production was something first class. Unarguably first class. You may not possess any knowledge of the Russian tongue, no understanding of the individual details of the events but after two minutes you knew that this was first class.' (Alfred Kerr, *Das Mimenreich*, Berlin, 1917, p. 225.)

Writing under the immediate impact of the performance, on the 25th, he was in no doubt that he had seen 'a chunk of history', and his views were shared. To his brother, Vladimir, Stanislavski wrote:

'There are over a hundred newspapers here, some of which carry evening editions. All, without a single exception, published huge articles and were beside themselves with joy. I have never seen such reviews. It's as though we were the revelation. Nearly all end their articles with the cry: we know the Russians are over a hundred years behind politically but, dear God, how far have they overtaken us artistically.' (*SS*, VII, p. 335.)

On the 12th the legendary virtuoso pianist, Leopold Godowski, wrote Stanislavski a letter of thanks for a performance which had given him more artistic pleasure than he had experienced for a long time. What struck critics and audience alike was the reality of the stage action and the presence of real characters quite unlike, as one writer put it, the posturings of the Meininger.

When *Uncle Vania* opened on the 15th, during one of the intervals Hauptmann declared loud enough for all to hear:

'This is the most powerful theatrical experience I have ever had, these are not people acting but artistic gods.' (Ibid.)

The Lower Depths opened on the 18th, with another personal triumph for Stanislavski:

'His Satin was unforgettable. . . . In any case, this man is a genius. The rest are capable indeed very capable artists, surrounding a genius.' (*Nationalzeitung*, March 3.)

Three Sisters followed on February 25 with equal success.

The Emperor, Kaiser Wilhelm II, and his family attended a performance of *Fiodor* on March 6, thus setting the final seal of approval on the tour. Talking to the cast the Kaiser displayed a knowledge of Russian history which few actors, in their nervousness, could match. The Crown Prince was a constant visitor, attending as many performances as he could.

The Berlin season ended with *An Enemy of the People* which opened on March 7 and produced the only serious critical reservation to appear in print. Kerr found Stanislavski's Stockman unforgettable but not really Ibsen's character; he was not 'a Viking' – perhaps a somewhat Germanic judgement.

On March 12 the company left for Dresden, where they again met Duse. She suggested that the time had come for them to play in Paris and that they should come to an arrangement with Lugné-Poë. Nemirovich investigated further but concluded that a Paris season would not be financially viable. The idea was dropped.

On the 19th they were in Leipzig, the 22nd in Prague and the 28th in Vienna where, for the first time, neither the welcome nor the audiences were perfect. Vienna lived up to its reputation of combining a rare cultural tradition with pettiness and intrigue. If Stanislavski expected help from the Russian embassy he was disappointed. When he called there the day after his arrival to recruit extras for *Fiodor* he was not well received. On his return to the theatre he discovered that there was trouble with the fire department:

'Quite awful day . . . trouble and strife . . . Visit Urusov [the ambassador]. His secretaries are nincompoops. Their reception was not very courteous. Urusov invited us all to breakfast. I declined.

I returned to the theatre. Exhausted. There, more trouble. The police have taken the play off. The sets have to be fireproofed.

Lunch and then back to the theatre. Chaos, no make-up or wigs. Everyone exhausted. Reception feeble. . . . During the interval the police daubed the scenery.' (*Notebook*, March 29.)

The performance was nothing like the success they had known elsewhere; a large number of people left before the end in order to avoid being fined for being out after curfew. There were also political tensions:

'Lay on the bed for hours. Read the reviews. Unexpectedly good notices. The town and especially the audience divided. Hostility between the Slavs and the Germans. Slavs 60%, ruled by 40% Germans. Germans stingy. They pay 50 crowns for a box but they won't pay a fine of 10 pfennigs for being out after 10 o'clock so at 9.30 many start leaving the theatre.

Life is expensive; company is grumbling. The crowns just fly away.' (*Notebook*, March 30.)

After Vienna the company returned to Germany, performing in Frankfurt on April 10 and in Karlsruhe on the 11th. On the 12th, by special command there was a gala performance of *Fiodor* in Wiesbaden. Ermolova, who was staying in the town at the time, was also present. After the performance both Stanislavski and Nemirovich were decorated with the order of the Red Eagle, Fourth Class. From Wiesbaden, the company moved to Düsseldorf on the 16th and Hanover on the 20th. While in Hanover Stanislavski received a letter from a group of émigré Russian intellectuals, thanking him and the company for representing the spirit of Russian life and the free spirit of art. The journey home began at the end of April, with a short season in Warsaw, beginning on the 23rd. They finally arrived back in Moscow on May 3.

The tour had been long and exhausting but – Vienna excepted – an unqualified success. It marked the beginning of the company's international reputation and influence. In contemporary terms the only comparison is the impact of the Berliner Ensemble when it began to visit abroad. In a short space of time the reputation of the Moscow Art Theatre spread throughout Europe and beyond. The financial losses of the early part of the season had been more than covered so that the theatre's future was assured – for the time being at least. For German and Austrian writers the Art Theatre seemed to offer a new way of thinking about acting and directing, a new concept of the nature of the theatre itself. It opened up a range of possibilities.

In Berlin, Hauptmann had given a rather chaotic lunch at his home in which conversation was somewhat inhibited by Stanislavski's poor German. Nonetheless the message Stanislavski received was clear:

'Hauptmann told us that he had always dreamed of seeing his plays acted the way we had – without effects and theatrical conventions, with simple, profound, rich, rounded playing. German actors had assured him that it could not be done, that the theatre, in their view, had its own conventions and its own demands which could not be denied. And now at the twilight of his literary activity it had been given to him to see what he had always dreamed of.' (*SS*, I, p. 292.)

Schnitzler, too, experienced the full impact of Stanislavski's thought and personality:

'That hour I spent with Stanislavski changed my whole inner life, my ambitions for ever. I finally found myself.' (Quoted in *Slovo*, Paris, December 25, 1923.)

Max Reinhardt went a stage further. Within a year he had opened the *Kammerspiele*, which was exactly modelled on the Art Theatre.

The tour had also been financially successful. More importantly, the prestige the company had gained attracted two important investors. It had, however, done little to improve relations between Stanislavski and Nemirovich. Whereas Stanislavski had been lionized, Nemirovich had been largely ignored by the press. Stanislavski was constantly referred to as the sole founder of the Art Theatre and its major director. Worse still, during a discussion on policy in Düsseldorf Stanislavski had announced his absolute determination to continue to experiment and build on the work of the Studio. A desperately angry Nemirovich drafted a letter in which he described Stanislavski as an amateur, a despot, mean-minded, brutal and morally weak. Fortunately he did not send it. But, once home, he started gambling heavily and losing. A loyal and discreet Stanislavski paid his debts.

Once the company returned to Moscow there was the task of recreating the 'lost' season. Stanislavski and Nemirovich, as ever, concealed their differences. Outwardly it was business as usual. Stanislavski put considerable energy into the rehearsals for *Woe from Wit* which began in late May, combining prescriptive directing and demonstration with an attempt to stimulate the actors' own imagination and creative force. At the same time he was working with the designers on the sets for *The Drama of Life*. But he was functioning in the midst of an overwhelming personal crisis. He was at pains to conceal it, because of its possible effect on morale. He even concealed it from his wife, who was confused by his behaviour. But the company picked up what he did not say, they felt that he was hiding something. It set him once more apart and this may well explain the suspicion and resistance he encountered when in the next two or three years he tried to introduce new ideas.

The crisis had indeed occurred during the tour. According to an interview with the magazine *Studia* in April 1912, during a performance in March 1906 he suddenly became aware that he was acting mechanically. The outer shell of the character was there, the body moved, the voice spoke, few people apart from himself would have realized there was anything wrong but there was no life, no inner impulse or feeling.

There is a good reason to suppose that the play in question was *An Enemy of the People*. The blow would therefore have been doubly heavy. Stockman had been one of his most spontaneous creations, a character which gave him deep satisfaction. The last two years had brought their problems and disappointments: Chekhov's death, the growing rift between him and Nemirovich, the failure of the Studio, his own inability to find a new artistic direction, but the one thing which remained, and which he prized above all, was his supremacy and power as an actor and as a creator. Now, it seemed, that was gone. What could the future hold?

There can be no doubt that a major cause of this creative drying-up was sheer exhaustion. In the eight years of the Art Theatre's existence he had turned out one major production or performance after another. It was inevitable that the system would give out some time. This he realized himself. As usual he committed his thoughts to paper – his method of having dialogue with himself. He tried to analyse what was wrong with the company, starting with his own case. What he required was an exercise in honesty:

> 'I'll start with the good points. I have talent as a director and an actor, a middling intelligence, a passion for what I do, energy and purpose in art, in which I endeavour to strive without compromise. In quiet moments there is an ability to adapt to people, for tolerance and even [*illegible*] and a recognized portion of administrative ability. But my nerves are not good, I am very spoiled, my temperament lacks restraint. These faults dominate me when I am overtired, irritated or bitter. . . . The sickness of my whole system, my nerves, is a result of my abnormal way of life . . . from the enormous number of things there are to do. Hence exhaustion and the need to do less work and get more rest. The circumstances of my life have demanded a reduction of my work outside the theatre. That leads to the question of my activity in the theatre. Can it be controlled and reduced? Of course it can.' (K.S. Archive, No. 3464/2.)

These notes were written in late May, a few days before the Alekseiev family left for Finland, where they spent the following two months. But tired and demoralized though he was, this was not to be a holiday in the real sense. As Lilina wrote to Knipper:

> 'He [Stanislavski] is happy that the northern air and climate agree with him. But between ourselves he has a strange way of spending his time. He doesn't walk or swim or even take fresh air. He sits in a half-darkened room all day, writing and smoking.' (*Maria Petrovna Lilina*, VTO, Moscow, 1960, p. 203.)

What he was working on was a draft *Manual on Dramatic Art*.

The examination of conscience had become a full-scale review of his artistic views and practice. With him in Finland he had all his notebooks which contained his ideas on acting since 1889, a series of unconnected jottings, ranging from notions of theatre and professional ethics to advice on how to dominate back-stage noise and keep the audience's attention. The time had come to put his intellectual house in order.

'Through my experience as an actor I had gathered together a rag-bag of material on the technique of the theatre. Everything had been thrown in willy-nilly, no system. . . . Some order had to be created, the material had to be sorted out, examined, assessed and, as it were, ranged on mental shelves. Rough matter had to be worked on and polished and laid down as the foundation stones of our art.' (SS, I, p. 285.)

The failure of his experiments with Meierhold and the Studio, all concerned with form, Briusov's emphasis on the actor as the centre, and his own insistence on the notion of the actor-creator, forced him towards a more thorough examination of the actor's process. If the play's meaning was to be realized principally through the actor then a prime concern must be to give the actor control over his creative method. That control, it now seemed, lay at the level of personal psychology. There had been hints of a new essentially psychological approach in his notes on Lopakhin. Since then he had gone a stage further. This is evident from the letter he wrote to his friend, the St Petersburg actress Kotliarevskaia, on July 1, 1905, giving her advice on how to prepare the role of Charlotta in *The Cherry Orchard*:

'First of all you must live the role without spoiling the words or making them commonplace. Shut yourself off and play whatever goes through your head. Imagine the following scene: Pishchik has proposed to Charlotta, now she is his bride. . . . How will she behave? Or: Charlotta has been dismissed but finds other employment in a circus or a café-chantant. How does she do gymnastics or sing little songs? Do your hair in various ways and try to find in yourself things which remind you of Charlotta. You will be reduced to despair twenty times in your search but don't give up. Make this German woman you love so much speak Russian and observe how she pronounces words and what are the special characteristics of her speech. Remember to play Charlotta in a dramatic moment of her life. Try to make her weep sincerely over her life. Through such an image you will discover all the whole range of notes you need.' (SS, VII, p. 315.)

This contains in embryo much that was to be developed later: the exploration of character through improvisation, setting the character in new, imaginary circumstances, not foreseen by the author, as a means of stimulating the actor's imagination. But it is still *ad hoc* advice. If the creative process was not to be left to chance or the fickle inspiration of the moment, the only way forward was the systematic formulation of that 'grammar' of acting which he had dabbled with for years.

Stanislavski's determination to create that 'grammar' was not the expression of a purely theoretical concern. He always lived in a state of the provisional. He was and remained profoundly suspicious of 'the definitive statement'. Hence his difficulty in ever completing a manuscript. He had moved on almost before the ink was dry. But now he was driven by a sense of desperation. He had to create a survival-kit for himself as an actor.

The basis of his whole 'system',* as he came to call it, was the conviction that in acting as in everything else nature, not the rational intellect, creates. What he had to discover was an artistic process in tune with the processes of the human organism at the level of the un- or super-conscious. By 'super-conscious' – a term which was to get him into a great deal of trouble later – Stanislavski merely meant those regions of the mind which are not accessible to conscious recall or the will. It had nothing to do with notions of latent content advanced by Freud, whose works he did not know. It followed therefore that whatever he proposed would have the status not of aesthetic theory or philosophical speculation but of natural law. Any grammar, method or system, was only useful as a stimulus to these organic processes. It was no more than a substitute for the instinctive, intuitive creation enjoyed by the truly great actors he had seen and of whom he did not count himself one.

Stanislavski undoubtedly over-romanticized great actors and insufficiently understood the difference between their working conditions and his own. In many cases they performed a limited number of roles to which they were temperamentally sympathetic and, like opera singers, took their interpretations with them wherever they went. The pressures of a working theatre like the Moscow Art Theatre were considerably greater. In any one month Stanislavski might be playing three or four major roles in the existing repertoire, creating new ones, directing new productions and discussing policy in addition to fulfilling his minimal but unavoidable duties at the factory. The problem was one of mentally changing gear. You could not expect to be able to walk into the theatre and automatically become Vershinin. Or, at least, he could now no longer expect it. Nor, as a company member could you always expect to like the parts you were assigned. More than ever now he needed a secure methodology, a new pattern of theatre practice.

Stanislavski founded his new 'grammar' on two basic principles. First, the actor's ability to use the totality of his experiences. If these

---

* Having opted for the word System, it seemed too dogmatic, so Stanislavski preferred to write it as 'system', without a capital letter and in quotes, to suggest the provisional nature of his findings. This is the practice followed here.

experiences do not come into play automatically when starting work on a part then the actor must develop a method which will provide access to them, otherwise, in desperation, he will be thrown back on externals and theatrical clichés.

The actor as Stanislavski saw him was a man divided against himself. On the one hand there was Kostia Alekseiev, with his mundane concerns and worries, his family, his meals, his children; on the other was Konstantin Stanislavski of the Moscow Art Theatre, who was expected to represent, nightly, extremes of human passion and feeling, to typify at the highest level the human condition. The prime task of any method or grammar must be to bring the two aspects of the personality together in a creative relationship. For the moment, Stanislavski was convinced that the key lay in stimulating the will. The actor must arouse in himself the urge to create afresh each time thus bringing other psychological mechanisms into play.

The second principle involved the breaking down of a role into its component parts. Where a role was not grasped globally, in a single intuitive act, the creative process must be broken down into a series of smaller, more manageable problems, which could be studied and mastered separately and then brought together again to form the whole. Stanislavski derived this principle, in all probability, from his knowledge of industry. He was familiar with the theory of Taylorism, the breakdown of complex manufacturing processes into a sequence of simple actions on a production-line. In his new approach to acting he transferred this theory albeit, perhaps, unconsciously to creative work.

He read his notes daily to Lilina and Kotliarevskaia in Finland. In Kotliarevskaia he found a sympathetic listener. Lilina was less convinced. On August 8 he returned to Moscow, knowing that he had done no more than lay down a programme of study. What he needed was a period of observation and analysis. He would watch actors at work and discuss their working methods with them.

CHAPTER FOURTEEN

A 'GRAMMAR' OF ACTING

The 1906–7 season began deceptively well. *Woe from Wit*, which had been abandoned in mid-rehearsal at the end of 1905, during the revolution, had its first public dress rehearsal on September 24. Stanislavski and Nemirovich worked together on the production although neither of their names appeared on the programme. Stanislavski, however, would appear to have exerted the dominant influence.

Griboiedov's play occupies a special place in Russian theatre. It ranks in cultural importance with the greatest of Shakespeare's plays or, perhaps more appropriately, Molière's comedies. Written in a complex stanza form it has defied satisfactory translation and is therefore less well known than it should be. For Russian audiences, however, a new production of the play is comparable to a new *Hamlet*. Stanislavski was well aware of what he was taking on and of the expectations that the audience would bring with it. He met the challenge head on, making no concessions, sticking to the principles he had laid out in his letter to Besnard (page 54). Mrs Gurevich, writing in the spring of 1907 when the play was on tour in St Petersburg, stated:

> 'The Moscow people revolutionized the play; blew all the expectations of the audience and the critics sky high.' (*Tovarishch*, May 10, 1907.)

Stanislavski repeated with this Russian classic what he had achieved in other standard works. He brought life out of literature. The tone was lighter; there was less bombast and rhetoric and more realism. The house in which the play is set was a place that was lived in, not a place where the actors recited verse. Professionals like Lenski, Ermolova and Fedotova were excited when the inexorable flow of the verse was broken up by the use of pauses in Act Three. Critics were suitably outraged. Nemirovich remarked that for the first time in Kachalov's performance Chatski, the rebellious young hero, was played as a human being and not as an illustration of every critical commentary ever written on the character. Stanislavski's own performance as Famusov, the merchant, was a triumph. He had again broken with tradition by playing the character not as an aristocrat, which was the practice at the Mali, but lower down the social scale.

Any feelings of euphoria were, however, short-lived. The differences between Stanislavski and Nemirovich broke out more virulently than ever and the gulf between them was patent for all to see. Nemirovich wrote to Leonid Andreiev:

> 'We have finally reached agreement on the season. I shall be doing *Brand* and Stanislavski *The Drama of Life*. We rehearse separately and independently of one another, although simultaneously, me in the foyer, him on the stage – when I am on stage he is in the foyer. This is the first time we have drawn a demarcation line – a necessity in view of the continuing artistic differences between us.' (N-D Archive, No. 11303.)

There had been continuous argument since July over the order in which the plays were to be given and the casting. Nemirovich wanted *Brand* to have priority as he regarded it as a revolutionary play, a 'once in a lifetime work of genius', far superior artistically to the Hamsun, which was 'a talented question-mark'. He also wanted Kachalov for the lead in both productions, whereas it had been understood that Stanislavski would play Kareno. Both plays went into rehearsal on the 27th. Within weeks the company had divided into rival factions. Nemirovich's hostility to Stanislavski's method of rehearsing *The Drama of Life* was undiminished. He openly described it as 'crackpot'. The more he saw of *The Drama of Life* as it was shown to him act by act the less he liked it. As for the ideas on acting which Stanislavski brought back after the summer he took them as further evidence that his colleague had gone off the rails, as did many other members of the company who had no desire to change their working methods or to be treated as guinea-pigs in Stanislavski's research. Stanislavski on his side considered that Nemirovich had made a fundamental mistake in not playing *Brand* in prose. His decision to use a verse translation transformed the play into a fairy-tale or a piece of Gothic tedium.

Nemirovich decided that in the interest of the future of the theatre he must take strong action and assert his authority in management. He could see no way of controlling his colleague and he became increasingly apprehensive that the theatre would become 'Stanislavski's club' as he later put it, rather like the Society of Art and Literature. He knew that commercially and financially the theatre could not succeed if Stanislavski were given a free hand: schedules would cease to exist and budgets would become a joke. Things finally came to a head in early November, with much manoeuvring among the shareholders. Nemirovich, having told Stanislavski on November 3 that he should not play Kareno, informed him on the 4th that the shareholders wanted him to take the part. He publicly humiliated Sulerzhitski, who was assisting Stanislavski on *The Drama of Life*, pointing out that he had no right to make any demands whatsoever on the management as his position was purely unofficial. Stanislavski reminded Nemirovich that they had agreed in private conversation that Sulerzhitski should become his personal assistant. He apologized for not putting in an official request and rectified the omission. He had no interest in power. All he wanted was a quick solution. He proposed that Nemirovich should become chairman of the board, if that was what he really wanted. The shareholders agreed.

He confided his sense of irritation to his journal on November 6:

'It's grotesque. I am paying Sulerzhitski with my own money. He is working all out and I still have to beg permission from V.I., who does nothing, to have his help. When Suler heard about it he almost walked out of the theatre.' (K.S. Archive, No. 746.)

Nemirovich took matters a stage further, writing on November 5, in response to Stanislavski's official request:

'Since you acknowledge me in your letter as chairman I will simply ask you to participate in a short meeting of the shareholders . . . so as to draw up the appropriate agreement. Then I will assume total *responsibility* for the current season and at the same time full *power* as chairman. . . . I ask you not to bring anyone to work in the theatre, even should it concern an assistant for yourself, without my permission or the permission of the management if any occasion should arise in the current season.' (N-D Archive, No. 1627.)

At least one of the shareholders was critical of Nemirovich's behaviour. Writing to Knipper from abroad, Stakhovich accused him of being far too full of himself to do what he should, namely renounce his own ambitions, support Stanislavski, and cover his weaknesses.

Stanislavski's conciliatory attitude seemed to do little to improve the overall situation. Nemirovich continued to treat *The Drama of Life* and Stanislavski's new ideas with cynical disdain and made full use of the new managerial powers. He was, moreover, no more reconciled to Sulerzhitski than before. At the end of January Stanislavski was ill, with a high temperature. Sulerzhitski took over rehearsals, working alone for the first time. Nemirovich stayed away from the first dress rehearsal, something unheard of in the whole history of the company. Stanislavski was outraged:

'The worst insult I have received. Today when I was still very ill I went to the dress rehearsal of *The Drama of Life* after ten days in bed. The play was announced in the press last Saturday without my being asked. On Tuesday and Thursday performances were cancelled because of dress rehearsals. I was ill. Suler had charge of a play for the first time. Before it even began I learned that neither Vladimir Ivanovich [Nemirovich] nor Kaluzhski [Luzhski] would be present at the theatre. They didn't even bother to inform us. This is theatrical filth, revenge. I can't stay in such an atmosphere any longer. I've decided to quit the theatre.' (K.S. Archive, No. 746.)

This was not an idle threat. Stanislavski was now thoroughly disillusioned and sick at heart. He could not work in an atmosphere of intrigue or one that was not 'clean'. But for the moment he soldiered on with a production and a role that were now poison to him.

Nemirovich finally attended a highly successful public dress rehearsal on February 6 and experienced a change of heart. The play opened on the 8th, when Stanislavski was still unwell. He wrote to Kotliarevskaia on February 15:

> 'The Drama of Life had the success I wanted. Half the people hissed, the other half were in raptures. I am satisfied with the results of a number of trials and experiments.
> They have opened up many interesting principles for us.
> The decadents are happy,
> the realists are outraged,
> the bourgeois are resentful.' (SS, VII, p. 364.)

His own performance as Kareno had a mixed reception. Efros condemned it as monotonous and boring and, on the whole, it did little to recommend his new ideas, his new grammar, to his colleagues, who could not see any positive result. His attempts to base the production on psychological action only, without gestures, conveying everything through the face and eyes, met with only partial success. There was still a basic contradiction between the production style and the ingrained naturalism of the acting. Even the faithful Suler did not fully understand. His idea of 'psychology' was to whip the actors into a frenzy. Going into rehearsal one day Stanislavski found:

> '... a tragedian bathed in sweat, rolling on the ground and roaring with every appearance of passion he could drag out of himself, with my assistant sitting astride him, yelling at the top of his voice and pushing him with all his might, "More! more! Go on! Louder!" . . . "Life, feeling! Feeling!"' (SS, I, p. 310.)

Stanislavski was nonetheless determined to pursue his researches. The season was drawing to a close. After that there would be the by-now annual St Petersburg tour. He had already fixed on the idea of directing Maeterlinck's The Blue Bird for the following season. Among other projects were Byron's Cain and Oscar Wilde's Salomé.

It was at this moment that he learned that Nemirovich had apparently been approached by Nelidov, the literary manager of the Mali Theatre, and offered a possible merger. He should not have been surprised. There had been moves to combine the Mali and the Art Theatre in 1905 and

Nemirovich had been party to the discussions. The authorities were worried by the decline in standards at the Mali, which was now not even a shadow of its former self. A fusion of the two companies would also give them an opportunity to bring the rebellious Art Theatre under control. Both companies got wind of the scheme and were opposed to it. The whole idea was shelved during the revolution. Now it was being reconsidered. Stanislavski felt that it was time to resign for his own sake and for the good of the theatre, which must at all costs survive. With him out of the way, Nemirovich could pursue his own policies unopposed. On February 23 he drafted a letter of resignation in his journal. It was never sent but reveals Stanislavski's state of mind and the low ebb he had reached. In it he refers to conditions, known to both of them, which would oblige him to leave the board of directors within a year. These conditions remain obscure. It is, however, the deterioration in their personal relationship and its effect on the theatre which concerns him:

'The exceptional feature of our partnership has been our mutual respect for the work we have each contributed.

That has now disintegrated. We are pulling our enterprise in different directions and are tearing it apart. That is criminal.

Married people can divorce, lovers, friends can part so as not to make each other's lives a misery. Cannot we (condemned as we are to torture each other for all our lives) find some *modus vivendi* which will avoid the worst thing of all, ruining each other's very existence?

To create this new relationship we must, first and foremost, part.

I don't want to play on gratitude or be over-modest. . . . I should be the one to surrender because I am a director without responsibility and a shareholder without influence. If I relinquish these functions the theatre will not go off course for a single day. But if you go, the theatre will cease to exist. . . .

There can be no solution until what is unique and creative in our enterprise is recognized. Regularize my position and everything will go smoothly, whatever position you envisage for me.

1. The theatre needs me as an actor in certain roles.
2. The theatre needs me as a director for one or two productions.
3. Sometimes it needs my tact and acumen in business.

All this will remain in a new role. . . .

As you see, I am not making demands but asking you, as a friend, to help me. . . .

Let us part friends, so that an enterprise of world renown may not, later, be broken up by its members.

It is our civic duty to support it.

To destroy it would be a barbarous crime.' (K.S. Archive, No. 746.)

In the event what he actually sent was a short, formal letter of resignation, followed some hours later by an even shorter letter asking Nemirovich to find some means by which it would be possible for him to retract.

Matters went no further but Stanislavski's scribbled draft accurately predicted both the timing of his departure from the board, which took place a year later, and the conditions of his future relationship with the company.

On April 2, Nelidov made Nemirovich an official offer to become the principal director of the Mali. Nemirovich insisted on seeing the director of the theatre, Teliakovski, and an appointment was arranged for 4.30 that afternoon. Teliakovski arrived half an hour late having been to see Stanislavski beforehand. The two men talked until 6.45. Nemirovich immediately went to see Stanislavski at his home but found he was asleep and decided not to disturb him before the performance. After the performance, however, he gave his colleague a full account of the discussions and of his feelings.

> 'I don't create at the Art Theatre, all I have really done is establish an institution where others create. If someone says to me: you founded a theatre, now found a state theatre, I can't do anything other than accept and try to bring the best artistic talents I can and exploit them. My attachment to one theatre, even one of my own creation, does not warrant my refusal, because that would diminish the progressive nature of what I am doing. It would be like a man refusing to go into parliament because he was a member of the local council. . . . (Letter to his wife, April 3, 1907, N-D Archive, No. 2088.)

Nonetheless he had suggested a year's delay. He had been quite blunt about the need for fundamental reforms at the Mali and had proposed that he should draw up a report outlining his conditions and that a final decision should be taken some time in 1908. There the matter rested. A few days later the company left for St Petersburg where, on April 29, it gave the hundredth performance of *Three Sisters*.

The new productions were far more controversial. *Woe from Wit* caused a critical controversy of the first order, inciting the vituperation of conservative critics, *Brand* was condemned as socialist propaganda and *The Drama of Life* almost universally detested.

Returning to Moscow the company found itself in further trouble. The Synod banned Byron's *Cain*. Nemirovich, against Stanislavski's wishes, decided to replace it with Andreiev's *The Life of Man*, a drama possibly even more abstract than *The Drama of Life*. Stanislavski directed it under protest, ultimately describing it as rubbish and not a play at all. The première, which took place on December 12, was a success. This was almost entirely due to its production values and to Stanislavski's chance discovery during preliminary work on *The Blue Bird* of a method of making things appear and disappear as if by magic.

'I needed a piece of black velvet which I had just been looking at but it had disappeared. We looked everywhere, turning over drawers, boxes, tables, the whole room in fact – but no black velvet. At last we saw it, hanging right where we passed by, under our very noses. Why hadn't we seen it before? Because behind it on the wall hung another piece of black velvet of the same size. You can't see black on black.' (*SS*, I, pp. 317–18.)

The result was a series of spectacular designs, considerably indebted to Beardsley, and effects, using the black velvet, which impressed the public. But Stanislavski wrote off the production. As far as he was concerned there was nothing new here, nothing that would provide the basis for experiment or for a more deeply inward acting technique. He wrote as much in the theatre's daybook straight after the play's hugely successful first night.

The production was, however, important in terms of artistic polemics. In late November, Meierhold, who was directing *The Life of Man* himself in St Petersburg, had delivered a lecture denouncing the Art Theatre as obsolete, bogged down in naturalism and literal realism. It was Efros' opinion that Stanislavski by his own, superior, production had given Meierhold the lie in the most effective way possible. Nor was Efros alone. A few months later Lunacharski, subsequently to be the first Commissar for Enlightenment after the 1917 Revolution, published a violent attack on Meierhold, denying that he was in any genuine sense revolutionary, accusing him of being fundamentally bourgeois and decadent in his thinking, and describing his writings as 'immature scribblings'. Andreiev himself was quite clear that Stanislavski's was the best version of his play available, although he would have preferred the designs to be based on Goya rather than Beardsley.

This was of little interest to Stanislavski who was now concentrating all his efforts on *The Blue Bird*. His obsession with Maeterlinck had not diminished. He was determined to solve the artistic problems which had so far defeated him. *The Blue Bird* was almost an international event before it got into rehearsal. Work had already begun in April 1907. After the first reading Stanislavski addressed the company, appealing for unity and criticizing the divisions and dissensions of the preceding few months. He reminded them of their mission to humanize an ignorant and insensitive mass and raise the level of moral awareness. His speech was sent to Maeterlinck and published in the *Mercure de France* on June 15. A Russian version, apparently translated back from the French by Efros, appeared in the *Stolichnoe Utro* on July 27.

'Man in his animal nature is brutish, cruel and vain. He kills his own kind, devours animals, destroys nature and believes that everything about him has been created solely for his pleasure. Man rules the earth and imagines he has captured its secrets. In reality he knows very little.

The most important things are hidden from him. People live among their material goods, becoming ever more remote from a spiritual and contemplative life.

Spiritual happiness is only given to a chosen few. They listen intently to the minute rustling of a growing blade of grass and turn their eyes on the mystical contours of worlds unknown.

Having seen or heard these secrets, they reveal them to people who look at geniuses with wide eyes, a cynical smile and a wink. Centuries pass and the clatter of the cities and villages drowns out the tiny rustle of a growing blade of grass.

The smoke of factory chimneys hides the beauty of the world from us; industrial prosperity blinds us and moulded ceilings cut us off from the sky and the stars.

We fight for breath and look for happiness in the stench and grime of the world we have created.

Once in a while we catch a glimpse of real happiness, out there in the fields, in the sunlight, but that happiness, like the blue bird, turns black once we return to the darkness and stench of the town. . . .

Children are closer to nature from which they have but lately come. . . . Let *The Blue Bird* in our theatre delight the grandchildren and provoke serious thoughts and deep feelings in their grandparents. . . .

Let the old people cleanse their soul of its accumulated grime and perhaps for the first time in their lives look into the eyes of a dog and stroke it gently in gratitude for its dog-like loyalty to man. . . .

If we succeed in getting such a response from the audience, even in the smallest measure, I believe our dear friend, the author of *The Blue Bird*, would be full of praise for us.

But the problem is how to get such a response from an audience a thousand strong? . . .

Things abstract are not easily accessible to the bulk of the bourgeois and that makes our task quite complicated. . . .

Luckily we have new methods which are the opposite of the old. Our theatre has become strong enough through the combined creative efforts of interpreters in all the arts and back-stage workers.

Creative effort of that kind is invincible. . . .

Directors have learned how to make a harmonious whole out of all the elements in a show. The theatre had become strong thanks to this harmony. The new theatre is strong because of it. Through it we shall try to arouse the audience when the curtain raises on our new play. . . .

The dominant chord in that general harmony is you, ladies and gentlemen of the company. . . .' (*SS*, V, pp. 363–70.)

No such harmony was forthcoming, nor could it exist until some settlement had been found to the differences between Stanislavski and Nemirovich. Rehearsals for *The Blue Bird* started on December 16 but on the 19th Knipper was writing to her brother Vladimir expecting trouble. By the 28th Stanislavski was writing protests in the daybook about the lack of technical cooperation and the absence of the property-master.

Stanislavski, it is true, was making complex demands on the technical side. He wanted new methods, new materials. He set aside Maeterlinck's stage directions since in his view they would introduce the wrong kind of theatricality. He wanted neither gauzes, nor cut-outs, nor trap doors, none of the paraphernalia of the ballet, but designs and sets that would be nearer to the child's vision. For the music he wanted new sounds and new combinations of instruments, not the usual symphonic orchestration. All in all, he envisaged several months of work and experiment before the play opened. These experiments included exercises and improvisations for the actors and the extras. On August 21 Nemirovich had written to his wife with cynical amusement that they were all imitating dogs, cats and cockerels and were mewing, barking and crowing all round a delighted Stanislavski. *The Blue Bird* enjoyed the longest period of rehearsals the theatre had as yet ever deliberately undertaken. It was an omen of things to come.

Stanislavski became increasingly isolated. The company, encouraged by Nemirovich, continued to regard his new ideas as an aberration potentially disruptive to the running of the theatre. The shareholders tried to get a grip on the situation before there was a total collapse. Early in February 1908, Nemirovich wrote to Stanislavski a letter, now lost, which was evidently intemperate in tone. On February 8, Stanislavski resigned:

'Dear Vladimir Ivanovich,
As our ten years of effort have ended with the letter I have just received, any belief in my *infinite* devotion and love for you, the theatre and our association can only be futile.
    I ask you to take note that at the end of the current season I shall cease to be a shareholder and a director.
    As to the future I offer my services, gratis, as an actor in my old roles and as a producer – under conditions of which you are aware.' (K.S. Archive.)

What Stanislavski's conditions were is not clear.

The shareholders set up a committee of enquiry which met on February 15. Luzhski immediately raised the problem of the breakdown in relations between Stanislavski and Nemirovich. Whatever Stanislavski might write in private correspondence, he was concerned to conceal the depth and rancour of the quarrel in public. The minutes of the meeting report him as saying:

'I understand Vasili Vasilievich [Luzhski], who has put his finger on a very sore spot. But I see no discord. I repeat, I am very fond of Vladimir Ivanovich [Nemirovich] and consider that it is impossible for us to split up under any circumstances. If there have been differences they in no way indicate a break. I repeat: should Vladimir Ivanovich leave I would not be long in following. . . .

Two years ago Vladimir Ivanovich said he felt crushed by me. It was essential at that time to go our separate ways so that later we could stimulate each other with what we had discovered through our individual work. That's not discord or splitting up, that's artistic freedom. . . . Can we close the theatre? No, that's not possible. Quite apart from the large number of employees in the theatre we must not forget its social significance. . . . The whole of Russian and even European theatre is centred on us.' (K.S. Archive.)

Methods of cutting costs were discussed. Stanislavski criticized the over-elaborate staging in recent – by which he meant Nemirovich's – productions.

Nemirovich again condemned Stanislavski's scheme for a network of provincial theatres as an extravagance at a time when the theatre needed to reduce the number of productions and use the talents of its members more effectively.

The committee, which was unable to complete its business, was reconvened on the 27th. Stanislavski had failed in his attempt to play down his dispute with Nemirovich and the whole matter was raised once more. Stanislavski made a forthright statement on his artistic position and reaffirmed his view of the actor not as a passive interpreter of words but an active creator:

'The committee is wrong if it thinks that the director's preparatory work in the study is necessary, as previously, when he alone decided the whole plan and all the details of the production, wrote the *mise-en-scène* and answered all the actors' questions for them. The director is no longer king, as before, when the actor possessed no clear individuality. Work in the study can even be harmful and a positive hindrance. Even work on the décor and technical problems was impossible before general discussions. The director is accused of extravagance but he must, of course, want everything to be as good as possible. Above all the Art Theatre must not stop experimenting.

What is called the director's inefficiency is more often than not attributable to the cast. For instance the absence of method among those playing the major roles during rehearsals arises from *our lack of professional artistic ethics. . . .*'

Do not forget, the time has passed when the actor did not have to worry about anything – K.S. would teach . . . and Efros would praise. It is essential to understand this – rehearsals are divided into two stages: the first stage is one of experiment when the cast helps the director, the second is creating the performance when the director helps the cast.' (K.S. Archive, No. 1098/4.)

The shareholders reached a decision on March 1. Stanislavski would be allowed to mount one 'experimental' production of his choice per season and would be required to direct no more than two other plays single-handed, although his help and advice might be sought for other productions. His work as an actor would continue. The present membership of the company was to be guaranteed for three years but responsibility for its administration would be handed over to a committee of five with Nemirovich as chairman. Stanislavski's conditions were accepted.

The question of a possible merger with the Mali remained. In September 1907, without waiting for Nemirovich's proposals, Teliakovski had made a direct approach to Stanislavski, who had stated bluntly that he was not interested. Now, following the shareholders' decisions, on March 6, Nemirovich wrote both to Yuzhin-Sumbatov and Teliakovski at the Mali saying that he could not leave the Art Theatre since that would entail nothing less than its demise.

The new management structure, although it did not satisfy Nemirovich's desire for absolute control, was, in the long term, a liberation for Stanislavski. The kind of research he wanted to undertake could not be contained within the constraints of a theatre which had to be commercially viable. For the next thirty years he would work on the periphery of the Art Theatre, in one of its Studios or in opera. The whole pattern of his activities changed. His productions, highly successful as most of them were, were part of his research. The rehearsal process and the discoveries it produced became more important than the actual performance. Stanislavski never forgot that the ultimate purpose of his work was to have an effect on an audience, but to produce the *right* effect on an audience the actors had to produce the right truth and that could only be attained by the right methods which enabled the raw material of behaviour to be transformed into significant theatrical statements. It was the results produced by this search for human truth and the 'system', pursued for its own sake, that resulted in even greater fame and recognition. Although he might, in strict legal or administrative terms, be on the margin of the Art Theatre, there was no doubt in anyone's mind, in Russia or abroad, where the artistic and creative centre of that theatre lay. At the moment when his nominal power was being reduced at home he was becoming a world figure.

CHAPTER FIFTEEN

THE CREATIVE WILL

Stanislavski's 'grammar' of acting was beginning to take shape. It evolved slowly, not as a result of theoretical speculation but empirically, through rehearsal and the analysis of practice. It was as yet only the 'system' as we know it in embryo. Indeed, the term 'system' did not come into common use until two or three years later.

Stanislavski pressed on with his *Manual*, developing the notion of the creative will conceived in Finland. In December 1907, he drafted a chapter in which he defined its nature, function and relationship to other elements in the creative process. At the same time he received fresh stimulus to his ideas from Isadora Duncan, who was giving a season of special matinées at the Art Theatre. Her impact was enormous. Even Sulerzhitski, the dour revolutionary, came under her spell, taking to her, as someone put it, 'like a cat to cream'. Isadora was deeply impressed by Stanislavski's work and found his ideas on dramatic rhythm illuminating. On his side, he found her artistic energy and fresh approach revitalizing. At the very moment when he had rejected anything redolent of classical ballet for *The Blue Bird*, she came forward with a concept of physical expression and scenic movement which would release personal energy. They discussed the possibility of starting a school, attached to the theatre.

Isadora made no secret of her wish to take Stanislavski as her lover. He made it clear that he would always remain entirely faithful to Lilina. Fortunately, his rejection of her advances did not impair their artistic relationship. Isadora determined that Stanislavski and her ex-lover, Gordon Craig, must work together and immediately wrote excited and somewhat exaggerated letters to Craig in Italy.

Stanislavski now began to put his notions on the creative will into practice during rehearsals for *The Blue Bird*. The urge to create, he decided, could be stimulated through the discovery of motivations. When an actor knew why he was performing a particular action his will to perform it would be aroused. The action would then become his.

He gave his actors a first indication of his notion of motivation, and the need to define what later became known as the 'task' or 'objective':

'The blocking is not understood. Everyone moves because the director has said "move" and because the move corresponds to the director's ideas. Nobody is digging around and so there is no search for inner motives. All the moves are false because they are unthinking. It's not enough to understand, you must take your positions and moves to your heart.'

'The will is perhaps only strong when there is a definable goal for it.' (Notes to *The Blue Bird* cast, January/February 1908, taken down by Sulerzhitski, K.S. Archive, No. 1392.)

As always, he overestimated the speed at which his colleagues could change direction. They had achieved success by obediently following their master and now he was trying to push them out on their own. He was introducing unfamiliar ideas and expecting his actors to apply them without preparation. *The Blue Bird* was the wrong play with which to start introducing new acting techniques. It was a director's play and, as it turned out, a technical nightmare. By the time it opened on September 30 it had received some 150 rehearsals and generated a great deal of irritation. When at a final read-through on September 25, with full chorus and orchestra, the woodwind and xylophone failed to arrive, Stanislavski threatened to report the whole matter to the board. Close to midnight on the 26th, still sitting at the director's table, he wrote a letter to Sulerzhitski, saying he had been shouting and yelling from eleven in the morning to eleven at night. New music had been provided which the cast must adapt to. He had been told that an effect he had been working on for six months would have to be scrapped. Small wonder then if he had behaved badly:

> '*I* am the only one who is doing any thinking, *I* have to galvanize the will of every single actor. I am living for everyone, sitting here at my table.' (*SS*, VII, p. 413.)

Despite a first night when the intervals were too long, the audience's concentration overstretched and the atmosphere back-stage far from cheerful, *The Blue Bird* became Stanislavski's most famous production. In October, Beerbohm Tree sent a request through the Russian ambassador in London, asking if his assistant, Stanley Bell, might come to Moscow and study the production. Tree's later presentation owed much to this visit. Sarah Bernhardt, who saw the play in December, insisted that it be seen in Paris and, indeed, two years later Sulerzhitski was sent over to reproduce the production move for move for Réjane.

Stanislavski felt he had finally achieved his goal of expressing the abstract on stage, of moving beyond the literal surface, yet with *The Blue Bird* he was not dealing with pure abstractions, or wholly symbolic figures, as he had in *The Drama of Life*. Maeterlinck's play provided a psychological framework – the mind of a child which, for all its capacity for fantasy, is essentially concrete, observable, reproducible. By insisting that the cast enter the imagination of the child and that the production as a whole should reflect that world, Stanislavski made the invisible comprehensible. He also arrived at a new and extended notion of Realism. *The Blue Bird* was his last 'spectacular' as a director and it was a fitting culmination to a brilliant series of productions. That phase was now behind him.

In his report on the tenth anniversary of the Art Theatre, which he delivered on October 14, he gave his version of the theatre's artistic trajectory and also stated the current position as he saw it:

'Having made a whole series of preliminary experiments and investigations into the psychology and physiology of the creative process we have come to a whole series of conclusions. In order to study them we shall have to go back for a time to simple, realistic forms of staging. Thus, having started with realism, having followed the development of our art, we have come full circle and are back to realism again, enriched by our work and experience.' (*SS*, V, p. 414.)

His approach to Gogol's *The Inspector General*, currently in rehearsal, amply illustrated not only his growing perception that motivation provided the impetus for truthful action on stage, but his intuitive conviction that an actor's past experience, his 'affective memory', was a means of achieving that symbiotic relationship between the actor's personality and the character. The expression 'affective memory' first occurs in a letter to Kotliarevskaia on May 5:

'I've got on to the track of new principles. These principles may turn the whole psychology of the actor's creative process on its head. I am making daily experiments on myself and others and have come up with some interesting results. What fascinates me most is the rhythm of feelings, the development of affective memory and the psycho-physiology of the creative process. With the help of these experiments I have managed to achieve much greater simplicity and strength in existing roles and I am able to fortify my creative will to such an extent that even when I am ill, or have a temperature, I forget about my illness and find energy on stage. As a result the company respect these new ideas and have stopped laughing at my experiments and listen to what I have to say with considerable attention.' (*SS*, VII, pp. 386.)

Chance brought Stanislavski scientific confirmation of what he had perceived instinctively. In July he went to Germany for the opening of the Chekhov monument and to take the water at Homburg.

'I met a very cultivated and well-read man, who, in conversation, quite by chance, produced this statement: You know that an artist's experience and creativity are based on affective emotion and memory? I said nothing but immediately wrote off for the literature dealing with the subject.' (Material for *My Life in Art*, K.S. Archive, No. 42.)

The books in question were Ribot's *Les Maladies de la Mémoire* and *Les Maladies de la Volonté* which had appeared in Russian in 1900.

Two of Ribot's notions were of particular interest. First, that the will has a positive role to play in the patient's recovery and that the rate of convalescence may depend on the desire to get better. Second, that all memories of past experiences are recorded by the nervous system and, although not immediately available to the conscious mind, may be evoked by an appropriate stimulus: a touch, a sound, a smell may enable a patient to relive not just one experience but a grouping of similar experiences which merge to create a single emotional state. The actor's problem was to remove the chance element and find a technique whereby his memories could be made available to him.

Stanislavski's marginal notes show his attempt to apply purely medical knowledge to a creative process. For the moment it was still the problem of the will which occupied him:

'Failures in creative art disappoint and in a given role produce the very same symptoms as in illness.'

'Automatic action is apparent in the daily routine of life.'

'Weakness of motive does not stimulate action. What must be the actor's motive – to convey the life of another person.' (Marginalia in *Les Maladies de la Mémoire, Les Maladies de la Volonté,* K.S. Archive.)

Apart from ideas drawn from or confirmed by Ribot, his own process of self-analysis had yielded results. Concerned as ever by the problem of relaxation and control on stage, he discovered that his own tensions disappeared if he concentrated his attention strictly on the specific action the production demanded. When his attention slipped physical tension returned.

The Inspector General, which went into rehearsal immediately *The Blue Bird* had opened, provided the perfect opportunity to draw these ideas together and work at an almost exclusively psychological level. Stanislavski made use of Gogol's notes on the play which he had studied twenty years earlier. A primitive terminology began to emerge. Actors were suddenly confronted with terms such as 'nail' – taken directly from Gogol – and 'circle', which in the final 'system' became the through-action and circles of concentration.

Stanislavski did not wish to fall into the error of merely imitating external behaviour or the psychopathology of daily life. He noted in his journal:

Explain the fact that every play needs the quintessence of life, not life itself. For instance: read some long-winded novel that doesn't appeal to you. You shut it at page ten. Cut the novel, leaving in what interests you and you respond. There's a great deal that is uninteresting in life. What interest is it to me how a man eats, drinks and washes, if he does not do it in a special way?' (K.S. Archive, No. 764.)

Gogol's play demands a kind of enriched realism which Stanislavski was anxious to achieve. He maintained that exaggerated external action could only be justified by a counter-balancing intensity of inner drive. The degree of his success is evident from Efros' review. Placed between the stage and the audience, Efros said, was a powerful magnifying glass. Everything was blown up but this exaggeration was not merely external, it encompassed the characters' thoughts and feeling. Everything Gogol had written, all his comments and stage directions, had been pushed to the limit. As for the moment when the central character, Khlestakov, crushed a bed-bug against the wall with the end of his nose, that was surely destined to cause as furious an argument among audience and satirical journals alike as the notorious crickets in *The Seagull*.

Nemirovich was certain this was a pivotal production in Stanislavski's development:

'I would say that no production at the Moscow Art Theatre up till now has been in the hands of the actors to such a degree. Not one production detail was allowed to get in the way of the actors. Stanislavski is no longer the kind of director he was previously, as, for example, in *The Blue Bird*, but has become a teacher. The essence of all the work on *The Inspector General* consisted in deep psychological investigation of the characters and the rediscovery of direct, simple speech.' (Interview with Nemirovich in *Russkoe Slovo*, November 18, 1908.)

Nemirovich was right, although he could not have realized the far-reaching implications of such a change.

Stanislavski's concern indeed was now with research and teaching, with restoring creative control to the actor – but the actor had to be equal to the task. Stanislavski was depressed by the decline in standards of behaviour, the increased amount of drinking, the lack of discipline and sense of purpose. He had tried direct protest. Only a radical overhaul of working method, which included notions of personal and artistic responsibility, could turn the situation round.

On August 23 he had come home frustrated from a rehearsal of *The Blue Bird*. The cast had appeared neither to know their lines nor their moves, although the scene had been rehearsed at least ten times. Nobody seemed worried. He returned to his notes for the *Manual* and drafted a chapter on professional ethics. It was indicative of his isolation that he found the most sympathetic response outside the theatre in men of advanced ideas. Two days later on the 25th, he read his draft to Lunacharski. Discussion went on well into the night.

He tried, with varying degrees of success, to persuade his colleagues and contemporaries, the 'veterans', of the value of his new methods but it was increasingly to the up-and-coming generation and to young actors and directors in training that he turned his attention. He continued to play the parts he had made famous and to create the occasional new role, but the last thirty years of his life represent one continuous, deliberate effort to develop a set of training exercises and rehearsal practices, to produce an historical overview of various schools and theories of acting, and to apply his 'grammar' to the creation of new roles. Individual productions and performances, while important in themselves, take on their real meaning when seen as part of the evolution of the 'system'.

CHAPTER SIXTEEN

THE 'SYSTEM' EMERGES

Isadora succeeded in bringing Stanislavski and Gordon Craig together. Craig arrived in Moscow on October 15. He first greeted Stanislavski lying naked in a freezing cold bath in his room at the Hotel Metropole although there were several degrees of frost outside. With his romantic disdain for the vulgar realities of nature, he had turned up with only the light clothes he wore in Italy. His hosts, anxious to show him the city, the theatre and generally give him a good time, had first to express the warmth of their hospitality by fitting him out with a complete wardrobe, including a fur coat, taken from the stock of *Woe from Wit*. On the 18th he attended a performance of *An Enemy of the People* accompanied by Stanley Bell, who had once again been sent over by Beerbohm Tree. Subsequently he saw *The Blue Bird*, *Uncle Vania*, and *The Life of Man*, which because of its unremitting black-and-white designs and claustrophobic atmosphere practically made him ill, as it had Isadora. Nonetheless his admiration for the theatre and for Stanislavski, despite basic aesthetic disagreements, was profound. Writing to himself in the guise of a fictitious correspondent, John Semar, Craig stated:

'The Art Theatre . . . is alive, is possessed of character and intelligence.

Its director, Constantin Stanislawsky [sic], has achieved the impossible: he has successfully established a non-commercial theatre. He believes in realism as a medium through which the actor can reveal the psychology of the dramatist. I don't believe in it. This is not the place to discuss the wisdom or folly of the theory. . . .

It is quite enough to say that what these Russians do upon the stage they do to perfection. They waste time, money, labour, brains and patience like emperors. . . .

They give hundreds of rehearsals to a play, they change and rechange a scene until it balances their thought. . . .

Seriousness, character, these two qualities will guide the Moscow Art Theatre to unending success in Europe or elsewhere. . . .

Less of a spontaneous whirlwind than Grasso, their first actor Stanislawsky is more intellectual.

This is not to be misunderstood. You are not to imagine that this actor is cold or stilted. A simpler technique, a more human result, would be difficult to find . . . his performances are all remarkable for their grace. I can find no better word.

I have been most pleased by the performance of *Onkel Vanja*. . . . In *The Enemy of the People*, Stanislawsky shows us how to act Dr Stockman without being "theatrical" and without being comic or dull. The audience smile all the time that they are not being moved to tears.
. . .' (Edward Gordon Craig, 'The Theatre in Russia, Germany and England' in *On the Art of the Theatre*, Heinemann, 1956, pp. 133–6.)

Stanislavski knew almost nothing about Craig, although Isadora had procured him a bad German translation of Craig's two dialogues, *The Art of the Theatre*, which he had recently completed. There could, in any case, be no question of their coming to an agreement on basic questions of principle. Both were far too committed to their ideas for that. But each could supply something of what the other needed. Craig was happy to have found a theatre that took theatre seriously; Stanislavski needed stimulus, a fresh mind, controversy, anything rather than the back-biting and derision to which he was so often subjected. In their correspondence various ideas for plays had been floated but both men harboured a desire to do *Hamlet*. On January 19, 1909, the board decided to mount *Hamlet*, *A Month in the Country* and Leonid Andreiev's *Anathema*. *Hamlet* would be under the general artistic control of Gordon Craig. *A Month in the Country* would be directed by Stanislavski and *Anathema* by Nemirovich. The Turgenev and the Andreiev were scheduled for the 1909 season, *Hamlet* for 1910. It was agreed, however, that given the complexity of the undertaking, work on *Hamlet* was to begin at once.

Stanislavski's decision to work in tandem on two plays so disparate in style, the one intimate, domestic, subdued in tone, working in psychological hints and half-lights, the other spread across a huge canvas, combining intimacy with moments of extreme action and violence, the one in contained prose, the other full of intense and passionate poetry, was central to his purpose, which was to demonstrate that the 'system' was a universal approach that could be applied to any play, whatever its formal demands.

Preliminary discussions and plans for *Hamlet* began immediately, prior to Craig's return to Russia in the spring. Although Craig's designs were essentially geometric, made of blocks and cubes and giant screens, Stanislavski engaged a second designer, Egorov, who was sent to collect authentic material from Denmark, Sweden and Norway. The results of his travels were examined on February 24. On the 28th Stanislavski outlined his ideas on the play to the production team. Preliminary rehearsals began in March and on April 1 Stanislavski wired Craig asking him to be in St Petersburg, where the company would be on tour, by the 15th. He also advanced two months' salary.

With Craig's arrival everything started all over again. He and

Stanislavski went through the play scene by scene, building up a production plan, including basic blocking, sound and lighting, and then went over the text line by line so that Craig could check and if necessary improve the translation. Their discussions, all of which were scrupulously noted down, were conducted in a hotch-potch of English and German. While Stanislavski had no English, Sulerzhitski was able to manage a little and acted when necessary as interpreter. Work continued in Moscow in May. Despite their agreement on matters of staging, divergences in approach and interpretation soon became evident. Craig's Hamlet was largely a self-projection, a pure spirit in a grossly material world. Stanislavski's Hamlet, also in part a self-projection, was another of his crusading individuals, a Christ-like figure sent to cleanse the world from corruption – an active Russian Hamlet as opposed to the philosopher-Prince of German criticism. Stanislavski made it clear that whatever degree of abstraction or symbolism the production might ultimately achieve, he intended to rehearse, in the first instance at least, using the 'system'. It was the only way to prevent the actors from falling back into their old habits and delivering standard bombastic 'classical' acting. Their final discussion took place on June 2, before Stanislavski's departure for Paris. After that *Hamlet* would have to be set aside while he concentrated his attention on rehearsals for *A Month in the Country*.

He returned to Moscow in August and spent an evening going through the casting with Nemirovich who was pleased to report to his wife the next day that the atmosphere had been 'harmonious'. He was, therefore, not a little surprised when Stanislavski then virtually cut himself off for the next four months.

It was one of the rules of the Art Theatre that all rehearsals should be open. They were considered the principal means by which members of the company could learn. Stanislavski broke with this tradition. The rehearsals, conducted in the small rehearsal theatre, were closed. No one not directly connected with the production was allowed near it. This was neither pique nor paranoia. It was the direct result of his new working method.

Gone now was the carefully, minutely pre-established production plan. The sets were reduced to a strict minimum, just enough to suggest the milieu. Production values were not the main concern. The process of creating the performance depended on delicate collaborative work with the actor. For the first time Stanislavski's production book shows the action broken down into sections or 'bits'. The rehearsal process consisted in finding the feelings, the psychological states, contained in those sections and in relating them, through emotion memory, to personal experience.

Stanislavski elected to work in a small rehearsal studio, rather than on the main stage, in order to emphasize the intimacy of the play. He further broke down the space into smaller rooms suggesting the house. He kept the actors under tight control, using what he was later to call the 'sitting-on-hands method'. They were not allowed to speak their text either in full or with full voice. Cuts were made in the longer speeches and used as sub-text, to be thought only. In this Stanislavski was influenced by certain notions drawn from yoga which had become fashionable. Great emphasis was laid on what is now called non-verbal communication. The actors were expected to 'radiate' their mental states. He was, in fact, as he was aware, returning to some of the experiments he had made when directing *The Drama of Life*. This time, however, the technique was to be applied not in order to convey the abstract and symbolic but the reality of psychological action.

> 'What we needed was a kind of invisible radiation of feeling and creative will – eyes, facial expression, fleeting elusive tones of voice, psychological pauses. . . . We had once more to return to immobility, absence of gestures, we had to get rid of all superfluous movement; we had to cut down, cut out entirely all director's moves and leave the actors motionless on their chairs; let them speak, think and communicate their suffering to the thousands in the audience.' (*SS*, I, p. 326.)

This stripping down of the acting style matched the sets which were symmetrical and unobtrusive.

Stanislavski provided a psychological outline for each character, not merely an overall profile, but the stages by which feelings and attitudes develop and change. Nowhere is this more evident than in his notes, made in late August, on the leading character Natalia Petrovna Islaieva, to be played by Knipper:

> 'Because of Beliaev's arrival she, above all, with increased energy, observes, notes and even criticizes in Rakitin and her husband things she let pass before. Not irritation, but mild caprice. She is much more observant, concentrated, attentive. An outward smile.
>
> She is concentrating and therefore seems outwardly distracted. Something has appeared in her which draws her into herself. When she is at her embroidery, she becomes easily lost in thought, but this love which she still does not recognize, does not disturb her and therefore she can remain entirely concentrated on herself.
>
> . . . Must bear in mind that it is better for the actress to start the role quietly and keep the brighter colours for later. So for the moment there is no need to show irritation, nor excessive absent-mindedness, nor venom. All that is necessary, precisely to explain her state, but all in moderation. Only Verochka and Beliaev pay attention to her; the rest do not. So, these are the basic elements of her state, the starting point of her experience.
>
> 1) She has inward concentration, which is not disturbed by any thoughts which can draw her attention.

2) Nothing external can hold her attention, although it can attract it for a moment.

3) Critical attitude towards Rakitin (particularly) and to some extent her husband. They all become irritated, being interested in cards or the everyday things of life. She, as it were, is not disturbed by anything. Above all remind Olga Leonardovna [Knipper] of the restraint "of being in corsets" (of the period). Olga Leonardovna may want to move towards external etiquette but in this case she can't. It is essential that, for her posture, she listen and answer very attentively (i.e., that she achieves "being in corsets" out of *inner concentration*).

. . . In the first act Natalia Petrovna loves Vera's youth. In the second act she becomes irritated by it and in the third act she hates it.' (K.S. Archive.)

He insisted on the essential charm of the woman. Knipper was still battling unsuccessfully with the role in October. Using his somewhat uncertain vocabulary of 'circles' Stanislavski explained the Act Three conversation between Natalia Petrovna and the young Beliaev:

'[Natalia Petrovna] continues to probe him but the essential factor is jealousy. Having changed the circles of trickery, she wants to get from him a promise that the meetings, etc., with Verochka will cease. All her lines, therefore, are tinged with that inward state of trickery. The outward appearance she gives is that she is mistrustful. Using in turn mockery, irony, an open and frank tone, the tone of a great and upright gentlewoman, with folded arms, she gets what she wants. All that is not a little dishonest, of course, but it is also charming in a woman who is in love, who realises it is impossible not to fall in love with Verochka, who has no right to love another man, who deceives her husband and insults Rakitin.

This whole scene is about the agitation which the actress creates out of a desire energetically and clearly to change the circle of inner trickery.' (Directorial notes, October 17, 1909, K.S. Archive.)

The intimate, analytical work, accompanied by exercises in focusing attention and silent communication, went on until the last ten days of October, when rehearsals had to transfer to the large stage. Stanislavski was aware that his 'system' was on trial: Knipper and Nemirovich remained unconvinced of its value; even Lilina had made it clear during *The Blue Bird* rehearsals that she did not find his new ideas helpful. The move from the small to the big theatre proved catastrophic:

'When we got on to the stage it wasn't rehearsal, it was hell. Everything just disappeared. What had seemed fine at the table, emerged as weak. They all spoke quietly, could not expand their voices . . . Knipper drove us mad with her obstinacy, Koroneva by her bad character. . . . Boleslavski out of inexperience turned into a complete idiot. The enemies of my system spread gloom and doom, said it was boring and brought the whole rehearsal down to a low point.

It's a long time since I have felt such torment, despair and a slump in energy (not since *The Drama of Life* and *The Life of Man*).' (Late October 1909, K.S. Archive, No. 545.)

When Nemirovich attended a reading on October 31 he too, was in despair. As he wrote to his wife, the play, which had already been given eighty or ninety rehearsals, was nowhere near ready and what he had seen was totally feeble. He had decided to keep a tactful silence rather than try to sort things out and so revive all the old quarrels with his friend.

The main problem was Knipper. She had begun well enough but she was completely thrown when Stanislavski started to apply his new method. He had been in conflict with her before. He had accused her of being lazy, of never being ready on the first night. This was a little unfair since he himself was far from being a first-night actor. Indeed, his own performance as Rakitin did not fully mature until the St Petersburg tour in the spring of 1910. But the difference between them was that he had a working method and she had none. She was an instinctive actress but her range was limited. When her instinct failed, as it had in this case, she was lost, and since she found Stanislavski's new ideas too 'intellectual' she was not prepared to be helped. She was attempting, as Stanislavski had suspected she would, to approach the role from the outside. Psychological analysis was lost on her. Of the fifty rehearsals that had taken place by the end of September, nineteen had been devoted to Knipper privately in Stanislavski's flat.

Inevitably Nemirovich was drawn in. He had always had a close relationship with Knipper and when, on November 6, he arrived for a rehearsal in make-up and costume, matters came to a head. Knipper broke down in tears in Act Three and left the theatre. She had hoped that once she got into costume everything would come together. It had not. Her confidence was now completely undermined. Nemirovich crept out of the auditorium not wishing to become involved.

Stanislavski handled the situation with delicacy and tact. The following day he sent Knipper flowers and a letter, gentle in tone but offering no concessions. He expressed his affection for her and his respect for her great gifts. If he appeared cruel it was only because he loved her talent too much to allow it to be degraded. The letter contains an offer, a piece of advice and a criticism. First he proposes a painless, jargon-free introduction to the new method:

'If you need my help I will break your part down into sections. I promise not to frighten you with technical jargon. That's probably where I went wrong.'

Next he advises her to use her own personality, her own psychology as a base and stop thinking about her effect on the audience and whether they liked her or not:

> 'At every point in the role look for some desire which concerns you and you alone and banish all other, vulgar desires concerning the audience. You will quickly find this inward work will carry you away.
>
> Once that has happened you will turn from something which is unworthy of true artists, the desire to serve and ingratiate oneself with the audience.
>
> In the same measure that you are not logical in that instance, you will become logical by being carried away by genuine feelings.'

Finally he sugars the pills with a piece of flattery:

> 'You are lucky, you have a charm on stage which makes people listen to you and so it is easy for you to do anything you want.' (*SS*, VII, pp. 453–4.)

Above all he told her not to give up the fight since only through struggle could she achieve great art.

The letter had the desired effect. Knipper responded warmly and work began again. But the crisis was not over. A series of depressing dress rehearsals followed. Act Three was still weak. Yet when the play opened on December 9 it was accounted a success. Stanislavski and Boleslavski were much praised although Knipper's performance was accounted a failure. The favourable reception of the production as a whole was of the utmost importance to Stanislavski. He had proved the value of his new method in the most effective manner possible, by success.

The production nonetheless provoked criticism, in particular the accusation that there was an excessive concern with the trivial and the commonplace. A series of discussions took place in St Petersburg in the first week of May 1910, during the annual tour. The production was compared unfavourably with 'true' theatre, as represented by Greek tragedy, which strove to create an 'event', something which had a liturgical and religious thrust. Could the Turgenev really be compared to that? Stanislavski avoided any theoretical response. He could only point, empirically, to the actual audience reaction the Art Theatre had experienced over the years. If what they did was insignificant, not an 'event', how did his interlocutor explain the stunned reaction of audiences in Berlin, when people had remained seated long after the curtain had fallen, still under the impact of what they had seen? Or how to explain the many hundreds of letters from appreciative theatregoers? Stanislavski was aware that he would always come under this sort of attack. As he wrote two years later:

> 'They will attack my system for driving conventions and clichés out of art. . . . In order to discredit my opinions they will, of course, call me

a realist-naturalist, etc. They'll say I'm a photographer, because I am dealing with the greatest of beauties, nature, while they are refined people of culture because they work with all the errors which arise from copies of nature – actors' conventions and clichés.' (1912, K.S. Archive, No. 931.)

Stanislavski needed to prove the validity of his new method with a classic play. *Hamlet* provided him with the opportunity.

Craig returned to Moscow on February 15, 1910, so that he and Stanislavski could pick up rehearsals where they had left off. They would work together with the company until Craig returned to Italy at the end of April. Stanislavski would then work alone until the summer break. Craig would return in August and the play would open in November.

The company did not find rehearsals easy mainly because Craig did not know how to rehearse. He kept himself aloof from the company except for Alisia Koonen, to whom he had taken a fancy. This champion of the Übermarionette was prepared to allow the actors total freedom of choice in the means they selected to convey his abstract ideas. Thus, while the cast were willing to try anything he cared to suggest to them, he suggested nothing. Craig, like his hero, Hamlet, was pure spirit, dealing only in pure abstract concepts which somehow had to be materialized in actors' bodies. Similarly his designs took no account of practical issues. Many of his sets proved technically impossible to construct, although huge sums of money were spent, and wasted.

There was a mismatch between Stanislavski and Craig and the Art Theatre which events were to accentuate. Craig, unable to give any precise direction himself, found Stanislavski dictatorial and manipulative as a director, and merely complained that the acting did not match the mood of the sets. Stanislavski tried everything he knew to find a new approach demonstrating various styles of acting – French, Italian, German, traditional Russian – none of which were to Craig's liking. Craig also created problems by his endless demands for money which he thought owing to him, whether he was present in Moscow or not. At one point he even took legal advice. Disaster struck in August when Stanislavski went down with typhoid. It became apparent that he could not return to work until the beginning of 1911 at the earliest. The whole production had to be postponed until the following season.

When he returned to rehearsal in April 1911 Stanislavski pursued his own line, applying the system. He made a number of cast changes. Craig had disappeared, giving him a free hand, although he did, as far as he could, respect Craig's basic ideas. His fear was, as he had indicated to Craig at the very beginning, that the actors would fall back into a conventional style, that the speaking of the verse would become the mere mouthing of sounds, that the moves would be reduced to mere parading about in costume. The audience could all too easily, and willingly, become mesmerized by the visual aspects of the production and lose the meaning of the play. The actors must be clear as to the motivation and purpose of everything they said and did.

> 'The hidden essence of a soliloquy in verse can only be made comprehensible through clear and precise shaping of the bits. Without that it is lost in a welter of rhetoric, elocution, rhythm and pounding metre.' (K.S. Archive, No. 924.)

He accordingly broke the play down into bits, with a specific 'task', or in the accepted translation, objective, and mood for each bit. When rehearsals resumed after the August break the company was still nonetheless confused, caught between Craig's abstractions and Stanislavski's own clear perception as to what the character of Hamlet was about. Kachalov had been brought to the point of nervous collapse by the conflicting direction he received. Any ambiguity was dispelled when, in a fit of exasperation, Stanislavski made his meaning clear in the most direct possible fashion, by demonstrating. During a rehearsal of Act Three scene two, the Players' scene, he leapt on to the stage. He seemed instantly to be transformed. The Hamlet he demonstrated was the active Hamlet he had conceived from the start:

> 'This was a brilliant Hamlet. Hamlet the artist, the teacher, the preacher, who knew so much more than those around him.' (Gzovskaia, in conversation with Chushkin, August 3, 1945.)

> 'This was not Craig's Hamlet, lit by the rays of death, striving to surmount his unreal, earthly existence. In rehearsal Stanislavski showed Hamlet to be so virile, full of human nobility and controlled passion. His demonstration obliged Kachalov to play Hamlet with enormous *spiritual* energy, with tragic élan . . . Stanislavski's Hamlet was active and virile . . . passionate, emotional, full of conflicting shifts of feeling, from tenderness and love for other men to angry sarcasm and hate.' (Chushkin, *Kachalov–Hamlet*, Isskustvo, Moscow, 1966, p. 31.)

On another occasion he demonstrated the scene with the recorders, venting Hamlet's anger on his erstwhile friends, Rosencrantz and Guildenstern:

> 'In the Third Act, in the episode with the recorders, he hurled himself around the stage, making them pursue him like foxhounds. He led this "chase" at a frantic speed and then suddenly came to a halt, throwing a line at them, so that Rosencrantz and Guildenstern, unable to stop themselves, crashed into him full tilt. In general, in Act Three, Stanislavski's Hamlet was full of tragic bitterness, enormous spiritual tension and strangeness.' (Ibid.)

Demonstration, however useful, was in a sense a return to old and rejected methods. The actors still had to be given a framework within which to work. Where necessary, therefore, Stanislavski broke the bits down into a series of precise actions. Rehearsing the Mousetrap scene, he analysed the action for Kachalov, who was trying to be 'tragic' in the abstract and was getting nowhere:

> 'Kachalov puffed himself up, he tried to be subtle, merry, malicious, ironic. In a word he was playing results – despaired because it wasn't tragic.
>
> STANISLAVSKI: This scene is a heap of pearls, sort them out individually and you will find:
>
> a) Pearl number one. Hamlet is full of energy and therefore wants to cover the distance boldly and effectively; b) Hamlet wants the king to have a slap in the face but without revealing that it is a slap in the face; c) same thing for Polonius; d) same thing for Ophelia; e) Hamlet wants to watch the king unobserved (but you demonstrate that you are watching). Hamlet is afraid of alarming the king too soon; f) the king rises. Hamlet runs across and leaps on the throne, wanting to see the king; g) Hamlet shouts to the king "Why, let the stricken deer go weep" and very much wants him to hear; h) Hamlet runs downstage to get another glimpse of the king as he rushes out; i) Hamlet wants to get his cloak on quickly and properly (because he has a burst of energy and at such moments [people] act quickly and properly); j) Hamlet wants to declaim effectively; k) Hamlet wants to make Horatio tell what he has seen.
>
> The tragic elements will arise from a series of simple, mechanical tasks.' (K.S. Archive, No. 912.)

Stanislavski was clear that under no circumstances was the play to become a series of set-pieces or 'arias', delivered for their own sake. A case in point was Hamlet's speech to the Players, which everyone knew and which could easily become detached from the main action and turn into an actor's credo. It had a dramatic function, a specific objective, and it was that which had to be played:

> 'This scene with the Players has a specific relationship with what has gone before and doesn't simply stand as a lecture on dramatic art . . . Hamlet pronounces his advice in the light of his main purpose, that "The Mouse-trap" will be staged so truthfully, seriously and realistically that it will stir the conscience of the king. Without that Hamlet cannot discover the truth.' (K.S. Archive, No. 924.)

A major preoccupation in rehearsal was the relationship of the physical to the psychological. At this stage the psychological was pre-eminent and Stanislavski insisted on the primacy for the actors, as in the more intimate Turgenev play, of establishing contact with one another, mainly through eye-contact. The physical served mainly to illustrate and fix emotional states which the artist discovered, intuitively, under the director's prompting. Precise physical action was essential to prevent too great a variation from one performance to the next. The assumption was that once an emotional state was represented or realized in a physical action, the repetition of that physical action would evoke the emotion:

'The object of the director-artist is to be able to stimulate the actor's talent, to lead him along the right path.

The creative process is unconscious. The most precious things about it are those flashes of unconscious inspiration. But inspiration is not enough, you must be able to fix those flashes.

Otherwise the actor will play in an inspired fashion today and feebly tomorrow . . .' (Conversation with Stanislavski, *Rampa*, March 15, 1909, p. 171.)

If, however, the actor took premature refuge in conventional or theatrically false physical moves he could block the flow of genuine, authentic feeling. This is what happened to Massalitinov, who was playing Claudius. During the prayer scene he got off to a bad start, falling immediately into a conventional posture:

'CLAUDIUS/MASSALITINOV: Pray I cannot.
STANISLAVSKI: You got down on the floor so conventionally, in such a clichéd posture that nothing can come of it but stagey conventions and not living truth. Honestly aren't you yourself aware that only clichés of body, voice, rhythm, speech, diction habitually associated with such a clichéd posture can come if you do that? Try, instead to discover for this mood – a tormented prayer – another, much more simple posture, far removed from any stagey picturesqueness, and you'll see it will result in a life-like body and a tone of voice and a manner of speaking which is habitually associated with that posture in real life.
(*Massalitinov tries.*)
STANISLAVSKI: You see how much nearer you are to the truth. There are still some clichéd elements – root them out. The main thing is you are not living the reason for which Shakespeare wrote the king's words but the words themselves, you're spelling out their direct meaning. You illustrate "smells" and "offence" with a display of disgust but that prevents you from experiencing the truth fully. Don't live smells or offence but the impossibility of praying to God, the helplessness, the despair. Then you will experience the real truth inside and outside and will live it. . . . You must abandon the periphery and go to the centre; external clichés are too firmly rooted in you. They are so blatant in their unnaturalness and falseness that they squeeze out the truth. Find the truth of inner feeling, then you can talk about external truth.' (K.S. Archive, No. 911.)

Stanislavski worked on remorselessly, obsessively, leaving the long-suffering Sulerzhitski to mediate between himself and Craig, ward off Nemirovich, who once again was becoming understandably worried, and sort out the many technical problems concerning the sets. When the play finally opened on December 23, it provoked, inevitably, a mixed reaction. Moscow had not seen anything like it, nor, for that matter, had anyone else. Craig's cubes and screens produced enthusiasm, bewilderment, irritation and derision. Neither audience nor critics were aware of his original intention to have visible set changes, with scene flowing into scene. The technical problems of constructing any sets at all produced a clumsy compromise.

The acting also encountered a mixed reception. Briusov, writing a year later, pointed to the contradiction between the abstract design concept and the acting style. Knipper as Gertrude, Massalitinov as Claudius and Gzovskaia as Ophelia got bad notices and Stanislavski immediately thought of recasting. Of Kachalov's Hamlet there was no doubt. It was recognized as a genuine achievement, effacing the memory of Mochalov's turbulent, romantic mid-nineteenth-century performance of which most people had heard but few had seen. The months of painful and sometimes despairing effort, under Stanislavski's mercilessly critical eye, had paid dividends.

The production received, in reality, few showings but its fame and influence spread across Europe, mainly because it was described in *The Times* and the French press as an unqualified success. Thanks to this legend, which Craig was careful to foster, it came to be regarded as a seminal event, influencing the whole history of production style, although as the years went by Craig took a more and more jaundiced view of the whole affair. As far as Stanislavski was concerned he had proved the relevance of the 'system' to a major classical text. He now intended to move on, both as actor and director, to another classic author, Molière.

CHAPTER SEVENTEEN

THE FIRST STUDIO

Even as he worked on his production Stanislavski attempted to provide a coherent written account of his 'system'. By 1910 a number of drafts existed besides the *Draft Manual* begun in Finland in 1906. The *Reference Book for the Dramatic Actor*, and *Practical Information and Good Advice for Beginners and Students of Dramatic Art*, date from 1907. The *Notebooks* for 1908 and after contain a series of individual entries on specific topics which were later listed, in 1913, under the following headings:

'Introduction, Hackwork, Performance, New Trend (Foundation), Being [Experiencing], Truth, Logic of Feelings, Emotional Feelings, Roots of Feelings. Will, Muscles, Eradicating Clichés, Tasks, Desires, Communication, Adaptation, Kernel, Through-action of Action, Circles, Tempo, Characterization, Analysis, Self-analysis, How to Use the System, Annotation, Terminology.' (K.S. Archive, Nos. 906–934.)

On March 8, 1909, he was sufficiently confident of the general shape of the 'system' to deliver a paper to a theatrical conference. There is great emphasis here and in the later *History of a Character* (1915) on the use of emotion memory and on what came to be known as the Magic If. The actor knows, intellectually, that everything around him is false; it is wood and canvas and papier mâché. But *what if* it were true, *what if* the given circumstances laid down by the author were reality, how would he react?

In his preparatory notes Stanislavski sets out a six-stage process: first the stimulation of the 'will', the creation of a commitment to the author's text; second, the personal base, the inner search for psychological material; third, 'experience', the private process of invisible inner creation, when the actor comes to terms with a character, an 'image' which is not his own and merges his own personality with it; fourth, 'physicalizing', the process, still private, by which the actor gives the image bodily existence; fifth, the bringing together of the inner and the outer, the psychological and the physical, as a synthesis; sixth, making an impact on the audience.

The problem of implementing the 'system' was still to be resolved. In

November 1910 he was able to give Nemirovich a summary of how far he had got:

'. . . before you start work with my system you must:
a) stimulate the process of the *will*; b) begin the process of investigation with some literary discussion (your expression) – how to maintain and develop these investigations, that I know: c) how to stimulate the process of lived experience, I know; d) how to help the process of physical characterization, I don't yet know in detail but I am aware of the fundamentals and seem to be getting close to the right track; e) the process of *synthesizing* and *influencing* are clear.

Now I have to find a practical way to arouse the actor's imagination in all these processes. This aspect of psychology has received little attention, especially the creative imagination of the actor and the painter.' (*SS*, VII, pp. 484–5.)

In addition to working out the detail of the 'system' he proposed to survey the art of acting and the theatre in general. Starting in 1909, he gave the work a number of titles, according to the draft he was working on: *Trends in Art, Two Trends and Hack-Work in Art, Introductions, Three Trends in Art*, etc. He continued work on the manuscript, on and off, until 1922 when he finally abandoned it although most of the material found its way, later, in modified form, into the opening sections of *An Actor's Work on Himself*. The manuscript is now published under the title *Various Trends in the Art of the Theatre*.

The three trends Stanislavski defined were the school of the proficient or hack actor, the school of representation and the school of lived experience. To judge by the section on the hack actor there had not been much general improvement in acting style since Shchepkin's early days. There was still the same mechanical colouring of words: 'sad' was delivered sadly, always, 'love' amorously, always, without regard to context or real meaning. Words like 'big', 'small', 'tall', 'wide' were carved out of the air with the hands. As for stage movement it was always 'theatrical' and majestic:

'Let's start with the solemn, measured gait of the actors. They do not walk, they advance across the stage, they do not sit, they ensconce themselves, they do not lie down, they recline, they do not stand, they adopt a pose.' (*SS*, VI, p. 48.)

Magniloquence of speech and grandeur of movement were amply supported by stock gestures which were available to express all the important feelings:

'Agitation is expressed by pacing up and down the stage very quickly, by the hands being seen to tremble when a letter is being opened or by letting the jug knock against the glass and then the glass against the teeth when the water is being poured and drunk.

Illness – a hacking cough, the shivers or vertigo (theatrical medicine only recognizes consumption, fever and anaemia).

Death – clutching the chest or tearing at one's shirt collar (the hack actor only recognizes two causes of death, cardiac arrest and asphyxia).' (Ibid., p. 51.)

Many of the stock gestures were simply copies of copies of actions performed once by actors of genuine talent at dramatically appropriate moments, now slavishly imitated and handed on as law:

'One very famous French actor used a highly effective bow at the end of a costume play. A Russian actor who was with me at that particular performance remembered it and brought it back to Russia. Now this manner of bowing is taught in schools and is considered essential for costume plays, whatever the period.' (Ibid., pp. 54–5.)

The acerbity of Stanislavski's tone is attributable to the fact that even as he was drafting this section he was complaining to his colleague Leonidov that performances of *The Inspector General* had declined into mechanical hack-work.

The second trend, the School of Representation, commanded much more respect. Stanislavski identified it with the best in French acting which he had so much admired in earlier years. Its method consisted in finding emotional truths during the preparatory period, observing the external features of those truths and then reproducing them faithfully, technically, so as to give a perfect representation of feeling without actually experiencing it during performance. This is in essence the approach of Shchepkin's 'actor of reason'.

Finally, there came the School of Lived Experience, the school of Shchepkin's 'actor of feeling'. Here the actor is required to recreate emotions and states of being afresh at each performance. This fell short of total identification with the role for, as Stanislavski pointed out later, actually to believe that one is someone else is a pathological condition. He never succeeded satisfactorily in defining the extent to which an actor identifies with his character and how much of the mind remains detached and maintains theatrical control. He was clear, however, that these schools rarely existed in pure form. In practice each performance was a mixture of all three trends. The crucial question was that of the proportion of one to the others. Only where the School of Lived Experience was dominant could there be real theatre. There could only be real theatre, too, when a company was dominated not by the author, as Nemirovich wanted, or by a single star actor who imposed his personality, but by an ensemble of artists, working sensitively and responsibly together towards a common creative purpose.

He was also thinking forward to new forms, notably the effect of the cinema. Film was still at an elementary stage of development and he could see only a limited role for it. The absence of the live actor seemed to have a crippling effect:

> 'The theatre and the cinema belong to different spheres and the things by which the theatre excites, attracts and charms us can never be provided by the cinema. It is really naïve to imagine that what currently has meaning in the theatre for audiences is outward form. That is not the life of the theatre. Theatre lives by the exchange of spiritual energy, which goes continuously back and forth between audience and actor; that contact of feeling that unites actor and audience with invisible threads. That will never and can never occur in the cinema where the living actor is absent, where the flow of spiritual motions is effected by mechanical means. In the theatre it is a *living* man who delights us, saddens us, disturbs us and calms us but in the cinema everyone and everything is *only apparently real.*
>
> The cinema cannot replace the theatre, but it can, if it is understood and takes on board the question of people's spiritual progress, introduce the popular masses to the generality of cultural life. Then it is undoubtedly an important and beautiful thing.' (Interview in *Peterburgski Kurior*, May 1, 1914.)

He sensed, nevertheless, that the screen would have an influence on acting technique and would, in fact, confirm the superiority of the School of Lived Experience:

> 'You want to see the difference between the art of representation and the art of lived experience? – go to the cinema. The audience is beginning to understand the difference and very soon will be demanding it from actors. Are you ready for it?' (In *Voprosi Kinoiskusstva*, 1962, p. 283.)

More new ideas came from Maksim Gorki. In December 1910 he suggested that Stanislavski complete his convalescence by joining him in the Mediterranean where he was living, for health reasons, on Capri. On December 18 and 19, Stanislavski read his note and discussed the problems of training a new kind of actor. Gorki was sympathetic to Stanislavski's basic notions. He himself was fully convinced that a proper exploration of personal experience could lead to political insight just as well as abstract theory. Stanislavski's combination of the purely subjective with a concern for the historical and social was entirely in line with his own thinking. He suggested establishing a company of young actors who would devise plays through improvisation, working with a writer, just like the strolling players of the Middle Ages and early Renaissance. Strength was given to this idea when, on the 20th, the two men went across to Naples and attended a performance at a popular theatre, which was attempting to work in the *commedia dell'arte* tradition. There was no written script. The actors improvised. The performance captured Stanislavski's imagination but there was no time to see it again before his departure on the 23rd. Back in Moscow he met Efros and discussed the notion of this new way of creating plays and its implications for productions where the author's text was poor:

> 'If the words are poor, as for example in bad writers or translations, and a talented artist finds his own words which are better and correspond to the tasks and the writer's intentions – why not take advantage of better words?' (*Notebook* 927.1 16.)

In January and again in September 1912 Gorki invited Stanislavski to come down with a group of colleagues and create a play. That was impractical. In any case it is questionable whether Stanislavski, who, despite his reservations on the supremacy of the author, remained devoted to the scripted and indeed the classic play, would have wished to go very far down this road. Gorki's ideas did, however, find an important place later in the First Studio.

Having left the official management, Stanislavski's power to influence decisions or promote change had been seriously diminished. His reputation among the company for being something of a crank persisted and Nemirovich did little to discourage it. On the contrary, in private correspondence to Knipper and Luzhski, he made no secret of his own scepticism about the direction his partner had taken. But Stanislavski was not to be deterred. He made several attempts to promote his ideas among his colleagues. He gave a series of lectures outlining the 'system' but soon realized that you could not compress an active process into one hour's talk. When he was directing, the cast attempted to use the 'system'. They were compliant, if nothing else, when he introduced classes in Dalcroze's eurhythmics in 1911 and elements of yoga but on the whole they maintained a reserve. He came to realize that his main hope lay in the rising generation, but he had only limited contact with young actors. Having no status in the Art Theatre School he could only teach, privately, any student who showed interest. With time an increasing number of them came forward but there was no stability or continuity in the arrangement. As Sophia Giatsintova points out in her reminiscences, many young actors came upon the 'system' by chance – in her case by finding some pencilled notes in a dressing-room. Misunderstanding and half-truths abounded.

By the beginning of 1910 Stanislavski felt that with the success of *A Month in the Country*, he had proved his point sufficiently to make demands. He wanted the opportunity and the facilities to teach the 'system' officially. He drafted a seventeen-point statement to the board which Stanislavski read to Nemirovich over a meal on January 19, 1910. It is highly personal, not to say emotional, and shows quite clearly how aware he was of his poor standing in the company. The main points were:

'3. . . . I want total freedom for all those who are possessed of a pure and disinterested love of the theatre. Let whoever will make his own trials and experiments. I want the same right for myself.

4. . . . I am now persuaded as never before that I am on the right track . . . [and] will discover simple forms of words that will sum up everything and help the theatre to discover what is most important, that will point it in the right direction for many years.

5. I want not only to discover the fundamental principles of the creative process, I want not only to formulate its theory, I want to put it into practice.

6. The man who knows the difficult, uncertain, primitive nature of our art will be aware of the difficulty, scope and importance of this task. Perhaps it is insane arrogance. So be it! Then it will prove to be beyond my strength and I shall get a broken head. And deserve it. . . . Perhaps I am a madman and a dreamer but I cannot be and do not wish to be otherwise. At my age your roots are your roots.

7. The task is complicated and long and I am not young in years. . . . At the very most I have ten years' work left in me. . . . It's time to think of one's will. After all, every man wants to leave some small mark behind him. That's understandable.

8. I need material for my plan, I need help. It's impossible to count on everyone but there are a few people whom I have trained with great difficulty or who believe in my dreams. Of course I prize their help greatly.

9. The paths of our art are pitted with ruts and holes. They are deep and you can't get past them without falling. In moments like those you ought to help and pick up those who have stumbled and not think of them as already dead. . . .

10. . . . There was a time when there was not a single young person who was a real hopeful. Now there are such young people and our first task must be to teach them to find satisfaction in plain work, unless, of course, they turn out to be a real find – and there must always be a place for that in our theatre. . . .

12. I would like to forget just for a while many hurtful expressions used in respect of me – "scatter-brain", "a bundle of whims" – because they are unjust. I don't get into a mess all the time, sometimes I pull it off and my whims are not always unsuccessful.

13. If these expressions are dropped perhaps the result will be greater faith both in me and in the people I have trained to help me. . . .

15. It may be that the people I have chosen are failures, or that I have harmed them or that I am a bad teacher. If it is the case then it is better to tell me so straight out and not use hidden weapons against me. . . .

17. For my research I need a variety of material, not only what is artistic but also what is flawed. It is more difficult to eradicate faults than simply to develop secure talent. I need both people who are

artistically dull, static, somewhat anaemic and weak and also those who are on fire. I can only verify the things I am working on with a range of differing pupils. . . . If you do not deny others the right to have pupils who are thick, I would also like to be allowed that privilege.' (*SS*, V, pp. 456–8.)

Nemirovich's response was to try and head him off with flattery. The theatre, he wrote, was enjoying great success, becoming internationally famous; box-office receipts were good; he was at the height of his powers; he had *Hamlet* – why bother with trifles?

Seeing Stanislavski's determination to follow his own path, Nemirovich decided he must, once and for all, take absolute control of the management of the Art Theatre.

On February 24, 1911, the management committee met to discuss the future of the company. Kachalov, sensing a move to exclude Stanislavski, reacted strongly. He stated, quite categorically, that without him the theatre would not be the same:

> 'Yes it would be a good theatre, the best of theatres but not the Art Theatre.' (N-D Archive, No. 2248.)

Finally he lost his temper and threatened to quit.

Stanislavski then submitted a document setting out in thirty-eight paragraphs the conditions under which he would work for the following three years: a restricted workload, proper holidays, a decent attitude towards his immediate associates, particularly Sulerzhitski, and no more tragic roles. What he wanted, he repeated, was the possibility to teach. He further made it quite clear that he would, under no circumstances, assume any management responsibilities. This left the way open for Nemirovich and on May 7 new statutes were voted giving him full control. The powers of the management committee were reduced to a minimum. He was to all intents and purposes answerable only to the full meeting of the shareholders. Stanislavski raised no objections.

Nemirovich now had all the power he needed to get things back to normal, but he had to proceed with caution. Kachalov's outburst had been a warning. If Stanislavski left the theatre the chances were that senior members of the company would go with him. It was the old problem – how to control Stanislavski without incurring the accusation of exerting 'tutelage'. Personally, too, Nemirovich was in a cleft stick. He admired the positive side of Stanislavski's work, i.e. those aspects which concurred with his own practice. But there were other aspects which were deeply inimical to him. He rebelled against the notion that acting, an essentially mysterious and poetic process, could be reduced to a set of individual operations or, as he was to describe it later, in one of his periodic diatribes, to 'a crude, manufactured, artificial surrogate'. Worst of all, in his efforts to release the actor's creative potential, Stanislavski was distorting the author's intentions. Obedience to the letter of the text was central to Nemirovich's approach. The warning he had given Stanislavski at the beginning of their partnership, that there was to be no directoral tampering with major plays, was being consistently ignored.

Strategically, his first step had to be to gain access to Stanislavski's *Hamlet* rehearsals from which he had been more or less excluded. In August rehearsals both for *Hamlet* and for Nemirovich's production of Tolstoi's *The Living Corpse* began. Nemirovich proposed a return to their earlier partnership. He would attend the *Hamlet* rehearsals and Stanislavski would collaborate in the production of the Tolstoi.

Hamlet rehearsals began on Tuesday, August 2, with Nemirovich duly in attendance. He participated quite effectively in Stanislavski's exercises, then, doubtless to establish his authority in the matter, took it upon himself to give a lecture on the 'system' while its creator sat listening. Stanislavski felt that Nemirovich's explanation was no more than adequate but was nonetheless encouraged by this display of support, feeling that the *Hamlet* cast had finally been won round to his new method.

For Nemirovich the week was pure torture. Now he could only think of the 'system' as a kind of disease – the Stanislavski sickness (*stanislavshchina*) – that endangered the life of the theatre and threatened to infect him too. Since a direct confrontation was impossible he would need to employ more indirect, not to say devious, means. By Thursday the 4th he had found the solution. He would make the 'system' the official working method of the theatre which would bring it under his control as manager. Accordingly, on Friday, August 5, he made an announcement to the cast of *The Living Corpse*: they would work according to the 'system'. The week had taken its emotional toll. Nemirovich took refuge for the weekend in a hotel at the Chernichovski Monastery to calm down and sort out his ideas. On Sunday he was able to give his wife a lucid account of his strategy:

'The "Stanislavski-sickness", i.e. his awkward side with his per-sistence, or rather, his obstinacy and absurdity, is not so easy to get rid of. But as, when all's said and done, there is always some underlying artistic purpose, you are carried along. And that's one of the reasons why I came here, to spend some time alone, to find out whether I have not been dragged in and am not in danger in the future. I have reasons to be suspicious. I already feel it is the case. How I have unwittingly drifted away from the [original] plan. It's time to back-track before it is too late. We are a little off course. We have to go back to the beginning but that means a huge detour. . . . I have to agree that what he says is good, right, beautiful. . . . The trouble is I can't leave him alone with the actors. . . . I spent two days, Thursday and Friday, on something that Stanislavski has no way of refusing – that we apply his system to everything we work on (which is impossible). . . . Keep him within bounds in such a way that he will not notice and rear up, arrange things so that we can take what is useful in his theories. Others will be persuaded by his example. My intention is this, not to do it right away; Stanislavski will be obstructive all winter. . . . Better to delay at first so as to proceed calmly later.' (N-D Archive, No. 2286.)

Had Nemirovich been able to stick to his strategy he might have been successful. As it was the application of the 'system' to one of his own productions proved too much for him to take. He could be tolerant, indulgent even, during *Hamlet* rehearsals, but when it came to his own work it was another matter. Rehearsals for *The Living Corpse* resumed on August 8. On August 10 the cast spent the whole day, from 8 a.m. to 10.30 p.m., on the first scene – four pages. Stanislavski encountered strong resistance. Nemirovich then delivered another lecture on the 'system', probably to try and smooth things out, but what had begun reasonably enough turned into a diatribe.

An angry and bitter Stanislavski wrote to Lilina on August 13:

'. . . For a full hour Nemirovich stated that he had said all this before but that he was far from being in agreement with everything. Then in more heated tones – barking like some general – he went on to say that if we applied my system not only would we not finish analysing the play this year but not even next. I rejoined that it was each individual's responsibility to do this analysis at home and that it was easy. After that I had to endure another barrage. I was told I was a child, and credulous, they all talked nonsense at me. . . . In other words out came all the old stereotypes and clichés that have made my life in the theatre a misery.' (*SS*, VII, p. 532.)

Nemirovich's loss of control is surprising, considering how carefully he had worked out his strategy over the preceding weekend. The source of his irritation, to judge from Stanislavski's letter, seems to have been his perennial concern with schedules and time. Thanks to his efforts and his stringent control, the theatre was out of the red for the first time since it opened but this was not the moment to let things slide. Delays meant losses. *Hamlet* had been in preparation for three years already and still needed considerable rehearsal. Was *The Living Corpse*, under Stanislavski's influence, to go the same way? What would the financial effects be?

Stanislavski's response to Nemirovich's outburst was unexpected and devastating. He did not argue – that, he decided, was a waste of time and energy. He simply stopped going to rehearsals. Within forty-eight hours work on *The Living Corpse* came to a virtual halt. In a letter to his wife a shocked and shaken Nemirovich admitted that the ground had been cut from under his feet.

Fresh from his quarrels with Nemirovich, Stanislavski spent the remainder of the summer with the Kachalov family, including the young Vadim Shverubovich (Kachalov's real surname), whom he affectionately called Dima. In his *Memoirs* Shverubovich recalls that Stanislavski and Efros spent days discussing acting and the theatre in general. Stanislavski hoped that Efros would help him sort out the chaotic ideas that were in his head, and would find a more interesting way of expressing them. Stanislavski played his usual game: I am uneducated, I don't read and don't make notes. This was untrue as his notebooks are full of comments and his library contained many closely annotated volumes. But it soon became evident that his thoughts could not be reduced to the kind of clear, linear exposition in which Efros specialized. His thinking, as Shverubovich noted, sometimes seemed to defy logic, it was never dogmatic, the connections he made were untuitive, as in dreams. Above all, it was Stanislavski's talk, his gestures and movements, that gave richness to his ideas. This was almost impossible to contain within measured prose. The problem of getting his ideas down on paper was, and remained, a major obstacle in passing on his legacy in book form.

The summer over, a compromise had to be found at the theatre. At a board meeting on September 5, Nemirovich responded to Stanislavski's earlier demands for proper teaching facilities and recommended he be given support for his classes and his experiments with young actors. Again, this apparent concession was manipulative since these activities too, as part of the Art Theatre, came, on paper at least, under Nemirovich's jurisdiction. He could still, technically, intervene and apply his 'correctives'. But technically was not actually, as he discovered all too often. Whatever management structures he might set up everyone knew where the real creative power lay.

This incident prompted Stanislavski to a decision concerning his relationship to the Art Theatre. Hitherto he had been passive, responding to the management changes which Nemirovich organized, attempting to carve out a corner for himself where he could pursue his experiments. Now he decided that he could only teach effectively outside the main Art Theatre. He must turn to the young.

He decided, with encouragement from Gorki, to found not a school but a studio as he had done years earlier with Meierhold, a centre for learning, experiment and research. Rather than teach raw beginners he would form young actors who had sufficient experience of professional theatre to recognize their difficulties and know the problems involved but who were not yet fixed in their ways.

The obvious person to take charge of the Studio would be Sulerzhitski. Discussions on policy began:

'At one of the meetings Konstantin Sergeievich, explaining the purpose in establishing the Studio, said roughly the following:

The Studio exists thanks to the Art Theatre and for the sake of the Art Theatre, to help it.

It is concerned with the problems of the actor's creative process (system), the educational formation of the artist, providing him with a set of practices, help through daily exercises and, perhaps, in future, parallel performances.

. . . It provides new experiments on the creative process common to authors, actors and directors in the making of plays (Gorki's method). Experiments in décor, lighting effects and the possibilities of the stage. Experiments in mime for large-scale productions. Experiments on the management side. Research into proper methods of theatrical management.

. . . For that purpose, so as to learn who among the company of the Moscow Art Theatre wished to take part in these activities, Konstantin Sergeievich put up a list, on which each member of the company was to indicate his wishes by signing in the appropriate column.' (Sulerzhitski, Notes on the Studio, September 1912. Sulerzhitski Archive, No. 6477/47.)

Who were to be the founder members? Boleslavski was a natural candidate. Sulerzhitski drew up a list of others. At the top came two names: Evgeni Vakhtangov and Michael Chekhov. Stanislavski added his own comments. Of Vakhtangov he said, 'Can turn himself into a good teacher and director. Forget him as an actor.'

Vakhtangov had entered the Art Theatre in March 1911 as a result of an interview Sulerzhitski had arranged with Nemirovich. He very soon attracted attention by the completeness and accuracy of the notes he took during rehearsals. He learned and mastered the elements of the 'system' with amazing speed so that by August Stanislavski was using him to take classes and direct exercises with small groups of young actors who were involved in Tolstoi's *The Living Corpse*. Stanislavski, aware that allegiance to the 'system' could be damaging to his career, and learning from Sulerzhitski's unfortunate experiences, warned him of the intrigue which existed in the theatre, and put him under his personal protection.

Stanislavski had auditioned Michael Chekhov in April, 1912, when he had seen two pieces – an extract from *Tsar Fiodor* and one of Marmeladov's speeches from *Crime and Punishment*. He had immediately asked him to join the company. Adding his comments to Sulerzhitski's list he noted, 'Talented, has charm. One of the real hopes for the future.' Also included on the list was Maria Ouspenskaia, who, with Boleslavski, was to found, in 1925, the highly influential American Laboratory Theatre. The original group of members was small but Stanislavski tried to open out the work of the studio as much as possible. He put up the following notice:

'Anyone wishing to give a reading, perform an extract, submit model sets, show the results of their research into stage techniques, or offer some literary material for staging, should kindly inscribe their names in the book specially provided in the hall of the studio. The book is lodged with the porter, Baranov.' (In *O Stanislavskom*, p. 366.)

The new young company were subjected to a gruelling workload. They had to fulfil their obligations to the main company, attend classes at the studio and rehearse any plays they wished to put on in whatever free time was left to them, mainly late at night. The facilities they enjoyed were modest: some rooms over a cinema, the Cinematograph (later known as the Lux). The theatre was tiny; a small stage on a level with the front row, a low ceiling, almost no wing space and a raked auditorium with room for about fifty people. But this time Stanislavski had judged the situation aright. He had succeeded in attracting major talent and provided the opportunity for a release of fresh creative energy.

The First Studio did not get off to an entirely propitious start. In October 1913 Vakhtangov directed his first production, Hauptmann's *Das Friedensfest*. It was extremely tendentious, stressed all the negative aspects of the situation in terms of overt social criticism, thus violating Stanislavski's basic tenet that a production should always present counterbalancing forces and reveal its meaning to an audience, not force it on them. After the dress rehearsal, a white-faced Stanislavski, more angry than anyone had ever seen him, threatened to cancel the show. Sulerzhitski and Nemirovich backed him. It was only Kachalov's intervention that persuaded him to let the production go forward. The incident caused a breach between Stanislavski and Vakhtangov that was never entirely healed.

The Studio rapidly took on a life and character of its own, shaped by the talents of its members. New students, however, still needed training and it seemed to Stanislavski that he had to start afresh with each new generation; the Second Studio was created in 1916, the Third, which was in fact a school created by Vakhtangov, in 1920 and the Fourth in 1921. An Opera Studio was started in 1918.

Such developments had damaging side-effects on the Art Theatre proper. It meant that genuine new talent was being siphoned off. As for Stanislavski, he continued to act and to direct plays of his choice but his heart was with his students. His productions were, essentially, a way of teaching. For this reason, rehearsals for *Le Malade Imaginaire* in 1913 were conducted at the Studio rather than the main house. They were open to anyone interested in the practicalities of the 'system'. Many actors not connected with the production did turn up. In a letter to Vladimir Gribunin, written in March 1916, Nemirovich noted ruefully that once he had a powerful ally in Stanislavski; now he had lost him to the Studio.

CHAPTER EIGHTEEN

PHYSICAL TECHNIQUE

Stanislavski the actor was not necessarily restricted to the 'system' he taught. His own working method was more complex than his theories and his response to his own needs as a performer inevitably pushed him beyond anything he had formulated as a teacher. Even if justifiable claims can be made for the scientific nature of the 'system', the fact remains that its formulation depended on Stanislavski's capacity to analyse his own practice and that practice could not, except within certain general limits, be anticipated. It always produced change. There is a constant time-lag between personal practice as recorded in the *Notebooks* and the 'system' as publicly proclaimed. The result of this evident discrepancy between words and deeds produced some sharp criticism, notably from Vakhtangov, who felt he was betraying his own ideals.

His first attempt to put the 'system' into practice, as Rakitin in *A Month in the Country*, had been a psychological exercise. He had deliberately kept the character within narrow physical bounds. A year later, in 1910, he was confronted with a character, General Krutitski in Ostrovski's *Enough Stupidity in Every Wise Man*, which posed the whole question of the relationship of internal and external characterization. Stanislavski the actor could not get away from the highly developed visual imagination of Stanislavski the director. Despite his insistence on the supreme importance of the psychological aspects of a role he had a strong sense of any character's appearance and an exceptional capacity for physical transformation. Yet, knowing the errors a purely external approach had produced in the past, he was suspicious of using it. Even so, in October 1909, when preparing Rakitin, he had allowed Stakhovich to demonstrate the role to him and had then copied him. This had led him along a false path, away from Turgenev. In the end he had had to start afresh, using himself as a base. Yet he had been right in one important respect. Clarity concerning internal processes did not, as he had assumed, automatically lead to clear physical characterization.

He started work on General Krutitski in January 1910 with Nemirovich directing. The rehearsals followed Nemirovich's usual pattern: literary analyses, study of period material and photographs. Out of all Nemirovich's brilliant exposition Stanislavski retained only one phrase, a reference to Ostrovski's 'epic calm'. It was an expression he hung on to. He did his own independent research. He began to develop an external image but the part would not come together psychologically. The problem lay in the very first stage of the creative process as he then defined it: the stimulation of the will, the engagement of the actor's interest and personality. Yet the answer came not from psychological investigation or from 'affective memory' but, as so often in the past, from an accidental external stimulus:

'How many photographs, sketches, portraits I was show, how many did I find for myself that seemed to correspond with the external appearance of the role. We even managed to find out which general Ostrovski had taken as a model when creating Krutitski. But I did not know him and for all this material could not feel my Krutitski.

Then the following thing happened. I had, for professional reasons, to go to what is called an "orphans' court". . . . The house, its customs, the people were bowed down under the weight of the ancient moss that covered them. In the courtyard of this institution . . . a small additional rickety, moss-covered building, and in it an old fellow (who did not look in the least like my make-up) writing, writing, writing, like General Krutitski, plans which were of no use to anybody. The overall impression I received from the building and its solitary occupant suggested to me what the face, make-up and bearing of my general should be. And there too *epic calm* had its influence. The external and internal forms of the role, which I had found by chance, came together, so that a role which had started following the line of "the interplay of forms and passions" was suddenly transformed into something else, following the line of "intuition and feeling", for me the only one of any value.' (*SS*, I, pp. 427–8.)

Once the block had been removed the historical and period aspects of the role fell into place. When the play opened on March 11, 1910, the role was recognized as one of his most significant achievements. Not only had he created the individual personality of this decaying general, who had power without sense, but had symbolized a whole era and a whole section of Russian society.

The role was also a masterpiece of physical transformation. In April, during the St Petersburg tour, Mrs Gurevich met Stanislavski in the wings. She did not recognize him. She wondered who this old general, who was holding out his hand to her, could be. It took a short conversation to make her realize whom she was really talking to.

Yet Stanislavski could still go over the top on externals and this he did in his next production, *A Provincial Lady*, which formed part of a Turgenev triple bill. He was cast as Count Liubin, the sophisticate from St Petersburg who goes down to the country and is humbled. He worked out the internal logic of the character's development in scrupulous detail but when it came to the make-up he allowed himself to be carried away. When the play opened on March 5, 1912, Efros commented:

> 'There was laughter all the time in the house. People had never laughed so much, or so it seems, at the Art Theatre. And the exaggeration was subtle, brilliant, with many exquisite details.
>
> Only Count Liubin's external appearance was overdone by Stanislavski. He had gone too far with the make-up so that the Count ceased to be a real character and the acting became laboured.' (N. Efros, in *Rech*, March 8, 1912.)

Stanislavski's difficulties became particularly acute when he was alone, preparing the annual production of his own choice. It was nothing new for him to work simultaneously as actor and director and negotiate the difficult balance of interests involved. Now, in addition he was attempting to justify, teach and verify the 'system'. This meant that, at a moment when he was making more demands on himself as an artist, energies which should have been devoted entirely to the creation of a role were being dispersed. It also meant, more importantly, that he could not fulfil the primary objective of the 'system' itself: to use conscious means to stimulate unconscious creative processes and then give them free rein. Involved as he was, inevitably, in endless verification and analysis, he was continuously inhibiting the free run of his imagination, or if his imagination was functioning he was unable to accept unquestioningly solutions which he had instinctively or intuitively found.

He was also beginning to confuse rehearsing and teaching, to the detriment of the production as a whole. Rehearsal was no longer work towards a performance but an end in itself. In Nemirovich's view Stanislavski wasted a great deal of time, and money, by turning every working session into an acting class. At the end of August 1911 he had come into a rehearsal where Stanislavski was working with a young actor, Sushkevich, on his one line in Tolstoi's *The Living Corpse*. It was a simple announcement but Stanislavski made his pupils speak it a dozen different ways, in a dozen different characterizations, from the adolescent to the senile, on the grounds that a creative actor should be able to offer the director a choice. Nemirovich made it clear that he was not interested in a gallery of characters but in a straight line delivered straight.

Having tried out the 'system' on classic tragedy with *Hamlet*, Stanislavski turned now to classic comedy, *Le Malade Imaginaire*. He was still looking outside the company for other collaborators. An entry in his notebook in the autumn of 1907 advises him to keep an eye on the theatre designer Alexandre Benois and his group in St Petersburg. The two men met in 1908 and, in 1909, discussed the possibility of working together. The interminable preparations for *Hamlet* and Stanislavski's illness kept the two men apart until 1912. When they did come together they had some initial difficulty in reaching agreement on the sets. Benois' preliminary sketches were too ornate, too 'theatrical' for Stanislavski's taste. They seemed to veer towards the School of Representation and the Molière 'tradition' he had been fighting for years. As with previous productions, he refused to glamorize an essentially bourgeois milieu. Writing to his wife on September 15, 1912, the day of the first read-through, Nemirovich, who was also to collaborate with Benois on *Le Mariage Forcé* which was to complete the evening, stated that he felt he had found a genuine ally. Benois put Stanislavski in his place much as from time to time he himself did. Nonetheless, although Benois was responsible for the staging of the last act, it was Stanislavski's views which prevailed.

As was now his accepted practice the play was broken down into bits during the first session. Stanislavski's final bits for Act One were:

'1. Argan's exposition (analyses his illness);
2. Subjugation of everyone by the petty tyrant (Argan) to his illness;
3. Toinette's opposition;
4. Angélique's personal life counter to her father's life (revolution);
5. Despotism over daughter;
6. Exploitation of the petty tyrant (wife overcomes him; subjugation of petty tyranny by the insolence of the wife);
7. Conflict between two plots (camps) Toinette and Béline (Béline won, wife robbed);
8. Plot of second act – Toinette's campaign.' (Rehearsal daybook, January 19, 1913.)

As far as his own work as an actor was concerned, Stanislavski also developed a method of working within and through the bits which would appear to show the influence of his conversations with Gorki. It consisted of a kind of personal, internal improvisation:

'Studying the text of a role. In the current year (1912–1913) I divide the work into *large bits* clarifying the nature of each bit. Then, immediately, in my own words, I play each bit, observing all the curves. Then I go through the experiences of each bit ten times or so with its curves (not in a fixed way, not being consistent). Then I follow the successive bits in the book. And finally, I make the transition, imperceptibly, to the experiences as expressed in the actual words of the part.' (Notes, K.S. Archive, No. 1586/1.)

There remained the problem of physicalizing the role. Stanislavski turned once again, rather surprisingly considering his earlier experience, to Stakhovich, asking him to demonstrate the characteristics of French behaviour. Why Stanislavski, with his extensive knowledge of France and the French, should have needed this is not at all clear. It may simply be that as an actor in the throes of creating a role he needed some kind, any kind, of outside eye. The results were no better than before.

Towards the end of March 1913 he noted:

'Stakhovich showed me how to play a Frenchman (*Malade Imaginaire*). I easily seized on the external aspect from a visual impression and then during the process of experiencing the part in terms of my own personality I slipped over into an external imitation of Stakhovich. The result was clichés, everything became a muddle. To get back to a living state I had to 1) either cut free from Stakhovich and go back to myself or 2) capture in the French psychology Stakhovich had outlined for me what it was that made him [Argan] precisely what he was and not just wave my hands and rush about. . . . I tried to discover in myself, in my own individual psychology, fused with the role, and add to the common state (or kernel) [elements of] conceit and despotism. 3) I tried to discover in myself a completely different external image (Stakhovich portrayed an aristocrat, I was a bourgeois). During subsequent attempts things came together by chance, i.e. the psychological side experienced earlier merged with the external image I had discovered quite separately. A character is sometimes formed psychologically, i.e. from the inner image of the role, but at other times it is discovered through purely external exploration.' (K.S. Archive, No. 927.)

This recognition of the creative function of external elements, of the interpenetration of outward and inward, of the notion that an external action might subsequently be justified internally represented a marked shift of position. The 'system' as taught to his pupils stated that physical action was always the reflection of a previously discovered psychological truth. This move away from the purely psychological did not immediately get into the official version of the 'system'.

The production as a whole ran into a more fundamental difficulty. Stanislavski had misunderstood the central message of the play, the 'supertask' as it came to be known. It is the 'supertask' which determines the contents of the individual bits and the nature of the characters' motivations. Stanislavski saw the play very clearly as a mordant satire on the medical profession in Molière's time. He could not understand, therefore, why the production was increasingly plunged into gloom. The fact was that he had defined a wrong 'kernel', as he then called it, and taken the wrong through-line on his character:

'Initially we approached the play in a very simplistic fashion defining the supertask as "I want to be ill". The greater my efforts to achieve that and the more I succeeded, the more it became obvious that we were turning a satirical comedy into a pathological tragedy about illness.

But we quickly grasped our error and defined the despot's supertask as "I want people to think I am ill". With that the comic aspect of the play suddenly came alive, the basis for exploitation by a group of charlatans from the medical world had been created and a tragedy was suddenly transformed into a malicious comedy.' (*SS*, II, pp. 336–7.)

The play finally opened on March 27, 1913, to overall if not universal critical acclaim.

Stanislavski's own personal success as Argan, and Lilina's as Toinette, were immense. Reviewing the production on the 29th, Efros noted Stanislavski's capacity to exploit all the traditions of farce, to indulge in all the *bouffonades* and at the same time create a living character possessed of an inner emotional logic. He also considered the make-up and general physical characterization one of Stanislavski's finest achievements and, indeed, just as the skinny Stockman had replaced the overweight Astrov, so the scraggy Krutitski with his wispy hair and beard was replaced by a human dumpling. If there was a qualitative difference in the more recent performances it was in a move towards the realm of the grotesque but a grotesque which was inwardly justified and had nothing to do, as Stanislavski had written to Mrs Gurevich on March 14, with Meierhold's stylized offerings.

Stanislavski did not anticipate any personal difficulties with his next production, Goldoni's *La Locandiera*. He had already directed and played in it in 1898. His prime intention, as he had announced in April 1913, was to provide a showcase for Gzovskaia. The designer would once again be Benois while he himself would resume the role of the self-styled woman-hater Count Ripafratta. The 1898 performance had been a somewhat perfunctory affair, staged fairly rapidly. General critical opinion at the time had been that the role did not develop after Act One. Yet he assumed that he would more or less be able to walk through the part. He was wrong. Neither here nor in *Mozart and Salieri* of 1915 nor in the disastrous *Village of Stepanchikovo* of 1917 did he have anything but an agonizing struggle.

He was happy with the first reading which took place in the first week of September 1913 and felt equally at ease during early rehearsals. He was taken aback when one or two colleagues, including Vishnievski, pointed out that he was merely producing clichés. His immediate, somewhat paranoid reaction, was to assume they were merely attacking the 'system' but he had to admit, finally, that they were right. The 'system' aimed at producing acting that was natural and simple but he had made the fundamental error of trying to play the results of the 'system' and not its process. He was playing not the character but 'simplicity'. Just as he had discovered earlier that it is possible to gather together a set of clichés that superficially look 'natural' so it was possible to collect a set of clichés that looked 'simple':

'The greater half of our work was aimed at being simple, as in life, and nothing else. . . . When you want to be simple, all you think about is being simple and not the basic tasks of the role or the play and so you begin to act being simple. What you get are clichés of being simple, the worst clichés of all.' (*SS*, V, p. 521.)

He, no less than the rest of the cast, had to go back to basics. He had to establish a set of concrete tasks and look for elements of the character in himself, and find the 'affective kernel'. This was not easy. He was a man who was fond of women and enjoyed their company. He did, however, recall an uncomfortable acquaintance of his wife's who had made him uneasy and remembered how he disliked overweight, overbearing women. He also came to the conclusion that he could be very naïve when it came to the affairs of the heart. But progress was slow and Nemirovich did not help the situation by coming in to the rehearsal and suggesting a quite different and, from Stanislavski's view, quite unworkable, line on the part. Vishnievski suggested that the cast should familiarize themselves with the inn itself, its lay-out and contents. He also suggested to Stanislavski that he should rehearse the play in his own person, believing in the situation and believing himself actually to be afraid.

Many sleepless nights were spent going through the part, scene by scene, allowing the imagination to wander and suggest ideas. But all too often what had seemed clear in the darkness of the bedroom disappeared in rehearsal. Recalling perhaps his encounter with the *commedia* three years earlier, he began to see the character in terms of Captain Spavento, the loud-mouthed but essentially cowardly soldier. Benois suggested that there were also elements of Don Quixote in the Count and provided him with a sketch which was half one and half the other. Stanislavski achieved the remarkable feat of combining both sets of characteristics.

At fifty-one, Stanislavski was essentially too old for the part. He found a vocal solution, concentrating on the head-notes rather than the lower register to give the voice lightness and youth. Yet good as his work on his individual role might be, the play, like *Le Malade Imaginaire*, had ceased to be funny. The problem once more lay in the overall concept. Stanislavski needed to step back from his detailed work and redefine his through-line, his 'kernel' or supertask:

'. . . at first we defined the supertask as "I want to hate women" (misogyny) but this stopped the play from being either funny or effective. Once I had understood that the hero liked women and did not actually wish to be a misogynist but only appear so, then the supertask became "I want to woo them secretly" (simulating misogyny) and the play suddenly came to life.' (*SS*, II, p. 337.)

By the time the play opened on February 3, 1914, it had received 112 rehearsals, as opposed to seventeen for their original production, but the time, effort and struggle payed off. This time Stanislavski succeeded in making the character develop, presenting new facets with each succeeding act. His performance also gave the impression of being effortless. In a review in *Odesskii Novosti* on February 9, Efros described the performance as almost improvised, 'it sparkled with unexpected and beautiful comic details'. Stanislavski's application of his ideas was superior and more consistent than any other member of the cast. Lvov, writing in *Novosti Sezona* on the 4th referred to a 'cascade of glittering nuances'. Instead of the usual loud-mouthed upstart, Stanislavski had presented a noble, simple man, 'a great big boy in his love for the lady of the house'. The reaction to the performance during the spring St Petersburg tour confirmed his success. Whatever his private difficulties he still remained for the public the supreme actor of his time.

CHAPTER NINETEEN

THE VILLAGE OF STEPANCHIKOVO, MY TRAGEDY

The period preceding the outbreak of the First World War was rich in promise for the theatre's wider, international reputation. While both Nemirovich and Stanislavski declared themselves depressed when they thought of the future, though for entirely different reasons, the rest of the world was still catching up with their achievements. Apart from staging its own productions the Art Theatre had served as host to concerts and musical evenings. Besides Rachmaninov and Chaliapin, who were already his friends, Stanislavski had attracted musicians of the calibre of the conductor Serge Kussevitsky and the harpsichordist Wanda Landowska. All the people he drew to him shared one thing in common: high energy, drive, and an almost obsessive sense of purpose.

The Art Theatre increasingly attracted visitors from abroad. In January 1913 Beerbohm Tree arrived in Moscow specifically to see *Hamlet*, which he attended on the 16th, accompanied by Isadora. According to Lilina, who was still in correspondence with Craig, the performance was below par. Kachalov was ill and played very slowly. Knipper was also ill and had been replaced by an understudy. After the show Stanislavski gave a supper party at the Hermitage Theatre where Isadora improvised a dance with Scriabin at the piano. A year later H. G. Wells arrived and on January 21 saw Stanislavski, who was playing despite a very high temperature, in *Three Sisters*. Wells immediately tried to persuade the company to come to London on tour with a repertoire of Chekhov. This invitation was matched on March 12 by a telegram from Norman Hapgood inviting the Art Theatre to New York. In the interim Harley Granville-Barker paid a visit, arriving on February 14, with the intention of studying the theatre's working methods. He held a long conversation with Stanislavski during which it was decided that he would send over two pupils. Significantly he chose to place them in the Studio rather than with the main company.

One can only conjecture what the history of western theatre might have been had these plans come to fruition, had not the war and the revolution intervened. In the event it was ten years before the Art Theatre went to the United States and forty-three years before it set foot for the first time on a London stage.

In June 1914 Stanislavski joined Lilina in Marienbad, where he found Kachalov and his family, Efros, Mrs Gurevich and Leonidov. They were joined later in the month by Nemirovich-Danchenko and on July 15 (July 2, Old Style) they all marked the tenth anniversary of Chekhov's death.

Stanislavski once again used the summer break to marshal material for his book on the 'system'. Central to his concerns was the question whether the actor feels any emotion during performance or whether he technically reproduces the external signs of emotion, the opposition between what Shchepkin had called the actor of feeling and the actor of reason. He was working on the manuscript of *Various Trends in the Art of Theatre* which he had started in 1909, and in which he outlined various approaches to acting. With Mrs Gurevich he embarked on a study of eighteenth-century French theatre. He read Luigi Riccoboni's *Pensées sur la Déclamation* (1738), which emphasized the need for the actor to experience feelings, and François Riccoboni's *L'Art du Théâtre* (1750), which advocated the opposite view, Rémond de Saint-Albin's *Le Comédien* (1747) and Diderot's notes on Sticcoti's *Garrick ou les Acteurs Anglais* (1769). This led to an examination of Diderot's *Paradoxe sur le Comédien* and a discussion of the conflict between Mlle Clairon, who represented reason, and Mlle Dumesnil, who represented feeling. Both had set out their views in their respective *Mémoires* (1798 and 1800). He also read Adrienne Lecouvreur's letters. Lecouvreur was famous for the simplicity, intelligence and directness of her style. In the margin of his copy he noted that Lecouvreur 'was the first to relate to her partner and not to the audience' and 'she instinctively followed Molière's advice: speak your lines the way people speak'. He also looked at Doré's *Les Déclamations Théâtrales* (1771) and Fournelle's *Curiosités Théâtrales* (1859) which further illuminated the conflict between the School of Representation and the School of Lived Experience. He made extensive notes on Coquelin's *L'Art du Comédien* (1894). He discussed the great tragedian Talma. Mrs Gurevich then surveyed for him the history of eighteenth- and nineteenth-century theatre, outlining in particular the ideas of Lessing, Goethe and Schiller. From Bram Stoker's biography of Irving he took over the notion of the perspective of a role.

The group of friends dispersed, agreeing to meet up later. Only Stanislavski, Lilina, Kachalov and Gurevich remained in Marienbad. Stanislavski became increasingly alarmed as Europe moved towards hostilities. On July 27 (July 14) he wrote to Nemirovich-Danchenko telling him he could not sleep for fear there would be a war. On the same day he wrote to Sulerzhitski about the difficulties of getting back to Russia. No train tickets were available as troops were being mobilized. He was, according to Gurevich, 'in a panic'.

He had good reason. On August 4 (July 22) Germany invaded

Belgium. The group left Marienbad for Munich so that they could make their way to the Swiss frontier and thence to Russia. There were posters proclaiming mobilization everywhere. They reached Immerstadt on the Swiss frontier on August 3 (July 21). German soldiers suddenly appeared in the train and, as Stanislavski later described it, 'in cliché-ridden military tones' yelled: 'Russian spies! Off!' Luggage was thrown out of the windows. They were the first prisoners of war. Stanislavski, with his limited German, understood that only lack of ammunition prevented them from being shot there and then. They were then put on a train first to Kempten and then to Lindau on Lake Constance. During the long slow journey through the night Stanislavski expressed his thoughts to Mrs Gurevich:

> '. . . in that moment he could contemplate life from a kind of imper-
> sonal height and nothing seemed frightening. He said that events of
> recent days had given him a clear impression of the superficiality of all
> that was called human culture, bourgeois culture, that a completely
> different kind of life was needed, where all needs were reduced to the
> minimum, where there was work – real artistic work – on behalf of the
> people, for those who had not yet been consumed by this bourgeois
> culture.' (L. Y. Gurevich, in *Russkaia Misl*, Bk X, p. 153.)

Once in Lindau, all the prisoners were put in the fortress. It seemed to Stanislavski that the Germans were determined to put on an impressive and intimidating display of their military smartness and strength. On August 5 (July 23), the day after Russia's entry into the war, they were put on a boat to cross the lake to Switzerland.

Stanislavski, Lilina, Kachalov and Gurevich eventually arrived in Bern where other Russian friends, equally stranded, joined them. Stanislavski calmed down after his adventures but he had been profoundly shaken. Sometimes he would not come out of his room for days. He was supplied with German, Swiss German, French and Italian newspapers and, with the aid of dictionaries, translated important passages into the notebooks usually reserved for his thoughts on the 'system'.

As for so many others, August 1914 was a turning point in Stanislavski's life. One world came to an end and another, much less certain, began. Indeed, these events were but the first in a series of upheavals that was to undermine his sense of security in almost every domain. Up till then, whatever the difficulties, the bitter battles with colleagues, he had always had a measure of control, a freedom to choose alternative paths; now he was for the first time in his life rich but penniless, powerless and dependent on events or perhaps even the whim of others. His mind was paralysed. He was, as his companions realized, incapable of making decisions. He was a bundle of nerves, tormented by endless anxieties. It seemed to him impossible to get back safely to

Russia but, at the same time, he was horrified at the thought of being imprisoned or interned.

It was his colleague Podgorni who decided to take the initiative. He produced a plan for their return which he hoped Stanislavski would approve. There was a boat of the Messagerie Maritime leaving Marseilles for Odessa in early September. First-class tickets were brought on credit. The journey to Marseilles, via Geneva, was paid for by friends. The task was now to persuade Stanislavski that this was a viable plan. Such a journey involved passing through the Dardanelles and Stanislavski, like so many of his generation, was terrified by the Turks, who, he rightly suspected, would enter the war on the German side. His companions drew up a list of his anxieties and agreed that certain subjects were never to be mentioned – German cruisers or any kind of naval activity in the Mediterranean, the Turks, or cholera and dysentery in ports of call along the way. The conspiracy of silence was successful and Stanislavski arrived back in Moscow on September 14 (Old Style).

If anything positive emerged from this traumatic experience it was a strengthening of Stanislavski's dedication to his own country, to his Russian-ness. Provided what was truly Russian was preserved, personal sacrifice did not matter. In Bern, in discussion with younger colleagues, he constantly stressed the need to understand the differences between cultures and civilizations. It was no good Russians emptily imitating the externals of other cultures, that could only lead to the destruction of Russian culture itself. At a more practical level, as his contribution to the national effort, he planned to switch the Alekseiev factories from the manufacture of gold and silver thread to electrical cables – a plan that was, in fact, implemented after the Revolution when the factories had been nationalized. This deep patriotism is evident in the artistic decisions he took immediately after his return to Moscow.

Within two days of his return to Moscow on September 14, ignoring the fact that he had no real authority to do so, Stanislavski called a special meeting, demanding that the theatre be even more strongly aware of its artistic mission. The repertoire must be examined and cleansed of all superficiality both in form and content. There was to be no running after cheap success just for the sake of making money. As chance would have it, the new season was to include a revival of Russia's greatest play, *Woe from Wit*. The theatre's next patriotic contribution to the war was a presentation of a triple bill by Pushkin – *The Stone Guest*, *A Feast During the Plague* and *Mozart and Salieri*. Stanislavski, Benois and Nemirovich were to be jointly responsible for the evening.

In Stanislavski's mind the task of presenting theatre purified of trivia was synonymous with the development of the 'system'. Only this approach, rooted as it was in the legacy of Pushkin, Gogol and Shchepkin, in the heart of the Russian tradition, could adequately present human truth at a time when that truth was needed.

The work he had done with Mrs Gurevich had clarified his mind and some of the major principles of the 'system' emerged in September/October 1914 during work on *Woe from Wit* and *Mozart and Salieri*. One of the rehearsals for *Woe from Wit* attended by Nemirovich, Lilina, Knipper, Sulerzhitski, and Podgorni, turned into something of a master-class. Stanislavski for the first time formulated in public his notion of the state of 'I am being', a verbal form which he coined.* The 'I am being' is a state of creative readiness, the moment in the preparation of the role when the boundary between the actor's personality and the character becomes blurred and a symbiotic relationship, the actor/role, emerges and the actor's subconscious takes over, allowing him to behave *as if* he were the character.

The initial, the crucial, problem for the actor is achieving that state. The trouble with most actors, Stanislavski told his colleagues, is that they try to force emotion out of themselves without reference to what is going on around them or to the other actors on stage with them. 'Be still,' he told them, 'look closely at the world around you, try to understand it, appreciate it, so to speak, through the senses, understand your relationship to it.'

He then explained the basic principle on which all his later work was founded: that a performance is based on a definition of action, not on a search for emotion. Stanislavski asked his visitors to consider very carefully the essential difference between two questions:

"'What would I be like, how would I feel, if this were May 31?" That is one way of putting the question, but there is a second way, "What would I do if this were May 31?". Can you see the difference between the two? It is of enormous significance. You must ask the kinds of questions that lead to dynamic action.' (Rehearsal notes from *Woe from Wit*, K.S. Archive, No. 1306.)

The revival of *Woe from Wit* did nothing to improve relations between Nemirovich and Stanislavski. They had been quarrelling for years and always on the same subject: the director's relationship and responsibility to the author. After a rehearsal of *A Provincial Lady* in February 1912, when Nemirovich had accused Stanislavski, who was playing Liubin, of distorting Turgenev's intentions, Stanislavski had retorted that the part as written was not interesting. Stanislavski had then blocked all Nemirovich's attempts to interfere in the production of *La Locandiera* earlier in the year. But *Woe from Wit* is the great Russian classic play and Nemirovich obviously felt that something drastic had to be done. When he failed to bring Stanislavski round to his point of view, he brought in a

* The verb 'to be' (*est'*) exists only in the infinitive in Russian. For the rest it is omitted. Stanislavski used the form *Ya esm'* which no one would normally use, thus marking the very particular state he had in mind.

literary historian, Professor Piksanov, who was insistent that an actor should follow the writer's directions:

'. . . it would be desirable to keep not only to the text of *Woe from Wit* but also to the *author's comments*; highly desirable to adhere strictly to the author's instructions.' (N-D Archive, No. 48/1-2.)

Stanislavski's reply was typical and robust:

'Stanislavski referred to Gogol's letter, in which, in reply to the complaints of one of his correspondents about the lack of new plays, he wrote that every old play, staged in a new, open way, was a work of art. Gogol wrote: "Take any play of Schiller or Shakespeare and stage it as contemporary art demands." "And that," Stanislavski said, "always gives me the courage to change things, adapting to what's needed, to the actor's inner experiences." Then he recalled that Chekhov had written Epikhodov [*The Cherry Orchard*] as old, fat and short of breath; Moskvin played him very young and not short of breath, and when Chekhov saw him, he was delighted and grateful because the actor had shown him the character he himself would have liked to create.' (K.S. Archive, No. 3328.)

After the opening, Nemirovich wrote to Stanislavski on November 10: 'The rehearsals for *Woe from Wit* show that we are as far apart as ever we were'. As a footnote it is worth recording that despite his theoretical agreement with Nemirovich, fifty years later Piksanov recorded his appreciation of Stanislavski's performance.

Relations between Stanislavski and Nemirovich deteriorated still further at the beginning of the following year. The cause was the First Studio. In the autumn of 1914 it had moved into more spacious premises and by the end of the season had established itself as the centre for original work and expressive acting. Efros considered the adaptation of Dickens' *The Cricket on the Hearth* to be the best production he had seen that season.

This caused Nemirovich great alarm. Like it or not, without Stanislavski's full involvement the Moscow Art Theatre lost its creative impetus and drive. In January 1915 he wrote two crucial letters, one purely formal, the other highly personal. On January 9 he informed Stanislavski, as a courtesy, that he would be putting forward certain proposals to the management committee, of which Stanislavski was no longer a member. He was not, he assured Stanislavski, avoiding a preliminary meeting with him but:

'. . . I think our discussions can only have essential meaning when there is a certain attitude on your side, one where there is no hostility and suspicion . . . In such cases it is better to keep things on a formal level and for both of us to rely on the decisions of the Committee. So, if you have a real need to have access to my plans . . . then please arrange a time and place at your convenience. I will always try to make myself available.' (*MATL*, No. 330.)

Nemirovich had good reason to conceal his plans from Stanislavski since the purpose of the meeting was to discuss the First Studio and its adverse impact on the theatre. The meeting revealed the depth of resentment the Studio had aroused, the feeling that it had done irreparable damage to the main company. The answer was to sever all connection between the Studio and the Art Theatre and get Stanislavski back, full-time, to the main house. It was also decided to set up a group to monitor the Studio's activities. On May 15 another meeting was held to which again Stanislavski was not invited.

Whatever measures Nemirovich might take at management level they did not reduce his personal sense of frustration and anger. This resulted in another of his huge, denunciatory letters in which he set out all his fundamental disagreements with Stanislavski, every grievance he had felt, his continuing sense that the vital contribution he had made to the theatre's and Stanislavski's successes were unappreciated, and that he was being excluded. The cause of all their problems lay in Stanislavski's character:

'Your monstrous ambition, which is ostensibly burned out but is not burned out and never will be – intolerance of anyone near you.
    . . . Why can't you come to terms with the fact that you aren't God? That you are just a man. And dear to all of us precisely because we know your great, human qualities, for the sake of which we forgive your simple, human faults.' (*MATL*, No. 329.)

Stanislavski does not appear to have replied. He had to all intents and purposes written off the Art Theatre except as a place where he could continue his work on the 'system'. He began rehearsals for *Mozart and Salieri* which he again used as a kind of laboratory experiment which would help him write the 'system'.

Whatever difficulties Stanislavski might have had with his previous two roles, they paled in comparison with the problems he encountered with Salieri. His concern to research the 'system' was having a damaging effect on his ability to perform. Nemirovich had seen the dangers. On November 10, 1914, he had written to Stanislavski, pointing out that his performance as Vershinin had gone off because he was over-complicating the issue:

'. . . either I really don't understand your 'system' or (*listen please*) you are so busy with the means that you lose sight of the end. Aren't you changing the role of prophet for that of sacrificial priest?' (*Iz. Pis.*, p. 321.)

A month later he was able to write again saying the performance was back to normal.

Stanislavski decided that the process of creating Salieri would form the basis of a book, *The History of a Role*, which would provide a practical illustration of his working method. He received almost no direction and consequently no challenge. Nemirovich was wholly occupied with *The Stone Ghost*, with Kachalov, while Benois was concentrated on design. Between the beginning of January 1915 and the opening on March 26 Stanislavski worked steadily on the role, making notes as he went. First came the problem of the through-action:

'1. Salieri is a villain, a man of envy. Straight to the point – to hate Mozart, censure, cavil at everything about him. He turns out to be a theatrical villain.

2. A more subtle notion of envy. I want to be first and therefore I get rid of Mozart, although I have nothing really against him.

3. The most characteristic thing for Pushkin is defiance of God. Struggle with God.

4. An assault on injustice and therefore a desire (cowardly) to escape from oppression and injustice.' (*SS*, V, p. 527.)

He then created a history of Salieri's artistic development, defining his attitudes to other composers, based on material in the soliloquies, filling the role out by imagining the character's memory of every incident. The result was a full biography, with every circumstance of the character's off-stage life vividly experienced. But, as with Vershinin, he had once more lost sight of the end, of the play itself. The subtext had taken over and had become so intense that it overpowered the text itself, which runs at most to a dozen printed pages, and it was the subtext that Stanislavski tried to play rather than Pushkin's actual words. The text was shattered into fragments as he tried to motivate every single word and relive in performance the background material he had so carefully worked out. Pauses were heavy and long. By the time a sentence came to an end the beginning was lost. The fact was that in trying to live the character Stanislavski had ignored the means by which the life of that character was principally to be conveyed, Pushkin's subtle, finely-wrought verse.

He had also become acutely aware of the inadequacy of his vocal technique. The mechanism could not take what he was trying to do and was suffering from it. On March 1 he even had Chaliapin, who was performing Rimski-Korsakov's operatic version, read over the part to him in an attempt to capture some of the true musicality of the verse but the singer's genius made him even more depressed.

For his part Stanislavski noted how difficult if not impossible it was in the theatre of living experience to be ready on the first night and went on working. In the end, after three months of struggle, it was an act of desperation, born of the actor's instinct for survival, which got him out of trouble. On April 1 he wrote to Benois:

'I felt so awful all day that I decided to go . . . for hypnosis. When I woke up in the morning and thought about the previous evening's performance I went red and was overwhelmed by a hot, burning depression. I stayed that way until they came to get me up. I acted the part all night, tormented by insomnia and the more I went through the lines the more I forgot them. During the day, in the street and in the carriage I wore myself out with the same relentless, stupid repetition of the lines. During the day I was worn out, I lay down but could not sleep because I was still going through the lines. I arrived at the theatre completely exhausted. I made changes to the make-up in order to convince myself that I had discovered something and so give myself courage. I drank a double dose of drops and (horror of horrors) a secret glass of wine to cheer myself up. But I only needed to put on the white breeches to feel corpulent while the painted thinness of my face seemed like a caricature. My heart sank and I was in such total despair that I felt clumsy, superfluous, stupid, above all *ridicule*. God knows how I acted, I stumbled through the lines and almost came to a complete stop. The more I tried to overcome my apathy the more the audience coughed. Yesterday I went to the wardrobe in a state of nothing short of anguish and felt that I could not put on white breeches or, more precisely, could not bring myself to go out on stage. Confident in your basic agreement, I sent someone to get me some black breeches and stockings. After I had put them on I felt as though I had been set free. Confidence returned, gestures. With my inner plan in pieces I decided, in actors' jargon, to pull out all the stops, let fly physically and vocally. And did I not!! It was so easy but I knew that only sheer desperation could push me to such shameful lengths. The audience listened to me as never before. They even tried to applaud after the first scene. Moskvin rushed round during the interval and said that this was the only way to play it. I don't understand a thing.' (*SS*, VII, pp. 610, 611.)

Stanislavski had, in fact, played the through-action, letting all other detail fall naturally into place. It was a lesson which, even if he did not fully understand it at the time, he was later to impress on others.

The production was by and large savaged by the critics, both conservative and avant-garde, and not even the sympathetic Efros could find anything good to say for it. Stakhovich wrote an encouraging letter but his appreciation of the performance depended on his willingness to forget what Pushkin had actually written. Both his own difficulties and the adverse critical reaction made Stanislavski realize that he needed to study the nature of spoken and written language more closely. Thanks to his study of singing and especially his classes with Komissarzhevski he was already aware of the mechanisms of voice production, but that was only sound. There remained the question of the structure and layout of the text, of the thing spoken – punctuation, phrasing, key words, emphases, pauses and the laws which governed them. He turned to his colleague S.M. Volkonski's book, *The Expressive Word: An Introduction to the Science of Language* which had been published in 1913 and to Uksakov's *Brief Introduction to the Science of Language* that had appeared in the same year.

Stanislavski's obstinate insistence on keeping literature, as literature, out of the theatre is nowhere better illustrated than in his complicated but amicable relationship with the symbolist poet Aleksandr Blok, whose play, *The Rose and the Cross*, set in the Languedoc at the time of the troubadours, was accepted by the Art Theatre in 1915, with some reluctance. At thirty-five, Blok was the outstanding poet of his time. In his youth he had thought of becoming an actor but the publication of his first volume of poetry *Verses on a Beautiful Lady* set him on a literary career. His first play, *The Puppet Booth*, was staged by Meierhold in 1906 but their relationship, for both artistic and personal reasons, was an uneasy one. The following year he approached the Art Theatre in the hope that Stanislavski would take an interest in his work.

In May 1908 he read his new play, *The Song of Destiny*, to Stanislavski and Nemirovich. Stanislavski at first seemed enthusiastic, immediately suggesting some ideas for staging. He also made some suggestions for rewriting. On September 11 a revised version of the play arrived. Stanislavski did not answer until December 3 and his letter was full of polite reservations. He had read the play four times but while he appreciated the quality of Blok's poetry it seemed to him that, as drama, the play lacked consistency both of plot and character and often contravened psychological truth. With characteristic courtesy, however, he ascribed his failure to appreciate the play more to his own limitations. He was, he said, 'an incorrigible realist' and unable to go beyond Chekhov. This was manifestly a polite fiction since he had spent the last four years trying to do precisely that. He had, of course, in his recent tenth-anniversary speech proclaimed a return to an enriched realism but what Blok had to offer, apart from fine writing, did not represent then, or indeed later, any real advance in terms of Stanislavski's artistic search.

Blok did not give up. When in the summer of 1912 he completed *The Rose and the Cross* he refused offers from the Aleksandrinski and from Meierhold and again contacted Stanislavski. In late afternoon of April 27, the following year, during the St Petersburg tour, he read his script to Stanislavski and fellow-writer Remizov. Remizov left almost immediately but Stanislavski stayed on until a quarter to midnight while the two men tried to come to an understanding. Blok has left a full account of their discussions in his diary.

Each man decided that the other needed educating at the most elementary level in the arts which they respectively practised. Blok found himself obliged to explain the meaning and the action of his play 'in more crude and simplistic terms' as Stanislavski had found it grey and monotonous. He was amazed that:

> '. . . an intelligent man, in whom I have great faith, who has done important things (Chekhov at the Art Theatre) *understood nothing, "took in" nothing and felt nothing.*' (Blok. *SS*, VII, p. 246.)

Stanislavski, for his part, explained in great detail the work of the Studio and, in explicit terms, what he thought Blok had to learn about writing for the stage. Blok's script was too allusive. Paying audiences wanted concrete action. Thus he suggested that the degradation of Bertrand, the principal character, should be established not by dialogue or description but concretely by his carrying out some menial task. He would be ordered to get rid of the slops. Down would go his sword and shield and he would pick up a bucket or even a chamber-pot. This was the way, Stanislavski assured him, to make the play work and offer an actor a meaty role. The arguments are deliberately pitched high in an effort designed to shock a lyric author out of his private world and bring him nearer the footlights. Stanislavski was not and never had been confined to a world of slop-buckets nor was he indifferent to broader more philosophical issues. If anything, during the period 1915–1920 he was too concerned with the 'symbolic' and the 'cosmic', to his own detriment, but for him abstractions were perceived and communicated through a selective, clear, 'transparent' theatrical presentation of the living world. What he could not accept was the notion that it was sufficient to clothe ideas, however interesting and relevant they might be, in insubstantial forms which had no genuine, independent reality but were merely representative of different aspects of the author's own mind.

After the conversation Blok was not at all certain if he could or should go down the road of the overtly 'theatrical'. Two days later he did, however, have an opportunity to see the First Studio at work in *The Wreck of 'The Hope'*. He recognized and appreciated the working method Stanislavski had described. He saw the emotional effect on the audience. He still believed an understanding could be reached and kept the offer of the play open. He did not have a happy time. Stanislavski applied himself. He discussed the question of music with Rachmaninov, who suggested that his friend and fellow pianist-composer, Nikolai Medtner, might be suitable. In the event responsibility for the production was bounced back and forth between Stanislavski and Nemirovich for three years, with constant changes of designer and design-concept. Rehearsals came to a halt during the October Revolution but were picked up again with a complete change of cast the following year. The last rehearsal Stanislavski took was on December 3, 1918, after which the whole project was finally dropped.

By April 1917 it had in fact already become obvious to Blok that the play would not be staged and that Stanislavski, for all his protestations that he liked the play – 'self-deception' Blok called it – was finding the script impossible. Blok's diary entry for April 17, 1917, nonetheless contains a generous tribute to Stanislavski whom he describes as 'the only truly great artist in the Art Theatre' and in a letter to his mother, written the same day, he said that while Stanislavski might say stupid things from time to time he 'really loves art because he is art.'

Early on in his conflict with Stanislavski, Nemirovich had once written that circumstances had become so combustible that it only required a spark to set off a conflagration. That spark was now *The Village of Stepanchikovo*. Stanislavski had adapted Dostoievski's novella in 1891 and had played Colonel Rostanev, the role in which he was cast again. However, the adaptation had now been made by the young Vladimir Volkenstein and Nemirovich himself. In Nemirovich's mind, his function as co-author gave him the absolute right to make all final artistic decisions. However, Stanislavski had not changed his position since *Woe from Wit*. If anything, he was even more determined and when at 12 noon on January 11, 1916, he addressed the assembled company he set out his 'modest but difficult work as a director' in almost crusading terms. He made it clear from the outset that they would be working according to the 'system' and that concentration would be on the actor and his process:

'Fashionable innovators, who want to be gods in the theatre, need not bother to come to me. As a director I will attend to the proper working of your creative nature and help it. I must protect you from any kind of forcing, and stimulate your creative energy with compelling creative tasks. I must help you recall what's been forgotten, and cultivate the unknown; I will try to feed your imagination and discreetly channel your creative efforts, bringing out what should be conscious and hiding what should be unconscious. I will try to guess the secret desires of your creative nature, each one of you, and create the right creative situation for all of you and the harmony of creative group work for you. And only in the extreme cases, when it cannot be avoided, when you have to be saved from false, harmful, actorish habits and conventional acting will I, like a doctor, perform an operation which, alas, cannot but be painful.' (K.S. Archive, No. 1353.)

Before Volkenstein read the text of the dramatization, Stanislavski added a few further introductory remarks. Each actor, he stated:

'. . . must experience the play not only in the terms laid down by the author but in all the circumstances which only his own imagination can create. It is that mastery of the inner, living spirit of a role which constitutes the actor's creative state. When a role is created in such a way it is better to avail oneself of the life laid down by the author than to create an inferior life for oneself. And then once more the author comes together with others who are creating the performance so that they flow together for ever, meet and can never again be separated. We start with the author's creation and come back to the author.' (K.S. Archive, No. 1351.)

The first rehearsal took place the following day, on January 12. Stanislavski and Volkenstein discussed the very special qualities of Dostoievski's story and the relationships among the characters. As they started to break down the play Stanislavski warned the cast against a mere dry-as-dust analysis. This, presumably, was a reference to Nemirovich's working method. What was important for the actor was to 'feed the subconscious', to try to understand the 'emotional facts, inner and outer, of the role', starting by creating his or her childhood. Then the problem for the actor was to find those compelling creative tasks he had referred to in his opening address:

> 'Only the creative tasks should be conscious, the means of achieving them, unconscious. *The unconscious through the conscious*. The is the watchword which must guide our coming work.' (K.S. Archive, No. 1353.)

Stanislavski seemed curiously unaware of the potential conflict he was creating. He was not merely confronting Nemirovich as a fellow director but as an author, or part-author. It did not appear to have occurred to him that Nemirovich was bound at some moment to challenge his direction if he felt that it went against what Dostoievski had written, or his own understanding of what Dostoievski had written. For Nemirovich it was a matter of fundamental principle. But Stanislavski was now totally committed to the 'system' and nothing else mattered. For him, too, it was a matter of principle. The 'system' was the only way the theatre could come alive again and fulfil its civic and social duty. The actor's approach to a role must be concrete:

> 'Put yourself in the circumstances of the character as portrayed and put the questions: what would I do in such a circumstance, what do I want, where am I going; stimulate your will. Answer them with verbs which express actions and not with nouns which express ideas and concepts.' (K.S. Archive, No. 1388/1.)

Rehearsal, therefore, begins not with literary analysis but with an examination of the circumstances, the facts, the incidents, what happens. This acts as a stimulus to the imagination and the unconscious and evokes memories of personal experience:

> 'As an artist gets into a part, penetrates deep into it, unconsciously selects his feelings, the incidents, facts, which he knows and has

experienced in daily life, he becomes unconsciously entwined through feelings with the spirit and life of the part. With habit and time, believing everything he has been working on, the artist, unbeknown to himself, acquires, through proximity, some elements of feeling and motivations which the part has implanted deep within him. This conjunction, person plus part, begins to live on stage as natural, lived life but is distinguished from his normal everyday life. The more the person approximates to the part the stronger, tighter, more compact this connection becomes. This transmutation seems like a wonder but at the same time it is quite simple and real and can be observed in life every minute.' (K.S. Archive, No. 1350.)

His statements, taken down by a young member of the cast during the series of lectures Stanislavski gave between January 11 and 16, represent a significant shift of public position. Whereas action previously had been taught as the expression of a previously established 'mood', it is now action itself which predominates and is the key to the psychological. Indeed, within a few years, Stanislavski, somewhat perversely, was to deny having any knowledge of 'moods'. Throughout the rehearsal period the cast were given exercises to help the synthesis of the personal and the textual. It is important to note also that there is no suggestion of the premeditated use of emotion memory. Personal experience is brought into play unconsciously. Here, in embryo, is the 'system' in its final form, the Method of Physical Action, which Stanislavski was to evolve in the last years of his life.

Stanislavski had similar difficulties recreating Colonel Rostanev to those he experienced with Ripafratta. In 1891 he had found immediate sympathy with the brow-beaten officer, who was bullied by his mother and exploited by the Tartuffe-figure, the evil, hypocritical servant, Foma. It had been one of those rare occasions when he had stepped straight into the skin of a character. Now matters were much more complicated. He was demanding greater psychological depth and insight. The world, too, had moved on and the political context in which the play was being staged was very different, the atmosphere was more highly charged. It was no longer a matter of presenting a gallery of Gogolian grotesques. The play was about the conflict of two principles, good and evil, Rostanev and Foma. But the search for the through-action that would express that conflict concretely in terms of character became more and more difficult and more and more complicated. In the earlier production he had been able to change in one crucial scene from good-natured compliance to towering rage. He had been able to reconcile the opposing tendencies in the character. But he now found it impossible to play a direct conflict between good and evil. At the January 18th rehearsal he stated:

'It seems to me that we made a mistake last time in trying to discover the through-action in conflict, in war.

Conflict, war against evil, the eradication of evil demands a strong Rostanev of which I am not capable.

The through-action may well be a longing for the idyll, simple love of life and a striving towards it.

This newly discovered through-action essentially alters the tasks and the content of the bits we have established. I, Rostanev, do not even attack, I defend, I surrender to judgement – take me, devour me. I do not destroy evil, but defend the idyll. Striving for love of life and protecting it puts me in the position of defending goodness.' (Rehearsal notes, K.S. Archive, No. 1388/2.)

By 'idyll' he had in mind a Tolstoian notion, a longing for the preservation of peace, harmony, quiet and goodness, which he may well have derived from Sulerzhitski. He began to see the character in Christ-like terms. Rostanev:

'. . . can say nothing but stands like Christ before Pontius Pilate.' (K.S. Archive, No. 9924.)

On the 19th he noted that perhaps the through-action was his love for his fiancée, Hastiénka, and his desire to protect her. That would give the spine of the play. He felt that his imagination was more deeply engaged. However, by the beginning of February he had returned to his notion of the idyll but in a more active sense: it was the striving towards the idyll which was important.

The play was also beginning to acquire contemporary overtones. On January 22 he stated that Foma shared certain traits with Rasputin and, indeed, Dostoievski's text, published in 1859, is strangely prophetic in its description of the character. On March 18 he announced:

'The village of Stepanchikovo is Russia itself. It even has its own Rasputin. (Foma).' (Rehearsal notes, K.S. Archive, No. 1388/5.)

He worked in equal detail on Foma's through-action, helping Moskvin to build his performance, in counterpoint to his own.

The shareholders met on April 2, 1916, and, faced with Stanislavski's refusal to return to the board, reaffirmed the 1911 agreement. Nemirovich was re-elected as managing director with full powers.

Rehearsals of *Stepanchikovo* continued through the summer with Moskvin in charge while Nemirovich and Stanislavski took a break. On August 8 Nemirovich wrote to Stanislavski stating that the play must be staged in September/October so that they could concentrate on other productions. The question was which? The letter is both professional in content and friendly in tone. Nemirovich was still looking for an accommodation, a return to their earlier close collaboration:

'Our discussions will be so very useful. They will unite our most important, personal endeavours, perhaps, and remove many of our radical disagreements.' (Iz., Pis., 2, p. 179.)

On August 11 Stanislavski replied, calmly setting out a detailed statement of his position, the many reasons for his disillusion with the current state of the Art Theatre:

> 'My indifference, etc., has its reasons. I was not always so. There was a time when I was afire. But a radical disagreement exists. . . . I and the shareholders have different goals, different paths to tread, different (how shall I put it?) ethics, upbringing, culture, views, habits, nature.' (MATL, No. 331.)

He then went through the various areas of disagreement.

First, there was the business side, the question of making a profit. He simply could not share Nemirovich's short-term thinking. In the long term, he explained, the most profitable businesses are those that build up a reputation for a reliable product of high quality. That means long-term planning and long-term investment and modest demands for profits in the immediate. There were other businesses that only thought short-term, over one year, and were ultimately far less stable. That, in Stanislavski's view, was what the Art Theatre had become. He had said it before and had been ignored. His answer was:

> '. . . to close my eyes, not to see and pass by as quickly as possible and deliberately develop that indifference which enables me to work in businesses which have other ends than mine in view.' (Ibid.)

Second, Stanislavski recognized that his financial situation was different from that of the other members of the company. That granted him a certain freedom of action, although he was fully aware of the derision he sometimes provoked:

> 'I am financially secure, others are not. It is easy for me to take risks, others not. I, in appearance, take no risks in the business and others, in appearance, do. In these circumstances I acquire the dangerous label of an impractical, addle-pated genius, etc. And it is true, as far as the current season is concerned I am impractical but I am practical as far as future profits are concerned. . . . For me the soundness and durability of our business is more important than future profits.' (Ibid.)

Third, there was the damage to his own reputation because of his continuing connections with the Art Theatre:

> '. . . I, as a Muscovite born and bred, surrounded by the traditional prejudices of a certain group of people on whom I and my family depend, financially and in other ways, must be scrupulous in another area, known as public opinion, the que dira-t-on. And the ethical side of the theatre is at present very low and more than once I am pained, embarrassed and get into an appalling state. Nowhere is there more

drinking, more drunkenness than in our theatre, nowhere is there such conceit and disdain for other people and such insulting outbursts. . . . Moscow is proud of us and certain people need to have a thought for their reputation. . . . In Rostov recently there was a poster which misled the public and the wool-merchants wrote on it: "Ask Alekseiev why he allows his actors such deceit."' (Ibid.)

Finally, Stanislavski summed up the absurdity of his situation. He had no executive or administrative power but as far as the public was concerned he was responsible for everything that went on in the theatre, even the things he disapproved of. Above all, he was the financial guarantor of the whole enterprise:

'. . . When I am useful I am wheeled out and my name is used; when I am not I do not even know what is going on backstage. . . . When a signature is needed at the bank I have to provide it. In a word I must give my name for risks the business takes. . . . Summing up. In my opinion you make two mistakes from which all misunderstandings flow:
1. You want forcibly to unite things that cannot be united. . . .
2. You are afraid to let go of power and want to keep a grip on everything big or small.
    Time is passing. Call the shareholders together. They must decide for themselves . . . and both of us must stand to one side but close together.' (Ibid.)

The solution to their problem was greater openness, giving young artists a chance, selecting and developing any good piece of work they produced:

'. . . They, i.e. the whole group of people, want to put on a bad play. Let them mount it and show it! If it's worthwhile we will finish it and help them. If not they will learn from their mistakes. *First and foremost we must revive a dormant sense of initiative.* And we must not be afraid of one thing, a season which is a large write-off. Otherwise it's misery, bankruptcy which I will defend myself against in every way.
    I gave an honest warning of this a long time ago. Were it not for the war I would have taken steps.' (Ibid. Emphasis added.)

This response was all the more devastating because it substantially removed the conflict from a personal to a business level. Stanislavski moreover reinforced his point by creating the Second Studio for another generation of young actors. Unlike the First, it was primarily a school and it was from his teaching here that Stanislavski built up the material on training that was to form the basis of *An Actor's Work.*
Rehearsals extended through the autumn. Stanislavski struggled to

bring coherence to his own character and to clarify the philosophical issues of the play. Progress was further hindered when Moskvin was mobilized into the army, although he was discharged shortly after.

Despite all that had been written that summer, Nemirovich persisted in trying to bring Stanislavski back on to the board. Stanislavski wrote to him on December 4:

> 'It is difficult and distressing for me to declare again *absolutely and categorically* that under no circumstances will I sign any document, official or legal, binding me to a new association. . . . My decision is sufficiently categorical for me to ask you not to return to the matter again. It is too difficult and painful.' (*MATL*, No. 332.)

There matters rested until January 5, 1917, when Nemirovich wrote a desperate letter. They could not just let events take their course as Stanislavski suggested. There had to be a plan, the plan he had been working on for fourteen months. They had to work together, their conflict was opening the door to all kinds of intrigue and plotting. Sentences are heavily underlined – *I cannot work except in full agreement with you. I remember everything you said. I am ready for the most radical decisions.* At all events, one of them had to be in charge:

> 'The first way out of my uncertainty is for you to take everything in hand and then *Tell me what I am to do.* . . . The second way out is the absolute opposite. I carry out the programme as I have conceived it and tell you what I require of you.' (*MATL*, No. 333.)

Again an impasse. Matters were coming to a head. *Stepanchikovo* had now been in preparation for ten months with 156 rehearsals and the end was still not in sight. There was no guarantee it would be staged that season. Nemirovich felt he had to get the play on somehow. Another year could not go by without a single new production. In February he took charge of the production. The result was a greater crisis than he could have foreseen. The 'literary' Nemirovich could not accept Stanislavski's interpretation of Rostanev. It was not what Dostoievski had written. After all his painstaking work, Stanislavski was supposed to turn his characterization completely round and to play Rostanev as a retired officer and a boor:

> '. . . a fanatic, in that when there is talk of good he forgets everything, the agitation in the household, etc., and is simply carried away by pleasure (the sense of goodness in caring for peasants).' (Stanislavski, Note written after rehearsals, K.S. Archive, No. 1562.)

On March 8, 9 and 10 he worked alone with Nemirovich, with negative results:

> 'I'm often so ill at ease that the whole part is flattened out, it becomes

muddy. We must [define] the through-action more clearly (in Dostoievski it is very clear).' (Ibid.)

Three days later Stanislavski was both angry and frustrated:

'I may not be able to give birth to Dostoievski's Rostanev but I can to a son we both produce, who will bear many resemblances to both mother and father. But Nemirovich, like all literati, wants this mother and father to produce another mother and father in their own image. What's the point if they already exist? I can only give Rostanev/ Stanislavski or at the very worst Stanislavski/Rostanev. Literary critics can give one Rostanev. He will be dead, like their critical essays. Let's absolutely not have that but something living. It's better than something that's identical but dead.' (K.S. Archive, No. 3174.)

By the dress rehearsal on March 28, Stanislavski had neither a fully prepared performance of his own nor had he adapted to Nemirovich's ideas. He was caught between the two and could not pull the role together. The evening, with an audience present, was a harrowing experience for all concerned. Vadim Shverubovich was in the audience and has provided an eye-witness account:

'The second act began. *He* made his entrance. . . . I was sitting at the front row and suddenly sensed a kind of fear, a kind of hesitation coming from Stanislavski's eyes, which flickered everywhere. There was bewilderment, terror, fear there, in the way he looked toward the prompter's box. . . . He didn't hear him, asked for the line, got it wrong, fluffed the text. There was a stir in the audience, someone giggled but was angrily hissed for his insolence.

In the interval my father came to see me, pale, his lips tight with pity, and took me on one side and said, "You'd better go home, something awful is happening to Konstantin Sergeievich." I refused to leave, although I knew I was letting myself in for a bad time, seeing him in such a dreadful state was terrible. Somewhere in the third act he got hold of himself and became Rostanev . . . but not for long, something was wrong with him, scaring him, I felt I was seeing something I shouldn't. Seeing this, taking part in it was a kind of blasphemy.' (V. Shverubovich, *Teatralnie Memuary*, Iskusstvo, Moscow, 1990, p. 174.)

Towards the end of the play the other members of the cast saw Stanislavski standing in the wings in tears. They waited for him to recover. Finally he said, 'On!' and the rehearsal was somehow completed. Immediately after the curtain came down Nemirovich took swift and decisive action. He removed Stanislavski from the cast and replaced him with Massalitinov. The cast waited for an explosion but none came. Stanislavski's iron sense of discipline prohibited any open disagreement.

The deep hurt he felt was endured in silence, in public at least.

Nemirovich's action was so iron-fisted that the question inevitably arises as to whether he was settling old scores. Yet in taking the line he did he merely remained faithful to his own aesthetic philosophy: the author first, last and always. That Stanislavski was in part responsible for his own dismissal is undeniably true. He was asking too much of himself. Endlessly self-critical during rehearsal, never believing he had got it right, always searching for some perfect but perhaps unattainable theatrical truth, he was prepared to go on until he did find it. Members of the cast who had watched the performance grow were convinced it was only a matter of time before it came together. But how much time? Nemirovich had been patient. In addition to the 156 rehearsals already taken prior to his taking over, Nemirovich took forty more rehearsals before sacking Stanislavski. The play had to open on schedule if the theatre was to retain any credibility. Another season could not be allowed to go by without a new production. There was no time to wait for Stanislavski to get things right to his own satisfaction.

Yet if Stanislavski was asking too much of himself, impossible demands were being placed on him. During the 1916–17 season, in addition to rehearsing *Stepanchikovo*, he was playing leading roles – Vershinin, Gaev, Satin, Krutitski, Ripafratta, Liubin – working on *The Rose and the Cross* and taking rehearsals for the Second Studio's opening presentation, *The Golden Ring*. At the same time he dealt with an industrial dispute at his factory and coped with a walk-out of props men at the theatre. At a more personal level he suffered the loss of his beloved Sulerzhitski, who died the previous December after a serious illness. At the funeral Stanislavski wept like a child.

In the circumstances, therefore, to succeed as Rostanev, Stanislavski needed sympathetic handling. But, as Stakhovich had remarked many years earlier, Nemirovich would always rather be one-up than help Stanislavski when he was in trouble. Lilina was in no doubt that Nemirovich's abrupt and in many ways insensitive handling of Stanislavski in rehearsal was the main cause of the catastrophe. In a letter to Mrs Gurevich, written after Stanislavski's death, she stated:

'I will give you a brief account of what happened. Vladimir Ivanovich wanted to instil something of his own attitude towards the role into a character that was already prepared, something very faithful from the literary point of view, but Konstantin Sergeievich really could not accept it or perhaps simply didn't understand how to deal with it and the whole part, or rather, all relish for the part was lost. The flavour was lost. But when he played without being told what to do, you could not watch his interpretation without tears in your eyes. The part was wonderful.' (In *M. P. Lilina*, VTO, 1960.)

Stanislavski stayed away from the theatre and Nemirovich did not refer to the matter again until early September when he wrote justifying what he had done. He appears to have suspected Stanislavski of criticizing him behind his back. He assured Stanislavski of his goodwill and reaffirmed the contents of the conciliatory letter he had written the previous January. As far as *Stepanchikovo* was concerned he had done what was necessary, in spite of personal feelings. Nonetheless he could not resist placing the blame for the whole unhappy business on Stanislavski's shoulders. Always the perfect manager, Nemirovich stated:

> 'Faced with an "affair" with a budget of a million, directors' vanities must give way.' (N-D Archive, No. 1724.)

Stanislavski, in reply, denied all charges of gossip, rebutted the accusation of vanity, expressed his pleasure at not being in the production but indicated that his days with the main company were perhaps numbered:

> 'I have no thought at all about future roles, there is nothing more I can do, not in the Art Theatre, at least. . . . Maybe I could be reborn in another sphere, another place. Of course, I am not talking about other theatres but about the Studios. *Othello free!* [in English in the text].' (*SS*, VII, p. 643.)

Later in the month Nemirovich wrote again, after the final dress rehearsal on the 24th, still, apparently trying to prove his point:

> 'This public dress rehearsal was a great success, especially with the literary part of the audience.' (N-D Archive, No. 1723.)

Nemirovich just had to be right. The same day all forty-seven members of the company, including Nemirovich, sent Stanislavski a letter, expressing sympathy and gratitude. A waxen-faced Stanislavski arrived at the theatre on the first night, September 26. He brought gifts for the young members of the cast. To each one he gave a parcel. It contained a large pear and an apple, rare treats in a period of wartime shortages.

Nemirovich could not have foreseen the long-term consequences of his actions, but Kachalov did. He had seen Stanislavski go to pieces in Germany in the summer of 1914. He knew that for all his reputation as a superman, Stanislavski was extremely vulnerable. He had lost his sense of living in a secure world, and now his sense of belonging to the Art Theatre was finally destroyed:

> 'Kachalov said that Konstantin Sergeievich would probably never recover from this blow. This trauma destroyed his creative ability for a long time, deprived him of his feeling of solidarity with the theatre, his total identification with it. The sense of security, of the impregnable nature of his position in art, in the life of the theatre, was shattered.' (Shverubovich, *Tealtralnye Memuary*, p. 175.)

Kachalov was right. Stanislavski's career as an actor of new roles was over. His confidence was gone. Nemirovich's comment that he had been dropped because he had 'failed to bring the part to life' obsessed him and he would refer to it months after, in private conversation. He never again created a new character, although he took over the part of Shuiski in *Tsar Fiodor* during the 1923–4 foreign tour. That, however, was a part he knew backwards. In his draft notes for *My Life in Art* there is a chapter-heading, *The Village of Stepanchikovo, My Tragedy*. It was never written.

PART THREE

THE REVOLUTION AND AFTER

CHAPTER TWENTY

REVOLUTION

As Stanislavski sat in his house at Carriage Row, trying to come to terms with his humiliation, the country was in turmoil. The February Revolution put an end to the reign of Nicholas II and of the monarchy itself. Factories were being taken over by workers' councils. Stanislavski saw his fortune disappear. He was not a political sophisticate. He had no conception of the ideological issues involved and no knowledge of Marxist theory. It was not, indeed, until 1926 that he even considered reading the basic texts of Lenin. But as an inheritor of the democratic aspirations of the nineteenth-century intelligentsia and as a patriot he believed that the Revolution was in the best interests of his country and he welcomed it.

In a letter to the literary historian, Kotliarevski, on March 3, 1917, he described recent events as 'the miraculous liberation of Russia'. He regarded the overthrow of an absolutist government as an opportunity to realize the goals he had set himself twenty years earlier – new plays, new audiences, the enrichment and enlightenment of the common people through art. That liberation, however, involved a high degree of personal loss. The Alekseiev factories were taken into state ownership and within a short space of time converted, as Stanislavski himself had planned, to the production of steel cables. His private fortune was gone suddenly and he himself potentially suspect as a member of the propertied classes, one of the 'has-beens'. In May he wrote to Kotliarevskaia that his house had already been 'done over' and he expected it would be again, this time thoroughly. He was looking for a new apartment not merely because he was about to be evicted but because he could no longer afford to live where he was. The rebirth of a nation, he wrote, inevitably involves disruption.

The February Revolution made little impact on the theatre. Only the extreme cold (minus 16 degrees) and food shortages distracted the company's minds from the problems of internal politics. An entirely new world was about to be created, powerful forces were to be unleashed, but the Moscow Art Theatre was entirely unequipped to meet the situation. It had to all intents and purposes ceased to exist as a creative force. It had struggled to stage one new production a year in 1915, 1916 and 1917. Only the First Studio, which Stanislavski had created as an alternative to the main company, was producing significant new work. All the new creative talent – Michael Chekhov, Vakhtangov, Boleslavski – was there.

All Stanislavski had now was his salary from the theatre. Modest as his lifestyle had been in comparison with the rest of the *haute bourgeoisie*, he could no longer maintain it. The stoicism he had developed when trapped in Germany in 1914 served him well. Just as he had then defined the patriotic duties of an artist in the war, so now, in the period of turmoil between February and October 1917, he defined the duties of the artist in a new society. His notes for an article, *The Aesthetic Education of the Popular Masses*, gave a clear message to the leaders of the Revolution: not by bread alone.

> 'Let there be no end to the opening of schools, people's universities, let there be general education classes and seminars, lectures, etc., to encourage the intelligent development of the masses. But knowledge alone is not enough. It is essential to educate the people's sensibility, their souls. One of the most important human senses, one which distinguishes him from the animals and raises him to heaven, is the *aesthetic* sense. That is a divine spark planted in man. . . .
>
> The aesthetic domain, that is our domain. Therein lies our most important work in the construction of Russia. It is in that domain above all that we must fulfil our civic duty.' (*SS*, VI, p. 23.)

Even in 1922, when as a result of Civil War and the War of Intervention conditions were worse than ever, he was still resolute:

> 'Theatre for the starving! Starvation and Theatre!
> There's no contradiction here.
> Art is not a luxury in the lives of the people but a daily necessity. It is not something you can manage without but something absolutely essential to a great people. The theatre is not idle pastime, or an agreeable plaything, it is a cultural undertaking of importance. . . .
> You cannot put the theatre in storage for a time, put locks on its workshop doors, bring its life to a halt. Art cannot go to sleep to be woken up when we feel like it. Rather it goes to sleep for ever and dies. Once stopped it dies. . . . And even should it rise from the dead that will be in a hundred years' time. The death of Art is a national disaster. . . . Time will pass and famine will be conquered. Wounds will heal. And then we shall be thanked for saving Art in a time of martyrdom.
> We are all the more happy that today we offer the Art which we are saving for people to aid those same starving people.' (*Theatre for the Starving. SS*, VI, p. 118.)

In August he drafted plans for the new Union of Moscow Artists in which he set out a policy for all theatres. He was quite clear that the theatre's work must be limited to purely artistic activities. In November he successfully opposed a call by some colleagues for a token strike against the new government, maintaining that it would be detrimental to their work. Their task was to preserve Russia's cultural heritage and hand it on in living form to the people.

Where the February Revolution had not even caused the theatre to change its schedule, the October Revolution, like the revolution of 1905, brought about its temporary closure. On October 25 the Bolsheviks staged a coup in Petrograd and Lenin proclaimed the overthrow of the provisional government under Kerenski. That night the Winter Palace was stormed. A guest performance of *The Cherry Orchard* was given on October 26, at the Theatre of the Soviet of Workers' Deputies. The audience dispersed after midnight to the sound of gunfire. In the streets outside the wounded were being carried away on lorries. The next day the theatre closed and the Studio was occupied by revolutionary forces. On November 5 the company assembled to consider its future. It was decided to send a representative to the Moscow Soviet to ask how the Art Theatre could best serve the people. The answer came back: start work again as soon as possible. The theatre reopened on November 17.

Stanislavski was convinced that without a radical change in outlook the theatre could not survive. Nemirovich had achieved the remarkable feat of paying off the debts and putting the theatre on a firm financial basis but in so doing he had abandoned the spirit of adventure which had characterized the company in its early days. The theatre needed revitalizing, rejuvenating. This would be difficult in view of the entrenched attitudes which prevailed.

On December 5, 1917, and at a later meeting on the 31st, Stanislavski and Luzhski presented a new plan to the board. All new productions, including those for the main house, should be prepared at the Studios. He proposed the partial separation of the First and Second Studio from the theatre and the creation of a Third Studio. He made it clear that he would neither prepare new roles nor direct new plays except under this arrangement. Nemirovich stood firm. The Studios and the main theatre were different establishments, with different methods. The Studios could never supply more than interesting experiment. They could not have the impact of the main house. Not all plays needed lengthy preparation. Rather unkindly, perhaps, he cited *Stepanchikovo* as an example of an unnecessarily time-consuming production. He also pointed to the adverse effect on the budget.

Stanislavski continued to formulate new plans and on May 22 of the following year delivered one of his most critical speeches ever to the shareholders. The theatre had lost its soul, its sense of social purpose, it was complacent, concerned only with full houses and the box office, and was failing to keep up with recent artistic developments. Their task was to save Russian theatre. His solution was an updated version of schemes he had put to Nemirovich many years before and which Nemirovich had rejected. Whereas then he had proposed a network of regional theatres, under the aegis of the Art Theatre, he suggested now the creation of a 'Pantheon' of Russian theatre, with the Art Theatre at its centre, controlling a series of studios and youth theatres which would play in Moscow and the surrounding districts, go on tour, and teach by giving seminars for professionals. He spoke of creating fifteen new Studios.

His dreams, however, extended far beyond the confines of Russia. In October 1916, Jacques Copeau had written to him describing conversations he had held with Craig and others which had convinced him that there was much in common between the Vieux Colombier, which he had launched in 1913, and the Art Theatre. Stanislavski was now convinced that the time had come to create an international Studio, bringing together artists from all over the world to study the 'system'. The Revolution had only increased his enthusiasm.

Nemirovich's objections still stood: the theatre had not been able to spread its resources too thinly thirteen years before and it certainly could not do so at a time of revolution, war and economic collapse when even the bare necessities of life were unobtainable. Stanislavski could not offer any practical suggestions as to how his plan might be implemented. He probably had not thought about it. As far as his colleagues could see he was once again displaying all the traits of character which had caused them to mistrust him in the past as an impossible dreamer, a 'muddle-head'. His idealism was impossible to live with but he made no demands on other people that he did not make on himself. He had accepted the loss of his privileges and property. He made constant efforts to make sure members of the company had food and fuel but asked nothing for himself, not even in 1920, when he was about to be evicted. He wept in private but made no application for the eviction order to be withdrawn. It was only when Lunacharski went directly to Lenin that it was agreed he could stay until he could be rehoused.

Justified as the theatre might be in practical terms to reject his ill-thought-through schemes, where was its alternative response to the situation created by the Revolution? It was more vulnerable to attack than it had ever been. Meierhold had been an unrelenting critic over the years, never losing an opportunity to challenge the contemporary relevance of the Art Theatre's work. In May 1915 he had attacked the First Studio's highly successful production of *The Cricket on the Hearth*, adapted from Dickens' story, describing it as 'key-hole theatre'. He followed that up by an assault on the Pushkin evening when Stanislavski played Salieri. Benois had, unwisely perhaps, gone into print in *Rech*, to defend the Art Theatre's style and approach to the three classic plays. Meierhold replied with a long and devastating article in which he deployed the full force of his intellectual gifts and polemical skill. But it was the theatre and, in particular, Nemirovich whom he loathed, that he attacked, not Stanislavski. He had told Aleksandr Blok very firmly in December 1912, 'I am a pupil of Stanislavski.' It was a position he maintained albeit not uncritically. Indeed, it was a standing joke among his friends in the 1920s that when he went to see Stanislavski he put on his best clothes like a schoolboy. Meierhold's insistence that theatre should be theatrical received support particularly among the younger members of the intelligentsia including, in time, Vakhtangov and members of the First Studio. A work of art should not attempt to present itself as 'natural', but should reveal itself as a human construct, as an artefact, making its means of communication evident. This aesthetic found its theoretical formulation in the work of Viktor Shklovski, who developed the notion of *ostranenie*, 'making strange', the precursor of Brecht's *Verfremdung*. By the 1920s the movement had emerged as Formalism.

Meierhold received, initially at least, support from another emergent director. Aleksandr Taïrov had founded the Kamerni (Chamber) Theatre in 1914 in a search for a style of presentation that was more formally structured and choreographed. His leading actress and also his wife was Alisia Koonen, who had left the Art Theatre in 1913 after playing a number of important roles including Mytyl in *The Blue Bird*. She had originally been scheduled to play Ophelia in the Craig *Hamlet*. Her greatest quality as an actress was expressive movement and she used this ability to give life to her husband's conceptions. By 1916 the Kamerni was using Cubist design, pointing the way towards developments in the 1920s. Taïrov and Meierhold collaborated in 1917–18 on a production of Claudel's *L'Échange* and there was some discussion with Evreinov concerning the creation of a new left-wing theatre.

A new generation of critics had also to be reckoned with. Prominent among them were Mikhail Zagorski, later a close friend of Meierhold at the Meierhold Theatre, and Vladimir Blum who represented the sharp ideological edge of the opposition. Blum was uncompromising in his attacks on the Art Theatre, its Studios and all they stood for. Apart from a grudging recognition of Stanislavski's personal gifts as an actor, which he could scarcely deny, he had nothing positive to say. All the Art Theatre's opponents agreed on one thing, it was no more than a nineteenth-century relic, a monument to a now-outmoded naturalistic style, essentially reactionary in its attitudes. Blum summed up the general judgement in 1923:

> 'The Art Theatre died a natural death on that same night, the 25 to 26 October, when a mortal blow was dealt to that class whose finest essence its magnificent productions distilled. That theatre carried the banner of Russian bourgeois theatre high until the end of its days.' (*Zrelischa*, 1923, No. 59, pp. 8–9.)

Such conflicts were, however, contained within a common set of cultural and aesthetic references; they assumed a certain historic context. But the Revolution had released forces of a much more radical kind, such as the

Proletkult. The notion of the Proletarian Cultural and Educational Organizations had been launched by a conference of revolutionary exiles in Capri in 1909 attended by Lunacharski, Gorki and the philosopher and scientist Aleksandr Bogdanov who became its leader. It came into being officially early in 1917. The intention was to create an organization which would operate in parallel with revolutionary political groups and create a new, working-class, cultural consciousness that would match social and economic changes. For Lunacharski this new culture would be based on two major elements: the traditions of the past, rethought and restructured, and new creations springing from the as yet untapped creative potential of the working masses. There was, however, a hard-left faction within the movement which demanded no less than the total abolition of all pre-revolutionary art and the creation of a new art which would spring from the masses and be comprehensible to them.

Proletkult was well organized and ready for revolutionary change. It moved fast. It held its first Conference in February 1918 when it drew up a programme for the creation of a network of Workers' Clubs and Studios based on works and factories. Where they could, they took over existing amateur groups. The intention was to train actors, directors and writers who would remain in vital contact with the masses and replace the current 'professionals'. The next fifteen months were spent implementing that programme as rapidly and effectively as circumstances would permit.

The leaders of the Revolution, Lenin and Trotski, were not sympathetic to either of the tendencies within Proletkult. Lenin had already attacked Bogdanov and the Capri group for departing from orthodox Marxism in what he considered to be one of his most important works, *Materialism and Empiriocriticism* (1909). When he revised the work in 1920 he included a specific attack on Proletkult, mistrusting above all its claim to independence from party control. Trotski was equally sceptical of the notion of a 'proletarian' culture in a post-revolutionary, and therefore classless, society. How can you have 'proletarian' culture if there is no 'proletariat'?

As he pointed out, the bulk of the population were either illiterate or semi-illiterate, and needed educating before they could form adequate judgements.

The polemic surrounding the Art Theatre was thus a paradigm for the debate on the relationship of post-Revolutionary art to the pre-Revolutionary past and the problem of the means by which Russia's cultural heritage was to be assimilated into a new society if at all. Uncomfortable it might be, but it was natural for Stanislavski to find himself in such a position. He had been perceived as early as the mid-1890s as the one individual who could transmit the best traditions of the past to the future. He did, however, need support. This he received from Lenin who was quite clear that audiences needed more than bully-boy slogans. They needed the lyrical; they needed living truth; they needed Chekhov. In conversation with Gorki he stated quite categorically:

> 'If there is a theatre from the past that we must at all costs save and preserve it is, needless to say, the Art Theatre.' (Quoted by Lunacharski in his Address on the 30th anniversary of the Art Theatre, 1928.)

When Russian theatres were reorganized in December 1919, the Art Theatre, like the former Imperial theatres, was designated a state 'Academic theatre' with full independence, thus acquiring official, and subsidized, status. Like all other 'Academic theatres', it was, however, controlled by the newly created Glavrepertkom (Main Repertoire Committee) that replaced the old imperial censorship. Under the new statutes Stanislavski was drawn firmly back into management.

During the two years following the revolution Lenin became a regular visitor, catching up with those productions which he had missed during his long years of exile – *The Village of Stepanchikovo, The Seagull, The Cherry Orchard, Uncle Vania,* and *The Lower Depths* which he found theatrical in the wrong sense and lacking in authenticity of detail. He particularly admired Stanislavski's performance as General Krutitski in *Enough Stupidity in Every Wise Man* which he saw on December 15, 1918, and in conversation after the show implicitly endorsed Stanislavski's refusal to indulge in didactic theatre:

> 'Stanislavski is a real artist, he transformed himself into the general so completely that he lived his life down to the smallest detail. The audience don't need any explanations. They can see for themselves what an idiot this important-looking general is. In my opinion this is the direction the theatre should take.' (Quoted in N. I. Komarovskaia's *Videnoe i perezhitoe*, Iskusstvo, 1965, p. 139.)

Whatever support Stanislavski might receive from the leaders of the Revolution, there were elements in the Bolshevik administration ideologically hostile to the Art Theatre and all that it stood for. On August 29 Stanislavski was arrested by the secret police, the Cheka. The order came from the top, from Dzerzhinski himself. Moskvin was also arrested, as were some sixty others, all suspected of being anti-Bolshevik. Nemirovich was away at his country dacha but his apartment was raided. Smishliaev, a member of the First Studio, learned what had happened and spent the whole of the next day trying to discover where Stanislavski was being held and effect his release. He knew the devastating effect the incident would have on him. He went to the Cheka and managed, with some difficulty, to see the officer in charge. Smishliaev had all the right political credentials as a member of the Proletkult studio and so expected to get quick results but the officer merely waved an order at him which stated that any officers failing to carry out their duty would themselves be arrested. Smishliaev went to see Dzerzhinski. He was sure that had Lunacharski (now People's Commissar for Enlightenment) been in Moscow the situation would have been rectified immediately. Stanislavski was such a child in political terms that any notion that he would engage in subversive activities was absurd. He learned later that both Stanislavski and Moskvin had been released that same day.

Other arrests followed. Everyone at the theatre was terrified. On September 11 Andreieva, Gorki's mistress, now People's Commissar for Theatre in Petrograd, and Lunacharski managed to get most of the prisoners released.

The incident was obviously a concerted attack on the Art Theatre at the highest level and explains the careful steps taken over the next three years to keep it out of trouble.

Nonetheless, Lunacharski, although fully aware of Lenin's private views, pursued a pluralist educational and cultural policy. His ambition was still a new culture which would be a fusion of the present and the past. The Communist Party was not yet committed to a particular line on the arts. The moment had not yet come when a word from a party leader could cause a work to be banned. Only in May 1925 did Lunacharski venture a preliminary statement on the party's attitude to literature and this amounted to little more than a warning against two dangers: at one extreme, statements that supported the idealist notion of universal human verities; at the other, attempts, for narrow ideological reasons, to muzzle genuine artistic expression. The battle for the artistic soul of the newly created Soviet society was on and faction fought with faction in a struggle of almost Byzantine complexity. The Art Theatre was ill-equipped to engage in such ideological in-fighting. It had always been proud of its refusal to commit itself to any one tendency, political or artistic. It had relied on the superior quality of its product to assure its position. Where was that superiority now?

Unable to obtain any planned or coherent support from his colleagues or to drag them out of their inertia, Stanislavski pursued his own campaign of reform. He was inspired by his own idealism but, at a more personal level, it is clear that he was anxious to prove, as later letters to Vakhtangov and Luzhski demonstrate, that he was not a parasite on the new Soviet state but was making a full contribution to its development.

In the years 1918–22 Stanislavski was active on many fronts: he continued to play major roles particularly for new popular audiences, taught the 'system', directed or revived productions both at the theatre and in the Studios, launched an Opera Studio and was active in the new Professional Union of Moscow Actors of which he became a chairman. All this in the worse possible material conditions.

The Revolution gave Stanislavski the opportunity to fulfil a lifelong dream: to bring the classics to a wider, popular audience. Performances were now given for factory workers and the army. But they were often uncomfortable occasions. Early in the life of the Art Theatre Stanislavski had had to educate his largely well-heeled audience into his notion of the theatre as a place that must be respected, a temple, persuading them to arrive on time and to listen. Now he had audiences who had, by and large, no experience of theatre-going. They talked noisily, ate and drank, seemingly unaware that they could be heard on stage. For once the illusion of the fourth wall was not helpful.

Stanislavski was driven to deliver a sharp rebuke. The daybook for February 15, 1920, records that after Act Two of *Uncle Vania* Stanislavski went out in front of the curtain in full costume and make-up and asked for silence during the action as the noise made it impossible for the actors to do their job. His little speech worked. The rest of the performance was heard in silence. In *My Life in Art* Stanislavski maintains that he made similar appeals on a number of occasions. The result was that as he arrived the schoolboy cry, 'He's coming!' could be heard and a respectful hush would fall.

He was similarly displeased by the audience's habit in cold weather of keeping their fur hats on. The fact that there was no heating made no difference. Hats are not worn in a temple. He endured it as best he could but when he came across a company member, in November or December, wearing his hat he remarked that what might be tolerated among a largely uneducated audience could not be excused in someone who should know better. The offending garment was quickly removed.

Stanislavski saw the Studios as a means of creating a new generation of actors and directors who would take over the Art Theatre and all its related activities. A major concern was to ensure a proper organic relationship between the 'old brigade' and young talent. This meant teaching the 'system'. It would be the means by which the older and younger generations could be welded together. A continuous tradition would be created, starting with Shchepkin and going through, unbroken, into the new Soviet society, guaranteeing for future generations the survival of Realism in its highest form.

In January 1919 he inaugurated a series of seminars at the Art Theatre, known as Creative Mondays, where broad issues of theatre aesthetics were discussed. He followed this up with a series of lectures on the 'system' from October to December. His notes reveal his implicit criticisms of the overall work and standards of his older colleagues. At the same time he lectured at the Second Studio, where he was also working on *The Blue Bird*. Significantly he did not attempt any classes at the First Studio which was resolutely, not to say aggressively, following its own line of development. He watched Boleslavski's rehearsals of a Polish play, *Balladina*, taking one session but disappearing three weeks before the opening, apparently displeased.

His most consistent teaching, however, took place outside the ambit of the Art Theatre. Part of it was directed toward the members of the recently formed Habima Theatre, a company of Jewish Palestinian actors living in Moscow. He had seen a preview of their work on September 30, 1918, nine days before their official opening. He agreed to start a Studio for them and put Vakhtangov in charge. Vakhtangov had just, as it were, come back into the fold and his own studio had become the Art Theatre's Third Studio. Between September 1920 and April 1921 Stanislavski gave over twenty sessions at the Habima, sometimes dealing with specific aspects of the 'system', such as Bits and Tasks, Role Analysis, Rhythm, and on other occasions using scenes from *Woe from Wit* and *The Merchant of Venice* as teaching material. The culmination of this work came in 1922 with Vakhtangov's internationally famous production of *The Dybbuk*.

CHAPTER TWENTY-ONE

OPERA

In the autumn of 1918 Elena Malinovskai approached the Art Theatre to see whether it could not collaborate with the Bolshoi and help raise the standard of acting there. She had been given responsibility for the Academic theatres in Moscow and was determined to protect and develop them. She was also concerned to train a new generation of singers. What she foresaw was the creation of a studio.

A gala evening was arranged for December 30. After dinner, members of each company performed extracts from their repertoire. The occasion was a considerable success. Both theatres seemed more than happy to cooperate. In the event the collaboration merely highlighted the deep division that existed between Stanislavski and the Art Theatre. Nemirovich worked consistently on major Bolshoi productions while Stanislavski worked on his own in the two rooms that were set aside for rehearsals at the house in Carriage Row. In 1919 Nemirovich created the Art Theatre Music Studio with which Stanislavski had no connection.

Stanislavski proceeded with caution. It was many years since he had worked in the musical sphere although his own musical culture had continued to deepen. He was not at all sure how welcome his ideas would be. One of his duties was to help the lead singers. He was aware that many established opera stars were convinced that all they had to do was open their mouths and allow a magical larynx to do the rest. They could be resistant. On January 20, 1919, he gave a demonstration-lecture to senior members of the Bolshoi company. Some were genuinely interested and participated in the exercises; others listened politely on the sidelines. A month later a small but dedicated group made great efforts in the most adverse weather conditions to get to his house for lessons. The work was fragmentary. It was impossible ever to get a complete group together because of rehearsal schedules; tenor, soprano and baritone were present at different times and the final result had to be patched together at the last moment. Malinovskaia, according to Stanislavski's account, watched over the whole enterprise like a mother.

Yet he still needed convincing that he could be of genuine use. The only means of proving it was to submit his work to critical examination. At the beginning of March he began rehearsing a series of extracts from Dargomizhski's *Rusalka* and Rimski-Korsakov's *May Night*. The results were shown at a small private performance in June before Nemirovich and the Art Theatre company. Members of the Bolshoi were, evidently, not invited. There was no doubt in anyone's mind that the results were positive.

Stanislavski agreed to continue his work but subject to certain conditions. The kind of improvised arrangements he had been working under would not do in the long term. He had uncovered the full depth of the problems young singers encountered. They had voices but no sense of theatre. The Studio must be properly organized, with a coherent and comprehensive programme. It would accept young singers from the Bolshoi and students from the Moscow Conservatoire, who, once they had proved their worth in class, would be allowed to perform. His teaching was based on the fusion of two masters, Shchepkin and Chaliapin. the 'system' was the means, Chaliapin was the goal.

The study programme consisted of two main areas: exercises in the 'system' and in technique, which took place in the morning, and work on repertoire for the rest of the day. He drew on the resources both of the Art Theatre and the Bolshoi to bring in teachers. Volkonski was invited to give courses on diction and Pospekhin, from the Bolshoi ballet, to teach dance and expressive movement. Stanislavski himself attended the classes as part of his own research and retraining. He also took the opportunity to bring in his sister Zinaïda and his brother Vladimir to teach and supervise the general running of the studio. His own contribution was a series of thirty-two lectures on the 'system' delivered between 1919 and 1922.

The experience of working in music theatre revitalized him. He felt, as he wrote to one of his pupils, that he had been starved of music. Here was a chance to escape from the routine of the Art Theatre, to re-examine his ideas, to test them out on young artists who came because they wanted to and who were not yet caught up in back-stage or front-of-house politics. It was also an opportunity to refute the accusation that the 'system' only had validity for 'naturalistic' plays. If it could be made to work in opera, that 'irrational entertainment' as Dr Johnson described it, with its seemingly insurmountable conventions, it could prove its universality and its claims to be rooted in the real world of nature.

His objective was to create a synthesis of words, music, movement and gesture. Actions, motivation, he insisted, were to be found in the score, not in the stage directions which were often added later, without reference to the composer and in blatant contradiction to the music. A bar-by-bar examination of the structure of the music, its rhythm, and of the particular colour of the orchestration would supply the information needed for a truthful performance. It was essential above all for the singers to take the music into themselves, to experience its rhythm and tempo internally as their own. They were no longer to stand with their eyes glued on the conductor, waiting for his beat. They should feel the beat, not watch it. At the same time, in an ideal company, the orchestra would understand the 'system' and would be aware of the dramatic as well as the musical significance of the score so that there would be unity of intent throughout the company and the performance.

Such ambitions are not achieved overnight and Stanislavski proceeded slowly. A primary task was to make the singers sensitive to the full potential of the words they were singing. He began with singers from Tchaikovski's *Evgeni Onegin*. This opera makes two major demands. In the first instance the libretto consists almost entirely of lines from Pushkin's original poem and is therefore very demanding on diction and delivery; in the second, it is an opera of great psychological depth with solo and two-handed scenes where any failure of imaginative insight is cruelly exposed. Stanislavski explored the text as he would with a dramatic actor, refusing to accept anything that was vague or generalized, insisting that the words should have precise, vivid images behind them. To *Onegin* he added scenes from *Rusalka* and worked on both throughout the 1919–20 season. At the end of June there was a final dress rehearsal in costume and make-up without a public audience.

The students were, however, pushed into a public appearance rather sooner than Stanislavski wished. As a teacher he was unwilling to force the pace, he always wanted more time but the original intention had been to bring the Bolshoi and the Art Theatre closer together. By 1921 it was important to show some results. On April 18 members of the First and Second Studios and of the Bolshoi company presented a Rimski-Korsakov Evening at the Opera Studio. This was followed, on June 9, by another Rimski-Korsakov Evening given by the students of the Opera Studio, this time at the Art Theatre itself. Stanislavski wisely restricted his pupils to the presentation of songs, which he had prepared with the same meticulous attention to detail that he applied to full-scale opera.

At the same moment he began rehearsing Massenet's *Werther*. Here again the choice of material was crucial. Apart from a group of children, *Werther* contains no chorus and no big set-pieces. Instead there is close interplay between the characters and, as in *Onegin*, monologues and two-handed scenes. Work continued throughout June and July side-by-side with rehearsals for a Pushkin evening. This was presented at the Art Theatre for a run of six performances in a modest staging using drops and screens. They were out of season and attracted little attention. It was with a studio performance of *Onegin* in the following year, however, that the Opera Studio really made its mark.

The study of scenes from *Onegin* had run like a thread through all the Opera Studio's work. Now Stanislavski decided he would stage the whole work. Circumstances provided him with the ideal setting. He had received notice that he was finally to be evicted from Carriage Row. He had managed to stay there after the Revolution by letting out most of the house to members of the First Studio, who used the larger rooms as rehearsal spaces. Now he was to lose the small number of rooms he still occupied. Why the authorities should have chosen to take this step at this time is not clear, unless it was a further example of the resentment that had been displayed at the time of his arrest. Although he had always taken steps to ensure that the members of the company had food and shelter, he did nothing in his own behalf, neither reacting nor protesting against the eviction order, although he apparently broke down and wept now that after four years of apprehension and doubt, his worst fears were realized. Lunacharski attempted to intervene only to find himself blocked by an official in his own department. He was informed that, while Stanislavski's stature as an artist was not in doubt, his enormous house could provide much-needed space for transport facilities. Lunacharski found this argument entirely unconvincing. He pointed out that not only would this action alienate many intellectuals, it would have repercussions across Europe. He finally went direct to Lenin.

Lenin's solution was ingenious. He rehoused Stanislavski and his Opera Studio simultaneously, so that his official work-place became his home. A large house was found at No. 6 Leontievski (now Stanislavski) Lane, a few minutes' walk from the Art Theatre. Stanislavski moved in on March 5, 1921, and it was here that he lived until his death. The house was a modest but attractive building, constructed during the Napoleonic period. On the first floor there was a large ballroom, just across the corridor from what were to be the family's living quarters. At one end was a raised platform, originally intended for the orchestra, with four sets of double pillars. When Stanislavski visited the house in January his first comment was, 'It will be perfect for *Onegin*.'

The production was designed to fit within the space. It was to be a chamber performance. This meant that the peasant scene in Act One, with its singing and dancing, was severely curtailed. Stanislavski did not consider this a loss as he found the scene something of a conventional set-piece which held up the action. He wished to concentrate on the human drama.

Clarity of diction and the meaning of the words were a major concern. He wanted the singers to be aware, during ensemble numbers, of the important line and to adjust the balance accordingly, holding back where necessary to let one single, as Stanislavski called it, 'word-thought' voice emerge. Typical of this was the opera's opening number, a quartet, or rather a double duet, Larina and the Nurse, Filipievna, on the one hand, Tatiana and Olga on the other. Tatiana and Olga are singing a duet while the other two reminisce. According to the published score Larina and the Nurse are making jam. Stanislavski considered this quite specious and could find no justification for it in the music. On the contrary he invited the two to sit back and relax after a hard day's work – on the terrace suggested by the columns and not under a tree as indicated in the libretto

– and listen to the young people singing. Vocally the problem was to make both the duet and the conversation of the two older women intelligible. The solution was to place Tatiana and Olga inside the house, invisible to the audience, giving depth and perspective to both sets of voices. This also provided Tatiana with a more effective first entrance. Rehearsal time was devoted to ease and naturalness of movement so that the music for all its complexity could emerge from credible behaviour. The audience would be at close range and would detect any hint of artificiality.

Full rehearsals had begun in November 1921, transferring in March 1922 to Leontievski Lane. The performance was previewed in May and opened on June 15. The accompaniment was provided by a grand piano placed in the body of the hall. There was the minimum of set, no costumes and no make-up. The singers were on their own.

The evening created another Stanislavski legend. Two years later the production transferred with full orchestra to the Novi Teatr. Stanislavski's staging survived many years and many changes of cast. As for the famous ballroom columns they acquired the status of an icon. No production of *Onegin* anywhere in Russia was possible without them. They turned up in every set. So much so that in the 1930s Meierhold remarked that if there was one thing he wanted to do with Tchaikovski's opera it was to ditch them once and for all. As for the ballroom, from that time onward it became known as the Onegin Room.

Stanislavski's work at the Opera Studio had a decisive influence on the development of his own ideas and of the 'system', in particular on the importance he gave to the notions of tempo and rhythm. A musical score provides basic speeds, an inner impulse for each part or bit of the action. That impulse is integral to the scene. Stanislavski carried this notion over into the dramatic theatre and from this period onward he was increasingly concerned in rehearsal to find the appropriate tempo-rhythm for each moment in the play. His thinking on the subject is summarized in *An Actor's Work on Himself: Part Two*.

Stanislavski's activities at the Opera Studio during this period are well documented. Pavel Rumiantsev, who sang the title role in *Onegin*, kept a record of rehearsals from 1919 to 1932, which was ultimately published in 1969. Another singer, Konkordia Antarova, who sang Charlotte in the 1921 version of *Werther*, took detailed notes of all of Stanislavski's lectures on the 'system' and of the *Werther* rehearsals. They were intended only for her private benefit but in 1938 Stanislavski's sister, Zinaïda, tracked them down. They were edited by Mrs Gurevich and published the following year. Stanislavski delivered the lectures off-the-cuff, using brief jottings which appear in the *Notebooks*. They are, nonetheless, even allowing for some tidying up by Mrs Gurevich, clear and coherent.

It does not seem to have occurred to Stanislavski to publish them. This was a pity since he could have saved himself a great deal of trouble had an accurate statement of his views been available. He was continuously at a disadvantage in the ideological debates that raged from 1917 to 1934 because his opponents were for the most part working on hearsay or on half-understood, distorted summaries offered for the most part by people outside the Art Theatre. Everyone in the theatrical world knew about the 'system' and a minor industry grew up explaining it. According to Nikolai Efrod, a completed manuscript on the 'system' existed in 1918 yet Stanislavski could not bring himself to publish it. All he would agree to was the publication of the first section of *Various Trends in the Art of the Theatre* on the hack-actor in the magazine *Kultura Teatra*, but this was no more than a demolition job. It said nothing about his own ideas.

In 1916 Fiodor Komissarzhevski, the son of Stanislavski's old teacher, put out a volume *The Creative Actor and the Stanislavski Theory*. It was fulsomely dedicated to Stanislavski and, in the view of the dedicatee, totally misleading. Stanislavski's enraged comments are to be found in the margin. The word 'lies' makes more than one appearance.

Michael Chekhov had also gone into print in 1919 in the Proletkult magazine *Gorn* with a short article which was equally unsatisfactory. Stanislavski did not respond publicly. It was left to Vakhtangov who delivered a sharp attack on both writers in *Vestnik Teatra* accusing them of inaccuracy and of treating isolated elements of the 'system' out of context. It would take, he remarked prophetically, several volumes to describe the 'system' in its complete form. Nothing deterred, however, in 1921, Smishliaev published his *Theory of Stage Production*, also published by Proletkult. Stanislavski jotted down his adverse comments but did not make them public. He noted that Smishliaev was simply an inadequate and backward pupil.

The scope and volume of Stanislavski's activities and the attention paid to his ideas merely served to emphasize the inertia of the Art Theatre itself. Between 1917 and 1922 it staged one new production and that was Stanislavski's. Initially, while relations with the First Studio were still tolerably good, he worked there, supervising and revising productions prepared by young directors. The revolution of February 1917 put him in a mood of determined optimism and his work is characterized by a search for positive elements. In May 1917 he saw work-in-progress on *Twelfth Night*, directed by Sushkevich. The production was in a lamentable state. Both cast and director were depressed. The play was shrouded in gloom. Stanislavski took over rehearsals and rebuilt the production stone by stone, continuing his work in the autumn. He insisted that the play was light, youthful, without a shadow in the sky. He imposed a rapid pace on the whole performance, driving his young actors to a state of near exhaustion. For the first time in his productions the action spilled over into the auditorium, with characters appearing behind the audience and running down the aisles. It was an overt display of 'theatricality'.

Vakhtangov, who had not yet come under Meierhold's influence, was both shocked and bewildered by Stanislavski's almost exclusive emphasis on the externals of the staging. What had happened to the 'system'? Where was the inner psychological truth to justify the outer action? He felt that the image of the First Studio had been tarnished. At the same time he did not doubt that the production would be a huge success. And so it proved on the opening night, December 25. Three years later Lunacharski could still recommend it to Lenin as the best show in Moscow.

A similar determination to find positive elements in established works was evident in the reworking of *The Seagull* which was in rehearsal at the same time as *Twelfth Night*. Stanislavski was concerned to reverse the view of Chekhov as a pessimist. He took a much less negative view of Konstantin. For the first time he introduced the comparison between Konstantin and Hamlet. It must, of course, be remembered that he saw Hamlet as an active moral force and not as a melancholic intellectual.

'S. suggested an analogy between Hamlet and Treplev. For both of them at a difficult period in their lives there was only their mother. [The more his mother] was dear to [Treplev] in that moment, the more he desired to reform her and the more he controlled himself. He decides to kill himself not because he does not wish to live but because he passionately wants to live, he snatches at everything that would enable him to root himself firmly in life but everything collapses round him. For him – an aesthete – there is nothing in life to keep him back [from death]. His through-action: *to live* to live beautifully, aspiring to Moscow, to Moscow. Chekhov was a man of action, he was not a pessimist. Life in the 80s was such that it created Chekhov's heroes. He himself loved life, aspired to a better life, like all his heroes.' (Notes by P. F. Sharov, production assistant, in the rehearsal daybook, September 12, 1917. K.S. Archive, No. 4328/1.)

After *The Seagull* there was nothing: 1918 and the first half of 1919 were consumed by the vain struggle to push the theatre forward into the future. In October 1919, *Pravda* announced:

'The Art Theatre, which has not offered a single new production in the last three years, has decided to present Byron's *Cain* with L. M. Leonidov in the title role.' (*Pravda*, October 1, 1919, No. 218, p. 2.)

The decision to put on an obscure example of romantic drama, unknown even to British audiences, as a response to the post-Revolutionary situation in Russia might appear strange. But the material was not entirely out of keeping with the spirit of the time. Few people were Marxists, or materialists, or discussed the Revolution in abstract, political terms. Much of the writing of the period is couched in quasi-religious, biblical, almost apocalyptic language. Stanislavski had originally planned to stage Byron's play in 1907 but had been prevented from doing so by the church. This poetic expression of revolt suited him temperamentally. The initiative to take the plan off the shelf did not, however, come from Stanislavski himself but from Leonidov to whom the lead role had originally been promised. On April 19, 1917, he wrote to Stanislavski asking for permission to stage the play at the First Studio. His intention appears to have been not only to play the title role but to direct as well. Boleslavski would play Abel and act as assistant director. A full cast-list was supplied. Naturally it was hoped that Stanislavski would give all the help he could.

No reply from Stanislavski is recorded. In the autumn of 1918, however, Leonidov read the play to the First Studio by which time Vakhtangov had taken over. He had written to Stanislavski in July with a final cast-list, slightly different from Leonidov's original. Ideas on staging had begun to form in Vakhtangov's mind. In his diary entry for November 24 he noted the importance of putting the play on. Interest in the project spanned the generations. This Mystery, for all its religious connotations, was felt to be relevant to current conditions. But in August 1919 the play was taken away from the First Studio and transferred to the main house. Stanislavski later, in *My Life in Art*, described the whole production as 'doomed from the start' and 'an abortion'. On June 1 the bulk of the Art Theatre company, including such key figures as Kachalov and Knipper, had started a tour of the Ukraine. They were immediately cut off by the Civil War and could not get back. They spent the next three years touring Europe. An emergency meeting was called for August 6. Stanislavski travelled back overnight from Kimri, near Moscow, together with Moskvin and Vishnievski, the only senior company members left, arriving at eleven in the morning. They had to walk across the whole of Moscow to get to Nemirovich's office. Decisions had to be taken as how best to deploy the theatre's remaining forces.

Under the circumstances it would have been logical to merge the studios with the main house and form one company. But Nemirovich had no wish to go cap in hand to the First Studio which he continued to regard with suspicion. As for the Studio itself, it was split into warring factions. The result was a stand-off: on the one hand, the Studio waiting to be asked to help, on the other, the Art Theatre waiting for help to be offered. Inevitably the two companies remained apart. The Art Theatre took its fate in its hands and decided that Stanislavski should direct *Cain*. Work was to begin immediately. Stanislavski retired once more to Kimri to work on the production plan.

He saw Byron's Mystery play, like *Stepanchikovo*, as a conflict between the cosmic principles of good and evil and his intention was to bring out the contemporary relevance. God is conceived as a 'conservative' and Lucifer as an 'anarchist'. The problem was, as with the Dostoievski, that he was trying to make the text bear more than it could reasonably carry and so, despite his statements early in rehearsal that what was needed was not theological discussion but a factual analysis of the action, as work progressed more and more time was spent on philosophical issues. In September Stanislavski read I. A. Illin's book, *The Philosophy of Hegel as Doctrine of the Concrete Nature of God and Man*, making extensive notes as he went along. The central issue was the origin of evil. If God is perfect and His creation is perfect, how does evil come into being?

Cain is conceived as the archetypal rebel. He is dominated by a feeling of injustice and futility, marking him off from his family. His sense of alienation is the counterpart of Lucifer's own opposition to God, the opposition of the spirit of absolute freedom to the spirit of compromise. God simply wants to side-step the problem of the origin of evil:

'. . . God says: No, good and evil have to be, i.e., we must allow compromise. Lucifer responds: compromise begets rules and regulations, etc., which diminish and destroy freedom. There must be truth and freedom. Though mankind should perish and the world fall apart, when all is said and done, they will come to the truth and know everything. God affirms that such freedom leads to egotism and only through goodness and non-resistance to evil, etc., can goodness come through. Lucifer affirms that but for the existence of good and evil there would be bliss, paradise.' (Rehearsal notes, September 5, 1919. K.S. Archive.)

In Stanislavski's concept of the play, Cain and Lucifer enter into a symbiotic relationship:

'. . . in that moment when the first man appears asking intelligent questions, saying "Why?", Lucifer (*lux ferus* the bearer of light) appears. Lucifer is an extension of Cain. That is "Why", "What for". Those spirits who created the earth with God, having created it, could not agree as to what it should be. Lucifer wanted to people the earth with gods but God created Man. And thus Lucifer approaches, goes to Cain. . . . Don't you feel what that encounter means when a man is approached by a super-being, how he fears it, how he recoils from it, how he is drawn to it even though there is no enticement. [Lucifer shows him] all the beauties of the world, the boundlessness of space and leads him to the highest ecstasy. . . . And then Cain comes to life again. He is now someone quite different. He is filled with the spirit of denial.' (Stenographic record, November 21, 1919. K.S. Archive, No. 834.)

There are therefore two fundamentally opposing views in the play: those who, like Adam, Eve and Abel, say, 'Wonderful are Thy Works, O Lord' and those who, like Cain and Lucifer, reply, 'Not so, the world was created imperfect.' The extension of the conflict between Cain/Lucifer and God is the conflict between Cain and his brother Abel. If Cain's through-action is 'Why?', Abel's is, 'I believe':

> 'The secret lies in this, that for Cain the most important thing is cognition (the tree of knowledge), for Abel it is life as it happens to be.
>   The fact is there are two truths. For Cain the truth is in enquiry, for the others the truth is absolute.' (Ibid.)

It was important not to see Abel as a purely passive or a weak character. Gaidarov, who was playing the role, had his own views:

> 'Gaidarov (Abel) detects in Abel hints of the future Christ. Abel's last words – of reconciliation – are Christ's own words ("they know not what they do")
>
> > "Oh God! receive thy servant and
> > Forgive his slayer for he knew not what
> > He did – Cain, give me – give me thy hand. . . ."' (Ibid.)

From this flowed the idea that mankind is descended from Cain, since Abel died childless. Abel returns in the form of Christ.

These theological issues had then to be translated into political terms. Lengthy discussions took place on the nature of revolution and the class war. These discussions, in turn, had to be expressed in the performance. Despite all the metaphysics the actors were given concrete, practical tasks. Stanislavski insisted that thought must be a direct, lived experience, an idea must be a 'living vision'. 'Thought,' he stated, 'cannot be understood by thought alone.' This was crucial in a play such as *Cain*, which is set in the childhood, the innocence of the world, when sophisticated intellectual processes did not exist. There was no sense, except for Cain, of today and yesterday. Everything was a permanent now. There was no division between what was thought and what was said. In consequence he ruled out any question of subtext. Impulse and expression were directly linked. Equally he ruled out a suggestion from Shakhalov, who was cast as Lucifer, that he should play the character as more than human. An actor, Stanislavski replied, could not escape his human status. A superman could only be an extension of a man.

In his attempt to make the play relevant, particularly to the Civil War, Stanislavski would provide contemporary analogies. In Act Three, towards the end of the play, Eve has a climactic scene in which she realized that Cain has murdered his brother and curses him:

> 'Let us assume that a depraved German soldier raped you during the offensive and then vanished. Having given birth to a child you try to forget the appalling truth, you pray, you resign yourself. The child is your first born. All the time, all your life you fear that the German will

come out in him. Finally, one beautiful day, with your own eyes, you see in your son that very German in whose face you could not spit. Therefore you curse not the son but his father.' (Rehearsal notes, September 4, 1919, K.S. Archive.)

If the cast entered happily and willingly into the complicated rehearsal process, the atmosphere on the technical/design side was far less happy. Although, in *My Life in Art*, Stanislavski claims that he was aware of the need to be cost-conscious the production was conceived on the grand scale. He intended to use a full orchestra and chorus but to keep expenses down by having one adaptable set. The theatre, including the auditorium, was to become a cathedral. The actors would be dressed as monks performing a Mystery play. The set would be elaborately architectural, with statues of saints and gargoyles. The flight of Cain and Lucifer through space would be represented by their climbing a large staircase while the stars and planets would be represented by lamps at the end of poles held by the officiants. Changes of time of day or night would be indicated by the light which filtered through giant stained-glass windows. A huge tree with shining fruit would represent the tree of the knowledge of good and evil with two stones on either side to serve as an altar.

The idea had to be scrapped. There was not enough money either to build such a set or to employ the number of extras that would be needed. Stanislavski and his designer, Andreiev, then came up with another approach. They would make use of one of Stanislavski's favourite earlier devices, black velvet. Against this background architectural elements for Act One and movable statues for Act Two would be set.

'In the scene in Hell the tormented spirits of the Great Figures of the past who had lived in an earlier world, were represented by huge statues, three times life-size. . . . We found a very simple method of making these movable statues. Andreiev modelled heads with torsos and arms. We placed them on the end of long poles and draped them in ordinary scenic canvas of a yellow very close to the clay from which statues are made. The material fell in large folds and spread out on the floor.

When these statues were placed against the background of black velvet, by dimming everything down and lighting them in a special way they seemed transparent and produced a weird impression. To show the flight of Cain and Lucifer, in the second act we built high platforms covered in black velvet which were in consequence invisible against a background of identical material. When Cain and Lucifer were on them the audience had the impression that they were floating between the ceiling and the stage floor. Extras dressed in black carried huge lamps of translucent mica on the end of long black poles to represent dead planets. The black extras and the black poles disappeared into the background of black velvet so that the planets seemed to float in the air.' (SS, I, p. 380.)

Even this proved impossible. There was simply not enough black velvet in the whole of Moscow to black out the entire stage. It had to be replaced by black canvas. Unfortunately canvas does not absorb light in the way velvet does. The carefully calculated lighting-effects did not really work.

If Stanislavski's frequent complaints are to be taken seriously, there was a lack of coordination on the technical side which meant the sets were not ready. People were not consulting each other. By the end of December Stanislavski was threatening to decline responsibility for the production and only to answer for the acting.

Even the acting, however, was proving problematic. There was a serious lack of discipline. Worse, the sets, compromise though they were, had the effect of highlighting the technical inadequacies of the cast, with the exception of Leonidov. A high standard of diction was achieved, with clear incisive speech, but the giant statues, and such architectural structures as could be managed for Act One, revealed the serious limitations of the actors' bodies and their inability to extend out from mere day-to-day movement into a more poetically expressive dimension. If there was one serious flaw in Stanislavski's training at this period it was in the area of physical expression. Despite his experiments with yoga and Dalcroze eurhythmics he had not studied the problem systematically enough. It was precisely in this area that younger directors, Meierhold, Taïrov and Vakhtangov were making advances. The hastily assembled cast, particularly the younger and inexperienced members, had no skills with which to respond to the demands of the production.

In My Life in Art Stanislavski claims that the play was put on before it was ready. In reality it was he who forced the issue. He was fully aware that another season could not be allowed to go by without a new production. In January he wrote in the rehearsal daybook:

'For the salvation of the theatre and its children it is *imperative, imperative, imperative, come what may*, for *Cain* to go on in the immediate future.' (Daybook, January 13, 1920.)

Cain opened on April 4 and survived eight performances. The audience was simply bewildered. Stanislavski had made a futile attempt at a public dress rehearsal on the 2nd to explain the play's relevance; from the opening music and chorus to the end the audience sat in numbed silence. Stanislavski tried to blame the production's failure on the audience who consisted largely of workers and peasants but then why did the cultivated people, the 'intellectuals', stay away? The fact remains that the decision to stage the play had been a huge error of judgement on everyone's part. The critics were hostile. The theatre seemed once more to have proved its irrelevance to contemporary life and its incapacity to break with its 'bourgeois' past. Zagorski concluded that not only was the Art Theatre incapable of 'revolution' it could not even achieve 'evolution'.

Meierhold came to Stanislavski's defence. In an article, 'The Isolation of Stanislavski', published in the spring of 1921, he described the production of *Cain* as a tragic failure but saluted Stanislavski's attempt to stage something large-scale and ambitious. He was still the Michelangelo of theatre art. If only he had chosen something else, not *Cain*. Meierhold spoke with the experience of another kind of Mystery play behind him. In the autumn of 1918 he had staged three performances of Maiakovski's *Mystery-Bouffe*. Shunned by professional actors, put on with the help of almost anyone who made themselves available, Maiakovski's aggressive, irreverent, iconoclastic text, bristling with contemporary allusions, made its mark. In its 1921 version it was destined to become one of the classics of early Soviet theatre. Lenin might call it 'hooligan communism' but it spoke to audiences in a way that *Cain* could not. Meierhold argued that Stanislavski was a genius whose flair and originality were stifled by the mediocre ambitions and petty atmosphere of the Art Theatre. There was a theatrical animal waiting to be released. The price of salvation was for him to go it alone.

Meierhold was not alone in this view. Among Stanislavski's younger associates and pupils there was a growing sense that he must somehow be rescued. In conversation in November 1921 Vakhtangov expressed the need to get Stanislavski to break with the main house and move permanently into the First Studio. Someone had to open his eyes but who was that person to be?

The following year Vladimir Volkenstein published an eighty-page monograph, *Stanislavski*. Volkenstein had been at the very heart of the Art Theatre's affairs. He worked there as a dramaturg and had been responsible, with Nemirovich, for the adaptation in 1917 of *Stepanchikovo*. From 1913 to 1921 he had charge of the literary department of the First Studio after which he became Stanislavski's secretary. The book caused Stanislavski acute embarrassment. It underplayed Nemirovich's contribution to the Art Theatre and the final sections, 'A Spiritual Portrait of Stanislavski and Stanislavski's Fate', depicted him as a lonely figure, isolated in his conflict with Nemirovich and shackled by a dead realism. Volkenstein provides a graphic description of Stanislavski sitting alone on social evenings, like a votary, with a yawning void all round him. Stanislavski felt impelled to write to Nemirovich to disassociate himself from what his secretary had written. In his letter of September 22, 1922, he told Nemirovich that he had discussed the problem with several professional colleagues and had been advised that it would be a mistake for him to reply directly as it would only inflate the whole business further and make it seem as though he was putting on a rather coy display of nobility. He suggested that someone should be found to write a suitably sharp review. Yet Stanislavski was perhaps less embarrassed by the truth or falsity of Volkenstein's statements, which were not entirely without foundation, than by the fact that his often bitter quarrel with Nemirovich, which both men had resolutely tried to keep private and 'within the family', had suddenly become public knowledge. From a contemporary point of view Volkenstein's book is significant in its description of the 'system' for the emphasis it places, even at this early period, on physical action rather than on the search for emotion, thus undermining the notion that Stanislavski's work in his final years represents a total break with earlier practice.

After *Cain* no further new productions were scheduled for the foreseeable future. The Art Theatre had to fall back once more on restaging old productions. Yet it was with Gogol's *Inspector General* that Stanislavski was able to re-establish his right to be heard in the debate on new theatrical styles. Officially it was a revival of the production of 1908 in which Kachalov had scored such a great success, but in reality it was a complete reworking of the whole staging. It was essential in Stanislavski's view to rethink the play in terms of changed circumstances. With Kachalov still abroad, the lead was given to Michael Chekhov. The 1908 production had been considered remarkable in its time for the degree of exaggeration it had displayed. By the early 1920s the obsessive preoccupation with 'non-naturalistic' acting focused on the concept of the Grotesque, defined by Vakhtangov as acting that was both tragic and comic but which went beyond normal 'character acting' to extend into new dimensions of fantasy. An alternative definition was Imaginative Realism. Vakhtangov's approach was demonstrated in Strindberg's *Erik XIV* which opened on March 29, 1921, with Michael Chekhov in the lead. The style was typified by the exaggerated, non-realistic make-up. Stanislavski wanted to demonstrate his own view of the Grotesque, which he passionately advanced to the sick and dying Vakhtangov late in 1921. In 1929 Stanislavski, who was then ill, dictated an account of this discussion to his doctor, now published under the title *From the Last Conversation with Evgeni Vakhtangov*.

His view was that the Grotesque is a rarity, something only experienced and highly talented actors can achieve, not a style that can be applied indiscriminately to any text. It has to be the expression of enormous creative energy, springing from the unconscious.

'. . . real Grotesque means the vivid, external, audacious justification of enormous inner content, which is so all-embracing as to verge on exaggeration. Not only must human passions be felt and lived through in the full vigour of all their essential elements but they must be concentrated and made manifest, graphic, irresistible in their expression, outrageous, bold, going to the brink of over-acting.' (*SS*, VI, p. 256.)

Without a compulsive inner drive the Grotesque is

'. . . a pie without filling, a bottle without wine, a body without a soul.'
(Ibid., p. 257.)

Gogol is an author who can withstand, indeed demands the Grotesque
and in Michael Chekhov, Stanislavski had an actor of genius who could
achieve it without losing his essential humanity to become a mechanical
clown or a gesticulating puppet. Chekhov had an exceptional ability to
invent and execute stage business. Stanislavski cut all this away. All
effort went into the creation of inner tasks, motivations, which would
generate extraordinary, eccentric behaviour, the Grotesque as he
understood it. To most people the performance seemed endlessly
improvised; no one could tell what he would do next. Nemirovich found
himself endlessly checking the script as one new reading after another
came at him. Gogol's text was untouched.

For the rest of the cast, Stanislavski conceived the play as a study in
mass hysteria, a madness which overtakes a whole community and
swamps its reason. That he intended this interpretation to apply to his
contemporaries is clear from one effect which he introduced at the end of
the play. On the Mayor's line, 'What are you laughing at? Yourselves,
aren't you?' the lights came full up not only on the stage but also in the
auditorium. Moskvin threw the words straight out front, to the audience.

The production, which opened on October 8, 1921, provided a much-
needed success. For the first time in many years an Art Theatre
presentation provoked a serious public debate. This was conducted in the
tradition of the old 'thick' magazines in the pages of the first issue of the
newly created *Teatralnaia Moskva* and in the *Vestnik Teatra*, once an
innocuous journal but now, under Meierhold's influence, the voice of the
radical left.

It was Michael Chekhov's performance that was the most widely
discussed and *Teatralnaia Moskva* launched the debate by calling
attention to the wide and unremitting coverage it had received in the
Moscow press, most of it highly favourable. The counterattack was led
by the *Vestnik Teatra*. One critic described Chekhov's performance as
that of 'a total nonentity, insolent, loudmouthed, without a brain in his
head'. An equally negative judgement came from Vladimir Blum who
defined the performance as 'the same old snub-nosed little idiot
Petrushka'. Earlier in the year he had described it as one of the most
unpleasant spectacles the European theatre had put his way in the last
eight to ten years. One positive voice was that of Meierhold's
collaborator, Zagorski. He found the performance 'stupendous, awe-
inspiring, Hoffmanesque, like a chimera' and at the same time 'joyful,
endearing, full of light and fascination'. Meierhold himself disliked the
production as a whole but confided to a friend that Chekhov's
performance had provided a revelation of new methods of achieving the

Grotesque in acting. Just how many people realized the contribution Stanislavski had made to Chekhov's success is not certain.

Four days after *The Inspector General* opened Stanislavski began work on a revival of Tolstoi's *The Fruits of Enlightenment*, hoping perhaps to repeat his success, but despite several months of effort he could not discover a line on the play which could speak to a modern audience and the production was abandoned.

CHAPTER TWENTY-TWO

AMERICA

By January 1921 Nemirovich had to admit that the Art Theatre was almost defenceless in the battle against what he later described as near-hooliganism. He himself had made a serious tactical blunder and provided fresh ammunition to his enemies by opening his new Music Studio in the summer of 1920 with a French operetta, *La Fille de Madame Angot*. Meierhold gave expression to the contempt felt by the avant-garde:

'Now we know what the Moscow Art Theatre audience consists of, leftovers of the bourgeoisie who couldn't managed to get a boat out . . .' (*Vestnik Teatra*, Nos 834/4, 1921.)

Maiakovski too had added his powerful voice to the opposition. In 1920 he wrote an open letter to Lunacharski describing the theatre of Anton Chekhov and Stanislavski as 'putrescent'. In the Prologue to the revised *Mystery-Bouffe* he proclaimed the virtues of overt theatricality and, with a direct quote from Meierhold, poured scorn on the Art Theatre.

'For other companies
real theatre doesn't matter:
for them
the stage
is just a key-hole.
Sit down, shut up, relax now
straight or skew
we have a slice of life for you.
Listen, look at
Auntie Mania
Uncle Vania
sitting on the sofa whining.
But we don't give a hoot for
aunt and uncle
Uncle and aunt you've got at home.
We can show you real life too
but now
transformed by theatre into a super-show.'
            (Maiakovski, *Sobranie Sochinenii*, ix, pp. 107–8.)

He was not to know, nor was anyone at the time, how disenchanted Stanislavski himself was with Chekhov, how irrelevant he felt him to be. He kept his feelings to himself but finally, from the safe distance of Berlin, in the autumn of 1922, unburdened himself to Nemirovich:

'. . . It would be ridiculous to take pleasure in the success of . . . the Chekhov productions or be proud of them. When we play the farewell to Masha in *Three Sisters* I am embarrassed. After all we have lived through it is impossible to weep over the fact that an officer is going and leaving his lady behind. Chekhov gives no joy. On the contrary who wants to play him?' (*SS*, VII, p. 29.)

When Efros tried to defend the Art Theatre as a living and valuable tradition he was accused in the *Vestnik Teatra* of 'demonstrating his White [anti-Revolutionary] nature'. Even Lunacharski was attacked by Vladimir Blum for 'propagating bourgeois culture'. Taïrov entered the fray, publishing a collection of his writings, *A Director's Notebook*. In it he distanced himself both from Meierhold and Stanislavski. He could not accept Meierhold's reduction of the actor to a mere mechanical function. On the other hand he was not willing to endorse Stanislavski's thesis of a necessary connection between emotion as experienced in life and emotion as experienced on the stage. Stage feelings were essentially imaginative creations. Nor was there any conscious, systematic way of evoking them; they were spontaneous and mysterious. What he sought was a freely creative imagination, contained within a tightly choreographed stage pattern. Stanislavski, as usual, contented himself with writing caustic comments in the margins, Meierhold went public with a critical article.

For a time, it seemed as though Meierhold's views were to be translated into political reality. In the autumn of 1920 he had assumed charge of the Theatrical Section (TEO) of the Commissariat for Enlightenment. He was one of the few members of his profession to have experienced the Civil War at first hand. Caught by the hostilities in southern Russia where he was convalescing, he had been imprisoned by the White Army. He was subsequently liberated by the Red Army and joined its political section. Lunacharski then called him to Moscow. He arrived in September with a radical plan of reform to eliminate the Academic theatres and replace them with popular, non-professional and Red Army theatres – a Theatrical October – a term invented for him by Vladimir Blum.

The time seemed right for a tactical retreat. Nemirovich approached Lunacharski with a plan to split the Art Theatre company into three. One group would remain in Moscow, another would tour the provinces and a third would take advantage of the many outstanding invitations to Europe and the United States, some of which dated from before the war. Yet even as the far left seemed to be triumphing, Proletkult's claims to

9a *The Cherry Orchard* (Chekhov)
Stanislavski as Gaev, 1904.

9b *Ivanov* (Chekhov) Stanislavski as
Shabielski, 1904.

10 Stanislavski as Satin in *The Lower Depths* (Gorki), 1902.

11 Stanislavski, Gorki, Lilina. Yalta, 1900.

12a *Woe From Wit* (Griboiedov)
Stanislavski as Famusov,
1906.

12b *Woe From Wit*
Stanislavski as Famusov,
1914.

13 The house at
Carriage Row where
the Stanislavskis
lived from 1903 to
1921.

14a *Le Malade Imaginaire*
(Molière) Stanislavski
as Argan, 1913.

14b Stanislavski as
Cavaliere Rippafratta
in *La Locandiera* (Goldoni).

14c *Enough Stupidity in
Every Wise Man*
(Ostrovski). Stanislavski as
Krutitski, 1910.

15a Stanislavski
and Sokolova
at work, 1924.

15b Lunacharski,
Stanislavski and
George Bernard
Shaw.

16 Stanislavski.

independence were being undermined. Its attempts to create a network of studios and clubs had failed, mainly for practical reasons, and the tendency now was to centralize its activities in a workers' theatre. At its first All-Russia Congress Lenin had pushed through a series of resolutions bringing it under the control of the Commissariat for Enlightenment.

Lunacharski had not by any means given a free hand to Meierhold whose authority did not extend to the Academic theatres. Within three months of his appointment they were in public disagreement. The December issue of *Vestnik Teatra* carried articles by each of them, published side-by-side. In a response to his detractors on the left, Lunacharski made it plain that whatever Meierhold's other qualities he was the last person to be entrusted with the preservation of the treasures of the past. The tone was heavily sarcastic. Meierhold replied with an article entitled *J'Accuse*. He was caught in a double bind. On the one hand, he was rapidly losing sympathy for the Proletkult, as despite his populist ideological flourishes, he was never really interested in the kind of open-air and street theatre Proletkult advocated; on the other, as an artist he was interested in professional theatre of the highest standard. On the other hand, the professional, the Academic, theatres were outside his control. On February 26, 1921, he resigned.

Nemirovich took the view that he had, in fact, been dismissed. By the summer he was claiming, over-optimistically, that the left-wing bubble had burst. This apparent improvement in the overall situation did not induce him, however, to abandon all his plans. The original idea of three groups had been scrapped but the foreign tour remained. Although Lenin and Lunacharski had agreed to the scheme in principle there was considerable mistrust lower down the line. What guarantees were there that once out of Russia the Art Theatre would ever return? If the so-called Kachalov group could not be persuaded back why should their colleagues? Even the young Boleslavski had slipped out of the country, disheartened, so he said, by the increasing level of political interference in artistic matters. His production of the Polish play *Balladina* which had originally been well received came under attack when Poland invaded the Ukraine and was withdrawn. Boleslavski and his wife managed to get through the lines and made their way to Berlin.

Nemirovich continued to press for official approval. There were practical reasons for his persistence. The beginning of 1921 saw the introduction of the New Economic Policy, whereby market forces were allowed limited play within a hitherto state-owned economy. One consequence was the withdrawal of all subsidies to theatres. The result was a financial nightmare. The running budget of the Art Theatre and the Studios was just under 1.5 billion roubles and could not possibly be covered by box-office takings which, despite full houses, were only in the region of 600 million. As Nemirovich saw it the company could stagger on for a while but with no new productions on the stocks the outlook, in competitive terms, was bleak. A tour would at one blow reduce expenditure and allow time for reorganization. A successful tour abroad might also be profitable and bring in foreign currency at a time when the rouble meant nothing on the world market. Therein lay the cause of Stanislavski's constant and, for him, exceptional preoccupation with finance throughout the tour. The restoration of subsidies to the Academic theatres in November 1921 changed nothing. The company still had to regroup.

A tour and any restructuring of the theatre was, however, impossible without the return of the Kachalov group. In July, October and November 1921 Stanislavski wrote pleading letters to his colleagues, setting out all the difficulties they were encountering at home, both financial and political, but at the same time painting a picture of economic recovery and improved conditions. On April 2, 1922, in desperation he sent a telegram: the tour was under active preparation, an immediate answer was imperative. On May 21 the whole company, residents and exiles alike, met for the first time in three years. The pleasure of this reunion was quickly overshadowed, for Stanislavski at least, by the fact that his favourite pupil, Vakhtangov, died a few days later at the tragically young age of twenty-nine.

In his later accounts, Stanislavski describes the opposition to the Art Theatre in purely artistic terms. He either did not see or chose to ignore the political issues involved. His tone is rather that of a disappointed teacher faced with a set of talented pupils who have steadily gone astray. He saw that in their ideological zeal these talented young people were mindlessly rejecting the past and trying to run artistically before they could walk. They were simply not willing to admit that work in the theatre demands long and patient preparation and training. They were always trying to jump a stage. As a result, actors were being manipulated by new directors, each apparently more green than the last, who simply made them leap through the latest theoretical hoop. How could a revolutionary theatre be developed without major new writers and performers of talent who were treated with respect? In the days when the Art Theatre had appeared as a revolutionary force it had had Chekhov. Where was the new Chekhov? He could not create another literary genius but he could bring the company back to some semblance of its former self. His prime task was to rebuild it, to marry the 'old brigade' with the new, to restore the sense of ensemble. His main fear was that the younger members of the Kachalov group who had not been given a basic grounding in his working method would have acquired slick and facile habits. His fears were justified. Indeed one of Kachalov's own reasons for returning, apart from his deep sense of nostalgia for Russia, was his realization that the company's standards had deteriorated. Even his own acting had suffered. The iron, almost monastic discipline, the dedication to the performance, unique to the Art Theatre, had disappeared. Actors were being dragged from the buffet just in time to make their entrance and a casual attitude towards their work was now considered 'chic'.

Stanislavski had three months to weld a company together out of disparate elements. In a farewell letter to his group, Kachalov regretted that despite their having been together for so long, there was no real respect or genuine trust among them. Nonetheless, as Stanislavski recognized, their common experiences set them apart. They had suffered none of the hardships that the others, including himself, had endured. Somehow an ensemble had to be created out of the 'old brigade' and the younger actors who had joined the Art Theatre since 1919. He had to revive, rework, revitalize *Tsar Fiodor*, *The Lower Depths*, *Three Sisters*, *Uncle Vania*, *Cherry Orchard* and *A Provincial Lady*.

Rehearsals began on August 15, 1922. Stanislavski was intransigent, almost fanatical in his demands. He had not changed his low opinion of the company's attitude and behaviour that he had expressed to Nemirovich in August 1916. To that now was added his sense that they were to represent Russia, and Russian culture. He was all too aware of the tendency in the West to regard his fellow countrymen as charming but feckless children.

They had to be disciplined and they had to be better than good artistically. They had, too, to adjust to a new work pattern. In Moscow they played in repertoire, sometimes two or three plays a week, and so were able to keep fresh. On tour they would have to give six to eight consecutive performances in the same week. When Vishnievski boldly announced that he could give as many performances as they liked, Stanislavski was merely plunged into gloom at such conceit.

In rehearsal he would frequently fly into a rage, laying about him indiscriminately. A particular target was Knipper. For the most part she left *Cherry Orchard* rehearsals to her understudy. When she did appear, Stanislavski, who had always considered her lazy, bullied her mercilessly. He had always concealed his true opinion of her from the company. But he did find her profoundly irritating. In his Notebook for 1908 he described her standing in the wings waiting to go on as Ranevskaia, fiddling with her frock and her hair without a thought for what she was going to do on her entrance. She did not really get into the mood of the scene until her exit, at which point she swept off to her dressing-room to the adulation of the stage-hands. That would no longer do. After one Act Three rehearsal, he suddenly yelled at the top of his voice, 'Amateur! You never were and never will be an actress!' He then gave a devastating parody of her performance, making her appear sentimental and stupid. The younger members of the company were terrified. These outbursts of rage continued throughout the next few months, during the tour.

The general management of the tour was entrusted to Sergei
Bertenson, the son of a physician-in-ordinary to Tsar Nicholas II who
had until the Revolution had a senior post in the administration of the
imperial theatres. Stanislavski knew the family. In 1918, Bertenson was
invited to join the Art Theatre and soon impressed Nemirovich. He rose
to the top quickly, being given responsibility for repertoire and the
actors. It was he who managed the Kachalov group during their exile. He
was not entirely trusted by the company. They felt that he had secretly
hoped the Civil War would end in the defeat of the Bolsheviks and the
restoration of the monarchy, after which he could continue his broken
career. They suspected that under his show of support and loyalty there
lurked a contempt for 'bourgeois intellectuals' like themselves. He had
the advantage of speaking fluent English. Podgorni was given some
responsibility for finance while the ever-ambitious, ever-pushing
Leonidov tried to make himself indispensable.

On September 14, 1922, Stanislavski, his wife, his son, Igor, his
daughter, Kira and his granddaughter, Kirilla, boarded a train for
Petrograd where they took ship for Riga. From there they went by train
to Berlin. The rest of the company was to follow on a few days later,
travelling by ship from Petrograd to Stettin. After Germany the full
company planned to go to France and from there to the United States.
The projected tour of England had not materialized.

Stanislavski arrived at Berlin Friedrichstrasse at 9 a.m. on September
18 after a day and a half of travel. The US tour was being arranged by
Morris Gest, a Russian-born impresario, who was interested in promoting cultural relations between his native and adopted countries. He
had been promoting the tour ever since the spring and had succeeded in
getting a long article in the September 17 issue of the prestigious *New
York Times Book Review*. His brother Simon was waiting at the station in
Berlin with a battery of photographers and cameramen. Stanislavski was
then initiated into the first law of news reporting: once for real and once
for the cameras. As he came down the steps from the station to a fairly
moderate round of applause he was duly filmed and photographed. He
got into a waiting car and drove off. The car immediately had to be turned
round again. The reporters wanted pictures of his wife and family. His
son, Igor, was with him but Lilina and his daughter had stayed over in
Riga because his grandchild was ill. Publicity mattered more than truth
and Stanislavski found himself suddenly saddled with a stand-in wife
and daughter and had to repeat his descent down the station steps with
bows, applause and flowers as before. This polite fiction was screened
both in Germany and the United States.

He had been booked into a suite at the palatial Fürstenhoff, as befitted
his status. Everything had been laid on to make him feel welcome,
flowers, delicacies, great baskets of fruit, but all this attention merely
served to embarrass him. In any case, the splendour of his surroundings

contrasted markedly with his own shabby appearance. This once elegantly turned-out man kept to his room rather than show his torn overcoat in public. However, there was a great deal of work to do. A management team had arrived from Moscow to tackle the intricate problem of preparing to transport a company of sixty, plus costumes, sets and props across Europe to America. At the same time extras had to be found and rehearsed, mainly for *Tsar Fiodor*.

Stanislavski set out on the tour in a state of high tension and that tension persisted throughout. He was always doubly nervous abroad. He was the ambassador of Russian art and whatever was presented must be of the highest quality. He was aware of the Russians' reputation in western Europe as strange, wild, essentially unpredictable people beneath a veneer of civilization. To that now had to be added the suspicion with which the new revolutionary Russia was regarded and the revulsion at the execution of the Romanov family.

The tour began with tantrums and crises. Stanislavski was having trouble with his voice which was now quite husky. The cause may simply have been tiredness and physical tension. He turned for help to two Russian singing teachers living in exile. His vocal exercises were not appreciated by his neighbours at the Fürstenhoff and there was a certain amount of banging on connecting walls until Stanislavski toned down the volume of his exercises. Rather more seriously, the company were delayed by storms in the Baltic. Five days went by before news came that they had finally disembarked at Stettin. When they reached Berlin they were in no fit state to work. Valuable rehearsal time was being lost. When work did begin conditions were not ideal. The Lessing Theatre, where they were to play, had to be shared with another company. Max Reinhardt came to the rescue offering his workshops for morning rehearsals. Stanislavski kept everyone hard at it from 9 a.m. to midnight. It would be idle to pretend he used the patient, exploratory methods of the 'system' to achieve his results. He whipped the company into shape. The correspondent of the *Berliner Tageblatt* wrote that he was like a conductor with an orchestra and, indeed, employed musical terms. It was hard work breathing new life into old productions. *Tsar Fiodor*, with which the season was to open, was twenty-four years old and it showed. In addition Kachalov had to be rehearsed into the lead. *Cherry Orchard* was in not much better shape. Things came to a head at the *Fiodor* technical rehearsal on September 24. The largest of the bells which formed part of the chimes to greet the Tsar's exit from the Kremlin had been deliberately left behind. It would have been impossible to transport; it weighed about 1600 kilos. At the appropriate moment all the other bells pealed out. Suddenly Stanislavski's voice came from the auditorium, 'And when are we going to hear the real chimes?' When the situation was explained to him he exploded. All his anxiety and tension were displaced on to the missing bell. Suddenly nothing else in the production mattered. Emergency meetings of the Moscow Art team and the Lessing Theatre management were called and all manner of musical instruments tried out. Stanislavski rejected them all. His parting shot at the end of the day was, no bell, no performance. A member of the stage management team came up with what must be one of the most original solutions in production history. He located some eight or nine circular saws in a nearby factory. They were suspended, tried out for sound. The most appropriate of them was selected and two double-bass players were invited to play on it. Backed up by a gong they provided the necessary deep tones. The crisis was over.

The play opened the next day to great acclaim. In the audience was Jacques Hébertot, who had come especially from Paris to see the show. That evening a contract was signed for a season of eight performances in Paris at the Théâtre des Champs-Elysées from December 2.

Cherry Orchard opened successfully on September 28 but *The Lower Depths* which opened the day after made the greater impact. *Three Sisters* followed on October 2. On the 3rd, between Acts Two and Three of *The Lower Depths* Stanislavski gave his first interview for the American press. He was very cautious in all his statements, side-stepping specific issues. He was not prepared to make facile observations on complex artistic matters for the sake of a quick quote. Neither was he prepared to discuss the situation back home. He simply declared himself politically illiterate and kept his own counsel. It was a wise policy although it did not keep him out of trouble.

The last performance of the Berlin season took place on October 10. A sudden decision by the Americans to postpone the US tour, planned for October or November, to the following January meant that there was a gap to be filled. Logically, after Berlin, the company should have gone to Vienna as they had in 1906. Stanislavski would have welcomed that. Whatever his private anxieties, success in Berlin had almost been a foregone conclusion. The company were celebrities before they arrived. The city was full of Russian émigrés all of whom claimed to be ex-members of the Art Theatre and Stanislavski's pupils. A band-wagon was rolling. Vienna was another matter. An Austrian tour, unfortunately, made no economic sense. The schilling was too unstable. They would simply lose money they could ill afford. On the 17th the company took the train for Prague.

The tour was arranged at great speed and with considerable warmth and generosity. Schedules were rapidly reorganized to make room for these unexpected visitors. The company were given a rehearsal room in the magnificent National Theatre. The season opened with four plays on four successive nights starting, as usual, with *Fiodor* on the 20th. It ended with *The Lower Depths* on the 31st.

Brief as his stay was, Stanislavski found time to attend a rehearsal of Janacek's opera *Katia Kabanova*, based on Ostrovski's *Storm*, which was about to have its première. His reactions are not recorded. What he saw of the dramatic theatre, however, he found disappointing, too many '-isms', too many sterile experiments, too great a concentration on production values which distorted actors' work and pushed it back into the past. It was much more rewarding and profitable to watch ordinary people going about their daily business, to note their characteristic tempi, their rhythmic patterns and ethnic differences.

On November 3 the company travelled to Zagreb where they played until the 20th. There Stanislavski took over the role of Shuiski, which he continued to play in Paris. It was his first 'new' part since *Stepanchikovo*, and his last. From Zagreb they returned to Berlin, travelling, as always now, third class. There Stanislavski had to say goodbye to his family. Lilina, Kira and Kirilla returned to Russia. Igor, who was suffering from tuberculosis, went on to Switzerland for treatment. On the 29th the company took the train from Berlin to Paris. The sets and costumes had already been sent on separately, direct from Zagreb. The train arrived at the Gare du Nord at 1 a.m. on November 30. Jacques Hébertot, Lugné-Poë and Jacques Copeau were there to meet them. Stanislavski gave a brief press interview. On the 2nd he visited Copeau and the veteran André Antoine whose work at the Théâtre Libre and the Odéon had frequently, and superficially, been compared to his own. After lunch with Hébertot and Louis Jouvet, at which they discussed the creation of an international centre of theatre art, all three went to visit Isadora Duncan at her studio.

The cordiality of the welcome offered by leading members of French theatre was not matched by the authorities who disapproved of the presence of dangerous subversives. The tour, in fact, had only been made possible by a considerable amount of string-pulling and legal evasion. The whole operation was now threatened, however, by a crisis far more serious than the absence of a single bell. All the sets, props and costumes had been lost somewhere between Zagreb and Paris and no amount of telephoning to stations along the line could locate them. Stanislavski was concerned that the sets should be as impressive as possible. He had counted on touching-up the backcloths on their arrival. They had been deliberately painted in very broad basic strokes. Any elaborate over-painting would have flaked off during the journey. The answer was to do it after their arrival. He was aware of the high standard of scene-painting in France and was anxious to avoid unfavourable comparisons. The opening could not be postponed. The company saw no alternative to cancellation at a disastrous financial loss.

This time Stanislavski kept his head. A telegram arrived to confirm that the sets were on their way, although nobody could say when. The build-up to the first night, December 5, was gathering momentum. There were tributes on the 4th in *Paris-Journal* from Georges Pitoëff and Jouvet and in *L'Eclair* from Lugné-Poë who described Stanislavski as 'the apostle of all daring'. Lugné-Poë had also cancelled the performance at his own theatre on the 5th so that the cast could attend *Fiodor*. On the evening of the 4th there was a welcoming ceremony at the theatre and still the sets had not arrived. Despite pressure to cancel Stanislavski stood his ground. If there was a chance that the sets might arrive in time, as he had been assured there was, they would go ahead.

The ceremony was long and elaborate, including a lecture on the foundation of the Art Theatre as well as formal tributes. When it came to Stanislavski's turn to reply he was already nervous, wondering how, under the circumstances, the company could live up to their reputation. At the crucial moment in his speech as he planned to draw to a fitting close, he dried. He began to improvise. He was more than surprised to hear his own voice inviting everyone present to the opening performance the following day. He recovered control in time to warn them that the sets and costumes had not arrived but promised that the play would go ahead without them if necessary. The audience responded warmly, his colleagues less so. They had already drawn up a notice announcing cancellation. At that moment, as if on cue, a dishevelled, dusty figure arrived to announce that the sets were in Paris. After some telephoning it was established that they would be at the theatre by 10 a.m. the following morning.

At four in the afternoon there was still no sign of them. At 5.30 news arrived that the trucks were stuck in a traffic-jam. The first van arrived at 6.15. There was a panic to find costumes, get dressed and made-up. The technical staff finished the set-up in record time but the curtain was delayed for thirty minutes by which time the audience was demonstrating its impatience by clapping. There had been no time for a lighting rehearsal and all the elaborate effects had to be sacrificed. The entire performance took place with the lamps full up.

The first act was well received. The company stuck to its practice of not taking a curtain and Stanislavski used the time to rehearse the crowd scenes with the hastily recruited extras who had not even seen the sets before. During subsequent intervals Picasso, Prokoviev, Stravinsky and Kussevitsky came round to offer congratulations. After the performance Stanislavski sent Nemirovich a telegram:

> 'Colossal success, general acclaim, fantastic press.' (*Ezhegodnik* MXAT, 1943, p. 504.)

The Lower Depths followed on the 7th and *The Cherry Orchard* on the 13th with equal success. On the 15th there was a special performance of the Gorki for the profession when the cast was once more greeted with speeches and flowers. Such honours were, of course, very flattering but there was considerable discontent within the company. There were more performances than the eight originally scheduled and lead actors, like Leonidov, were feeling the pressure. Junior members were complaining that they were underpaid and underfed. Their complaints met with little sympathy from the older members of the company who pointed out that they had toured to Berlin on 1906 on half salary.

But there were other tensions, over casting, over the payment of extras, over standards in general. There was the usual back-stage rivalry and bitchiness particularly with regard to *Cherry Orchard*. Podgorni threatened to resign if he did not replace Leonidov as Lopakhin. There was a dispute over who was to play Ania. Knipper wanted Tarasova. Lilina and Stanislavski chose Koroneva. Wagging tongues in the dressing-rooms suggested the reason was that Lilina, who was fifty-six, playing Varia, did not want to be on stage with the twenty-four-year-old Tarasova.

Cherry Orchard also provoked another of Stanislavski's rages. On December 18, on his way to his dressing-room, he passed the sets that were stacked and ready and noticed that the trees for the orchard were dressed with bits of white cloth instead of real flowers as was usual. The fact that from the auditorium the bits of cloth were more effective meant nothing. He berated the stage management, comparing them to the 'pseudo-innovators' and 'Futurists' whom he hated. They were only fit, he told them, to stage 'pot-boilers' – his ultimate term of contempt.

On the next day, the 19th, as a result of dispute over money, many of the extras failed to turn up for *Fiodor*. A number of Russian émigrés had been recruited for the crowd scenes. They had approached Podgorni for more money, explaining that food was much more expensive around the Champs-Elysées. Podgorni refused any increase point-blank. The extras' representative then spoke to Stanislavski who apologized for Podgorni's behaviour and promised the increase they had asked for. Podgorni dug his heels in and insisted that he was in charge of all financial matters and again refused.

On the 19th, anyone in the company who was free was mobilized to swell the crowd. Stanislavski insisted that those extras who had turned up should be paid a bonus and would not take no for an answer. A furious Podgorni qualified Stanislavski's behaviour as typical of Alekseiev, the factory owner and tradesman. The rest of the company, however, were glad to see Podgorni put in his place.

There were, however, more general resentments. First, the feeling that within the company there were 'them' and 'us', the stars and the rest. While Stanislavski was lionized, and endlessly ushered into Hébertot's office to meet celebrities, the rest were treated like subject colonials by theatre management and stage staff alike. They were not to know that this was the typical attitude Parisians display to anyone who does not actually live and work in their city. There was also the feeling that for all the brave words, for all the temper tantrums, standards had not been maintained. Too many props had been missing for too many performances, and, because of the quarrel between Stanislavski and Podgorni, costumes were either not cleaned or not in a proper state. And they were not encouraged when they saw Stanislavski himself on December 19, going through his lines as Shuiski at the last minute both before the performance and during the intervals. Was this what he meant by proper preparation? It seemed that he had been totally seduced by the attentions the French had showered on him.

The feeling of 'them' and 'us' was further accentuated by the contract that had been agreed with Gest. For the purposes of the tour a company had been created with shareholders who, in addition to their salary and expenses, were to receive dividends ranging from 15% for Stanislavski and Nemirovich to 1% for the others. Bertenson, Leonidov and Stanislavski's secretary, Olga Bokshanskaia, were also shareholders. The rest of the company were to receive salary plus expenses.

Gest had advanced $15,000 to cover the European tour. He guaranteed $8000 a week and also agreed to cover transport to and within the United States, the rental of theatres and the salaries of technical staff and the extras. Once all these expenses had been covered, the shareholders were to receive 25% of all clear profits.

Stanislavski continued to study the theatre around him. Prior to the opening of the tour he attended performances by the Italian tragedian Ermete Zacconi. What struck him most was the economy of effort displayed by an artist who was used to touring. There were moments of psychological truth which were genuinely inspiring, moments when the role was experienced, there were others of technically masterful imitation, moments when the role was represented. There was a marked qualitative difference between the two approaches although given the technical accomplishment of the actor there was never anything that was less than satisfactory. The essential lesson to be learned was that of planning, to know when and where to switch the approach so as to conserve energy and apply it when it was most needed.

He kept in close touch with Jacques Copeau and on the 21st there was a midnight reception at the Vieux Colombier. Just before his departure for the United States he once again discussed the possibility of an international studio, a society 'for the preservation of European theatre'. Copeau gave a dinner at a restaurant next to the Vieux Colombier to which he invited Firmin Gémier, who had created the first Théâtre National Populaire, was director of the Odéon, and had introduced plays by Gorki and Tolstoi to French audiences. Also present was Harley Granville-Barker who had come over especially from London. There was unanimous approval of the idea in principle but, as ever, there was the problem of finance. America might be the answer.

Stanislavski and the Art Theatre company sailed from Cherbourg on December 27 on the RMS *Majestic*. The extremely rough crossing took nine days and many people's thoughts turned to the fate of the *Titanic*. On New Year's Eve Mr Stanislavski and Mr Kachalov played, or rather, as Stanislavski put it, yelled, their way through a scene from *Julius Caesar* as part of the ship's concert. It was with great relief that they sailed into New York harbour at first light on January 4. Gest had wanted Stanislavski to travel first class, but he refused to be separated from the rest of the company. This worried Gest, who did not want the colleagues to belive he could not afford a first-class ticket. To save face, he made sure that Stanislavski disembarked through the first-class exit.

Stanislavski was besieged by newsmen and reporters. Indeed, he was kept so busy that he missed seeing the Statue of Liberty. Again he was wary in his answers. He felt that questions concerning the choice of repertoire were loaded:

"'Why did you choose these particular plays for inclusion in the repertoire? I mean *Tsar Fiodor*, *The Lower Depths* and *Chekhov?*" asked one reporter. I understood right away what was behind the question, recalling what had been said and written in Europe, that we had chosen *Tsar Fiodor* to show a weak Tsar, *The Lower Depths* to demonstrate the strength of the proletariat and *Chekhov* to illustrate the feebleness of the intelligentsia and the bourgeoisie.

"We've brought precisely the plays that were precisely asked for and no others," I answered firmly. "And they were asked for because they are typical of an earlier period of the Art Theatre and because we performed them in Europe in 1906 and just recently. America wants to see what Europe already knows." (*SS*, VI, p. 182.)

When Stanislavski went through immigration and customs he was apprehensive. Hostile articles had already appeared in the press. He could be refused entry or even, if he were let in, the tour could still be a financial disaster. As if to confirm his fears the planned quay-side greeting was a masterpiece of mismanagement. Gest, blissfully ignorant of the political consequences, had invited a Russian bishop or some other spiritual dignitary to come down in full canonicals. Fortunately the invitation was refused and Bertenson succeeded in persuading Gest that a religious display of any kind would not be helpful. Gest had also intended the Mayor of New York to present Stanislavski with the keys to the city but that had been mistakenly arranged for the 3rd. Everyone was at an important meeting on the 4th. The boat was so long docking that the officials who had arrived with gifts had to leave. The presents were piled into Stanislavski's car but later taken away for the inevitable photographs, after which they disappeared. Perhaps, Stanislavski wrote to Lilina, they had simply been hired. There were friends to meet him, Rachmaninov's wife and daughter and Boleslavski, who, after a stay in Paris, had come to the United States on tour. A letter from Stanislavski asking him to act as assistant director had enabled him to extend his visa. Later that day Stanislavski met his nephew Koka, who was an official member of a Soviet trade delegation, at a special performance given at the *Chauve-Souris* theatre, run by an émigré and former colleague, Baliev.

Some adjustment was necessary to American theatre practice. Stanislavski had not realized that when you rented a theatre that was precisely what you got, an empty building, nothing else. On his arrival at the Jolson Theatre on 59th Street he walked on to a bare stage with a solitary working light. It was soon apparent, moreover, that there were problems with the back-drops and larger pieces of scenery. Although the auditorium held two thousand the stage and wings were small and storage space inadequate. Dressing-rooms were difficult to reach, some of them located on the tenth floor. The technical problems of the get-in were complicated by the extremely rigid demarcation lines that operated among the back-stage staff. Once they had been briefed no one else was allowed to interfere. Stanislavski was impressed nonetheless by the cheerfulness and efficiency of the American crew as he was to be throughout the tour. He particularly appreciated the lighting designer Jim Brown, a Jew of Austrian origin, who managed at short notice to produce some impressive effects. On one occasion in a desperate attempt to break through the language barrier and express his appreciation he told him 'Je vous danke, very.' Vadim Shverubovich, who spoke fluent Yiddish, managed to communicate with those members of the stage crew who spoke German. Bertenson fared less well with the hard-working, highly democratic New York crew. His imperious manner and upper-class English accent soon earned him the name 'high-brow shorty'.

Boleslavski had recruited the extras from the mainly Jewish Russian community on the Upper East Side, where Gest had rented rehearsal premises. Some had emigrated after the abortive revolution of 1905, others had seen the Art Theatre on tour in Odessa in 1913. They started rehearsals on January 5 while Stanislavski rehearsed individual scenes at his hotel on West 56th Street, very near the theatre.

The New York season finally opened on January 8 after three days of chaos. The first performance of *Fiodor* was marked by a minor mishap when the curtain went up too soon on the second scene revealing stage-hands trying to adjust the ceiling and actors scurrying to their places. The actors froze, the audience laughed, and the curtain came down again. A white-faced Stanislavski gave a few quick words of encouragement and the curtain went up once more. The incident was soon forgotten and the evening was, as Stanislavski wrote to Lilina, the greatest success the Art Theatre had ever known. There were flowers and telegrams from Rachmaninov and Chaliapin and the veteran director David Belasco, Gest's father-in-law, constantly shook Stanislavski's hand. The next day he sent a telegram of congratulation – 'the world is proud of you'.

That, however, was first-night euphoria. While the Russian émigrés in the gallery appreciated a reminder of their lost culture, Rachmaninov, Chaliapin and their friends had reservations. They felt the company had gone soft, lost its edge and was verging on the sentimental. They were also worried by the heavy cuts that had been made and the absence of certain familiar, key scenes. Stanislavski had been told cuts were necessary to meet the tastes of American audiences. His friends, however, suspected that Gest merely wanted to get the curtain down by 11 o'clock, because after that he would have to pay overtime to the staff. They were right. Gest's constant concern throughout the tour was to avoid overtime costs.

Financially, too, the tour had got off to a bad start. Takings were poor. The theatre was half empty. Gest had set ticket prices too high. The first four rows of the stalls cost $5.50 when a good pair of shoes cost only $6 and a suit $16–$18.

The Lower Depths opened on the 15th and was a triumph but only after a furious row with Gest, who, when he discovered at the dress rehearsal that the play would be over at 11.15 and not 10.45 as agreed, harangued the company. There was nothing he could do, it was too late for cuts and the intervals could not be shortened. The company, however, realized why cuts had been imposed in the first place. But, they reasoned, Gest was an American and business is business.

A special matinée was given for the profession on the 19th, with John Barrymore in the audience. Knipper wrote to a friend that the papers were saying that Rembrandt, Hogarth and Shakespeare himself would be bowled over by such perfection. On the 20th the New York press published a letter from Barrymore to Morris Gest stating that he had had the greatest theatrical experience of his life. He had left the theatre shaken and intoxicated and with a very modest opinion of his own abilities. The same day the *New York Times* published an open letter from David Belasco to Gest thanking him for his initiative in bringing the Art Theatre company over.

The third play to be presented was *The Cherry Orchard* which opened on January 22. It provoked an extraordinary incident.

It was the custom at the Art Theatre for the cast, wherever possible, to make their own sound effects. This included the birdsong in *The Cherry Orchard*. Stanislavski wanted to run them through and called a rehearsal for 2.30. It was scheduled to last for about one and a half hours so that the company could rest between 4 p.m. and 6 p.m. Having heard the company's efforts, white with fury Stanislavski berated the actors, comparing their sloppiness unfavourably with the dedication of the American technicians. He then rehearsed the 'birds' as though they were characters, giving them tasks, 'Tell your mate what a beautiful morning it is.' The rehearsal went on for the whole afternoon, to the amazement of the American crew. The incident produced its effect. Even if there was mockery in some dressing-rooms the bulk of the company were galvanized into greater efforts.

Knipper was running a high temperature throughout all sixteen performances, including a special matinée for the profession on the 26th. On opening night, during the last act Gest once again appeared backstage saying she and Stanislavski had to play faster. He wanted the curtain down by 11 o'clock.

Stanislavski repaid the adulation he received by seeing as much American theatre as he could fit into a busy schedule. As he wrote to Nemirovich, any notion that there were no actors of the first quality in the United States must be abandoned. He saw Komissarzhevski's production of *Peer Gynt* in which Joseph Schildkraut, who was later to make a distinguished and undervalued career in Hollywood, played the title role. There was not his equal, he wrote to Nemirovich, in the whole of Russia. He found David Warfield in Belasco's production of *The Merchant of Venice* the best Shylock he had ever seen. As for Barrymore's Hamlet, it was not ideal but 'absolutely spell-binding'. In a later interview he did, however, express the worry that if Barrymore did not learn to pace himself and control his nervous energy he would burn himself out.

It is impossible to overestimate the impact of the company on the profession. In those brief weeks in January and February 1923 a seed was planted that would come to fruition in a new approach to acting in America and one which would ultimately feed back into Europe. Actors went to performances, Bertenson reported to Nemirovich, to study and learn. But they also wanted more concrete information. With Stanislavski's permission Boleslavski gave a series of lectures on the 'system', which were later published in the October issue of *Theatre Arts Monthly* as 'Acting, the first Six Lessons'. These lectures established Boleslavski's authority as a teacher and launched his career in America. Yet while Stanislavski was by now placing greater emphasis on physical tasks and physical actions, Boleslavski stressed the importance of emotion memory, developing the technique beyond Stanislavski's original practice. His teaching laid the grounds for a bitter dispute ten years later between those who emphasized the personal, emotional basis of the actor's craft and those who advocated the use of physical action.

One direct result of these lectures and the interest the Art Theatre tour aroused was the American Laboratory Theatre, which Boleslavski created with another Russian colleague, Ouspenskaia. An early member was the twenty-two-year-old Lee Strasberg. The impact of Stanislavski's acting decided Strasberg to go into the theatre. He saw both Stanislavski and Kachalov play Vershinin and realized that whereas Stanislavski *was* Vershinin, Kachalov, for all his accomplishment, still had a trace of the actor about him. Moreover, Strasberg did not share the popular opinion that Stanislavski was unable to play tragic roles.

Stanislavski had mixed feelings about New York, set out in long letters to Nemirovich and his brother, Vladimir. In his imagination he had conjured up a city like Fritz Lang's *Metropolis*. The reality was much more mundane. He was bewildered by traffic lights and almost got himself killed by standing in the middle of the street and examining them. The American people he took to immediately. He found them open, vital, impervious to social distinctions, free from snobbery and above all ready and eager for the new. On the other hand, he soon recognized the power of the success-ethic. It was wonderful to be successful but God help you if you flopped.

Musical life impressed him greatly. The opera was superior to anything he had known and the orchestras were outstanding, in particular the Philadelphia under Stokowski, which realized all his ideals of the perfect ensemble performing with commitment and energy. His old friends Rachmaninov and Chaliapin added to the riches available. At the end of February Rachmaninov, who had been away on a concert tour, returned to New York. On March 1 he attended a performance of *A Provincial Lady*. On March 13 Chaliapin, who was in town for a recital, saw *The Lower Depths*. In return, on the 25th, the entire Moscow Art company went to hear him in recital at the Met. It was not only the classical repertoire, however, that interested Stanislavski. As he came to know America better he became interested in popular songs and dance music. The syncopated rhythms were unknown in Russia and before he left in 1924 he asked friends to collect suitable recordings for him to take back to study.

The New York season closed on March 31 with a performance of *Three Sisters*. Artistically it had been all that could have been hoped for. Its success was due in part to the publicity campaign Gest had mounted with its endless flow of press releases and photographs. Full scene-by-scene synopses had been included in every programme. Everything had been done to attract audiences. Gest himself appeared very satisfied but the sad fact was that the company had made no money.

On April 1 they travelled to Chicago, going from there on the 23rd to Philadelphia and then on May 6 to Boston, where they encountered for the first time a hostile press campaign.

CHAPTER TWENTY-THREE

MY LIFE IN ART

While in Boston, Stanislavski signed a contract with Little, Brown & Co., to write his autobiography. He had been pressed by Oliver Sayler, one of Gest's publicity team and also one of the few foreigners to have worked at the Art Theatre, to bring out a book. This would help create interest in the second tour which, it had already been agreed, should start in September. Stanislavski, ever a reluctant author, agreed to write something simply because he needed money to pay for his son Igor, who was suffering from tuberculosis, to continue treatment in Switzerland. He was making nothing out of the tour. Earlier that year he had hoped to make money out of a film script based on *Tsar Fiodor*. True to his view that the cinema was only suitable for subjects on a wide canvas he decided to create a single epic out of the two Aleksei Tolstoi plays in the Art Theatre repertoire, *Tsar Fiodor* and *The Death of Ivan the Terrible* with the Russian people at the centre, hence the title: *The People's Tragedy*. He set to work on the treatment.

The prospective producers were only interested in a love story. This being silent cinema, the heroine would be played by Bebe Daniels. Moskvin, who was not considered photogenic, would have to be replaced. The good had to triumph and the bad be punished. That was the iron rule in the movies. It was agreed that Aleksandr Kairanski, an émigré, who had been engaged as Stanislavski's guide and interpreter, would write the new script. After two abortive script conferences on February 22 and March 5, Stanislavski pulled out. There was no alternative, therefore, to a book.

His first thoughts were to complete his account of the 'system' for which copious, if confused, notes already existed. The completed 1918 manuscript referred to by Efros had been cut up, reordered and pasted into notebooks. The completed draft was submitted to Little, Brown & Co., who rejected it as they rejected Stanislavski's second suggestion, a history of the Art Theatre and its aesthetic philosophy. They made it clear that what they wanted was a popular biography about Stanislavski himself, the man behind the star, with as many personal details as possible.

This was precisely the kind of book Stanislavski did not wish to write. He had expressed his contempt for works of this kind in no uncertain terms in 1911:

'I have been asked to write my autobiography but I have resolutely refrained from doing so as there is nothing more tedious than an actor's biography. I shall be asked, of course, to write stereotyped, irritating phrases like, "I felt within me a passion for art that I inherited from my grandmother who had been a well-known French actress."

I shall be asked to write on every line, "*I* played this or that, *I* was a success or a failure, *I* had so many curtain calls, they wrote this or that about me *personally*." This unending declension I, my, me, is particularly distasteful and actors should be banned from talking about themselves and forever trotting out how they were praised.

But actors should write, more than anybody. Why? Because their art lives and dies with them. Just think. If actors did not make a secret of their art but shared it with their successors we should have established the law of art all true artists pine for long ago. . . . We would be less gossipy and talk less nonsense.' (K.S. Archive, No. 1052.)

He had nonetheless no choice but to suppress his distaste. Kairanski claims it was he who produced an outline, based on Stanislavski's notebooks and diaries, which finally gave the publishers what they wanted. The contract stipulated a length of 60,000 words and a deadline of September 1. Kairanski's claims are difficult to verify but Boleslavski in his review of the book regretted that Stanislavski had not acknowledged his contribution.

Stanislavski did not attempt, nor had he the time, to write the book out in full. He made notes in long-hand which he then dictated to his secretary, Olga Bokshanskaia, straight on to the typewriter.

'He wrote out his first text of all in long-hand then dictated it to me in a free and relaxed manner. Then he would revise what he had done and I would type up a fair copy. Often he would revise it again and I would type it up once more . . . It was agreed that the days we played Chekhov and he was not needed (and sometimes after the third act of *The Lower Depths* in which I was an extra) I would go to his hotel and take dictation.

Armed with a portable typewriter, I made my way from 58th Street to 56th Street where he was staying and we would get down to work. K.S. didn't know what the word "tired" meant. We wrote page after page . . . At two o'clock in the morning and sometimes later when he was still fresh and ready to go on he would stop nonetheless and say: "Pardon me, what time is it? I'm sorry, we must stop. It's a pity but we must."' (Bokshanskaia in *Ezhegodnik MXAT*, 1943, p. 582.)

The same gruelling routine continued on the *Laconia* on which Stanislavski sailed to Europe on June 7. There was no point in returning to Russia for only two months. Stanislavski decided to meet his family in Freiburg in the Black Forest, not far from the Swiss border, so that he could visit Igor in Wernwald. There he learned that Igor would need treatment for at least four or five years. That would be expensive. On July 29 he took time off from the book to travel to Berlin and from there to nearby Warren, where he met Nemirovich. It was a dismal conversation. The Studios, Nemirovich reported, including the Opera Studio, were in a poor state. On his side Stanislavski was obliged to admit to discontent among the company: they did not want to learn or develop. Kachalov, especially, was restless, complaining that the tour was preventing him from tackling new roles.

After this brief interlude work on the book continued throughout August up to the deadline, with the end nowhere in sight. Stanislavski was seriously worried by the indemnity clause in his contract. Failure to deliver on time would result in his having to return money already spent.

By September 1 he was preparing the second tour. It was not possible simply to repeat the previous year's offerings. *La Locandiera* and Nemirovich's massive adaptation of *The Brothers Karamazov* were revived. All Stanislavski's energies went into rehearsals. He decided to take the company in hand. He drove them hard, reverting, when necessary, to his habit of demonstrating, even to experienced actors like Kachalov, to get quick results. On September 18 they travelled to Paris.

Stanislavski was soon disenchanted with the city he had once loved. He condemned the whole atmosphere as corrupt. Hébertot he found devious and unhelpful. Everything seemed to conspire against them. First, he was obliged to rehearse at night because the theatre was fully occupied during the day; second there were problems with *Karamazov*. Originally planned to be played over two evenings, it soon became apparent that it could not be squeezed into a single performance. On October 13, three days before the opening, Stanislavski made drastic cuts. Then, as if to repeat the *Fiodor* cliff-hanger of the first tour, the sets for *La Locandiera* were lost on the way from Berlin. Stanislavski immediately contacted Benois, the original designer, now living in Paris, to see whether substitutes could be rushed together. The sets eventually arrived on the 18th just in time for the opening on the 20th which, unfortunately, was received with less than rapture. A number of critics accused the cast of vulgarizing Goldoni, of not being 'Italian'. Finally, the rate of inflation and the high cost of living swallowed up the takings. Far from making a profit, Stanislavski confessed to Morris Gest that they were in debt to the tune of $25,000.

Gest proposed a new and apparently more favourable contract. He would offer a weekly guarantee of $5000 instead of $8000 as previously, but the Art Theatre could take 50% to 60% of clear profits. He would also charge $2000 a week for his administrative services. This deal appealed to some of the shareholders who, once the tour was under way, started to take $200–$300 a week against future dividends. They did not endear themselves to the rest of the company by trying to reduce the living allowance and so increase their own income.

On October 31 the company sailed once more to New York on the *Olympic*. They arrived on November 7. There was much less ballyhoo than had greeted their first season and Stanislavski had the impression that Gest was skimping on publicity. Rehearsal conditions were poor but work began on *An Enemy of the People* which was being added to their repertoire. This was a painful experience for Stanislavski. He had to hand over Stockman, his favourite part, to Kachalov. He was now sixty and could not do everything.

The day before opening night, Stanislavski went through the play with the cast, concentrating on the rhythm of each bit, taking them through exercises. The rehearsal worked for some but others were either bored, or smiled and giggled. Stanislavski persisted and finally lost his temper, only to be told the whole exercise was a waste of time and that everyone, including Kachalov, was confused. Pale and angry, he left the rehearsal. A full dress rehearsal that same evening, which, contrary to general expectation, Stanislavski attended, was no better and the cast suggested they rehearse Act Three before the opening. Stanislavski agreed.

It was not only the company who were frustrated. Stanislavski, too, was discontented. He was tired of being a manager. All he wanted, at times, was to be a simple actor, to have a moment's peace to think of his own performances. Stockman apart, he continued to perform all his major roles.

Karamazov opened on November 19. Duse, now very old, who was in New York playing in *The Lady from the Sea* came for the first act but left immediately after as she needed to rest before her performance the following day. Reinhardt was also in town with *The Miracle* and made contact.

Locandiera opened on the 21st and, in marked contrast to Paris, was a 'smash'. *Enemy* opened on December 3, *Enough Stupidity in Every Wise Man* followed two days later and rehearsals for *Cherry Orchard* began, although not without incident. Knipper's unwillingness to rehearse a role which she thought she knew all too well provoked another furious outburst from Stanislavski who was not prepared to allow anything to endanger the success of the season. His letters to Lilina gave details of box-office takings, show by show, indicating his preoccupation with finance.

The tour went on remorselessly. First Philadelphia where Rachmaninov, anxious to do all he could for his friend, arranged seats so that Stanislavski could hear Stokowski and the Philadelphia with Joseph Hoffman as soloist. But there were now political rumblings at home. The second season had confirmed all the suspicions that the company, or some of its leading members, would not return. Stanislavski felt obliged to emphasize in an interview for the *Novoe Russkoe Slovo*, published in New York, that he had every intention of going back to Russia, where his heart and duty lay. The satirical magazine *Krokodil* however, published on October 28 what purported to be an interview with Stanislavski in which he is supposed to have said:

> 'What was our horror when the workers invaded the theatre with dirty clothes, uncombed, unwashed, with dirty boots, demanding the performance of revolutionary plays.'

A worried Nemirovich asked for an immediate denial and on November 24 *Pravda* published the following telegram:

> 'The report of my American interview is lies from beginning to end. Repeatedly, and before hundreds of witnesses, I stated the very opposite about new audiences, boasting about, taking pride in their sensitivity, citing as an example the philosophical tragedy *Cain* which was splendidly understood by a new public. I thought that my forty years of activity and my long-standing dream of a people's theatre would have protected me against scurrilous suspicions. I am deeply hurt, cut to the quick.'

The allusion to *Cain* is quite at variance with the facts but Stanislavski's private perceptions did not always coincide with the real world outside. Stanislavski was tired of the political crossfire. On December 28 he wrote to Nemirovich:

> 'Moscow accuses us of disloyalty. But we get even blacker looks abroad. France just about lets us in. We only managed to get a favourable result by circumventing French law. In Paris a considerable amount of people, both French and Russian, boycotted us because we came from Soviet Russia and therefore were communists. Now they won't let us into Canada, officially declaring us Bolsheviks, and all our plans have collapsed. Who knows how many more difficulties lie ahead of us? You only have to think of recent persecution in the press stirred up in the Boston papers . . .
>
> Here we are attacked by both Russians and Americans for using our theatre to glorify present-day Russia. In Moscow they are slinging mud at us because we are preserving the tradition of bourgeois theatre and because plays by Chekhov and other authors of the "intelligentsia" are successful with Russian émigrés and American capitalists; they think we are rolling in dollars while in fact we are up to our ears in debt. Believe me, it's not for my own pleasure that I am spending almost two years going from place to place, from city to city with absolutely no time for the things I love and dream about and that I am losing what remains of my health. My spirits are low, I'm depressed, I've almost lost heart and at times think of giving it all up. . . .
>
> Seeing all the abuse that's heaped on me in Moscow I am refusing all kinds of good offers coming my way from Europe and America and

yearn with all my heart for Russia. . . .' (December 28, 1923, K.S. Archive.)

One of the offers to which he refers was an invitation to found a Studio in the US at a salary of $1500 a month plus a percentage. He did, however, later express a willingness to teach a group of American students if they came to the Art Theatre. It was, he explained, a question of providing a proper working atmosphere. That was something which took years to create; it could not be drummed up overnight. It was Moscow or nothing.

The New Year brought fresh political embarrassment. The company returned to New York on January 13, 1924, which they had left on the previous December 30 to play Boston, New Haven and Hartford, Connecticut. On the 18th, against his better judgement, together with Knipper and Luzhski he attended a fund-raising bazaar in aid of unemployed Russian émigré artists in the USA, organized among others by Rachmaninov's wife. Stanislavski knew almost nobody present but asked for and received an assurance that no photographs would be published. On the 20th he received an anxious telegram from Nemirovich stating that a photograph had appeared, showing Stanislavski and Knipper in a group with the caption 'What White émigrés are up to', and an article referring to the sale of valuables smuggled out of Russia. Would he please explain? Stanislavski was so shaken by the incident that he began to be worried by chance encounters in the street, particularly when the odd Kodak camera appeared. As he wrote to Nemirovich on February 12, it was not unusual for people to come up and talk to him. For the most part he had no idea who they were. What was he supposed to do?

Public and even official appearances could not be avoided. On February 15 he was invited to the studios of Famous Players. He was taken on to the set where Rudolph Valentino and Bebe Daniels were filming *Monsieur Beaucaire*. His hosts, knowing that he had at one time been involved in textiles, pointed to the care that had been taken to obtain the right materials from Lyons and Paris. Stanislavski only half heard his interpreter (the unfortunate Vadim Shverubovich) and thought they were asking his opinion of the acting. He answered in one word, 'Abominable'. He was particularly incensed by Valentino. He was unable to put on his 'full-dress' smile but launched into an angry commentary on the importance of learning how to wear costumes properly, to make them your own. Instead, they looked like dressed-up cowboys. Shverubovich tried to cover up Stanislavski's anger by saying that the bright lights hurt his eyes. Bertenson arrived at the critical moment and explained to Stanislavski that good public relations were essential. Stanislavski then put on his 'official' smile, toured the rest of the studio and was duly photographed with the stars, who appear not to have detected the cause of his anger, since they sent him a signed copy of the picture. But for days after he continued to inveigh against the 'cowboys'.

Illness continued to dog the company. Not only was Knipper unwell, but Podgorni fell ill, as did his understudy, so that Boleslavski had to take over in *The Lower Depths* at a few hours' notice.

On March 16 the company travelled to Washington having given performances in Brooklyn and Newark, New Jersey. On the 20th they were received by President Coolidge at the White House. This was something of a coup since the newly created Soviet Union did not enjoy diplomatic relations with the United States. The visit was arranged by Herbert Hoover, then Secretary of Commerce, who had worked as an engineer in Russia and knew the Art Theatre well. At the reception Stanislavski met his future collaborator, Elizabeth Reynolds Hapgood. Mrs Hapgood spoke good Russian and had been invited to perform the introductions to the President since no one in the White House could pronounce the actors' names. Stanislavski evidently took to her immediately since, to while away the time as they waited their turn to meet the President, he began to demonstrate to her elaborate eighteenth-century ways of greeting – perhaps he still had his encounter with Valentino in mind. It was Mrs Hapgood's husband, Norman, who had first suggested the Art Theatre might come to the United States in 1914. At all events, a firm foundation was laid to a friendship and to a collaboration without which Stanislavski's account of the 'system' would not have been published.

After Washington the company travelled to Pittsburg on the 23rd, Cleveland on the 30th, and Chicago on April 6. The theatre in Chicago was small, dirty and badly ventilated. There was also difficulty in finding extras for *Fiodor*. All available members of the company were used to swell the crowds, crawling on and off stage on their hands and knees and remaining kneeling while on stage lest they be recognized.

The tour had its lighter moments. At the first performance of *The Cherry Orchard* Ouspenskaia, playing Charlotta, was presented with a bulldog to serve as her 'little dog'. Unfortunately, this was a breed that had terrified her since childhood; but she steeled herself and made her entrance. The dog, startled by the brightness of the lights, began to bark very loudly, much to the audience's amusement. Ouspenskaia quickly deposited it in the wings and delivered her lines concerning it in its absence.

The company travelled from Chicago to Detroit on April 27 and finally returned to New York on May 4.

Stanislavski worked on *My Life in Art* as best he could during the tour 'in intervals, on trolley-cars, in the street'. A quiet room had been provided for him at New York City Library but it was not a facility he could use often.

On Kairanski's recommendation the publishers had engaged a young

American, J.J. Robbins, as translator. He had published an acclaimed version of Lermontov and, in consequence (or so Stanislavski was told) was in great demand. Robbins claimed to have been a pupil of Aleksandr Lenski, to have studied ballet at St Petersburg and to have worked as Stanislavski's assistant at the Art Theatre. Stanislavski, however, in his letters, speaks of him as a complete stranger.

The translation was completed chapter by chapter as they were made available to him. But the book continued to grow so that he was obliged to negotiate a further 30,000 words. This brought the total to 150,000 – two and a half times the originally agreed length.

By April 1924 the publishers were justifiably impatient. They issued an ultimatum: if the final sections of the book were not forwarded within two weeks the contract would be cancelled and the advance would be repayable. Stanislavski was distraught. It was Kairanski, if his claims are to be believed, who took over, shaped the final pages and even drafted one paragraph himself. Even at the last minute there was a hitch. Stanislavski had written a chapter for the end of the book in the form of an open letter to a young director (possibly Meierhold). It was on its way to the printer when Stanislavski sent a telegram withdrawing it. This was probably wise, as it would have made little sense to an American readership. The book finally appeared in early May with a print-run of 5,000.

On May 17 the company set sail for Europe on the *Majestic*. Holding the book in his hand, Stanislavski could only remark that the binding was better than the contents. Such had been the pressure that sometimes he had not written what he meant. Having no English, he could not realize how poor the translation was. His own natural, spontaneous, essential spoken style had been transformed into a totally unidiomatic language which nobody spoke and betrayed a translator in a hurry with no time to revise. What Stanislavski had managed to convey by speaking his book to Bokshanskaia, was precisely those vivid, instant personal qualities that the young Shverubovich had noted in the summer of 1911. Stanislavski's language can sound impossibly high-minded to us at moments but that was the language of his time, the language in which Chaliapin spoke of his art, the one in which many European critics wrote. But in the translation the authority has gone; he is made to sound quaint and simple-minded.

Stanislavski reached Paris on May 22. From there he travelled to Switzerland on June 9 to see his son, Igor. On August 8 he was back in Moscow to a much-changed world.

CHAPTER TWENTY-FOUR

THE THEATRE OF THE
REVOLUTION

Lenin was dead. The years of turmoil were over and the new state was
attempting to consolidate itself. The Soviet Union had formally been
created. In the arts, the avant-garde seemed unstoppable. Painting,
sculpture, architecture, posters, new ideas were bursting out with the
force of energy long pent-up. The theatre was swept along in the general
movement. The new cult was Constructivism and its high priest was
Meierhold. The dominance of the Art Theatre was, or so it seemed, a
thing of the past.

Nemirovich had watched the growth of Meierhold's influence with
alarm. He had sent anxious letters to Stanislavski and other colleagues
warning them of the new situation. His initial response to the danger had
been a managerial one. He and Lunacharski discussed a reorganization
of the Art Theatre and its Studios. Nemirovich wrote to Stanislavski in
July setting out the plan he and Lunacharski had agreed: the First Studio
was to become entirely independent and take the name of Second
Moscow Art Theatre; the Third Studio was also to go independent while
the Second Studio was to be merged into the main company. Stanislavski
gave his agreement in a letter written on August 10. His animosity
towards the First Studio – 'that long-standing sickness of my heart' – was
now considerable. His only objection was that it should be called the
Second Art Theatre since it had betrayed every basic principle the
original Art Theatre had ever stood for. He was also quite happy to see
the Third Studio go. Privately he thought of the Studios as Lear's
daughters: the First was Goneril; the Third, Regan; the Second was his
true Cordelia. On June 25 the Third Studio had written to Stanislavski
proposing he and Meierhold should run the Studio together. Essentially
this was a revival of Vakhtangov's plan of 1921 to 'rescue' Stanislavski
from the deadening clutches of the Art Theatre. Meierhold followed this
up with a letter on June 25 offering his help.

Within a week of his return, between August 15 and 19, he held long
discussions with the Third Studio. He was diplomatic, concealing the
deep suspicion that he felt. He told them he welcomed the idea but how
was it possible to abandon old friends and colleagues? Privately he

could not see himself finding common ground artistically with Meierhold. And yet, younger colleagues, the second generation as Stanislavski called them, could see the potential of bringing the two men together, and this was not merely motivated by a sentimental attachment to an old and respected teacher. Perhaps they were more perceptive than they knew.

In the event, certain members of the Third Studio chose to come over to the Second. Among these was the young director Nikolai Gorchakov who became an assiduous if not always reliable chronicler of Stanislavski's rehearsals. The newly combined group was then transformed into the Dramatic Studio and School with Stanislavski in charge. The students at the Studio were to be involved in main-house productions, playing small parts and walk-ons. Just how open Stanislavski's teaching methods were is indicated by the fact that there was no fixed syllabus, although certain classes were always given.

These reforms put an end to ambiguities concerning artistic policy by getting rid of 'dissident' elements. The Art Theatre was stripped down for action. But what action? The tour had given the Art Theatre a respite but none of its essential problems had been solved.

The apparently inexorable progress of the avant-garde had not, it is true, gone unchallenged. On April 13, 1923, at the celebrations to mark the centenary of Ostrovski's birth, Lunacharski had reasserted the importance of the Realist tradition with the slogan, 'Back to Ostrovski'. Meierhold made a defiant response a year later with one of the most revolutionary productions of *The Forest* ever staged.

Stanislavski's first concern was to reaffirm his artistic problem. This meant, in the first instance, revising *My Life in Art* for a Russian edition. He regarded the original American edition as mainly anecdotal, intended for the uninitiated reader. The Russian edition would discuss artistic problems seriously. He made it quite clear, in September 1924, in response to an enquiry concerning a possible German edition, that any translation would have to be made from the revised version when it appeared. He gave a similar response to Gaston Gallimard in 1928 when a French translation was under consideration.

Stanislavski had already cut up the manuscript during the return journey from America. He turned once more to Liubov Gurevich to help him put the material into a different shape. Before leaving Moscow in 1922 he had given her the keys to the cupboards in which his manuscripts were kept, asking her to put them in some sort of order. He worked with a sense of urgency and felt able to announce to a friend in January 1925 that the revisions were complete. In fact work continued throughout the whole of 1925 and the first two months of 1926. Mrs Gurevich suggested places where he might expand his account, such as the early St Petersburg tours. She also suggested combining a number of short chapters into one. Religious references were removed, for obvious ideological reasons. Other passages, such as the long account of Salvini's *Othello*, were cut. Stanislavski chose to expand the few paragraphs devoted to *Cain* into a full chapter. He was unrepentant in his conviction that the play was relevant to contemporary audiences and still harboured ambitions to restage it. He attributed the failure of the production to lack of rehearsal time and the endless compromises over the sets.

In the spring of 1925 Stanislavski showed the manuscript to Nemirovich, who as well as correcting a number of factual errors drafted several passages on the relationship with Chekhov (see chapter 6). These Stanislavski introduced into the text as they stood, without discussion. Nemirovich also suggested a re-write giving much more fulsome praise to his production of *Julius Caesar* but Stanislavski refused. The chapter 'Departure and Return' was introduced at Mrs Gurevich's suggestion but was not written until the last minute, in late February 1926. In it he gave his assessment of the developments which had taken place during his absence. He acknowledged the advances that had been made in the physical aspects of acting, the area where he himself was weakest. The expressive possibilities of the body has been explored and extended, but his fear was that such advances were merely external. As he had argued with Vakhtangov, physical skill must be justified by psychological depth. Much of this new chapter was a reworking of material he had intended for the American edition and had withdrawn. The reshaped version of this chapter was certainly directed against Meierhold, biomechanics and related techniques, although no one is named. The new, revised and, for Stanislavski, definitive *My Life in Art* was published in September 1926.

As to the Art Theatre, itself, it had to be relaunched. First, the management structure had to be reorganized. The problem of the relationship of the 'old brigade' to the younger members remained. Two important new arrivals were now on the staff: Pavel Markov, the most outstanding critic and teacher of his generation, and Ilya Sudakov, a dynamic young director, member of the Communist Party and of the Second Studio. He was ambitious, arrogant and considered something of a steam roller. Both men were now to play key roles in developing a new policy.

Stanislavski decided that management would now be divided into an upper committee, which would include Leonidov, Kachalov, Moskvin, Luzhski and himself, and a lower committee, chaired by Markov, that would include Sudakov and Gorchakov. In this way he hoped to balance tradition and innovation.

The question of repertoire was paramount. It had both to meet the new political situation and provide a means of revitalizing the company. Stanislavski proposed one or two plays which Nemirovich accepted. The material fell into two categories: first, plays which examined human responses to specific social circumstances, either contemporary or historical; second, plays which provided material helpful to the actors' development. Broadly speaking the plays in the first category fell into two groups, those that showed a corrupt pre-Revolutionary society and those that showed reactions to the new world of the Soviet Union and all the difficulties of adapting to it. In the second category he was willing to go to melodrama or even vaudeville. In 1925 there was only one new production, Treniov's *The Pugachov Rebellion*, which Nemirovich directed. The play, which was concerned with a revolt against the Tsar in the eighteenth century, opened on September 19 and was well received. It was seen as the Art Theatre's first step towards ideological acceptability.

By October 16 Nemirovich was in Berlin with the Music Studio, at the beginning of a tour that was to take them to the United States, including the West Coast and Hollywood. He did not return for two years. This meant that the burden of re-establishing the theatre as a significant force rested entirely on Stanislavski's shoulders. Gone now were the accusations of being a 'chaotic genius' or a 'muddle-head'. The artistic sterility of the Nemirovich years had not gone unnoticed. With no power struggle to distract him and a good supportive team around him which could help him realize his ideas, Stanislavski could function perfectly well. Between 1925 and 1928 he was responsible for nine productions, including three new Soviet plays, as well as four operas. A tenth play, Aeschylus' *Prometheus Bound*, was abandoned after more than a year's rehearsal. It was obviously impossible for him to undertake such a workload single-handed. Productions were assigned to young directors whose work he supervised, modified and, if need be, as in the case of *Prometheus*, scrapped.

His new programme was an ambitious one. During 1925 he laid the foundations of four new productions, all of which were shown during the following year. His young team of directors started rehearsals while he himself undertook a tour across the Soviet Union between April 27 and July 3 which included Baku and Tiflis in the south and Kiev in the Ukraine.

The first production to be seen was Ostrovski's *The Burning Heart*, generally considered a minor work. Stanislavski took over rehearsals from the young director Ilya Sudakov. The production was his response to 'Back to Ostrovski' and a further investigation of the problem of the Grotesque. The play was previewed on January 22, 1926, and opened the night after. It was received, the left-wing critic Zagorski apart, with an enthusiasm reminiscent of the theatre's early days. Nemirovich, in New York with his Music Studio, sent a telegram of congratulation. Meierhold shocked many of his supporters by turning to the audience at a performance of Tretiakov's agit-prop drama *Yell, China* and expressing his delight at the production by the 'wizard', Stanislavski, adding that young directors could not hope to equal the mastery the Art Theatre had shown that day. This was the second time he had made a public show of his support for Stanislavski. The first was in April 1923, at the jubilee to celebrate his own twenty-five years in the theatre, when he had insisted that a telegram of congratulation be sent to his old master in New York. This latest expression of his esteem, however, was too much for critics like Vladimir Blum who spoke of 'treason' against the avant-garde.

The problem of finding good new plays by new authors on contemporary subjects was still unresolved. *The Burning Heart* was a classic and *Pugachov*, in Nemirovich's words, a romantic historical drama. Stanislavski now established a new collaborative, working pattern. The task of finding new material fell to the young and exceptionally brilliant Pavel Markov who, with Nemirovich's departure, suddenly found himself in charge of the Literary Department. Markov was to the reborn Art Theatre what Efros had been to the old. His gift was his capacity to understand and to write about the art of the actor. Stanislavski, though retaining the final veto, treated him with respect and consideration, always publicly referring to him any manuscripts he was sent. Out of the authors whose work he knew and the hundreds of manuscripts he received Markov selected four writers, Ivanov, Leonov, Kataiev and Bulgakov.

Two instalments of Bulgakov's *The White Guard* appeared in the magazine *Rossia* early in 1925. The third and final instalment was not published as the magazine was closed down. The incomplete novel was nonetheless sufficient for Markov to propose a stage adaptation. Bulgakov was approached in April 1925 and agreed to start work on a script. By September a first draft was ready. It was overlong and without proper dramatic shape. Not surprisingly Bulgakov had tried to preserve as much of his original novel as possible. He spent the next three months reworking the script, with a great deal of advice from Sudakov, who was to direct, and other members of the production team. Sixteen scenes were reduced to seven. By January 1926 a rehearsal script was ready and work began on the 29th. The play very soon became the property of the younger members of the company. The members of the 'old brigade', like Vishnievski, who had originally been cast, fell by the wayside. Stanislavski was by no means averse to this; he wanted to see his second generation grow to maturity.

Rehearsals, according to Markov, were pure joy and very soon the spirit of Pushkino was being freely invoked. It was all happening again after almost thirty years. Bulgakov emerged as a second Chekhov and *The White Guard* as another *Seagull*. Like Chekhov, Bulgakov had a certain ironic detachment and a disconcerting sense of humour. He liked to debunk and had a propensity for what Markov described as 'philosophical sarcasm'. Unlike Chekhov, however, he was more than willing to discuss the content of the play. He could supply a biographical background for every character. A natural actor himself he was able, where necessary, to demonstrate what he meant. On March 26 Stanislavski saw a satisfactory run-through of the first two acts and sketches for the set of Act Three and urged everyone to work as fast as they could.

In the meantime he had two other productions to see through, *Nicholas I and the Decembrists* by Leonov and *Les Marchands de Gloire*, Marcel Pagnol's first play written in collaboration with Paul Nivoix. *Nicholas I* was another historical study of an abortive revolt against imperial power. It opened on May 19 and its success was in no small measure due to an outstanding performance by Kachalov, in the title role, which found favour not only with the critic of *Izvestia* but also with Vladimir Blum. Pagnol's play, premièred only a year previously at the Théâtre de la Madeleine, opened on June 15. This study of corruption in the local council of a small provincial French town, where the war-dead are exploited for commercial purposes, was a subject to which Stanislavski instinctively responded. The production was a further example of his extended realism, first developed in the pre-war production of *The Inspector General*, where a truthful portrayal of character and milieu expanded into the grotesque. Here, though, Gogolian satire was given the quicker, sharper rhythms of the French. A rival version which had opened at the Korsh Theatre in February appeared superficial and conventional in comparison. The Art Theatre presentation contained darker, more tragic undertones. *Pravda* praised it as an exposure of bourgeois hypocrisy, of a world of 'shady dealings and rogue politicians'.

Stanislavski now struck a blow for the rehabilitation of Chekhov, whose place in the repertoire had been the subject of considerable debate ever since the Revolution. A revival of *Uncle Vania* opened on May 11 with Stanislavski once again as Astrov. His performance was described as staggering. It seemed to have acquired more deeply tragic dimensions. The 'system' was now bringing personal dividends. At the age of sixty he still continued to improve as an actor and develop roles he had been playing for twenty years. Nemirovich had noted how much better his performance of Famusov had been in the 1925 revival of *Woe from Wit*.

From the company's point of view the reaction of a new generation to Chekhov was of paramount importance. If Chekhov could be justified then the artistic policy of the Art Theatre could be justified. Positive articles appeared in *Vechernaia Moskva*, *Izvestia*, and *Komsomolskaia Pravda*, which remarked that the time had come perhaps for the theatre to step out of its bombastic showcase and follow the path of more human and humane creation. The Art Theatre appeared to have found its ideological place.

Some time in late May or early June Stanislavski started attending rehearsals of *The White Guard* again to see what work still had to be done. He remained to be convinced of the play's merit. He had once asked Markov, 'Why should we stage this piece of Soviet agit-prop?' The run-through he saw removed his doubts. He was the most transparent of audiences; it was possible to tell what he was thinking at any given moment. He would laugh, cry, occasionally bite his hand when he was uncertain. Over the years, these nerve-racking occasions where Stanislavski would give his yea or nay acquired a certain format. After the run he would give his comments, he would thank the company and list the things he liked. Everyone then waited for the 'But', which at its worst could mean 'Scrap the lot and start again'. On this occasion he merely commented, 'Well now, tomorrow we can start acting.'

Stanislavski was able to walk in and take over, even make radical changes, because the group he was working with employed a common method, the 'system'. He could assume that basic problems of creating a character had been solved before he arrived. But problems of character-creation are not, as had often been assumed, the central issue of the 'system'. The central issue is the structure and meaning of the play itself. It was therefore problems of the through-action both of individual characters and of the action, of dramatic rhythm, tempo, that occupied him most. His major criticism of Act Three scene two was that it was emotionally self-indulgent – a constant danger of the 'system' misused. Actors were sentimentalizing their own feelings when they should have been thinking of positive, active responses to their situation:

> 'Well now . . . what's false here? You're playing feelings, your own suffering, that's what's false. I need to see the event and how you react to that event, how you fight people – how you react, not suffer. . . . What's the rhythm of this scene? You started playing it like a funeral. . . . You play a scene in which nice, kind, sensitive friends gather at home. The way you do it, they comfort their weeping hostess who is fast becoming hysterical and whom they all love very much. To do that you shed tears and suffer. To take that line on the scene is to be passive and sentimental. See everything in terms of action; *what we have here is an impassioned bitter argument. . . .*' (V. Toporkov, *O Tekhnike Aktiora*, VTO, 1958, pp. 25–7.)

Other problems, however, were beginning to surface. The free debate of the first years after the revolution was beginning to disappear. A new bureaucracy had been set up with its attendant abbreviations and acronyms. The Main Repertory Committee, the Glavrepertkom, now vigorously vetted all new productions. Inevitably its methods were cumbersome. It did not pronounce judgement until a play was at dress-rehearsal stage. Months of work could be lost if the judgement went the wrong way. At some time during March or April it would seem that the Art Theatre grew apprehensive about the reception that might be given to a play with a White, and therefore, *ipso facto*, anti-Revolutionary family at its centre. An alternative title was needed. Anything with the word 'White' in it was difficult. Bulgakov seems not quite to have appreciated the point since of the four suggestions he made – *White*

December, 1918, The Taking of the City, White Storm – two contained the word, 'White'. In May the management committee of the Art Theatre suggested *Before the End*, which both Bulgakov and Stanislavski disliked. Changes in the script were also asked for, presumably to head off any possible ideological criticism. Bulgakov could be strongly defensive about his work. On June 4 he sent a curt letter to the management refusing both the new title and the suggested changes, and threatening to withdraw the play altogether. The play was shown, unrevised, to the Repertory Committee on June 24. One of the principal spokesmen for the committee on that occasion was Vladimir Blum.

Remarks that were overheard were not propitious. By associating itself with Bulgakov the Art Theatre had placed itself in danger, just at the time when it needed to prove its political credentials. Bulgakov's flat had already been raided in May and the manuscript of *The Heart of a Dog*, which it had considered dramatizing, and his diaries seized. Stanislavski, however, was now determined to get the play on. If it was banned he threatened to close the theatre. He was particularly angry at this time since the Glavrepertkom had also put an end to his plans to direct *Othello*. He had done some very promising preliminary work with Leonidov in the title role. But Shakespeare, too, was 'out'.

On June 25 the Glavrepertkom met, with representatives of the Art Theatre present, Markov, Sudakov and Luzhski. Aleksandr Orlinski, one of the most hostile critics, set out in detail the committee's objections to the play as it stood and the changes that would be necessary. Markov and his colleagues accepted all the comments, promised rewrites and suggested another preview in late September.

In August Stanislavski took a short break, staying at a dacha near Moscow. He had to prepare for the reopening of the Opera Studio which was now to bear his name. Most of his time, however, he spent working on a book which, he wrote to a friend, was called *Work on Oneself: A Pupil's Notes. My Life in Art* now had an international reputation. Ellen Terry called it her constant companion. Given her own motto, Imagination, Industry, Intelligence, it was hardly surprising that she found a kindred spirit in Stanislavski. The new book was one of three about which he had written to Little, Brown & Co., in May 1925 – *Memoirs of a Journey to Europe and America, The Diary of a Student at a Drama School* and *The History of a Production*. He was uncertain which he would write first. The *Memoirs*, based on a journal he kept during his travels, were started but abandoned. They break off half way through the first American tour. The *History* was an old project for which there were many notes. It was the *Diary*, now *Work on Oneself*, on which he decided to concentrate, having now finally opted for a semi-fictional form rather than straightforward exposition.

He returned to Moscow on August 27 determined to get *The White Guard* on, not so much for Bulgakov's sake, it must be said, but because he considered it essential for the rebirth of the theatre; his Second Generation needed it. If the play did not go forward he would resign. He reworked the whole production, taking into account the comments of the Repertkom and managing to persuade Bulgakov to rewrite certain scenes along the lines he suggested. The result was inevitably an historical and ideological fudge but with luck it would be an acceptable fudge.

Arrangements were made to show the play to the Repertkom again on September 17. Only on the 16th was a new title agreed – *The Days of the Turbins*. Once again the play was rejected but the door was left open for possible approval. Stanislavski now went direct to Lunacharski. On the 23rd a closed performance was given for the press, a limited number of the public, and members of Repertkom. On the 25th it received approval subject to further, minor changes. Even so Lunacharski was aware how tricky the situation was and defended his decision in a public statement:

'*The White Guard* is an ideologically inconsistent and in places politically false play. However it comes together in the production and Soviet audiences appreciate it at its true value.' (*Vechernaia Moskva*, October 1, 1926.)

Maiakovski, happy to repeat an earlier joke and take a swipe at Stanislavski, replied:

'I think this is a proper logical culmination. They started with Auntie Mania and Uncle Vania and they end up with *The White Guard*. (Laughter) For me it's a hundred times better for it to come to a head and burst out in the open than to hide under the banner of apolitical art. Take that celebrated book of Stanislavski's, *My Life in Art*, that renowned book for connoisseurs – it's the same thing as *The White Guard*.' (*Nove o Maiakovskom*, AN SSSR, 1958, p. 40.)

The play opened on October 5. It was an immediate success. Box-office receipts went up and the theatre was once again solvent. The critics almost universally condemned it, displaying an animosity which may well be unique in the annals of the theatre. Nor did the violence of the attacks diminish with time. Over the years Bulgakov counted 301 reviews, 298 of them hostile, their tone achieving, at times, an almost eighteenth-century scurrility. *The Turbins* was categorized as the *Cherry Orchard* of the newly launched Art Theatre. Writing in *On Guard*, the magazine of the Association of Proletarian Writers (RAPP), Osaf Litovski asked why Soviet audiences should care about the tribulations of a bunch of émigrés and White counter-Revolutionaries any more than they should care about a property owner, Ranevskaia, having her cherry orchard chopped down? Against the nuanced complexities of *The Turbins* the critics set the 1925 production of Treniov's *Liubov Iarovaia* at the Mali, a much more straightforward piece, offering a conventional love/duty dilemma where loyalty to the Bolshevik cause comes into conflict with personal emotion. The play is an exercise in reassurance; its end is never in doubt. Nothing is left unresolved; there are no loose political ends to disturb. A public debate on the relative merits of the two plays was held at the Meierhold Theatre on February 7, 1927. Bulgakov spoke, as did Markov. Stanislavski, Nemirovich and the Art Theatre were attacked once again as bourgeois relics. Lunacharski was in combative form, determined to follow as far as he could a pluralist policy and not give in to the crude ideology of those he contemptuously termed 'Lefticrits' and 'snarling pug-dogs'. Blum was heckled and could not finish his speech but the general hostility to the Art Theatre and all its works was so intense as to verge on the hysterical and none of Lunacharski's careful references to Marx and Lenin could make any difference.

Two weeks later Lunacharski chaired a conference on the future development of Soviet theatre at the People's Commissariat for Enlightenment. Stanislavski held a number of preliminary meetings at home with Michael Chekhov, Meierhold and Markov, possibly in an attempt to find some common ground. If that was the case the attempt failed. He was called on the 21st. His speech was fully reported later in the journal *Zhizn Iskusstva*. His former pupils and younger colleagues were anxious for his approval and he would have given almost anything to be able to oblige but he could not. In February 1925 he had attended a performance of *The Flea* at the Second Art Theatre. He left the theatre in silence but was accosted by a student who was appalled that he should simply walk out without saying anything. 'That was splendid,' Stanislavski replied, 'but now we go our separate ways.' In October of the same year he had paid his first visit to Meierhold's theatre. The final act of his production of Nikolai Erdman's *The Mandate* impressed him. Not only did the stage revolve but so did the walls of the set. Meierhold had achieved, he stated, something he had dreamed of doing. But it was a moment of rare satisfaction. Michael Chekhov's Hamlet a month later upset him profoundly, although he readily admitted, as ever, Chekhov's extraordinary talent. As for Meierhold's production of Gromelynck's *Le Cocu Magnifique*, which he saw on September 26, 1926, it left him frustrated and disappointed.

The Day of the Turbins had revealed the division between popular and critical reaction. Audiences had received the play as an illumination of their own lives, of history as experienced at the human level. At one performance a member of the audience, in a voice choked with tears, shouted 'Thank you'. Such reactions were anathema to the ideologues, for whom history was a matter of abstract forces, progressive or reactionary, with which one could identify or not. They demanded that a play provide a clear-cut, not to say simplistic statement of position, pro-Revolutionary and therefore, of course, invincible. What was required was political tidiness.

Stanislavski could only restate his total opposition to such schematized views. He did not accept that avant-garde experiment was synonymous with revolutionary art or, more properly, with the art of the Revolution. He had witnessed, he said, his colleagues' attempts to create theatre according to a series of formulae, of -isms, either artistic or ideological. The result was sterile propaganda. It produced ideological tidiness by exploiting stock responses and hack acting. The crucial question was what was to happen when the new writers of talent, the real poets of the Revolution appeared, writers who would be able to confront the complexity and depth of the revolutionary experience in human terms? Such writers would require actors of genuine creative ability with a proper internal and external technique. 'We do not intend to kill that kind of actor and put a mere hack in his place,' he concluded.

In reality Stanislavski's attitude to the work of younger directors was less oppositional. In conversation with Pulitzer prize novelist Theodore Dreiser, he admitted that something might come of Michael Chekhov's and Vakhtangov's experiments. Stagnation was the real enemy. Behind this comment lay his disappointment that he had not been able to persuade the Art Theatre to establish an experimental group or laboratory.

About the same time as *The Days of the Turbins* was having its première, the newly-named Stanislavski Opera Studio opened. Rimski-Korsakov's *The Tsar's Bride* had its first performance on November 28, followed in January by Cimarosa's *Il Matrimonio Segreto*. Both had been in preparation for several months. Opera, happily, was less contentious than straight theatre and Stanislavski's productions were considered purely on their artistic merits. What struck critics about his production of the Cimarosa was his capacity to breathe life into works which were apparently only of historic interest.

His production of *The Tsar's Bride* was seen by the young Otto Klemperer, Aleksandr Glazunov, the doyen of Russian composers, and Rimski-Korsakov's son-in-law Maximillian Steinberg who taught composition and orchestration at the Leningrad Conservatoire where he counted Shostakovich among his pupils. Klemperer was impressed by Stanislavski's capacity to marry truth of character to musical form with proper theatricality. Steinberg felt that the production was faithful to everything his father-in-law had ever wanted both musically and dramatically.

After *Matrimonio* he turned to Puccini's *La Bohème*, which opened on April 12. This he updated from the 1840s to the turn of the century. Puccini's *verismo* suited him. The score contains many purely orchestral passages which accompany stage action. Stanislavski was able to push home the point that the motivation and shape of the moves were to be discovered in a careful study of the score.

The one production of the 1926–7 season for which Stanislavski took absolute responsibility was Beaumarchais' *Le Mariage de Figaro*. He worked as usual with assistants but of the 300 recorded rehearsals he took 82, an exceptionally high proportion. Work had started at the end of 1925, continued throughout the whole of 1926 and occupied the first four months of 1927. It opened on April 28.

Stanislavski's purpose was twofold: to present a classic play which was relevant to contemporary audiences and to direct it in such a way as to reaffirm his aesthetic principles. A battle of words was no longer enough. He had once challenged Nemirovich with the words, 'defeat me with work'. Now what he required was a spectacular, prestige production with a clear post-revolutionary message and equally clear pre-revolutionary production values. He had frequently expressed his misgivings at the disappearance of the artist-designer who created a visual world specifically for each play, helping the actors to believe in the given circumstances. This had now been replaced by a mechanical, constructed world, essentially a style in its own right, making statements in its own right, reducing the actor to a function of the set. He suspected, moreover, along with Lunacharski, that after the rigours of scaffolding and walk-ways audiences were ready for something more lavish.

His view of the play had been expressed as far back as 1915 when he had seen Taïrov's production at the Kamerni. He had disagreed with the interpretation. In his notebook he commented:

'Figaro is . . . a democratic play and certainly not decadent.' (K.S. Stanislavski, *Iz Zapisnikh Knizhek*, II, Moscow, 1986, p. 146.)

The action was to be seen through the eyes of Figaro and Susanna, not Count Almaviva, and set in a real not a theatrical world. The characters were not to be played as 'types' more or less derived from the *commedia dell'arte*, as they had been in the Mali production of 1920, but as individuals with historical and social roots:

'*Figaro* is a democrat, he's in the opposition, he's a rebel. . . . We know that he isn't a hero in the sense of our own recent turbulent revolutionary times but we won't "bring him up to date". But for his period he is a rebel, a representative of the people. And that's the effect he should produce today.

Susanna is Figaro in petticoats. Not a soubrette but a proper serving-maid who can work hard, spin, sew and cook – and she does it all easily and happily. Don't forget, she's the gardener's niece, a daughter of the people.

The Count is an egoist and a windbag but he's not stupid. A handsome man who knows he's handsome, the terror of all the girls in the district. . . . Inwardly amoral but outwardly attractive. . . . Even Susanna finds it difficult to resist his refined advances. . . .' (N. Gorchakov, *Rezhissiorski Uroki Stanislavskovo*, Moscow, 1951, p. 360.)

Figaro's attempt to deny the Count that last, degrading vestige of medieval privilege, the *ius primae noctis*, is a symbolic act of revolt. In defining Figaro's through-action Stanislavski insisted that it was not, 'I want to be married' but 'I want to be married in order to be *free*.' He decided to transfer the action from 'Carmen's Spain' to pre-Revolutionary France to show the people immediately prior to social upheaval.

The ruling idea behind the production was provided by the play's subtitle, 'la folle journée', the day of madness. This provided the rhythm of the action and the method of staging, which needed to be fast and free-flowing. From this decision others followed. He demanded of his cast that the 'Frenchness' of the play should be achieved by the quickness of their thinking, their nimbleness of mind, not through some vague notion that the French wave their hands a lot. This meant changes in the script. The same number of words takes much longer in Russian than in French and can appear heavy. He had the translation revised, cutting and condensing, while retaining the essential meaning, bringing the dialogue up to the lightness and pace of the original. He also insisted that Figaro's name should be pronounced, as in French, with the accent on the last syllable.

He decided to break Beaumarchais' five acts and five sets down into eleven scenes, moving freely throughout the house and grounds by means of the revolve. The last act, set in the garden, had four different revolve settings. The external pace with which the settings changed was to match the pace with which the inner action moved. As he told the cast, 'something new happens every second'. His use of the revolve may well have been influenced by Meierhold's production of *The Mandate* which he had admired a few months earlier.

For his designer he selected Aleksandr Golovin. Golovin belonged to the same school as Bakst and Benois; his designs recalled the splendour of Diaghilev's Ballets Russes. In 1910 he had provided opulent sets for Molière's *Don Juan* which he brought forward to the late eighteenth century and in 1917 he had designed Lermontov's *Maskerad* set in the same period. His palette was sumptuously polychrome. Stanislavski asked him to provide a contrast between the luxury of the salon and the poverty below stairs. To reinforce this contrast he also decided to change the location of Act Four, transferring it from one of the main state rooms to the servants' quarters. Golovin originally designed a splendid banquet with a table lavishly set. This is replaced by a small, shabby room with broken plaster. It is here that the wedding of Figaro and Susanna takes place.

Figaro brought two important developments to the 'system'. Stanislavski began working in terms of broad physical tasks, well illustrated by the Wedding scene, in Act Four, where the entire house-hold assembles for the festivities. Gone were the carefully choreographed movements and groupings with every pause timed; the cast were simply asked to respond truthfully to the cramped nature of the physical space. The action proceeded in three phases. Phase one: the servants were provided with a basic task: find yourself a good place. This left no room for the Count and the Countess. Phase two: make room for the master and mistress but still keep the best place you can. The question then arose, where were the Count and Countess to sit? Phase three: find two chairs and place them suitably. The scene staged itself through the identification of a series of basic physical problems, each requiring a new adaptation to changed circumstances but, from the servants' point of view, with a single task running through, to gain and keep an advantage.

Stanislavski then elaborated the notion of the Line of the Day. An actor's performance is constructed from a series of logically connected actions, justifiable in terms of probability. The naturalistic actor, concerned only with the imitation of the surface can, if need be, create the performance out of sequence, in isolated fragments. For the realistic actor, concerned with inner justification, this is not possible. What is seen on stage is only moments in a continuum which is the 'life' of the character. It was the actor's task to have a thorough and clear knowledge of all off-stage moments, so that when he comes on to the stage he comes *from* somewhere and is on his way *to* somewhere.

Figaro has been recognized as one of Stanislavski's most remarkable achievements. It owed its quality mainly to its rhythmic unity, which bound all the disparate elements together. It was the organic cohesion of thought, speech, action and scene change which gave the play its drive and force. It was also the last production for which he was totally responsible.

The opening night was a success, with ten curtain calls. Some thought the production would run twenty years. Others voiced criticism which was redolent of the theatre's early days. There were those for whom the play was still essentially a light comedy; they were disturbed by the way in which the dialogue was broken up with realistic pauses; they found the production a little heavy. Stanislavski did not demur. He merely pointed out that a play of this kind takes time to settle down; it has to be run in. The production received the inevitable thumbs-down from Vladimir Blum who accused it of failing to mark the class conflicts sufficiently. Stanislavski's principle of finding the good in an evil character and the evil in a good character – an essentially dialectical notion – meant nothing to Blum. He thought in crude ideological categories. It was simply unacceptable to him for Almaviva, the class enemy, to be presented as in any way sympathetic. First the *Turbins*, he wrote, now *Figaro* – the Art Theatre was incorrigible.

CHAPTER TWENTY-FIVE

THE ARMOURED TRAIN

The tenth anniversary of the October Revolution was approaching. Lunacharski attended the second night of *Figaro* with a number of colleagues and discussed plans for the jubilee celebrations. Stanislavski had decided ideas concerning the Art Theatre's contribution. He rejected an evening of dramatized extracts from contemporary writers. He wanted a single play, and a contemporary play, to contrast with the classic *Figaro*. He felt that while the theatre had presented works which dealt with the reactions of the privileged and middle classes to the revolution, it had not shown the lives of the people who had actually made it. There were apparently no new talented dramatists who could fill the gap. He was, however, attracted by a collection of short stories dealing with the partisans during the Civil War and, in particular, by Vsevolod Ivanov's *The Armoured Train No. 14–69*. The story deals with the capture of an armoured train from counter-Revolutionary troops by the partisans and with the transformation of the central character, Vershinin, from a politically indifferent peasant farmer into a hero of the Bolshevik cause.

He asked Sudakov and Markov to collaborate with the author on an adaptation. They were to concentrate on the human content but at the same time to strip away any superfluous naturalism in order to achieve 'simplicity raised to the level of a clear symbol'. Having set the project in motion he turned it over to Sudakov, who was to supervise the production, and Litovtsieva, who was to take rehearsals. He was himself committed to a tour in Leningrad. During his stay in Leningrad Stanislavski was introduced to the painter Chupiatov, whose designs for a ballet he had admired. The artist's work seemed to open up new possibilities. It was three-dimensional and made interesting use of perspective. The original intention had been to engage Simov to design *The Armoured Train* but now Chupiatov seemed their man. He worked on the preliminary sketches throughout the summer.

A script had been ready in late June and a reading given at the Bolshoi on the 21st. In Art Theatre terms the play was a rush job. It received only seventy-six rehearsals, less than one third the number for *Figaro*. Everything needed to go like clockwork. It was inevitable at this point that things went wrong. Chupiatov delivered his preliminary sketches in August when the play was well into rehearsal. Stanislavski was disappointed. They seemed very flat and lacking in energy. Above all they did not provide the opportunity for the dynamic staging in which the Art Theatre specialized. He made the necessary excuses and told Sudakov to contact Simov. There were barely two months to go to opening.

There were, however, more serious difficulties. The Repertkom was once again expressing its hostility. On August 12 Fiodor Mikhailovski, a member of the management team, wrote to Stanislavski, who was at a sanatorium in Kislovodsk, in Georgia, informing him that *Turbins* had been categorically banned and that a large number of changes were required in *The Armoured Train*, including a complete reworking of the final act. There were, furthermore, suggestions that *Uncle Vania* should be replaced by *The Cherry Orchard*. In other words the season as planned was on the rubbish heap.

On September 13 Stanislavski wrote to Lunacharski, asking for help.

'The presence of *Turbins* in our current repertoire would act as a guarantee that other new plays would come forward. Now we must either risk not being able to mount a show for the jubilee of the October Revolution or deliberately suffer financial losses.

I would like also to inform you that *Armoured Train* has still not been finally approved. We need extensive and complicated changes from the author who is abroad on holiday. We have sent him a telegram and all we now await is his arrival.

It is almost impossible to rehearse a much-needed show when there isn't a final script. Uncertainty is the worst enemy of work in the theatre; it saps energy and creates difficulties and delays by the minute.' (K.S. Archive, No. 6424.)

Early in October he was asked when it would be possible to arrange a showing for the Repertkom. On October 3 he wrote, displaying admirable restraint, to the department responsible for state Academic theatres informing them that he would be able to oblige once the author and Repertkom itself had agreed the two final scenes; the first seven were ready. He was careful to assure them that he would personally assume responsibility for the final rehearsals and for the performances. On the 13th he received a letter from Lunacharski assuring him that there were unlikely to be any difficulties over the script for *The Armoured Train* and that the problem of the *Turbins* had been resolved – 'for this year at least'.

Lunacharski was right to put in the proviso. In the end the opposition to the *Turbins* triumphed and, in 1929, the play was taken off but the ideological zealots were themselves wrong-footed. In 1932 it was discovered that Stalin not only liked the play but had actually seen it fifteen times. He detected no ideological problems. The play, in his opinion, finally proved the invincibility of the Bolshevik forces. The production was immediately revived and remained in the repertoire for the next nine years.

Stanislavski took over the production of *The Armoured Train* in September. He was then out of action for almost three weeks with a severe chill. He returned at the beginning of October and saw a run-through of several scenes on the 3rd. He was apparently pleased with what he saw. He made a speech of thanks for the good work done. The first complete run-through, staged for the benefit of the Repertkom, took place on October 31 in the foyer without costume or make-up; the sets were still not ready. Again Stanislavski seemed satisfied.

But, as on so many occasions, the more he became involved the less satisfied he became. The play was not progressing. The opening scene worried him particularly. Litovtsieva, he decided, had taken the wrong line. It needed to be tougher, harder, to set the tone for the rest of the play. What he was getting from senior members of the company like Knipper and Vishnievski was a kind of Chekhovian softness as a group of dispossessed White refugees considered their fate. It was the *Turbins* all over again, with the cast becoming involved with their own emotions rather than thinking of positive actions. What he wanted was murderous hate but the cast were unwilling to appear unsympathetic. Rather than adapt themselves to the characters, the actors were toning them down. Their unwillingness to show aggression was expressed in the over-relaxed physical action. At the root of the problem lay a degree of political anxiety. They did not, as artists, wish to be identified with the characters they were playing, something which is not unknown. Stanislavski understood but would have none of it:

> 'I'm not asking you to justify the characters either in political or human terms, far from it. What we're dealing with here is actors' feeling, a lack of courage to show the audience a so-called "negative" character. You've got to get over that.' (N. Gorchakov, *Rezhissiorskie Uroki Stanislavskovo*, Moscow, 1951, p. 481.)

The fact is the cast wanted the scene cut.

A long discussion ensued on the political and dramatic function of the scene but in the end Stanislavski resorted to a favourite strategy: he created a physical problem. He made them fight the furniture:

> 'Close in the greenhouse walls, pile all the furniture, crates and bundles on top of each other. Now I want you to clamber up on anything you like – the back of a chair, the piano crate, a pile of books. Help Olga Leonardovna [Knipper] on to the back of this armchair – it's strong. . . .
>
> KNIPPER: Look here, this is very uncomfortable.
> KS: That's just how it should feel. The others are uncomfortable too.
> KNIPPER: But really I do feel a bit of a fool.

KS: Good. They all feel they're in a ridiculous situation. Only you hide the fact that you feel silly from everyone and so you say the lines about how you're going to line this barn with silk.' (Ibid., p. 484.)

The strategy worked although a few days later Stanislavski complained that the cast had adapted to their piles of furniture. If they had been in any way artistically adventurous they would have made life difficult for themselves again to keep the scene alive and push it forward.

The crowd scenes suffered from the same lack of focus, in particular the scene known as the Bell Tower. What Stanislavski was getting was undifferentiated peasant 'rhubarb' instead of genuine reaction. The cast knew perfectly well what was expected of them. They had discussed it in detail with Sudakov. Rather than indulge in further talk Stanislavski set them an exercise. He used a device which was later to become one of the principal features of his rehearsal method, the technique which came to be known as Here, Today, Now. The actor is asked the question: what would you do, as a private individual, if such and such happened? In the case of *The Armoured Train* he set them the following problem: what would they do if Lunacharski unexpectedly turned up at rehearsal and said:

'Comrade actors of the Art Theatre, in order to defend the Soviet state against the most recent attacks by our capitalist enemies, you must go with me immediately to the broadcasting station and tell the whole world that the rumour in the bourgeois press that the Art Theatre has refused to play *The Armoured Train* is a base, common lie. Who's coming with me?' (Ibid., p. 507.)

Stanislavski's imitation of Lunacharski was sufficiently impassioned and convincing to produce an equally impassioned and spontaneous response. The block to the scene had been cleared.

Stanislavski continued to pull the production together, making cuts, changing sets, clarifying tasks and the through-action. As always for him at this stage it was the dynamic, the forward drive of the play as a whole, which mattered. After the first preview on November 3 he decided that the closing scene was too down-beat. He asked for more positive playing and again made changes to the set. The play opened five days later in a gala performance. Of the seventy-six rehearsals Stanislavski had only taken eleven, seven working on individual scenes and four run-throughs. There was, nonetheless, no doubt in anyone's mind as to who was responsible for the production in its final form.

Critics on the left apart, the production was received with enthusiasm both by the public, young and old, and by the authorities. For Lunacharski the Art Theatre had finally proved itself and demonstrated its ability to use high art to illuminate the revolution. *Izvestia* published a favourable article, rejecting the attacks of Blum and his colleagues. The

Vechernaia Moskva of December 13 reported that the Young Communists, the Komsomols, had warmly welcomed the progress the Art Theatre had made in moving ideologically from the *Turbins* to *The Armoured Train*. For Markov the 'system' had proved its relevance:

> 'Through the revelation of the psychology of character it leads to the revelation of the social nature of that character. It reveals the period through man.' (P. Markov, *Aktior Oktobriasksi Revolutsii*, in *Sovremeni Teatr*, 1927, No. 12, p. 179.)

Stanislavski surprised many of his colleagues, and shocked some, by working on a blatant melodrama, *Les Soeurs Gérard*, at the same time as *The Armoured Train*. This seemed ideologically inconsistent. He was, however, no artistic snob and he insisted that working on melodrama was good for actors. As a form melodrama relied almost entirely on plot. This forced the actors to make clear decisions about their sequence of actions. It also obliged them to use their imagination to flesh out the bare bones of the script and conceal the mechanics. At one rehearsal he gave a remarkable demonstration of what he meant. In the course of the action Constable Picard is meant to drug an old man, Martin. Stanislavski took over from the actor playing Picard and began to improvise with the actor opposite, Vladimir Mikhailov. A simple moment in the action was transformed into a ten-minute improvisation as each character tried to outwit the other. Stanislavski's point was not that such an exercise would ever be shown to an audience but that the logical pursuit of a goal, and adaptation to another character's reactions produced a richness of feeling and behaviour which would inform the final performance. The actors were no longer playing plot but situation.

After the success of *The Armoured Train* Stanislavski turned his attention to Rimski-Korsakov's opera *May Night* which had been in rehearsal for several months. It opened on January 19, 1928, though not before he had staged a walk-out from rehearsal apparently over the uncooperative attitude of the cast. The reviews in *Pravda* and *Izvestia* were excellent. The Stanislavski 'system' had, once again, according to *Izvestia*, proved its value.

The next two productions at the Art Theatre, however, dispersed much of the goodwill which had been created. *Untilovsk*, by Leonov, set in a remote community in Siberia, had been in rehearsal for some time but had been set aside during the latter stages of *The Armoured Train*. Stanislavski took the unusual step of holding a public reading before an invited audience of writers, officials and critics which was followed by a discussion of the play's merits. That seemed a wise precaution. Nonetheless when the recently reorganized management committee saw a preview on the 14th they disapproved of the play on ideological grounds. So, when it opened three days later, did almost everyone else. On March 14 Lunacharski published an article in the Leningrad journal *Krasnaia*

Gazeta stating that the play marked a step backwards. Everyone agreed the production was full of fine touches and the acting excellent but they could not save the play. Stanislavski was fully aware of the political deficiencies of the script but it offered good parts for actors from which they could learn.

Equally adverse reaction was encountered by Kataiev's *The Embezzlers* which opened on April 20. The play dealt with corruption among government officials in search of a good life during the early days of Lenin's New Economic Policy. The social themes of the play were denounced as superficial, as was the writing which, it was stated, offered trivial material for the actors to work on. The general view, expressed at an internal post-mortem discussion on April 16, was that the script could not bear the wealth of detail Stanislavski had lavished upon it. For his part Stanislavski could only ask what he was to do. New plays were thin on the ground. He had one, Bulgakov's *Flight*. What was better, to encourage young, inexperienced writers or to go on reviving classics? He lost the battle and the play was taken off after eighteen performances.

The failure of two productions produced a fresh wave of criticism. On May 5 an article appeared in the *Rabochaia Gazeta* accusing the Art Theatre of failing to give sufficient place to working-class groups and their interests, and of undervaluing the work of young actors. Particular criticism was levelled at Podgorni, of the literary department, and Egorov, one of the business managers. Stanislavski replied with an open letter in *Pravda* on the 16th which was also published by *Izvestia* and the magazine *Sovremeni Teatr*. He rebutted the criticisms and reaffirmed the theatre's concern for the future. That future, however, was no longer directly in his hands.

On January 22, 1928, Nemirovich had returned from the United States but the handover of responsibility does not appear to have taken place until May when the theatre's management committee was once more reorganized. The two-year period of Stanislavski's control had scotched the myth of his inefficiency. The fact is that with Nemirovich out of the way Stanislavski thrived and so did the theatre with him. The company were fully aware of their dependence on him and largely resented his involvement with the Opera Studio. They asked him more than once not to take on too many outside responsibilities. With Nemirovich back in command he was gloomy about future prospects and in May confided in his notebook:

'I cannot guarantee the further growth of the company and the actors.' (K.S. Archive, No. 814.)

He had set a number of projects in motion. Work had started on a production of *Othello* with Leonidov in the title role. He had proposed a stage version of Gogol's *Dead Souls* which Bulgakov was to adapt. Bulgakov's second play, *Flight*, was also scheduled.

In the field of opera he was already working on Mussorgski's *Boris Godunov* which he intended to stage in the composer's own second version with the original orchestration rather than the popular revised version by Rimski-Korsakov. Mussorgski's score had just been published and it would be the first time it had been heard since the 1880s. Stanislavski was on the look-out, too, for modern operas. He had seen Berg's *Wozzeck* at the Mali opera theatre in June 1927 and more recently had been interested in a one-act opera by Kurt Weill, *Der Tzar Lasst Sich Photographieren*.

From mid-June to mid-July he was on tour in Leningrad. He left soon after his return to Moscow for what had become a regular summer visit to the sanatorium in Kislovodsk. He was being advised to slow down; he was, after all, sixty-five. He stayed in Georgia until September 10 when he returned to Moscow. On the 15th, he went to Berlin. While there he held his last serious discussion with Michael Chekhov who had left the Soviet Union in 1927, having fallen foul of the authorities. Stanislavski tried to persuade him to return but to no avail. Chekhov never set foot in Russia again. Their conversation, he recalled, centred on the function of an actor's own personal emotions in the creation of a role.

Stanislavski also made contact once more with Max Reinhardt and on September 19 saw his production of *Die Artisten*. Reinhardt had been trying to persuade him to stage a play in Berlin for two years, suggesting either *The Dybbuk* or a Chekhov. There were other offers. Leopold Jessner, the Intendant of the Staats und Schiller Theater, invited him to stage *Figaro* with a German cast as part of the Berliner Festspiel in May 1929. There was also a plan to make a film to illustrate *My Life in Art*. He did not commit himself.

On the 22nd he left for Badenweiler where his family joined him. While staying there he received a telephone call from Leonidov telling him that Reinhardt had just spent 30,000 marks on a magnificent car which he intended giving Stanislavski as a gift. Was he, he wrote to Podgorni on October 5, supposed to drive to the theatre in it on the thirtieth jubilee in October? Kind as it was of Reinhardt the car was an acute embarrassment. How was he to get it to Moscow? What about the customs? What, more importantly, about running costs? Once back in Berlin he attended a reception given by Reinhardt at which the car was ceremoniously presented. Stanislavski gave a credible imitation of surprise, joy and gratitude and allowed himself to be driven back to his hotel, accompanied by Michael Chekhov. The car was not entirely wasted. In the event it served to chauffeur Reinhardt round Moscow on his next visit.

Stanislavski returned to Russia on October 16. He approached the forthcoming celebrations with a sense of foreboding. It would mean a heavy round of receptions, official ceremonies, meals, on top of what he had lived through in Berlin, getting to bed at three in the morning. He was also unhappy once again about the atmosphere in the theatre. He suspected that Podgorni and Egorov, who had been so heavily criticized in the press earlier in the year following the presentation of *Untilovsk*, were now working against him. Greetings began pouring in from all over the world. Reinhardt made him an honorary member of the Deutsches Theater. *Izvestia* reported messages from Gordon Craig, Mary Pickford, Douglas Fairbanks, Charlie Chaplin, Gloria Swanson. But even these happy events were overcast by ideological shadows. Stanislavski's address to the company on the 26th, which was no more than his usual idealistic appeal for dedication and openness to the future, was criticized for failing to reflect the contemporary mood.

On the 29th the theatre celebrated its jubilee with a gala performance consisting of extracts from its major productions. Stanislavski was due to appear as Vershinin in Act One of *Three Sisters*. He had once said to an actor, 'You can die on stage but you can't miss an entrance.' Like Molière, he remained true to that principle. His performance, according to eye-witnesses, was exceptional despite the fact that he suffered a massive heart-attack. Years later he recalled:

'. . . I come on, applause, I say the lines and suddenly I feel faint. I nearly collapsed but got a hold of myself, pulled myself together and finished the act. However, going upstage (as indicated in the prompt-book), you remember, to the dining-room, I sent for my doctors. They were both in the audience. Finally the act came to an end, I came out for two curtain calls and . . . I collapsed, they were already carrying me away. The audience knew nothing although they were surprised that I didn't take any more calls.' (Stanislavski's account, taken down by B. V. Zon, August 11, 1934. In B. Zon, *Meetings with Stanislavski*. K.S. Archive.)

He was driven home. As he wrote to his doctor later, he realized he might not actually reach there alive:

'I remember that fatal evening of the jubilee performance when you took me home in the car. I remember how you, in your dinner-jacket, took care of me, looking into my eyes searchingly and affectionately to see whether I was ill or already dead.' (K.S. Archive, No. 5103.)

In all probability Stanislavski suffered a second heart attack two weeks later. A third would undoubtedly have proved fatal. His career as an actor was over. He never appeared on stage again.

CHAPTER TWENTY-SIX

AN ACTOR'S WORK

Stanislavski lived the last ten years of his life on borrowed time. The heart was enlarged, he had emphysema, brought on by years of heavy smoking, and arterio-sclerosis, although the brain was not affected. Whatever his physical weakness his mental capacities were unimpaired but he could not carry through his ideas in practice. He suffered from periodic bouts of breathlessness, diagnosed as asthma. His natural propensity to colds, chills and flu meant that during the bad winter months the apartment was practically hermetically sealed. When he could he went abroad. At Leontievski Lane he had a nurse in constant attendance to make sure he took his medicine and did not overstretch himself. There was also the formidable Ripsime Karpovna Tamansova, 'Ripsi', his diminutive secretary, known to the outside world as Little Napoleon both on account of her stature and her fierce devotion to her employer.

His relations with the outside world were filtered through his entourage, domestic and professional; work was done at home, either in the flat itself or in the Onegin Room. Later, in the 1930s, he was able to make occasional visits to the theatre. If the doctors had had their way he would have retired but life without the theatre was nothing to him. He came alive when he could talk about the theatre or work on a scene, finding fresh reserves of energy. He did not reduce the scope of his interests – plays, opera, teaching, writing – but everything was done in snatches, often over long periods – the production of Bulgakov's *Molière*, from delivery of the manuscript to final showing, was spread over five years. His life became even more of a mosaic.

His health was a matter of national concern. On November 18 *Izvestia* published a bulletin giving details of his temperature, night and morning, and his pulse rate. They gave an assurance of general progress. He was confined to bed for three months. His attitude was exemplary. He was as disciplined a patient as he was an actor, almost as though he were being directed in a play, *The Sick Man*. He took the exact number of drops required and when he was finally allowed up asked how many steps a day he could take. Eventually he was allowed to go out for short walks. A chair was placed at each turn of the stairs so that he could sit down if he needed. These excursions were kept secret for fear that he should be approached by a colleague and get overexcited.

By the beginning of December he was well enough to write to the theatre to say what he thought should be done. He wanted work on *Othello* to continue with Leonidov in charge. He stipulated that there should be only a strictly limited number of performances, no more than one every fourteen days. He also directed that rehearsals should continue on Bulgakov's *Flight*. Work had begun in October but was abruptly terminated in January of the following year in a shower of vituperation from the authorities who had seen a run-through. For the rest, his thoughts turned back to the early days. He remembered with nostalgic pleasure the sense of ensemble among the original group, now the 'old brigade'. In contrast to what he had said in the recent past and what indeed he was to repeat not much later, he stressed the importance of revivals to weld the old and new members of the company together.

By the end of the month his condition had deteriorated, causing great anxiety. At the New Year Rachmaninov wired his good wishes from New York but the theatre's traditional celebrations were held under a pall.

As soon as he had recovered a little, he was asked to collaborate with Lunacharski and the new magazine *Iskusstvo* to try and solve one of the most difficult problems in Marxist thought, the development of an adequate aesthetic to counter crude sloganizing. Stanislavski's contribution would be his knowledge of the past and of the Realist tradition. A French publishing house, La Renaissance du Livre, requested permission to bring out a translation of *My Life in Art* with a preface by Jacques Copeau. Morris Gest renewed his invitation for another US tour, to include the West Coast. Stanislavski was still writing up the 'system' and was able to read Leonidov's draft chapters on 'Faith and a Sense of Truth' and 'Affective Memory' (later renamed 'Emotion Memory').

There was no question of his undertaking any rehearsal work, not even coaching actors or singers at home, but the production of *Boris Godunov* which he had planned and in part supervised opened on March 5 at the Stanislavski Opera Theatre. Moskvin had seen the work through its final stages. Stanislavski was telephoned between the acts and told how the performance was going. It was an unquestioned success. The experience of recreating the realities of Russian history displayed for so many years in *Tsar Fiodor* was transferred to the operatic stage.

By April he was working on a production plan for Tchaikovski's *Queen of Spades* and discussing sets for *Othello* with Golovin. *My Life in Art* had its third printing in as many years.

Stanislavski's long convalescence provided the perfect opportunity for him to complete a book on the 'system'. Mrs Gurevich had put all his papers in order, at his request, while he was absent in America. There was a pile of unfinished manuscripts in which he had made successive attempts to summarize his ideas, using various forms. *Various Trends in the Art of the Theatre* had been abandoned and the notes on *Mozart and Salieri* were mere fragments. From 1916 to 1920 he had worked on a book, *The Story of Role*, based on his rehearsals for *Woe from Wit*, in which he outlined his approach to creating a character. The book was planned in four sections: first, acquaintance with the play and the role; second, experiencing the role; third, physical characterization; fourth, the result. He completed three sections before abandoning the project.

Stanislavski's problem was to find an appropriate form. In 1923 he had told Gurevich that he had decided to use a 'semi-literary' form. The result was a theatrical novel, *The Story of a Production*. In it, for the first time, the persona who was to represent him, Tvortsov, appears. Following the tradition of writers like Gogol and Ostrovski, Stanislavski gave his characters names which indicated their dominant traits. Thus, Tvortsov means creator, the creative actor, from *tvorchestvo*, 'creativity'. Opposed to him is Remeslov, the cliché actor, from *remeslo*, 'stock-in-trade'.

Two years later, in June 1925, he wrote again to Gurevich to tell her he now had a plan for two books. The first was a student's diary, an actor's work on himself, the second, the history of a production, work on a role. The basic project that was to occupy him until his death was thus laid down.

Gurevich had always stressed the importance of publishing outside the Soviet Union in as many countries and in as many languages as possible. In September 1926 Stanislavski wrote to Baliev in New York informing him of the student's diary, asking what the possibilities for publication were, both in the United States and elsewhere. His earlier correspondence with Little, Brown & Co., in 1925, appears to have been forgotten.

Encouraged by Gurevich, he had continued to work until his heart attack in October 1928. He developed his idea of giving special names, like Tvortsov, to his characters. Thus, the student writing the diary was called Nazvanov, the chosen one, and bore a very strong resemblance to Vakhtangov, while Tvortsov's assistant was obviously based on Sulerzhitski. Tvortsov himself was probably based on Stanislavski's old teacher Fiodor Komissarzhevski.* Other students were given names such as Fatty, Brains, Beauty, Arguer. Gurevich saw drafts as the book progressed.

The combination of Gurevich and Stanislavski was an ideal one. Stanislavski suffered from an excess of adulation. Few were prepared to be open with him, he was too grand, too great, he was a kind of superman. While Gurevich had unending respect for him and was cautious and tactful in her editorial work, she was prepared to raise difficult questions and to challenge him when she thought it was in his own best interests. In particular, she would draw his attention constantly

* I am indebted to Dr Viktor Borovsky for this insight.

to the realities of Soviet life, of which he seemed totally unaware. Stanislavski still thought in pre-1914 terms. Had the two been able to work together consistently, many of the problems which overtook the writing and publication of his books could have been avoided.

On March 14, 1929, Stanislavski informed her of the progress he had made. He had managed to complete two more very difficult chapters, 'Affective Memory' and 'Communication'. His problem was that he was not sure who he was writing for: for specialists or for the general public. What did she think?

In a remarkable letter, dated April 8, while reaffirming her belief in the book as a source of inexhaustible secrets, she analysed its failings as she saw them. Criticisms came under five heads. First, in trying to reach a wider public he had become repetitious. He would have to complete his draft and then go back and cut drastically. Second, some of the scientific terms he used, as she had already pointed out, were inaccurate. She had consulted three psychologists on the matter and they agreed with her. Third, there was the problem of some of the exercises and improvisations he used. Two, in particular, she found troublesome: in one a student is given an expensive jewelled brooch so she can pay for her theatre studies, in another, a clerk is counting large piles of bank-notes and going through accounts:

> 'These examples with jewelled brooches and thousands in capital tell the reader that you, the greatest of living artists, are terribly out of touch with the real life of contemporary intellectuals, that you don't see them in your imagination and don't feel their joys and sorrows.' (K.S. Archive, No. 8056.)

She then painted a pitiful picture of the situation of the Russian intelligentsia. Once they had devoted their lives to higher things, without much concern for their material circumstances. They knew that in comparison to the really poor, they were privileged.

> 'The best among our young people did not dream of jewels, of a life without a care, but like Trofimov and Ania in *The Cherry Orchard*, of creating a new life. . . .' (Ibid.)

Now intellectuals are reduced to grubbing around to make a living and feed their families, compromising their most cherished principles:

> 'Young people without means of support are chronically under-nourished, chronically debilitated. Their hearts are weighed down with feelings of bitterness at the injustice of it all, the feeling that there is nothing to be done about their situation. I don't want to worry you with these pictures of the life of minor intellectuals . . . but having promised to tell you what I think of your book, I cannot keep silent: dear Konstantin Sergeievich, don't talk to starving, needy people

about jewels and money because it will provoke bitter anger in some and silent, nagging resentment in others. I already spoke to you about the undesirability of these examples last year. You replied that it was difficult to rethink your book. But this year the situation of the intelligentsia is even worse and the more I think about it, the clearer it becomes that these examples *must* be replaced by others, because they could ruin the book. And I really don't think it's all that difficult, if not for you, then for someone else to devise *psychologically similar* examples, but drawn from contemporary life.' (Ibid.)

He then needed to cut all references to particular periods, such as up to the First World War. Finally, there was the problem of the names, which seemed to her artificial and contrived.

'That is all I can say about an unfinished book which I am utterly convinced would be easy to reshape and, most important, without in any way affecting the essentials, neither its outline and structure nor the semi-literary form which I consider, as before, appropriate to the content.' (Ibid.)

Nonetheless, the semi-literary form seems to have been at the origin of many of Stanislavski's problems. There is a marked contrast between Stanislavski's style in his *Notebooks*, his letters, even in his early draft *Various Trends*, where the writing is direct, simple and clear, or *My Life in Art*, which was dictated, and the often tortuous, overwritten style of *An Actor's Work on Himself*.

At the beginning of May it was decided that Stanislavski was well enough to travel and on the 2nd, accompanied by his family and his physician, Dr Chistiakov, he left for Berlin. While there he received an invitation to give classes for an eight-month period at Boleslavski's American Laboratory Theatre. He was offered a fee of $5000 plus travel and expenses. At the same time, Elizabeth Hapgood wrote saying that many American friends wanted him to convalesce in the United States. She also informed him that she and her husband, Norman, intended living in France from 1930 to 1932.

While in Berlin, Stanislavski went down with flu but was well enough to travel to Badenweiler, the spa where Chekhov had died, on May 28, where he began work with his son Igor on a production plan for Rossini's *Barbiere di Seviglia*. In July, Knipper arrived, as did Elizabeth and Norman Hapgood. Stanislavski read them extracts of the *Pupil's Diary*.

Life was by no means easy in Badenweiler. Lilina wrote to 'Ripsi' telling her that they were staying in a small but clean pension, all of them, except Stanislavski, sharing rooms and living on $2 a day. Enough money was being paid regularly into Stanislavski's account in Nice to cover medical expenses but no more.

Stanislavski continued working on the book, which was now

becoming very lengthy. His health did not improve and on, September 1, Lilina wrote to 'Ripsi' requesting her to obtain permission for Stanislavski to extend his stay abroad. She was afraid of the effect of the Moscow winter. She was equally afraid that her request might be misinterpreted and that the authorities would imagine they intended to emigrate. On September 9 Stanislavski also wrote to her:

'I have been forbidden to do anything at all because, without realizing it, I have been tiring myself out. I'm not even making notes. . . . The American who invited me to the Laboratory Theatre learned that I can't go over and has suggested I accept a gift of $5000 so that I can live without worries and finish my book, which apparently is much needed in theatre circles in America.

Write to me. [Norman] Hapgood wants to translate my book and place it in newspapers. He is very experienced in these matters. . . . He assures me that newspaper articles will be good publicity.' (K.S. Archive, No. 5733.)

Two days later he wrote again:

'Mrs Hapgood was here. . . . She may draw up a contract. I have no other options. Conditions in Germany and France are quite different from America.' (K.S. Archive, No. 5734.)

Stanislavski appears to have been bewildered by the legal and financial arrangements he was supposed to make, confusing the contract Elizabeth Hapgood had suggested for the book and the outright gift of $5000 from someone whom he referred to as 'my unknown benefactor'. In a long letter to her he made alternative suggestions for the transfer of the money, either to the Paris branch of the Guaranty First Company of New York, or to his account with the Crédit Lyonnais in Nice. From there he could transfer money to an account he would open in his wife's name in Menton. Alternatively, the money could be paid to her and she could pass it on to him when they met. At all events, the money was to remain in dollars, which were more stable than the franc.

That same month he learned of radical changes in the Art Theatre management. To the two nominal directors, himself and Nemirovich, was now added a 'political' director, Mikhail Sergeievich Heitz, who would ensure that the theatre was on the straight and narrow ideological path. Stanislavski had given his reaction to this decision in a long letter to Leonidov on September 15. He had no objections in principle to the appointment of a political director. It was not the man's politics that worried him. What he was afraid of was an ignorant layman who would not understand the way theatres work and decisions are taken. He rejected Leonidov's notion that they would be better off with a second-rank official whom they could control. If there was to be a political appointee Stanislavski wanted someone with clout who could defend the theatre in the upper echelons of government.

A complex and difficult situation was developing. Stanislavski had to reassure the Soviet authorities, through Ripsi, that the book was ideologically sound. At the same time it was essential, he explained, to proceed immediately with the translation while he and Mrs Hapgood were together so that he could advise her on the technical aspects of the 'system'. Nothing, he stressed, would be published without Gurevich's approval.

By October Stanislavski was active again and wrote to 'Ripsi' asking her to find out from Gurevich how long it would take for her to edit the drafts and return them to him, in two fair copies. His concern at the moment was not the final Russian edition but the individual chapters that were to be published in the American press, subject, naturally, to the approval of the Soviet authorities. The Hapgoods in fact did a considerable amount of editorial work without reference to Gurevich to prepare the book for an American readership, for whom Soviet ideology meant nothing. Norman Hapgood would edit his wife's translation and suggest revisions, which she and Stanislavski would translate back into Russian. Stanislavski was thus working with two editors, who, as time passed, offered him conflicting advice. The idea for two editions, one American, one Russian, as with *My Life in Art*, was emerging.

In November Stanislavski succumbed to flu once again and on the 28th moved to the more congenial climate of Nice, where he started work with Igor on a production plan for *Rigoletto*, dictated *From the Last Conversation with Evgeni Vakhtangov* to his doctor, while Elizabeth Hapgood began translating the *Diary of a Pupil*. Stanislavski then turned his attention to *Othello*.

No single play occupied Stanislavski's mind more than *Othello*. The great challenge was Shakespeare. If he could demonstrate that the 'system' could be applied to one of the great tragedies, he would vindicate his position. When he had first directed *Othello* in 1896 the 'system' had not even been conceived. It was still embryonic at the time of the Craig *Hamlet*.

While on tour in the United States he had written to Nemirovich about his ambition to direct Shakespeare using the principle he had developed of working on the play through the logic of the action. He wanted to direct Shakespeare:

'. . . as he appears to me in my dreams, as I see him with my inner eye and hear him with my inner ear, Shakespeare based on harmony, phonetics, rhythm, on the feeling for words and diction, on the natural sound of the human voice, based on the simple, rewarding, step-by-step logical development of feelings and the course of the action.' (*Sovietskaia Kultura*, 1/XII, 1962.)

As he worked on the production plan he wondered whether he could not use it as the basis for the second of his books, *Work on a Role*. The plan is one of the most significant documents Stanislavski ever wrote, for in it we see, for the first time, his own practical application of what was later to be called the Method of Physical Action. Stanislavski's situation was similar to the summer of 1898, when he had written detailed plans which Nemirovich could then rehearse and stage. Now, many thousands of miles from home, he had once again to set out his intentions of how the roles were to be worked on. While Sudakov was nominally the director, Stanislavski did everything he could to circumvent him. He asked Nemirovich to allow Leonidov to supervise rehearsals, since much of the plan is concerned with his interpretation and approach to the role. The plan itself was supplemented by long personal letters.

The plan demonstrates that Stanislavski had lost none of his ability to visualize an intricate staging. Act One starts with a set of instructions on the creation of wave effects taken direct from the notes he had made in Bayreuth in 1902 when Cosima Wagner showed him round the set of *Der Fliegende Holländer*. There are signs both in this opening scene and, later, in the Senate, of earlier concerns with naturalistic effects – the lapping of waves and the beating of oars, the scratching of quills on parchment, which punctuate the dialogue. The essence of the approach is contained in the letter sent to Nemirovich in 1923, quoted above, the 'step-by-step logical development of feelings and the course of action.' He had now come to the firm conclusion that when the actor was not able to identify instinctively with a situation, emotion should not be approached direct. An assault on the unconscious produced a block. Emotion Memory had too often produced hysterics or self-indulgence. It is not possible to play Love. On the other hand, by recreating the stages by which a person falls in love, it is possible to induce feelings of love. The actions constitute the 'decoy-duck', as he called it, which lures the emotions.

In attempting to explain his new working method Stanislavski often used analogies of locomotion – trains, aeroplanes:

'Remember how an aeroplane takes off. It starts by running along the ground for a long time and then lifts off thanks to the momentum it has built up. A movement of air is caused which lifts the wings and takes the machine upwards.

The actor, too, moves and, so to speak, takes a run-up, thanks to physical actions, and gains momentum. At that moment, with the aid of the given circumstances and the Magic Ifs, he spreads the invisible wings of belief which carry him upwards to the realm of the imagination in which he sincerely believes.

But if there is no runway and no aerodrome how can you take a run-up or rise into the air? You can't, of course. Our first concern, therefore, will be to construct that aerodrome and runway paved with physical actions which are strong in truth.' (*Rezhissiorskie Plan 'Othello'*, Iskusstvo, 1945, p. 233.)

Stanislavski's experience in the period 1924–1928 had produced a shift of position, concerning not basic notions of training but methods of rehearsal and working on a role. Different productions had spotlighted different elements of the total process. Coming in at a late stage in rehearsal, after the ground-work had been done, he had developed a growing concern with the overall structure and dynamic of a play. He was conscious of the dangers of breaking a text down into too many small bits. While constantly emphasizing the importance of 'little truths', particularly to students, he was also aware of the importance of larger truths of which the little truths formed a part. What he was now anxious to emphasize was the distinction between the artist who *plans* and the actor who *performs* even though they are one and the same person. What an artist playing a major role must do is establish its dynamic, its 'economy', the curve of the action – where to hold back, where to play full out, as he had seen Zacconi demonstrate in Paris in 1923. The artist knows the end of the play, knows what happens next. When the actor, however, walks on stage he only *knows* one step at a time. The surest path, it now seemed to him, lay through a concentration on physical action. This he could only explain through his production plan and so, for Leonidov's benefit, he tried to pull all these emergent ideas together and summarize the process by which he now considered a role was created:

'When playing a role, especially a tragic role, you should think as little as possible about tragedy and as much as possible about simple physical tasks. Thus the plan for the entire role will consist roughly in 5–10 physical actions and the plan of the scene will be ready. In all five acts there will be 30–50 major physical actions.

Coming on stage the actor must think of the immediate physical act or the few immediately physical acts which fulfil the task or a complete bit. The others will follow of themselves in logical succession.

Let him remember that the subtext comes of itself, that when he thinks of physical actions he thinks, independently of any act of will, of the "Magic Ifs" and "given circumstances" which have been established during the working process.

. . . Physical actions which can firmly be fixed and are therefore useful for the overall plan, actually contain, independent of the actor's will, all the given circumstances and Magic Ifs. These are, in fact, the subtext. Therefore, progressing on the basis of physical actions, the actor, involuntarily, at the same time, progresses through the given circumstances.

Don't let an actor forget to use this approach only in rehearsal. With it he establishes, firmly grounds, develops that line, the line of physical actions. Only in this way can an actor master the technicalities of a role. The actor possesses a number of possible lines, as, for example, the line of the plot, the lines of psychology and feeling, the line of pure stage action and so on. But there are lines which are often forgotten which are nonetheless necessary to an actor's technique and lead to a proper approach.

The line of physical action, truth and belief is one of the most important lines out of which is woven the so-called "line of the day".

"The Line of the Day" is the external physical through-action. The line of physical actions is the line of physical bits and tasks.' (Ibid., pp. 230–1.)

Of particular concern to Stanislavski was Act Three, scene three, between Othello and Iago, the pivotal point of the play in which Othello becomes convinced of Desdemona's infidelity and swears revenge. In a section called 'The Scheme of Physical and Elementary-Psychological Actions', he broke this scene down into ten bits and provided a task for each bit, thus providing Leonidov with a clear set of intentions. Each bit was explained in detail and the total plan summarized at the end. In addition, Stanislavski sent Leonidov a long letter on February 10, 1930, setting out his interpretation of the scene, and Othello's psychological progression:

'Let us establish the circumstances as experienced by Othello. He has been indescribably happy with Desdemona. His honeymoon has been a dream, the ultimate height of passionate love. This ultimate height has been little presented by actors playing Othello, the writer himself pays little attention or space to it and yet it is so important if we are to show what Othello is losing and what he is saying farewell to . . . This scene marks, in essence, the dividing line. From here on Othello goes downwards. . . . Once there was happiness, how can one go on without it? . . . This is Othello's situation in the scene as I see it. And that was the reason for the set. That is why Othello flies to the top of the highest tower as in this scene . . . to live the moment when he says, "Ha, ha, false to me!"

I don't think that Othello is jealous. The petty jealousy with which Othello is usually portrayed belongs more to Iago. . . . Othello is an altogether nobler being. He cannot live in the world in the knowledge of the injustice men cause one another, or bear to see the sublime love that lives within them ridiculed or debased with impunity. And that under the mask of an ideal beauty, almost of a goddess of heavenly purity and innocence, of unearthly goodness and tenderness! . . .

And so, in relation to this scene, I think it is not a question of jealousy but a pathological disappointment in the ideal of a woman and a man the like of which the world has never seen. It is the most profound pain, unbearable sorrow. And so, when Iago comes up from below, cautiously, unseen, like a snake, and says, with unusual gentleness, like a doctor to a patient, "Why, how now, General! No more of that!", Othello begins to tremble in anticipation of the pain the torturer is preparing for him . . . Most actors playing Othello fall into a rage here. In reality it is still the most excruciating pain. . . .

So, "Farewell the tranquil mind! Farewell content!" etc., is a farewell, a lament, a lament for his second passion and not at all a sentimental panegyric over a life of war, as it is usually played. . . . Once he has bound up the wounds of his heart with this farewell, he feels the need to pour out his torment to somebody else. So he begins to reveal his pain to Iago. And when he has grabbed him and well-nigh thrown him off the tower, he takes fright at what he might do and runs up to the stone platform, throws himself down, racked with silent sobs. . . . At the end of the scene, when it is almost dark and the moon and stars are appearing in the sky . . . he calls the moon that is sinking below the horizon and the stars to witness and performs a terrifying ceremony, i.e., an oath of revenge.' (*MATL*, No. 351.)

This concentration on simple tasks and actions, even at moments of high tragedy, did not imply an indifference to the language of the play. On the contrary, language is paramount. It is stressed as the supreme form of integrated physical action. The prime consideration for the actor was the mastery of what Stanislavski called the 'active word'.

'To fulfil them [the tasks] (something extremely important and something actors always forget) he needs words, thoughts, i.e., the author's text. An actor above all must operate through words. On the stage the only important thing is the active word.' (Ibid., p. 232.)

The production plan was sent as each section was completed. Act One arrived in Moscow on December 24, 1929, Act Two was despatched in two parts in January 1930, Act Three on March 15 and Act Four scene one on March 18. The production plan breaks off abruptly. Events had overtaken it. Unknown to Stanislavski the production had actually opened four days earlier, on March 14, as Heitz informed him by telegram. A week later he learned that the production had been a disaster. At the same time he read in the French and German press that the production of Tchaikovski's *Queen of Spades* at the Opera Theatre had also flopped.

Stanislavski was totally unprepared for this turn of events. With the best of intentions, Lilina had written to the Art Theatre in the autumn of 1929 asking that Stanislavski be kept unaware of any problems the production was encountering. Her careful plan now misfired. Stanislavski was devastated.

The reasons for the failure are complex. One was Leonidov himself. He had shown great promise during preliminary work Stanislavski had done in 1926. Rehearsals went well, as did the early previews but he suffered increasingly from agoraphobia, which now extended to the gaping black hole he could see beyond the proscenium arch. His performance deteriorated during the later previews and by opening night was a shadow of its former self. The other was Sudakov, who for political reasons which only became clear later, rushed the play on, abandoning most of Stanislavski's work and altering Golovin's resplendent sets. Small wonder then, if Leonidov, who had been given responsibility for seeing that Stanislavski's wishes were carried out, collapsed under the strain.

A further factor in this débâcle is Nemirovich, who ignored the production altogether. While Stalin attended the second preview, Nemirovich attended none. Given the state of his relations with Stanislavski, it is understandable that he should not interfere with his plan, or feel able to supervise rehearsals, but his avoidance of any contact with the production looked studied.

On March 21, 1930, Ripsi wrote Stanislavski a long letter in which she set out her opinion scene by scene, set by set, of Sudakov's staging. It made dismal reading. At the end she went to great pains to excuse Nemirovich's behaviour. He had, she explained, been busy with three plays and two operas. He had asked Kachalov and Moskvin to see a full rehearsal and report back. Had their report been unfavourable, he would have intervened. As for his absence from the previews and the première, Leonidov himself had requested it. Nemirovich would make him nervous. This multiplication of excuses is suspicious. Busy as he may have been, it should have been in Nemirovich's power to ensure that Stanislavski's plan was carried out and that the leading actor had time to work through and digest a highly complex production plan, by insisting on adequate rehearsal time: the year everyone expected, not the two and a half months they got. But he did nothing. Even the ever loyal Bokshanskaia, who was now his secretary, found his attitude inexplicable. It is possible, however, that he was subject to forces which he himself, even as director, could not control.

As for the company, they awaited Stanislavski's return to rework the whole production. In a letter she wrote to Bertenson, Knipper admitted she was so embarrassed she did not know what to write to Stanislavski. They had simply gone off at half-cock. They should have simplified the production and made a complete set of new designs rather than half-stage a production which still bore Stanislavski's name.

On April 9, Stanislavski, still bitter and angry, replied to Ripsi:

'I am appalled. Why put on *Othello* like that? What's it got to do with me or my production? It's pure ignorance. I took on *Othello* precisely to try and correct such ignorance and now it has emerged worse than ever. Where's the new here? Where is there any sign of Stanislavski's production plan? I go hot with shame when I think of it.

... I am being hoodwinked. I'm being made to look a fool because I don't know what's going on in my own theatre, others do, but I, the director, don't. I'm not terribly fond of idiot parts. Send me the reviews, open all letters. Consult [Podgorni] as to how my name can be taken off the posters but without offending either Leonidov (I know what he's going through) or Moskvin (who worked on it). On the other hand, why should my name be linked with a pot-boiler? Poor Golovin. ... How low the theatre has sunk ...

Don't tell Leonidov how upset I am. Get him to write to me. But please tell me how his health is.' (*SS*, VII, pp. 242–3.)

Desperate as he was to get home, convinced that both the Art Theatre and the Opera Theatre were in decline, Stanislavski's only consolation was the book. Prospects seemed promising.

In a letter dated January 1, 1930, Ripsi had reported that she had been to Narkompros (the Commissariat for Enlightenment) to discuss the question of the American newspaper articles. There was, she was informed, no objection in principle but there were trivial publications in which a great man like Stanislavski should not appear.

Both Stanislavski and Elizabeth Hapgood concurred that they would need to be selective. In any case, the better newspapers also paid better, up to $1000 for a big chapter.

'In that way I could pay off my debts. ... Work on oneself and on the role are text-books. If they are published and catch on, that will give a small but permanent income for many years. This book is needed by people interested in art, and these people buy. ... Mrs Hapgood says there isn't a girl in America who doesn't dream of going into the theatre or the cinema. So she thinks there could be a large print-run. But my own private opinion is: I got a large sum in advance which gave me the chance to get better, thank God. I don't expect anything more from the book. I just want to pay off my debts and not lead people into disaster. If there's anything over and above that, well, let's say, it's a nice little extra.

One thing we have to accept – my heart is weak. It can't be mended. What's left can be trained and used. If when I return to Moscow I can so order my affairs that they don't worsen my condition, I can survive and I'll be able to write what I know and become part of young people's heritage, so that they don't forget me, and my wife and children don't die of hunger.' (K.S. Archive, No. 5748.)

By March he told Ripsi he had no money left and would have to return to Moscow in July. Every penny he could spare was needed for Igor's treatment, which had to be completed in Germany and Switzerland. In a separate letter, Lilina informed Ripsi that they did not venture out to the shops in Nice as their clothes were so shabby. They spent their time in their modest villa, except for the occasions when the Hapgoods came and took them out for the day.

Financial help was at hand, however. Unknown to him, Elizabeth Hapgood had set up a Stanislavski Fund in the United States and invited wealthy patrons of the arts to contribute. She opened an account in the Fund's name at Lloyds Bank in Menton in the sum of $7500. It may also be reasonably assumed that since the 'unknown benefactor' had never been identified, it was she and her husband who had earlier provided $5000 in the guise of the American Laboratory Theatre.

It was now the moment to make proper contractual agreements, above all to solve the problem of copyright. Copyright law was not universal and Russia had no copyright law at all. A constant preoccupation was to protect Stanislavski's rights and those of his heirs. Indeed, one of the last letters Stanislavski ever wrote was on that very subject. The history of the publication of Stanislavski's books world-wide is, in part, the history of the copyright problem.

As a Soviet citizen, Stanislavski could not establish copyright in the United States but Mrs Hapgood could. On April 22, 1930, on a sheet of writing paper headed 'Vista Bella, Menton, France', Stanislavski signed a document in English, granting Elizabeth Hapgood power of attorney to negotiate contracts for the translation and publication of a sequence of books he was writing – four at the time – in all languages, including Russian and also to negotiate magazine, serial and motion-picture rights. She was to hold in safe-keeping any royalties that might accrue to him. The following day the American Consul in Nice, George Armstrong, issued a Certificate of Acknowledgement of Execution of Document, confirming the legal status of the paper Stanislavski had signed. In fact, the assignment of rights within the Soviet Union was not legally enforceable, but then, Stanislavski could not expect to make any money from the Soviet edition.

The following day, Stanislavski wrote Ripsi a long letter outlining the manuscript material he was sending her, and including a list of chapters for the first volume and their order. He was, however, faced with a dilemma. Both he and Norman Hapgood were convinced that *Work on Oneself* should be a single book that would cover both the mental and physical aspects of actor training – inner experiencing, and outer physical characterization, the 'incarnation' of that experiencing. There was, however, a technical problem. The format used by the Soviet publishing house Academia was very small and the print large, so that *An Actor's Work* would run up 1200 pages, making the book unmanageable. It would be more practical to bring it out in two separate volumes, the first dealing with the psychological aspects of training, the second with the physical. A further book, *Work on a Role*, would deal with the problems of rehearsal. The three volumes together would provide a complete account of the 'system'.

The solution was not without its dangers, which Stanislavski acknowledged: spreading publication over a lengthy period would mean that the sense of the 'system' as a whole, the integrity of psycho-physical process, could be lost. The answer was simple:

> 'The book must begin with an outline of the whole scheme, i.e. of all three volumes. Otherwise we can't publish in separate parts. Because, when the first volume appears (The Diary of a Pupil. Work on Oneself. Experiencing) it could appear as though experiencing were ultra-naturalistic in character and the book will be slated for it. But if there is an overall plan at the beginning of the first book and it is made clear that the whole system leads to superconscious creation, then that justifies the naturalism of the early stages.' (*SS*, VIII, p. 244.)

He had another cause for concern: if they waited to bring out all three volumes simultaneously, that would mean a delay of at least five years, and would thus provide an opportunity for others, as they had done in the past, to publish partial and erroneous versions of his work. Financially astute as ever, Stanislavski also realized that few people either in the US or the USSR would have the money, or be willing, to buy all three volumes at once.

Unfortunately Stanislavski never wrote his synoptic view of the 'system' so that for many, even well-informed people, *An Actor's Work: Part One*, first published in America as *An Actor Prepares*, the inner process, represents the whole of the 'system'. The tortuous history of the publication of Stanislavski's works has reinforced this impression.

In July, Stanislavski, Lilina and the Hapgoods returned to Badenweiler where work on the manuscript continued. Never a man to work on one project only at a time, he was preparing a production of Rimski-Korsakov's *The Golden Cockerel*. In August, Leonidov arrived. Stanislavski read him the largely completed book. Leonidov responded: 'This is not "system", it is a complete culture.' In late October, Stanislavski said goodbye to Mrs Hapgood, whom he was not to see again for seven years, and started the journey back to Moscow, arriving there on November 3.

CHAPTER TWENTY-SEVEN

STALIN

When in 1924 Stanislavski had returned to Russia after the American tour he had found a society in a state of effervescence, exploring the possibilities of a limited degree of free enterprise. Now, in 1930, he returned to a country concerned with centralization. The first steps had been taken towards the enforced collectivization of agriculture; heavy industry was being developed with little regard to human cost. The era of false accusations and show-trials was not far distant. Lunacharski had been sacked by Stalin and Maiakovski had committed suicide. The world was being turned over to middle-ranking mediocrities.

Immediately after his return to Moscow, Stanislavski fell ill, although he continued working on the production plan for *The Golden Cockerel*. As to the book, he considered his work on it concluded for the moment.

Gurevich went through the draft he had brought back and reacted very critically. This did not seem to correspond to the book they had discussed. Writing to him on December 17, she stated:

'I cannot understand why you have selected so few chapters out of the vast amount of material you have written. Whatever your reasons may or may not have been, I have to say that in this form, without the chapters on transmission and reception, communication, adaptation, physicalization, the book does not give us a sense of your system as a whole and can only disappoint those who impatiently await an account of it. . . . To give a bit of the system – not even a part of it, presenting "work on oneself", but only a bit of that part . . . is to leave any reader profoundly dissatisfied. It is ESSENTIAL to include the missing chapters. . . . Above all it is essential to give the whole chapter on "Bits and Tasks" . . . the PURPOSE of dividing the play up into bits and tasks is just not explained. Finally, after much reflection, I am quite convinced that at the beginning of the book there must be a chapter using your earlier material on the art of representation and experiencing, and especially on "stock-in-trade" [from *Various Trends in the Art of Theatre*]. Without that, much that is in your book will be obscure for new readers.' (K.S. Archive, No. 8062.)

She then returned to her earlier warnings about his remoteness from Soviet life. He simply had, in his terms, to 'contact' and 'adapt' to reality.

Almost every page of his book revealed how out of touch he was. If he wanted to influence young people he had to be aware of their aspirations, their efforts to create a new life, he had to come out of his ivory tower, otherwise he would alienate them instead. Was it just that he had not thought about the matter sufficiently?

In, at times, desperate tones, she tried to make Stanislavski aware of the even greater shift in the intellectual and political climate that had taken place during his absence. When she now referred to young people's 'efforts to create a new life' she did not mean the kind of idealism she had written about earlier, the idealism of Trofimov and Ania, but a whole new ideology. This was the second year of the first Five-Year Plan, when the concept of the New Man, communist man, was taking shape. Just as nature would be mastered and controlled by political will, so would man be transformed. The central concept was engineered change. The most extreme example was to be found in the genetics of Lysenko, who claimed that he could produce new species in one generation. Those who dared to challenge him found their way to the gulags, if not worse. Man was seen as equally changeable. A favourite image of the period was the iron foundry where old scrap was melted down into new metal. New communist man would be born in the crucible of Soviet ideology.

All notions of universals, constants in human behaviour, were seen as reactionary. There were no latent contents in the psyche. There was no psyche. Man was the product of the interplay of social and economic forces and as these were controlled, so man would be controlled and transformed into an ideal social being. Stanislavski's vocabulary, with its 'Magic If', its talk of the subconscious, of intuition, its insistence that true creativity lay beyond conscious activity in the person of the actor, betrayed him as a dangerous relic of the past, just as he had been described after the Revolution by critics like Blum.

Stanislavski took five days, from the 18th to the 23rd to write a reply. His mind was not at all on the Soviet Union:

'Let me begin: I am writing a new book commissioned by New Haven University [Yale] who will use it to study the actor's art in their drama department. . . . I haven't thought yet about a Russian edition since I don't know whether it will be passed [by the censor] and published, as was the case with *My Life in Art*. So, for the moment I am only thinking of America, a completely bourgeois country. If I include even one of the examples you suggest for our young contemporaries then I can say with conviction that not only will my book not be published, I will never be allowed into America. So, for the moment, my thoughts take me across the ocean. Not all the student characters will be comprehensible to the Americans. There will be alterations over there, adaptation to suit overseas readers for which the Hapgoods will be responsible. He is a man of letters, she is my friend and is greatly concerned about the success of the book. When I think (or try not to think) about the Russian edition, I feel I won't be able to write it for the reasons you state in your wonderful letter. In the Russian edition, *all* the examples, *all* the characters will have to be changed. But the choice of examples and of people who can express not only the contemporary but the old, eternal, never-changing art of the actor-craftsman, and not just the actor-citizen is very, very difficult for me. I don't know if I can overcome this difficulty.' (K.S. Archive, No. 4738.)

What was Gurevich to make of this? She had been assured that she would have final editorial approval and this had been made clear to the Hapgoods. Now it appeared the Hapgoods would have control outside the Soviet Union and that their edition would have, for the moment at least, primacy of place. In Stanislavski's mind there were now clearly two versions of the book, *An Actor's Work on Himself* and *An Actor Prepares*. The confusion over the nature and contents of the book was to remain. For long periods neither Gurevich nor Elizabeth Hapgood really knew what they were dealing with.

Stanislavski followed this letter with another, running to several pages, written on the 23rd and 24th, in which he outlined his long-term plans. He now foresaw eight books, including the already published *My Life in Art*, which would cover all aspects of theatre, actor training, work on a role, directing and opera. He also provided a break-down of the various chapters of *An Actor's Work on Himself* as it then stood. Uncertainties, however, persisted. The decision to divide *An Actor's Work* into two parts, experiencing and physical characterization, presented problems of unity. Did not a full discussion belong more properly to *Work on a Role*? Was it worth while describing the art of representation before the art of experiencing had been fully discussed? At all events, he gave her 'carte blanche' to make any changes she liked. He also provided her with one of the many charts he made of the 'system'.

He had still missed Gurevich's essential point. It was his content, his terminology, that was the problem, not his grand design. So-called 'Marxist' ideologues were seizing on individual words and expressions, nit-picking and heresy-hunting with all the zeal of mediaeval clerics. Just as Stanislavski had been condemned just after the Revolution as a bourgeois relic by the Far Left and critics like Blum, so now a new generation, working towards the new man, were attacking him. Blum had his successors in the Association of Proletarian Writers (RAPP). A series of articles attacking the 'system' appeared precisely on the lines Gurevich had feared. Then, from January 25 to February 4, 1931, RAPP held a ten-day conference at which the 'system' was declared to be idealistic and inimical to proletarian art. Meierhold was given an opportunity to defend his system of Bio-mechanics as a viable alternative. Apart from an article written for the 1926 edition of the *Encyclopaedia Britannica* Stanislavski had published nothing about the 'system'. The attack, founded on half-knowledge and hearsay, was renewed when a second conference was held in December. The 'system' was accused of being 'an-historical', dealing in 'abstract timelessness', of reducing 'multiform social qualities into a few basic laws of the biological behaviour of man in general' and of translating 'socio-political problems into the language of ethico-moral concepts' and transforming the 'complex processes of the actor's perception of reality into primitive, childlike credulity, naïveté and the Creative If' – the word 'magic' was not allowed to pass their lips. At the December conference Meierhold also got his come-uppance. Bio-mechanics were declared to be no more than the obverse side of the Stanislavski coin. Yet if the Stanislavski 'system' was 'idealist' why was Pavlov, the determined behaviourist, interested in it? The attack in January had been led by the dramatist Aleksandr Afinogenov. He was intellectually more subtle than many of his associates. What he objected to in the 'system' was its 'biological psychologism', the suggestion of fixed qualities in nature. He saw personality as a product of the complex interplay of social forces. If the 'system' could be redefined in those terms it could be useful.

Following the RAPP conference, Gurevich again wrote urgently to Stanislavski on April 7:

'We must discuss things either in person or by letter. So far I have only set out the minor part of my doubts but the difficulties and DANGERS I wrote to you about begin to loom ever larger in my eyes than before: HOW TO RESHAPE YOUR INGRAINED – not only yours but mine too – HABITS and certain DEFINITIONS AND TERMS, which are obscure, inconsistent when I approach them as an "initiated" reader, or very hostile critic. . . . Doing that would remove the possibility of stupid cavilling and lofty phrases from various reporters and writers who will cut your Marxist legs from under you. . . . Psychological terms change and, I repeat, in that regard it is essential to consult people who are *expert* in science. That is crucially important because when the book comes out in America, it must be irreproachable from a scientific point of view: in the USA there are theatre studies which include the psychology of the actor's art, they have been highly developed in universities and control the practical work of theatre people there. And, of course, specialists in psychology always monitor any work on the psychology of creativity very closely and critically.' (K.S. Archive, No. 8064.)

The nub of the problem was still the 'Magic If' and its relation to the creative process and the subconscious. On April 9 Stanislavski wrote a lengthy response to Gurevich's arguments. In it he set out, in terms far clearer than appear in any of his books, his notion of the 'Magic If' and of the relation of the real world to the imaginary world, his insistence that the actor's feeling did not derive from some abstract, imaginary world but was rooted in human necessity:

'I, too, make a distinction between stage and real experience. Evidently I have not expressed that distinction clearly enough. What I say is that on stage the actor lives genuine feelings, but that they have their origins in affective memory, in which feeling is stripped of anything superfluous. This feeling is the quintessence of all similar feelings. Thanks to its purity and concentration it is often stronger than in real life.

I heard recently of a woman who had recovered from an operation . . . received a nervous shock not when they performed the operation or immediately after but when she went back home, to her own room and remembered the beginning of her illness and all that followed. . . .

Actors live on such memories of the past on stage and I call them real.

When we contact these affective memories on stage, they and similar memories come alive. Their quintessence, their synthesis, comes alive. For me that is stronger than the memory of a single incident. One small detail: why are actors so attached to the word "magic"? They say: if this were the case, what would you do? To give an honest answer as to what I would do today, I must do exactly what happens in life; I must both stretch my mind and reach out with the antennae of my intuition all round me. In these moments the actor forgets he is on stage and lives a truly human life. The only difference is that in these moments he feels the truth of his feelings more richly than in life itself. Does this lead to madness? Fortunately not. . . .

You know this just as well as I. But that's not the question. It's a matter of a stupid, uncouth, talentless audience that does not feel art but wants to approach it through their intelligence. I mean an unworthy audience that splits hairs over words, people like Afinogenov. . . .

You go on to say that [feelings] arise because the actor wants them to, through the magic if. But the magic of the if is that they arise not because the actor wants them to but because of real, living necessity.

The secret is the actor doesn't want or not want anything. He answers the question: what would I do, if . . ., etc. He does exactly what he does in life, and if he does anything else, it's false, it's playacting, it's not living the right way, not believing in the truth of what he is doing on stage. . . .

Again you say, they are accomplished in an impersonal way, through the magic if and don't touch personal concerns. That is just not true. The *only* creative moments on stage are those evoked by the magic *if*. So, I will talk about them. When I give a genuine answer to the *if*, then I do something, I am living my own personal life.

At moments like that there is no character. Only me. All that remains of the character and the play are the situation, the *life circumstances*, all the rest is mine, my own concerns, as a role in all its creative moments depends on a living person, i.e., the actor, and not the dead abstraction of a person, i.e., the role. . . .' (*SS*, VIII, pp. 283–6.)

He has nothing but contempt for ignorant audiences and critics who will nit-pick over words:

'Replace the *magic if* by the *creative if*. If we must. We shall have to have a footnote or put it in quotes, because it is very popular with actors, here and abroad. Not long ago I read an article by Charlie Chaplin who bases all his creative work on the magic *if* (which he claims to have discovered).

I absolutely agree, we need specialists. The curious thing is, I am talking about very difficult psychological problems, about the creative mind, and haven't read more than a couple of books on psychology. It amuses and bewilders me at the same time.' (Ibid.)

As chance would have it, even as Afinogenov was delivering his paper Stanislavski was reading his play, *Fear*. He recommended it to Nemirovich, who agreed to direct.

The attack on the Art Theatre's working method was, however, only one aspect of a much larger crisis.

The attack on the 'system' was overshadowed by a larger crisis at the Art Theatre, which Stanislavski had to deal with alone, as Nemirovich left for Italy where he received medical treatment for the next two years.

The 'red' director, Heitz, was, as Stanislavski had feared he might in 1929, allowing political considerations to take precedence over good artistic practice. Heitz and the artistic-political advisory group that came with him were undermining the very foundations of the theatre's creative life. They were bringing to the stage the same concern with output and mass production that characterized Stalin's first Five-Year Plan. The theatre was being pushed to put on more productions and give more performances. In 1928–30 it had played 795 times and, in 1930–1, 751 times. Given that the season lasted some 260 days this meant two performances a day. It was an old battle refought. The Proletkult had been succeeded by a number of groups, not least the Blue Blouses who specialized in topical Living-Newspaper productions. Their presentations soon fell into a predictable format of song, slogans and sketches. Audiences became bored. New groups, known as Agit-Brigades, had been set up as part of the first Five-Year Plan. They were putting together as many as twelve productions a year. While quantity was the prime consideration all seemed well. It was only a year later, in 1932, when an 'Olympiad' of these groups was held that the government realized how deplorable the actual quality of the performances was. The new policy was given active support by Sudakov, who was emerging ever more prominently as the leader of the younger members of the company. The reason *Othello* had been thrown on to the stage with such unseemly haste was now clear. It was not that the theatre could not cope with Stanislavski's plan, it was a matter of deliberate policy, following the new government line.

Stanislavski realized that the integrity of the Art Theatre had to be defended. More than that, the theatre needed to be reformed. Nemirovich's perception that their dispute opened the door to all kinds of manoeuvring and plotting was all too accurate. The Art Theatre stood for a set of values that had to be defended from attack both within and without. Stanislavski assumed, rightly, that he had Stalin's support, and still believed he represented the future of Soviet theatre. That future would be based on the Art Theatre and the 'system', whatever their detractors might say. In his last years Stanislavski developed an almost messianic view of his function.

There was dissatisfaction in the company. On January 12, 1931, he wrote to Heitz suggesting that he, Moskvin, Leonidov and himself should meet. As he was ill perhaps Heitz could come to Leontievski Lane? A meeting took place but Heitz did not attend; he did, however, take exception when he learned the contents of the discussion. Stanislavski then wrote excusing his colleagues from any blame and taking full responsibility for anything untoward that had been said. Nonetheless, he still went on to list the dangers of the new policy both for the company and the standard of work. The older actors were ill; sets and costumes for plays like *Fiodor* were worn out and the materials to replace them were no longer available; the company was being forced into making too many tours to Leningrad; lengthy delays over programming meant that no proper preparation was possible. Several new productions could be mounted in one season but only under certain conditions:

'I staged five plays in one season [1925–6]. . . . All these plays were thoroughly worked on, because the repertoire was worked on for a whole year [with one exception]. In our theatre it is essential that actors should have a certain amount of time to absorb the play. They can only act well in those circumstances. They're not good at pot-boilers.

In other theatres the opposite is true. They're good at pot-boilers, they're incapable of rehearsing and thinking a play through for any length of time. After ten or twenty rehearsals they don't know what more to do and think that the play should be on. . . .

It will be difficult to communicate with you by letter. I have no one to whom I can dictate and writing lying down, as you can see, is hard, forgive the handwriting.

We must get together and talk. When, what time? . . . (*SS*, VIII, pp. 281–2.)

Heitz did not reply. Stanislavski decided the only answer was to appeal direct to the artistic-political advisory board.

The appeal went through several drafts before being despatched in the summer. Stanislavski took great care, at the beginning of the document, to establish the political credentials of the Art Theatre and to stress the importance of its role in the building of socialism. He also stressed the link between the theatre and his 'system':

'No one can be unaware that in my mind the theatre is inseparable from the "Stanislavski system". The "system" is not an aesthetic tract but a theatrical technique which for its realization requires:

a)   large-scale, long-term organization;
b)   dramatic material of the highest quality, to make the theatre part of the general culture of our time;
c)   a planned programme of student training – in the broadest sense of the term, from pure artistic effect to political propaganda – in the possibilities of raising the cultural consciousness of the broad masses.' (*SS*, VI, p. 290.)

If the education of the masses was indeed the agenda of the board then they must realize their limitations, or acquire a greater understanding of the real nature of the theatre. They could not go on issuing orders that merely encouraged a superficial approach to new work.

Stanislavski then turned, as he had with Heitz, to the problems the actors were experiencing. He saw one way to avert the catastrophe that threatened the Art Theatre:

'1. the establishment of precise governmental and party directives concerning its place in the contemporary situation as a theatre of classical drama and of the best artistically significant plays in the contemporary repertoire;
2. the removal from it of tasks demanding above all hasty work or an inordinate dissipation of its energies in guest appearances;
3. the recognition of its right to compete with other theatres not in the quantity of contemporary plays produced but in the quality of its presentations.' (*SS*, VI, p. 300.)

The protest had its effect. By the end of the year Heitz had been removed and the committee with him. The Art Theatre was freed from the control of the Central Executive Committee and made directly accountable to the government with the title Moscow Art Theatre of the USSR. It is inconceivable that such a decision could have been made without Stalin's consent. Perhaps those fifteen visits to *The Days of the Turbins* had produced their results.

Stanislavski spent the summer of 1931 at a health resort, Uzkoe, where he was visited by Bernard Shaw. He continued working on the book, which he had assured Elizabeth Hapgood was nearly finished, but in an increasingly depressed mood. Also at Uzkoe was a young singer, Olga Sobolevskaia, from the Opera Theatre. She and Stanislavski talked almost daily and she realized that he was using her as a kind of contact with the younger generation. He needed to know how they thought and felt. In a moment of rare revelation, he admitted to feeling totally isolated and misunderstood. Sulerzhitski had understood him completely, Vakhtangov had half understood him, but both were now long dead and no one had replaced them.

Stanislavski was still battling with the problem of terminology. He was not supposed to use the word 'subconscious' or 'mind'. When he had taught her, had everything been clear, he asked. Could he have used other words? What other word could he use but 'mind'?

'– Konstantin Sergeievich, you often talked of the "inner-life of the person/role". Isn't that it?
– No. That's a process, Stanislavski replied almost sharply.
– Then what about your expression the "life of the human spirit"?
– First, that isn't it, second, what about the word "spirit"?'
    (Olga Sobolevskaia, *K.S. Stanislavski, rabotaet, beseduet, otdixaet*, Moscow, 1988.)

She then offered to lend him a recently published dictionary of philosophical terms. He accepted, but when she gave it to him he merely put it in his pocket without looking at it.

The new season was heavy, a large number of projects were launched – *Fear* and Bulgakov's adaptation of Gogol's *Dead Souls* at the Art Theatre, *Boris Godunov*, *The Golden Cockerel* and *Il Barbiere di Seviglia* at the Opera Theatre.

On September 15 Stanislavski set foot inside the Art Theatre for the first time since his heart attack. With Nemirovich absent, he had to take over supervision of the production of *Fear*, for which Sudakov was the nominal director. The cast were not happy with his tendency just to block and then repeat, precisely the method Stanislavski had been attacking.

His involvement with *Fear* enabled him to discuss the 'system' and the problem of terminology with Afinogenov. If Afinogenov wanted the 'system' with new words, could he find them? Stanislavski again played his 'ignorance' card: he knew nothing about psychology, in fact the only book he understood had been written for five-year-olds. He stressed the special nature of the actor's intelligence:

'I read with enthusiasm but in articles there's a lot about intelligence, however an interesting actor doesn't act abstract truth. His intelligence has to be visible in his feelings, in the simplest of human feelings.' (A.N. Afinogenov, *Stat'i. Dveniki. Pis'ma. Vosponimanija.*, Iskusstvo, 1957, pp. 57–8.)

For all his ideological orthodoxy, Afinogenov had no success finding alternatives.

Afinogenov's *Fear*, which opened on December 24, was acclaimed by the President of the Academy of the Science of Art with the words, 'I place this play among the outstanding victories of Soviet theatre.' The production was also remarkable for the fact that Stanislavski took Knipper out of the cast three weeks before the opening. She was too lightweight and refined for the role of Clara. The role was given to Sokolovskaia. For the rest, Rimski-Korsakov's *The Golden Cockerel* and Rossini's *Barbiere di Seviglia* were in rehearsal at the Opera Theatre while preliminary work began on Bulgakov's adaptation of *Dead Souls*.

Stanislavski's opera productions, destined for his own theatre, went comparatively smoothly. He retained total control so that the work done in the Onegin Room at Leontievski Lane eventually found its way on to the stage. He was sufficiently confident to ignore Nemirovich's proposal in February 1931 to merge his Music Theatre and the Stanislavski Opera Theatre. The dramatic productions for the Art Theatre were considerably more problematic. Stanislavski's new working method, the Method of Physical Action, was still a mystery to those who did not regularly attend rehearsals at Leontievski Lane and even then it was difficult to grasp. Leonidov, the first to be initiated into the new method, regularly summarized the 'system' in his notebook, and complained that Stanislavski made life difficult. He was also not a little disconcerted when, after he had struggled his way through the unsuccessful *Othello*, he was told that it was probably not possible to experience an entire tragic role truthfully but that there had to be moments when representation took over. But the real problem was that the work rehearsed by Stanislavski in the intimacy of his flat failed to transfer to the main stage. Working away from the main building, not confronting the day-to-day practical problems, Stanislavski could not ensure that his ideas were adequately realized. They were too subtle, too finely nuanced, too small-scale, and there was no director capable of expanding them into a larger space. Thus neither *Dead Souls*, which opened on December 9, 1932, after two years' work, nor Ostrovski's *Artists and Admirers* which opened on September 23, 1933, corresponded entirely to his wishes. The tense relationship with the theatre was exacerbated when on October 16, 1931, he paid one of his rare visits to the theatre to see a run of Acts Three and Four of *Dead Souls*. He took immediate exception to the sets. The furniture and props were distorted, exaggerated, 'hyperbolical'. They conveyed nothing of the claustrophobic atmosphere of a backwoods province. Everything was too grand. It was the now familiar battle over the Grotesque, the problem of directors attempting to make statements through design rather than through acting. Stanislavski demanded that the design be simplified. He was still arguing with Simov, one of the designers, in June of the following year.

Stanislavski continued his search for new Soviet plays that described the revolutionary experience. In September 1931 Gorki drew Stanislavski's attention to Nikolai Erdman's play *The Suicide*, already in rehearsal at the Meierhold Theatre. Gorki was convinced that Meierhold was turning it into a farce. In October Erdman read the play to Stanislavski who laughed uproariously. There was, however, the problem of getting the play past the Repertkom. Stanislavski, characteristically, went to the top and sent the script direct to Stalin, prompted almost certainly by the example of Bulgakov who, at a moment of extreme difficulty, had also written to Stalin and, it was widely – and wrongly – assumed, had reached an accommodation with him. Stanislavski requested that the theatre be allowed to work on the play and show it before a final decision was made.

In his letter Stanislavski was careful to stress Gorki's approval of the work – Gorki was, after all, *the* revolutionary writer in the Stalinist pantheon – and to put a positive gloss on the play's intentions. It was not to be seen as one of the 'anti-revolutionary' plays for which the Art Theatre had been so severely criticized.

> 'In our view N. Erdman has managed to lay bare the various outward signs and the inner core of the petite bourgeoisie who set themselves against the construction of our country. The means the author uses to show real-life petit-bourgeois people and their abnormality is totally novel and yet completely in accord with Russian realism and its best representatives like Gogol and Shchedrin and is close to the direction our own theatres take.' (October 29, 1931, MXAT Arch. No. 6537.)

It is difficult to see how Erdman's play can support such an interpretation. Did Stanislavski really believe what he said or was he, as in the 1920s, trying to rescue a good, new play which he knew was ideologically dubious? After all, Stalin had seen *The Days of the Turbins* not as White propaganda but as proof of the invincibility of the Red Army. Could he now be brought to see *The Suicide* as an attack on the petite bourgeoisie and, by implication, a call to toe the party line?

If such as Stanislavski's strategy, it failed. Stalin was not deceived and his reply of November 9 was politely discouraging:

> 'Most respected Konstantin Sergeievich!
> I do not have a very high opinion of the play *The Suicide*. My immediate comrades consider that it is fatuous and possibly harmful.

You may learn the opinions (and motives) of the Repertkom from the enclosed documents. It seems to me that the judgement of the Repertkom is not far from the case. Nonetheless, I have no objection to the Art Theatre's making an experiment and showing its mastery. It may well be that it will achieve its end. The Kultprop of the Central Committee of our party (Com. Stenski) will help you in this matter. Comrades more versed in artistic matters will arbitrate. I am an amateur in such things.

Greetings!

J. Stalin.' (MXAT Arch.)

Stanislavski let the matter drop. Meierhold, for reasons best known to himself, took Stalin's letter as a sign of encouragement and spent the next eighteen months working on a production that never got to a first night. He misjudged the times and was ultimately to pay for it. Gorki was also instrumental in persuading Nemirovich to include Bulgakov's *Molière* among the theatre's future plans. This was to prove as controversial as *The Suicide*.

Stanislavski continued to receive foreign visitors. In February 1931 the young Joshua Logan attended rehearsals for *The Golden Cockerel* where he saw Stanislavski applying the 'sitting on hands' technique, not allowing the singers to move until they had discovered the truth of their behaviour. Later he saw *Boris Godunov* which he considered superior to the production at the Paris Opera, notwithstanding Chaliapin's performance in the title role. When he informed Stanislavski of his ambitions to create a theatre on the Moscow Art model, he received the same reply Max Reinhardt had received so many years before: don't copy, find your own answers.

An Actor's Work in the meantime had run into severe problems. First, Gurevich's health was not good and her financial situation was desperate. Second, she and Elizabeth Hapgood were pulling in different directions, making conflicting demands on Stanislavski.

In May 1931 she wrote an unhappy letter to Stanislavski in which she explained that while she had tried to devote as much time as possible to editing his book, she, like all other writers who were not 'celebrities', had to take on every piece of work that was offered to eke out a living. This meant there was often a clash of deadlines. She was exhausted and a recent bout of flu had drained what was left of her energy. She had to rest, otherwise her doctors assured her she would never get better. Would it not be more practical to hand over her work to someone who could do it more quickly?

Her main problems were, first, that she still had no idea of what the book was like as a whole; second, that the American edition was taking up far too much of her time:

'It oppresses and unnerves me. It is better to slow down, not speed up because, *essentially*, our work must be *organic* and would evolve much more *naturally* if we were not constantly harassed over time. . . .

The American edition, which bears no relation to the real world we are living in, is a futile waste of time and energy for you and me. . . . And the less we are clear about this the longer the inevitable explanations to Hapgood will drag on and the more we shall waste our efforts.' (K.S. Archive, No. 8065.)

Stanislavski suggested that he should pay her a fee for her work, an offer which she accepted.

On her side, Elizabeth Hapgood was still pressing for an early delivery of the now long-overdue manuscript. If he could get it to her by January 1, 1932, the book could be published in the autumn. Otherwise they would have to wait until the spring of 1933. She was worried about the number of projects he was working on. Of course he had to reorganize the theatre, but should he not just concentrate on that and the book? Did he really need to direct so many plays and operas?

Gurevich resumed her work on the draft chapters she had so far. On October 30, 1931, she wrote to say that as there were still gaps she could not draw up an overall plan for the book:

'1) I don't have the major chapter on speech, which you read to me at our last meeting; 2) the form in which I have the chapters on gymnastics, fencing, etc., you tell me is incomplete; 3) in the list of chapters you gave me there are parts missing (or I don't have them): "Ethics", "General Theatrical State", "Discipline (how to use the system)". Generally the whole part of the book that relates to "Physical Characterization" . . . has not been fully developed and there are essentials missing.' (K.S. Archive, No. 8067.)

By mid-February 1932 she had enough material to produce a plan of sixteen chapters. Her main concern, in ideological terms, was that while Stanislavski always referred to the 'system' as a psycho-physical technique, the division of the book into two parts implied a mind/body split:

'I think . . . to divide the book into two parts, "Experiencing" and "Physical Characterization" would be highly misleading because 1) even in the first half of the book you are inevitably drawn to talk about the physical since "action", "physical tasks", "muscular release", "adaptation" are basic parts of the process of physical characterization; 2) such a division will only give our contemporaries grounds to accuse you of dualism, spiritualism, idealism, etc.' (K.S. Archive, No. 2400.)

She also questioned his definition of three separate, basic psychological drives – Will, Feeling, Intellect – which did not correspond to modern thinking:

'. . . will is not seen as an independent human freedom but as a complex process of the highest order involving emotional and intellectual elements and which is guided by a *conscious representation of the whole*. As to the role of the intellect in the creative process, it must be present in every chapter.' (Ibid.)

Even the title of the book had not yet been agreed. Gurevich suggested *My Theatre School* which might suit Elizabeth Hapgood who had still not, apparently, decided on *An Actor Prepares*.

Though bed-ridden with flu for almost ten weeks at the end of the year, Stanislavski continued to dictate the book. Gurevich, however, became increasingly frustrated. Stanislavski was still going back over chapters that had already been edited, making changes, instead of concentrating on the new chapters that had to be written. He wanted to write the perfect book, and that was just not possible. She simply could not cope any more. On May 25 she wrote:

'I shudder at the thought of you succumbing to your need for endless corrections, destroying your life with your own hands. It's a catastrophe for me, too. I wanted passionately to help you, was so sure I could do this great thing, and never thought that our combined work would encounter such insurmountable obstacles, created by you, and end so tragically. Words can't express how deeply painful this is for me.' (K.S. Archive, No. 8073.)

Gurevich's departure was indeed tragic. Without her, Stanislavski had no one who could advise him adequately on editorial matters. No one else concerned with the books had any genuine theatrical knowledge. No one else knew Stanislavski's mind so well. Had she been well enough, she might have been able to bring some sort of discipline to the writing and the books might have turned out better than they did. Stanislavski did not reply until July 5, on the day he was travelling to Germany:

'I understand you. You are like a director staging *Hamlet* with a complete beginner.

You are perturbed by my notes and variants. But they are not for you, *but for me*, only *for my own copy*. I have the writing craze, I'm obsessed; my book is a sickness. It's torture not to be able to express something you feel so clearly inside. I am like a pregnant woman who cannot give birth. In my search for words I thrash about on all sides. So be it!' (*SS*, VIII, p. 301.)

In her reply Gurevich repeated that he was not doing the book any real good by tinkering with details. She suggested they discuss it on his return in the autumn.

For once, Stanislavski received identical advice from Elizabeth Hapgood later in the year:

> 'I have nothing against your changing the way you express things. You can rewrite ten times if you keep finding better ways to convey your ideas to the reader. *But* what concerns me is that you are dragging the book out of yourself late at night, after a long exhausting day, when you are not really capable of work or of seeing what you have done with a fresh eye. You are forcing yourself to write. You are doing, as a writer, something you would never allow an actor to do. You are so tired you don't know which is better, the old or the new text. You can't throw out the first, second or third version because you can't feel the difference among them. You are piling up senseless sheets of paper, which is awful for you. That is why I passionately want you to find a clear-thinking *writer*.' (K.S. Archive, No. 2416.)

Stanislavski had been looking for a 'clear-thinking writer' since the summer of 1911 when he had approached Efros.

Stanislavski and Lilina stopped over in Berlin on their way to Badenweiler. There they stayed in the same pension as Nemirovich and his wife. Nemirovich was so short of money that he had asked that something be sent from Moscow to cover his living expenses. Stanislavski does not appear to have discussed his plans for the reorganization of the theatre. Their relations were purely social.

Kachalov and Leonidov joined Stanislavski in Badenweiler from mid-July to mid-August, during which time they held a number of meetings to discuss the future management of the Art Theatre now that it had achieved virtual autonomy. They proposed that a 'triumvirate' be created, consisting of Moskvin, Kachalov and Leonidov, who would deputize for Stanislavski and Nemirovich and help them in all organizational matters. The company would be divided into groups of ten who would work together to raise their technical standard. Above all, care had to be taken not to mount too many productions in any one season. All this Stanislavski duly reported to Nikolai Egorov in two letters written in mid- and late August. Egorov was ten years Stanislavski's junior. He had been an accountant at the Alekseiev factory. He had joined the administration of the Art Theatre in 1926 and left in 1929. He had returned in 1931. He was seen as an ambitious schemer, who had wormed his way into Stanislavski's confidence. It was evidence of Stanislavski's well-known gullibility. The question of the 'succession' was being openly discussed in the Art Theatre. Stanislavski was approaching seventy and in poor health. Nemirovich was also ill. To hold a position of command in a theatre Stalin was known to favour was to be at the centre of Soviet cultural life. It was, barring ideological blunders, a key to privilege and power.

In his letters Stanislavski spoke openly of Nemirovich's straitened circumstances and of the need to send him more money. Whatever his artistic disagreements with him, his personal concern for Nemirovich's well-being was sincere. He outlined all his plans for the repertoire and his concern for the future of the theatre:

> 'My life's goal is to guarantee the survival of the theatre and the position of the old brigade within it after my death. If they are given proper respect, their position will be stronger. Not only the "triumvirate" but all the rest of the old brigade as well. This isn't a matter of patronage but because they alone – without me and Nemirovich – can maintain the true tradition of the Art Theatre. If this doesn't happen, then Sudakov will seize power and as experience shows, in a few months the Art Theatre will turn into the former Second Studio with all its dreadful, actorish ways.' (*SS*, VIII, p. 304.)

He ends with an affectionate hug. The tone of all the correspondence is on a level of intimacy that is rare in Stanislavski's letters.

In two further letters Stanislavski began to sketch ideas for the Academy of Theatre Art which he had been asked to form as part of the Art Theatre reorganization. He rejected the suggestion that it should be open to actors from other companies. They would have to be taught separately. He also wanted a production-design department with Vadim Shverubovich in charge.

This reorganization still did not solve the basic problems of the Art Theatre. The combined staff, actors, directors, administration, and production department amounted to almost a thousand people. With Nemirovich absent and Stanislavski essentially based at home, and both of them at loggerheads, there was no real management, no central control. The door was open, as Nemirovich knew it would be, to all kinds of plotting and intrigue. There was also the problem of the younger members of the company who were both homeless and underemployed. Stanislavski felt that they should look into the matter of housing themselves. He provided, however, no answer to the increasing frustration the young actors were feeling. As in many permanent companies, leading roles were assigned to specific actors over many years. The young had to wait. The policy of long, slow preparation, of limiting the number of new productions in any one season, meant that there were few openings for young talent. The more rapid turn-over that had been practised in 1930 and 1931 had at least provided them with greater opportunities. A split was developing in the theatre between those, like the old brigade, who were interested in 'depth' and the young who were interested in 'breadth'. It was this division that Sudakov sought to exploit to his own advantage. It was an apparently insoluble dilemma. An Art Theatre that resorted to 'pot-boilers' was not the Art Theatre at all.

Stanislavski and Lilina did not return to the Soviet Union until late November, in time for the final rehearsals of *Dead Souls*. He was still not

satisfied with Simov's sets but his main concern was to find the right
rhythm for the production as a whole and the right inner rhythm for
Vasili Toporkov, a valued new addition to the company, who was
playing Chichikov. On the 25th, the day before the first public dress
rehearsal, Stanislavski gathered the cast together to discuss the play as a
whole. As so often, months of detailed work had led to fragmentation, to
individual moments that did not add up to an artistic whole. Stanislavski
concentrated on the meaning, the subject of the play, the supertask, its
dramatic thrust, the through-action and the sense of ensemble:

> 'The besetting sin of our theatre, a powerful and dangerous one, is that
> everyone is acting in isolation, trying to get laughs, and not
> concentrating on the through-action. . . . It will take a hundred
> performances for you to see how you will develop if you genuinely
> value the supertask and the through-action.' (K.S. Archive, No. 1325.)

Every episode had to be informed by a sense of the whole.

There was another reason for Stanislavski's insistence on the
ensemble and the quality of the performances: the Art Theatre was an
actors' theatre, it had to prove its worth in opposition to the formalists:

> 'We do Gogol in our own way, Meierhold uses props, we use actors.'
> (Ibid.)

The preview on the 26th was, according to Bokshanskaia, an evening of
wonderful acting, with some virtuoso performances. The audience
responded enthusiastically and when Stanislavski appeared in his box
after Act Four he received a huge ovation.

The critics, however, were less generous. Unfavourable comparisons
were made with Meierhold's production of *The General Inspector*.
Meierhold himself looked appalled, bored, angry by turns, standing in
the foyer during the interval, dispensing curt comments. This was the
year when Meierhold, Taïrov and Eisenstein still held sway. It was the
year Brecht visited Moscow for a screening of his film *Kuhle Wampe*.
Intellectually the Art Theatre was still 'out'.

Stanislavski was not prepared, this time, to let matters drop. The issues
were too crucial. He responded twice in the press. On December 23, the
Literaturnaia Gazeta published an article:

> 'Like any art, the theatre must deepen awareness, refine feelings, raise
> the level of culture. The audience must leave the theatre and see its life
> and times with greater insight than when it came in. Therefore, the
> theatre cannot adopt a frivolous or superficial attitude towards an
> audience's expectations or court applause and wild enthusiasm. The
> theatre, now, often obscures great ideas with cardboard acting or with
> an external imitation of life . . . The theatre must not "preach" but draw
> the audience into the ideas of the play through the characters. In our

country, the theatre has no right to lie – it must be inwardly truthful. That places an enormous obligation on the actor and great demands on his technical mastery. The most difficult of all is to show contemporary characters in depth and truth. Therefore, the MXAT concentrates its efforts on developing the actor's mastery of his craft.'

He then gave an interview to *Sovietski Iskusstvo*, which was published on December 27. Asked about the 'system', he replied:

'My task is to talk to actors in their own language. Not to indulge in philosophical discussions about art, which I regard as very boring. . . .

This is my last duty to art and to the rising and future generations, which I would like to fulfil before my death.'

In January 1933 Stanislavski reached the age of seventy. Among the many messages of congratulations was one from Harold Clurman on behalf of the Group Theatre in New York. Work continued on *Artists and Admirers* and *Barbiere* and preliminary work began on *Carmen*. In April Ernest Ansermet, who had founded the Suisse Romande orchestra, attended a rehearsal of *Carmen* and afterwards thanked Stanislavski for having made his visit to Moscow a memorable one.

By July 1933 *Barbiere* and *Artists and Admirers* were substantially ready but Stanislavski was already too ill to complete the work. He did not attend a private performance of *Artists* given on the 14th. The emphysema was worse and the attacks more frequent. It was imperative to go abroad. In August he left for Nice. He sent his final notes for the play from Berlin where, as usual, he broke his journey. He arrived in Nice on September 22. The play opened in Moscow the following day to no great enthusiasm. *Barbiere*, which opened a month later, enjoyed a considerable success.

Stanislavski was thus absent for the thirty-fifth jubilee of the Art Theatre. Nemirovich, however, had returned and was as depressed by the state of the theatre as Stanislavski had been. On that, if nothing else, they agreed. In his message to the company he accused them of indifference, of lack of commitment. They were, he told them, the most privileged of all theatres. Nothing was denied them, money, resources, anything. People abroad could only wonder at the level of support they were receiving. But did this lead to any better results than in the early years? The answer was no. Nemirovich blamed in part the attractions of the cinema, where members of the Art Theatre were in great demand. But this was an inevitable consequence of their being under-used in the theatre itself.

In Nice Stanislavski was able to resume work on the second half of *An Actor's Work on Himself*. During November and December he worked on the chapter on Diction. In January 1934 the French edition of *My Life in Art* appeared with a preface, as planned, by Jacques Copeau.

Stanislavski continued to work on *Carmen* which he saw more and more as a popular drama. Chaliapin, who was performing in Monte Carlo, came over to see him, the first time the two men had met since the American tour. Nemirovich kept in touch. He felt the need for reconciliation. The two men had had so little genuine contact in recent years. In March he wrote to Stanislavski giving an enthusiastic account of Shostakovich's *Lady Macbeth of Mtsensk* which he had just directed at his Music Theatre. Stanislavski replied that if Shostakovich was a genius that was a comfort. In May Nemirovich proposed that to celebrate a seventy-fifth anniversary of Chekhov's birth, Stanislavski should direct a new production of *The Seagull* while he himself staged *Ivanov*. Stanislavski replied that he was not interested in the past, although in the autumn, after his return from France, he did start rehearsing a new production of *Three Sisters* which, he insisted, had nothing to do with the original production but constituted a completely new approach.

In June Stanislavski went up to Paris where he stayed for some seven weeks. Stella Adler was in Paris with Harold Clurman, her then husband. She decided to call on Stanislavski and enlist his help: for some time all the pleasure had gone out of her acting, she had lost the creative urge. Stanislavski found himself confronted with a woman who he described as being in a state of panic, clutching at him and begging him for help. In response to her suggestion that she might have misunderstood the 'system' he gave her what was his normal reply: if the 'system' doesn't help you, forget it. However, he agreed to help her and to work on the role she had played in an unsuccessful production of *Gentlewoman*. Every afternoon for five weeks she and Stanislavski worked together, using French. Adler employed a secretary who took down Stanislavski's statements verbatim. What struck Adler most was Stanislavski's insistence on physical action as the basis for building a performance, his rejection of any direct approach to feelings and his abandonment, except as a last resort, of Emotion Memory, which, under the influence of Boleslavski, had become a feature of Stanislavskian acting in America. It has been suggested that Stanislavski deliberately played down the emotional aspects of acting because the woman in front of him was already over-emotional. The evidence is against this. What Stanislavski told Stella Adler was exactly what he had been telling his actors at home, what indeed he had advocated in his notes for Leonidov in the production plan for *Othello*. He could not foresee the furore this change of emphasis would cause when reported back to the Group Theatre in New York. Adler told Lee Strasberg he had misunderstood the function of Emotion Memory. He angrily rejected the new Method of Physical Action, declaring that either Adler had misunderstood what had been said to her, or that Stanislavski had gone back on himself. At all events he had no intention of modifying the version of the 'system' he had developed.

Passions ran high and the conflict persisted for many years. Strasberg was in Moscow in 1934, although he appears to have been more interested in Vakhtangov's productions than in Stanislavski's. Adler's version of the 'system' was confirmed by Harold Clurman, who visited Russia at the end of 1935 and discussed the Method of Physical Action with Stanislavski. Everyone could claim to be right. The battle for the succession, for recognition as the sole true heir to the master and his thought had spread beyond the confines of Russia.

Stanislavski would have found such concerns with doctrinal purity, based on mistaken notions of consistency, curious. He was never afraid to change his mind. Stella Adler assumed, mistakenly, that Stanislavski's position as he outlined it to her was the position he had always occupied. She was no more than the fortunate recipient of his latest thinking. Lee Strasberg had not necessarily misunderstood the exercises on Emotion Memory. He was using material passed on by Boleslavski and Ouspenskaia, neither of whom had any knowledge of the Method of Physical Action. Account must also be taken of Stanislavski's tendency to deny all knowledge of previous practice. Faced with one of his own long-abandoned exercises he asked, 'What idiot thought that one up?' The unfortunate actress who, during the rehearsals for *Tartuffe* in 1938, referred to 'moods' was sharply told that he had no idea what she was talking about.

He acknowledged, too, cultural and geographical differences. He had always been clear, for example, about the temperamental gulf which separated the French from the Russian actor, of the radically different role which the intellect played in the creative process as conceived within the French and Russian traditions. When he told Joshua Logan in 1931 to find his own way he acknowledged by implication that the needs of the American actor might differ quite specifically from those of his own compatriots. All the elements of the 'system' were valid and essential but the balance among those elements and the emphasis given to them changed with time and place.

He was equally aware that individual actors found the various aspects of the 'system' difficult or easy in varying degrees, according to their own natural gifts. It was impossible to legislate absolutely for all actors at all times. What was important was the end result. The 'system', he repeated again and again, only existed to provide access to truthful performances. It was not a moral obligation.

As always when he was away, Stanislavski's anxieties concerning the future of the Art Theatre increased. It was difficult to see where new ideas were coming from. Nemirovich had directed a number of new plays, most of them quickly forgotten. People were still looking to him for a lead. His black mood was not helped by a depressed letter from his brother, Vladimir. In his reply he repeated a complaint he had made to Nemirovich thirty years earlier: he had been forced into roles he did not like. How much happier he would have been just to go on being an actor, an actor and no more. But who among his colleagues could take over?

> 'People often say to me, why don't you tell us what's to be done? Tell us what's to be done and it will be. I said do *Rigoletto* five years ago and no one took any notice but said "Fine", "It'll be done". Is it the fault of my weakness and incompetence on the management side? All right, yes. That's my tragedy. All my life I have been someone else, not my real self. All my life I've played the part of the "Manager", the "Boss", the "tough-guy", the "hard-liner". Now I am old I'm not up to these roles any more and more often misfire and give up. These roles are hard for me and there's no one I can pass them on to. If you've worked on nothing this year then the fault is partly mine and partly because the whole of our staff are turgid and talentless. This turgidity and lack of talent drives me mad.' (*SS*, VIII, p. 377.)

On July 28 he left for Berlin and by August 4 was back in Moscow, already concerned by what he had learned of Hitler's Germany and the fate of colleagues like Reinhardt who had been forced into exile. Like others of his generation he had seen the Great War as the war to end all wars. Now it seemed the hostilities might break out once again.

On his return home, Stanislavski supervised rehearsals for *Artists and Admirers*, *Fear* and *The Tsar's Bride* prior to the opening of the season. He also began work on *Three Sisters*.

CHAPTER TWENTY-EIGHT

THE METHOD OF PHYSICAL ACTION

A few days after Stanislavski returned to the Soviet Union, the first All Union Congress of Soviet Writers, which replaced RAPP, held its opening session. Socialist Realism was proclaimed as the official party line and was to determine artistic activity for the next forty years. It was one of those dramatic reversals of policy that were to become familiar over the years and to cost many people their lives. The first Five-Year Plan was coming to an end and was regarded as a triumph. Few, if any, present in the hall realized what the human cost had been. Nonetheless, with Western capitalism mired in the Great Depression that followed the Wall Street crash of 1929, it was possible to present the Soviet Union as the land of the future and, in consequence, of the future of art and literature.

On August 17, 1934, Zhdanov, the Secretary of the Central Committee of the Communist Party of the Soviet Union, set out the new thinking in a triumphalist tone in a speech which is for the most part a hymn to Stalin. Stalin joins Marx, Engels and Lenin as one of the leaders of communist thought. Stalin has settled all matters of aesthetic principle and determined the writer's role in the construction of socialism:

'Comrade Stalin has called writers the engineers of the human soul.' (Stenographic record, Moscow, 1990, p. 4.)

Had he been present, Stanislavski might have wondered why, when *he* could not use the word 'soul', Stalin could.

In the new doctrine the task of literature and, by extension, of the other arts, was to encourage selfless devotion to the construction of socialism. The Soviet Union was a land without inequality, without unemployment, without organized crime, without prostitution. Soviet literature, therefore, should be without conflict, without contradictions. The classics were useful in revealing the injustices that had existed before the October Revolution, and presented 'positive' characters, who showed the way forward. The arts must reach, touch and transform the people, not remain the domain of a cultured élite.

Socialist Realism was a perversion of the nineteenth-century tradition of Realism which sought, precisely, to reveal the processes at work beneath the surface; it was a perversion of Tolstoi's view of the need for the arts to communicate directly to ordinary people, not become an intellectual game. The 1934 Congress initiated a systematic onslaught on the avant-garde art of the 1920s; Formalism became a blanket term of condemnation and its practitioners were labelled as 'cosmopolitan', which was a code word for Jewish. Western decadence, formal artistic experiment and the Jews were bundled together as some kind of anti-Soviet conspiracy. Meierhold and Taïrov were included in that conspiracy. Shostakovich and Prokoviev were soon to be condemned for 'formalist' music.

The one organization to emerge apparently unscathed from this wrecking operation was the Art Theatre. In 1933 it had been given the premises of the old Korsh Theatre, so it could expand, and Stanislavski had been given the task of creating a Theatre Academy. It was now obvious that the Art Theatre was to become a model for all Soviet theatres, and the 'system' the method of training in all Soviet theatre schools. Small wonder then that Stanislavski, putting Sudakov firmly in his place, felt able to remark: 'You take your line from the party fringe, I take my line from the Kremlin.'

In his concern to complete his book on actor training, Stanislavski had not forgotten the second half of his project, to establish a method of working on a role. As he had told Mrs Gurevich emphatically in his letter of April 9, 1931, the material for a role lay in the actor's personality and nowhere else. He recognized the distinction between the actor as a person and the character the author had written, the inescapable fact that the only emotions and thoughts an actor can have are his own. There are no emotions on the page, in the words. It was the creation of a third being, the actor/role, the child of the marriage between artist and author, that was the goal, with the director serving as midwife. The problem for the actor is to begin to become involved in the world of the play, to feel it as a reality. The critical moment is the first contact with the script, the first impression. This is the moment when the will to create is, or is not, aroused. This is the moment when the actor has a sense of the play as a whole, a single experience, just as the audience, later, will have a single, unified experience. That experience had to be fresh and in some sense 'naïve'. The standard practice at the Art Theatre had been to start the rehearsal period with prolonged discussions and study at the table. Stanislavski now felt that too much preliminary discussion cluttered the actors' minds, inhibited their creative energy. Their minds were so stuffed that their bodies could not move. The surest, simplest way into a play was to examine the action, what happens, to act out the dramatic situations in sequence so that they could discover what they had to do. Actors thus began with what they could best control and direct: the simplest physical actions. It was Stanislavski's basic principle that a sequence of actions which an actor believed to be true would automatically evoke a corresponding sequence of feelings and thoughts which were also true. As Stanislavski wrote later to Elizabeth Hapgood:

'This is what we now do: today we read a new play and tomorrow we're acting it already. What can we play? In the script it says Mr X enters and finds Mrs Y . . . Do you know how to come into a room? Then do it. In the play, let's say, two old friends meet. Do you know how old friends meet? Then meet. They exchange many thoughts. Do you understand the gist? Then tell this gist. Do you know the [author's] words? Never mind, use your own. You can't remember the sequence of the conversation? Never mind, I'll prompt you. We go through the whole play like this because it is easier to control and direct the body than the mind which is capricious. That is why the physical line of a role is easier to create than the psychological. But can the physical line of a role exist without the psychological when the mind is inseparable from the body? Of course not. That is why simultaneously the physical line of the body evokes the inner line of a role. This method takes the creative actor's attention off feelings, leaves them to the subconscious which alone can properly control and direct them.' (Quoted in *Minuvshe*, 10, pp. 317–20.)

This method was Stanislavski's final response to the literature/theatre debate that had dominated his relationship with Nemirovich. Now active, theatrical, actor's analysis came first. Questions of style, period and background were not ignored, they merely came later in the rehearsal process when the actors had made the action of the play their own and knew what it was they needed to research. The will to create produced the will to investigate. This was the principle he applied when he began to rehearse a new production of *Three Sisters* in October 1934. The actors were surprised when he dispensed with discussions 'at the table' about period and background and went directly into what he termed active analysis. The same approach was now applied to *Carmen* on which he continued to work through the winter, emphasizing the logical progression of the characters' behaviour, insisting that every action should be justified in the sense that it had to have a credible motivation, had to be genuinely human.

In February 1935, when the singers had worked through the entire opera, they were confronted with what was to become one of Stanislavski's favourite exercises. They were asked to think through their roles in ten or fifteen minutes.

'The overall shape of a role emerges when the actor, as a person, not as the character, knows the whole show, knows the whole sequence of his character's behaviour, what happens to it at every given moment.' (O. Sobolevskaia, *Stanislavski stavit "Carmen"*, K.S. Archive.)

Carmen opened on April 4 to mixed notices. Stanislavski's crime in the eyes of the more conservative critics was to have insisted on a real social setting, on a chorus of women who looked as though they might actually work in a cigarette factory and on gypsies who did not look as though they had strayed in from a second-rate *zarzuela*. A strange criticism at a time when social realism was supposed to be the order of the day. Stanislavski had done what he had always tried to do, present human beings in specific situations. Support came from an unexpected source, Meierhold.

Meierhold admitted that having read some bad reviews, he went to see the show with considerable reluctance. What he found was a production full of invention and insight, infinitely superior to Nemirovich's ten-year-old kitsch production *Carmencita and the Soldier*, which had been universally acclaimed. Stanislavski's women had real earth, not a stage floor, under their feet.

We can only speculate what the production would have been like had Stanislavski been able to cast the black American mezzo, Marian Anderson, in the title role, as he wished. On January 21 she had given a recital for the Opera Studio and Stanislavski had immediately made her an offer. She replied that she would be happy to do so in the future. Unfortunately she never returned to the Soviet Union. It was a missed opportunity she regretted. It might have been the first example of a black singer on a major operatic role. Because of colour prejudice Anderson had never been invited to sing at the Metropolitan Opera.*

Just before *Carmen* opened, Stanislavski turned his attention to Bulgakov's *Molière*. This was the most disaster-dogged, long-drawn-out production in the history of the Art Theatre. Bulgakov had read his play to the Art Theatre's Committee for Literary Affairs and Repertoire. As with *Turbins*, there were ideological problems. Some members felt that the play, though theatrically effective and good material for actors, did not have a clear attitude towards the class struggle. Sudakov wanted to turn the play into a 'monumental tragedy'. Bulgakov would have none of this. He had written a play about an incandescent genius, crushed by a league of hypocrites aided and abetted by a tyrannical monarch. This was the view that Stanislavski accepted.

The play was first banned; then, after Gorki had intervened, it was passed for performance. A contract was signed on October 15, 1931. Rehearsals began in 1932, with Gorchakov as director, Moskvin cast in the title role and the première scheduled for no later than 1933. The production was delayed to give priority to *Dead Souls* and again when Moskvin withdrew from the production. He was replaced by Stanitsin. These delays apart, the production made slow progress, according to Bokshanskaia, because for all his protestations Gorchakov was not really committed to it but busy elsewhere. Bulgakov, understandably, was

* She was finally invited in 1955, at the end of her career, but then only to sing a minor role in *Un Ballo in Maschera*.

becoming angry and impatient. His play always seemed to be bottom of the list. The greatest difficulty, however, proved to be Stanislavski himself.

On March 5, 1935, he saw a run-through and afterwards gave notes. The play, he felt, needed to be reworked. That meant starting all over again from the beginning. Above all he did not find the incandescent genius Bulgakov had promised. The play was too concerned with domestic detail, the force of genius was missing. Bulgakov responded that he wanted to show an ordinary man, not an international reputation.

The argument remained unresolved. On March 10 Stanislavski tried to pacify Bulgakov, patting him on the arm to smooth his 'ruffled feathers'. The tone was amiable but it was clear he wanted the central character, Molière, completely rewritten. Bulgakov refused but he did agree to write additional dialogue, which he headed, 'Inserts made at the insistence of the Art Theatre'. He described the whole, unwelcome process as 'putting green patches on a black dress suit'.

Bulgakov's discomfort increased as he attended rehearsals during April. Stanislavski was turning them into acting classes as he taught the actors his new approach. The records of the rehearsals show Stanislavski constantly urging the actors to sharpen and develop their technique. This merely irritated Bulgakov. No system, he felt, could turn a bad actor into a good one and by now it was obvious that Stanitsin was not up to the lead role. When Stanislavski suggested introducing scenes from Molière's plays, to show his genius, Bulgakov again refused.

Stanislavski, for once politically sensitive, asked Gorchakov if he thought the ending of the play was ideologically acceptable and they discussed alternatives. He also wanted to make other structural changes. When Bulgakov learned that Stanislavski was moving material around from scene to scene he wrote an angry letter threatening to withdraw the play altogether. (*MATL*, No. 367.) Stanislavski informed the cast that they had to respect the author's wishes.

The crisis over *Molière* developed within the context of a wider crisis. Both Stanislavski and Nemirovich were aware that the Art Theatre was in danger of bursting apart. Three generations were in conflict. One solution was to split the company in two: the traditional Art Theatre with its accepted policy and an annexe in which the younger members of the company could try out their strengths. Stanislavski was concerned that his idea should be kept secret from 'that crook Sudakov' who would try to turn it to his advantage. That 'crook' Sudakov had incurred Stanislavski's even greater displeasure by publishing, without consultation or consent, an article on the 'system' in the United States.

Stanislavski and Nemirovich agreed on the problem and, in principle, on the solution. Unfortunately, relations between the two men were now so bad they would not meet, talk or communicate directly with each other. They used Bokshanskaia, who was also a close friend of the Bulgakovs, as their go-between. On April 13, 1935, Elena Bulgakova recorded in her diary Bokshanskaia's account of the exchanges she had mediated between the two men.

'K.S. telephoned Olga [Bokshanskaia]: Ask Vladimir Ivanovich [Nemirovich] to telephone me.

Olga called Vl. Iv. He said: I don't want to talk to him on the telephone, he'll drive me crazy. I'll go and see him . . . on the thirteenth, say.

Olga called K.S.

K.S.: I can't see him on the thirteen. It's my rest day. My doctor doesn't even let me talk on the telephone.

Vl. Iv., to Olga: I can come on the sixteenth.

Olga calls K.S.

K.S.: My wife is ill, she has to keep walking about through the rooms. I can't throw her out.

Vl. Iv., to Olga: I'll only come for fifteen minutes.

K.S., to Olga: All right. I'll get rid of [my wife]. He can come.

Vl. Iv., to Olga: I won't go to see him. I just don't want to see him. I'll write.

Vl. Iv. telephones two hours later: I'm not going to write, because he thinks I'm a cheat and won't believe a word I say. Just call and say I'm busy on the sixteenth. (*Dvenik Eleny Bulgakovoj*, Moscow, 1990, p. 93.)

Lilina's illness was no mere excuse and by now, with all the stress and strain of the previous months, Stanislavski himself was seriously unwell. His nights were disturbed, he was talking, sometimes shouting, in his sleep. He suffered from blurred vision and the pain in his legs made it difficult for him to climb the stairs up to his apartment on the first floor.

In May his doctors ordered complete rest, advice which he substantially ignored.

His schedule was impossibly heavy but he was unwilling in a moment of crisis to let anything go. He still had to finish the book but he was afraid that if he did not continue to supervise productions at the theatre, he would lose contact with the younger actors who would no longer come and see him. Now he decided that he would probably never complete his books and that the only real way to pass on his legacy was to do what he had done before, create a Studio.

In April he had already expressed the view to Bokshanskaia that whatever they did with it, whether they divided it or not, the Art Theatre was a lost cause. The only hope for the future was a fresh start, with a new generation and a school. The new Opera-Dramatic Studio was based at Leontievski Lane outside the Art Theatre, away from the power struggles and the conflicting ambitions of younger directors, using those colleagues whom he could trust.

Early in 1935 Stanislavski's sister Zinaïda started to gather together a group of her private students, who had some knowledge of the 'system'. These were to form the teaching staff of the new Studio, and would work under Stanislavski's guidance. They met officially together for the first time on June 15, the day the Art Theatre season ended, and for a month worked on scenes with Stanislavski who introduced them to his new rehearsal method.

On July 15 Stanislavski finally left for his usual summer break at a health resort, where he remained until mid-October. While there, he continued writing *An Actor's Work*. In August he read extracts to one of the assistants who had come to report to him about the activities of the Opera-Dramatic Studio. Stanislavski was still concerned about his ideological position and the charge of idealism.

> 'I know that certain critics accuse me of idealism . . . even mysticism . . . But I want an actor's subconscious reflexes to be controlled by his conscious mind and will. Where's the idealism in that?' (Radomyslenskij Archive.)

He need not have worried. His orthodoxy was now being established by the party ideologues.

Stanislavski's new approach to rehearsal had caused a stir at the Art Theatre. It seemed a radical break with the past. Indeed, Stanislavski himself described it as 'new' but then Stanislavski was always finding something 'new'. His most recent conclusions, enthusiastically proclaimed, always seemed to represent a break with the past. In fact, he had, as his early production plans indicate, always started with action and in 1905 had already experimented with improvisation, with Meierhold, as the first step in the rehearsal process, and later with Gorki had considered the possibility of using it as a way of creating new plays. His fundamental approach to a script from before the First World War had been to break it down into sections, bits, and to find a basic task for each character within each bit. The Method of Physical Action, as his 'new' approach came to be called, was a re-ordering of the rehearsal process of which we see the first signs in the production plan for *Othello*.

The party used this apparent break with the past to establish Stanislavski's political credentials and to wipe away all the 'Marxist' criticism he had endured in the past. Thanks to recent advances in Soviet psychology, they maintained, Stanislavski had been able to abandon his subjectivist, idealist position and create a new, more materialist approach. The fact that Pavlov, the father of Soviet behaviourism, had expressed an interest in Stanislavski's work, seemed to confirm the truth of this statement. This was the party line, proclaimed throughout the

Soviet Union and later throughout the post-war socialist bloc. Stanislavski was 'sovietized'.*

Stanislavski used the eighteenth anniversary of the Revolution to make a public statement of his position in an article, 'The October Revolution and the Theatre'. In it he repeated some of the criticism he had voiced earlier towards the end of *My Life in Art*. Those criticism had now been endorsed by the government and he was able to speak with confidence:

'Much has been done in respect of outward forms and techniques. Every kind of conventionalized, stylized theatre has been tried. Every kind of acting space. . . . Every kind of directional device, some good, some bad. Original methods of stage movement and speech have been found. It is impossible to judge all these experiments. Everyone was given complete freedom to pursue their creative gifts and experiments. The means were not lacking. But, unfortunately, the inner nature of the creative process was ignored. I cannot remember a single major discovery concerning ways for the actor to master his psychotechnique, any practical methods for releasing ideas, emotions, wishes, when it is precisely these methods which progressive art requires.

What we need from the theatre now are not lavish productions, not the transparent tricks with which directors try to conceal the actor's inner emptiness. . . . The haste with which some directors work is caused by the paucity of their creative and intellectual material, which can barely last out two months. I do not want to drag out the rehearsal period. All my practical experience shows me that we need to speed up not only the production process but also the study of the basics of art. If the performers are masters of their art, then the director is not obliged to turn rehearsals into lessons, as is the case now. When the actors know how to work on their roles not only in rehearsal under the director's watchful eye but at home, using their own creative sensitivity and their own, finely honed technique, then the rate of work increases several times. Stakhanov achieved record speeds thanks to a detailed, profound knowledge of his own work processes. . . .

Our major task is to create a laboratory theatre, a theatre of masters, a theatre that is the model of the actor's technique. This theatre should establish the heights to which all other theatres aspire. But the laws of artistic mastery, the laws of realistic art, are not the property of one eminent theatre. On the contrary, all amateur clubs, all young workers' theatres, all studios must study them.' (*SS*, VI, pp. 338–40.)

* Gorchakov played a significant part in this process. In his book *Rezhissiorskie Uroki K.S. Stanislavskovo*, translated in a cut version as *Stanislavski Directs*, he puts statements of communist piety in Stanislavski's mouth that are quite incongruous.

This is such a politically astute document that it is doubtful if Stanislavski could have written it alone. His own long-standing objections to Constructivist, Formalist theatre, which were now the party line, are combined with an endorsement of Stalin's economic policy. The reference to Stakhanov is telling. Stakhanov was the worker who produced more, did more overtime than any of his colleagues, thus setting standards others were supposed to achieve. He became a Soviet hero and the search for more Stakhanovites went on. Stanislavski now promises to deliver theatrical Stakhanovites. That is the *raison d' être* of the new Opera-Dramatic Studio. His rehearsal periods did not, of course, get shorter. On the contrary, they got longer, but no one in the government objected.

At the same time as he published his article, Stanislavski took steps to bring some order into the running of the Art Theatre. He had referred in his conversations in April with Bokshanskaia to a Gordian knot which he was not prepared to cut. Now he was. Stalin provided him with an opportunity by writing a letter congratulating him on the anniversary of the Art Theatre. He responded by setting out with great frankness the weaknesses of the theatre as he saw them. (*MATL*, No. 368.) He stressed once more the role the Art Theatre had to play in setting standards, just as the Mali theatre had a century before. But the decline of the Art Theatre could not now be denied, the quarrels among the various factions could not be hidden. He was dedicating his last years to ensuring the theatre lived up to its ideals and was writing a book to hand on his teachings. He frankly admitted that he and Nemirovich were incapable of solving the problem since they could no longer cooperate adequately. His solution, given his experience with Heitz, was surprising. He proposed that Stalin should appoint a 'cultivated' communist director to arbitrate between himself and Nemirovich. He suggested M.P. Arkadiev, a senior member of the Central Committee of the Communist Party. They could then proceed to a shake-out of the company. There were those whose attitude to their work was trivial; others who were simply not good enough technically. The answer was to create a separate theatre for them, or let them go out on tour. The letter ended with a reference to Stalin's sympathetic attitude to the theatre.

Stanislavski's tone in the letter was extremely open. Like the many others he thought of Stalin as a benevolent figure, almost the mirror-image of himself, bringing the same care and concern to the Russian people as he brought to the members of the Art Theatre.

Stalin responded positively and Arkadiev took up his post in January 1936. He lasted, in fact, only one year, before disappearing in the first of the great purges the following year.

During Stanislavski's absence in the summer his assistants auditioned some 3500 students who had applied to join the Opera-Dramatic Studio. These were not, however, the standard auditions in which candidates present two or three pieces to a panel in the space of a few minutes. Zinaïda first weeded out the obviously untalented, some 500, while the assistants divided the remaining 3000 into small groups and worked with them in some depth. Twenty were then selected for the drama section. As Stanislavski explained later in the year to Elizabeth Hapgood:

> 'We are not just setting up a school to which people can come, do a bit of study and then go off to any old theatre. Our school will produce not just individuals but a whole company (operatic and dramatic). Our school creates *theatres* and produces efficient companies with a small repertoire, their own directors, wardrobe, make-up artists, managers and staff. These companies [operatic and dramatic] work together. Opera people can perform in plays and drama people in the chorus, in mime, in ballet-opera.' (Quoted in *Minuvshe*, 10, pp. 310–12.)

In the autumn Stanislavski took the assistants through the elements of the 'system' again and demonstrated his rehearsal methods once again. The first class with students took place on November 15, 1935.

Stanislavski's involvement in the day-to-day work of the Studio had to be balanced against his commitments as a director, the writing of *An Actor's Work on Himself* and his now rapidly declining health. He did, however, with his young colleagues, establish a four-year programme of study which more or less followed the pattern of his books: two years of work on oneself, followed by two years of work on the role.* It was made plain to the students that the Studio was indeed the laboratory of which Stanislavski had spoken in his article. There would be no fully mounted productions. There would only be work on technique and method.

With the Opera-Dramatic Studio firmly launched, Stanislavski returned to his work on *Molière*. His involvement with the production, however, came to an abrupt end. Whether he quit voluntarily or was simply removed is unclear. The reason may well have been ill health. What is certain is that Stanislavski and Stanitsin could not agree on the interpretation of the lead role. Nemirovich took over and tried to find a middle way but his first comments were yet another shot in his long-standing battle with Stanislavski:

> 'The besetting sin of the Art Theatre, one against which I have always fought, is that we agree to work on a play and the first thing we do is stop trusting the author. It was the same with *Three Sisters*. . . . This is trite, that's not right. Mostly people don't act the play, not even the character but what they feel like.' (Quoted in Smeliansky, *Bulgakov v Xudozhestvenom Teatre*, Moscow, 1989, p. 305.)

Nemirovich concentrated his efforts on Stanitsin, whom he recognized

---

* For a full account of the work of the Opera-Dramatic Studio see Benedetti, *Stanislavski and the Actor*, Methuen, 1998.

was inadequate. He analysed the character of Molière in terms of an artist's need for freedom, his feeling of anger when that freedom is crushed. Since Molière cannot show his anger to the king, he takes it out on others. He followed this analysis with a revealing comparison:

> 'Take [Stanislavski] for example. He is by turns vindictive, cruel, captivating, as suspicious and gullible as a young girl, an unbelievable bundle of contradictions. Only an obtuse critic would fail to understand such conflicting emotions.' (Ibid., p. 306.)

Nonetheless, in January 1936 he attempted a reconciliation, on the instructions of the government. (*MATL*, No. 369.) In the past, Stanislavski and his other colleagues had invested him with almost dictatorial powers. Now, Stanislavski had placed Egorov as a barrier between them. Stanislavski, Nemirovich wrote, did not know the tenth part of Egorov's high-handed behaviour, because it had been kept from him in the interests of his health.

> 'We both probably suffer from over-ambition. That is natural in those engaged in the arts. For 37 years, as you well know, this has been exploited by those who have no business to be in the theatre, and it is only thanks to you and my own immense love of the theatre, and our mutual respect for each other's work and our good breeding that we have saved the Art Theatre.' (*Iz., Pis.*, p. 445.)

Stanislavski did not respond. For the next few months he was able to work only sporadically. Most of the time he was confined to bed, either at home or at the sanatorium in Barvikha near Moscow. Lilina was also still ill and was sent abroad for treatment. He took a class here, a rehearsal there but no prolonged work. Though suffering from a high temperature much of the time, he managed to complete more chapters of *An Actor's Work* which he sent to Elizabeth Hapgood in January and March. At times his health caused the doctors considerable alarm, particularly the bouts of breathlessness.

The news from the theatre did not lighten his mood. *Molière* started previews on February 11 to a largely hostile press. Nonetheless, the play was a great success with the public and played to full houses. The party ideologues were, however, sharpening their knives. Crisis point came on February 29. Bulgakov's old enemy, Kerzhentsev, who had been responsible for the banning of *Flight* at its dress rehearsal in 1929, had become chairman of the Committee for Arts. He saw the play as a direct attack on Stalin. It is not difficult to see certain parallels: Louis XIV = Stalin, Molière = Bulgakov, the League of Hypocrites = the party. This was the interpretation he set out in a memorandum to Stalin, in which he suggested that rather than issue an outright ban, they should coerce the theatre itself into taking off the play by planting a series of hostile articles in *Pravda* and other journals. Stalin agreed. A press campaign was duly mounted. It was almost as though the critics knew of Stanislavski's own private criticisms of the play since they took issue with Bulgakov, just as Stanislavski had done, over the absence of Molière, the 'great man'. On March 9 an article entitled 'Outward Glitter and False Content' appeared. Even more shocking for the theatre was the fact that an actor in the company also published a condemnation of the play alongside three playwrights in the magazine *The Gorkiad* on February 22. The betrayals, which became essential for those who wished to survive in the Stalinist era, had begun.

It is surprising that no one in the Art Theatre had even considered the possibility of Kerzhentsev's interpretation of the play, but they had not. Pavel Markov had taken the view that there were no ideological problems. But the climate had changed greatly since the first reading of the play in 1931. Now, in 1936, on the eve of the great purges, the cult of Stalin was being established. Even the slightest breath of criticism of Stalin was soon to be punished by the gulag or death.

The theatre read the signs and acted as the government hoped they would: on March 10 the play was withdrawn. Stanislavski seems to have played no part in this decision. It was Nemirovich who had to bear the burden.

The withdrawal of *Molière* marked the effective end of Bulgakov's career as a playwright. It also marked the end of freedom for the Art Theatre. Not for thirty years would it be able to attempt any kind of adventurous repertoire. It could only stage exemplary works of socialist realism such as *Kremlin Chimes* or classics, and even they were subject to Stalin's personal tastes.*

At the same time the Second Art Theatre was closed down. The campaign against the 'Formalists' was now well under way. Stanislavski was asked to sign a letter requesting that the Second Art Theatre be saved, but the decision had already been taken, so his signature meant nothing. Some actors joined the Art Theatre, others were placed elsewhere. It is difficult to believe that Stanislavski saw the closure with any real regret. The Second Art Theatre had always seemed to him a betrayal of all he held dear. The political significance of the closure escaped him.

Immediately after *Molière* was taken off Stanislavski cast *Tartuffe*, with Mikhail Kedrov as co-director. It had been his original intention to perform *Molière* and *Tartuffe* in tandem. It was still important to him to prove that the 'system' could be applied to major classic plays, as he had tried to do with *Othello*, not just to so-called naturalistic plays.

In April he fell ill again. Bad news also came from the United States. Elizabeth Hapgood had translated the fifteen chapters she had and sent

---

* Stalin refused to allow the Art Theatre to stage *Hamlet* for the same reason he banned Eisenstein's *Ivan the Terrible Part Two*: leaders cannot have doubts.

them to Yale University Press. The new chief editor turned the book down on the grounds that there were not a dozen people who would know what it was about. The United States was still in full recession; people were not buying books, certainly not Russian books on the theory of acting. Elizabeth Hapgood immediately approached other commercial publishers who were equally negative. She finally turned to Theatre Arts Books, which originally had only produced the highly respected magazine, *Theatre Arts*. However, in 1933, they had turned to books, bringing out Boleslavski's *Acting, the First Six Lessons*. The chief editor, Edith Isaacs, accepted the book on condition it was cut, in particular the passages she thought 'too Russian'. The book, originally planned at 100,000 words, had expanded to 175,000. While these negotiations were in progress, Stanislavski revised the final chapter, entitled 'The Subconscious in the Actor's Specific State', which was, for him, the most important in the book.

He sent it to Elizabeth Hapgood on June 7, accompanied by a long letter which he had to dictate as he was too ill to write himself. He took the news of Yale's withdrawal philosophically, thanked her for finding a new publisher and gave her a list of chapter headings. The same day he sent her a telegram giving her permission to make cuts:

'I trust in your tact, your taste, your attentiveness. Correct, cut anything that is difficult to understand. Do everything necessary in your judgement . . .' (K.S. Archive.)

Elizabeth Hapgood then set about editing and cutting the book to the best of her ability. When she had finished, Edith Isaacs made further cuts of her own. Mrs Hapgood expressed concern over Edith Isaacs' editing in private but supported them in public in order to get the book out. Although we have Stanislavski's typescript, initialled on every page and marked 'Final Version for America', we do not have access to the edited copy of the translation, if indeed it still exists, so cannot determine which cuts are Hapgood's and which are Isaacs'. Whatever the case, the book which was published in New York in November 1936 under the title *An Actor Prepares* is not *An Actor's Work* but a pale shadow of it.

An Actor Prepares has been in print ever since it first appeared. Many have turned to it with enthusiasm, and all too often have turned away in disappointment. The publisher's dilemma is understandable. All the faults that Gurevich had listed in 1929 were still there: overwriting, over-explanation, confused terminology. By 1935, when Stanislavski was ill and writing against the clock, the writing had deteriorated. The metaphors he uses, sometimes spreading from chapter to chapter, become so convoluted as to be incomprehensible. What is the reader, professional or lay, to make of chapter headings such as 'The Subconscious in the Actor's Specific State' or 'The Lines of Force of the Drives of Psychological Life'? But he had no one to help him.

The need for cuts was indisputable. Gurevich had told him so in 1929. But on what basis were cuts to be made? Neither Elizabeth Hapgood nor Edith Isaacs had any direct experience of the 'system' or any professional experience as actors and therefore could not properly distinguish what was essential from what was not.

An Actor's Work had started as The Diary of a Pupil and remained so, a day-by-day, personal account of what happened in class. An Actor Prepares is not a diary. The cuts remove much of its humanity and its humour. The lively exchanges in the classroom have gone. Instead we have a 'Director' with a tendency to pontificate. Discussions are replaced by 'The Director stated . . .'. There is no Director in An Actor's Work; there is a teacher, called Tortsov, who responds to his students' ideas and problems, setting up classes and improvisations in response to their needs.

In reducing the book to half its original length, the editors made nonsense of certain chapters. In particular the chapter on Action, which is central to the 'system', entirely loses its logic and its force. Tortsov's careful, detailed exposition of the Magic If is reduced to a few paragraphs.*

Finally, there is the question of the words which Elizabeth Hapgood used to translate Stanislavski's terminology. Stanislavski tried to use simple, everyday words when describing the 'system', what he called his 'home-grown' vocabulary. He divided the play up into bits, and for each bit he found a task. Elizabeth Hapgood translated these words as units and objectives, which are rather more technical in tone. There is also a difference in meaning between a task, which is here and now, facing me, and an objective which is a project, something to work towards. Stanislavski often refers to a 'goal' (tsel) which corresponds more closely to 'objective'. More important, perhaps, Elizabeth Hapgood sometimes confuses 'objective' with 'action', the means by which the objective is achieved.

The word 'bit' did enter American theatre vocabulary but in a curious form. When teaching acting, both Boleslavski and Ouspenskaia used the word 'bit'. Unfortunately, because of their imperfect pronunciation, it sounded like 'beat'. Successive generations of American actors have used the term 'beat', unaware that it is the result of a phonetic accident.

Not speaking English, Stanislavski never realized what had been done to his book.

Mrs Hapgood took another crucial step. To secure American copyright, which was only available to United States citizens, when registering the book she designated herself as co-author, not, as stated in

---

* For a comparison between Stanislavski's original and the Hapgood/Isaacs edit, see TDR Spring 1993, pp. 38–42, in which an extract from An Actor Prepares is compared to my own provisional translation.

her contract with Theatre Arts Books, as the translator. Once she had done that, she could negotiate translation rights. She felt, wrongly as it turned out, that *An Actor Prepares* would never be as popular as *My Life in Art*, so Stanislavski's financial interests would best be protected through world-wide sales. Stanislavski gave his full approval:

'. . . do what you like with the book. If you want to take it under your wing I can only be infinitely happy that it has fallen into your own good hands. . . . Do with it what you will, translate into any language, sell it in other countries. . . .' (Quoted in *Minuvshe*, 10, p. 314.)

These expedient measures were to have long-term consequences that could not have been foreseen. Because of Elizabeth Hapgood's co-authorship and her being Stanislavski's legal representative, the cut version, not only of *An Actor Prepares* but subsequent books, published after Stanislavski's death, such as *Building a Character* and *Creating a Role*, became the standard edition, so that all their shortcomings were reproduced and continued to be reproduced in other languages.

By the end of 1936, despite his happiness that the book was out at last, Stanislavski was in a depressed mood. In November he went to Barvikha where he was joined by Kachalov, who was also in need of rest. He opened out to Kachalov, expressing his feeling of loneliness. Not the intellectual loneliness he had spoken of in the summer of 1931, but real personal loneliness. Gorki had died in June, news which his family unsuccessfully tried to hide from him. He felt, perhaps, he had neglected certain talented people. In his diary, Kachalov commented that Stanislavski's problem was that he did not really relate to people as people, only as artists.

In his depression and isolation it was to Meierhold that Stanislavski turned – the only director, in his opinion, himself apart, of any flair and imagination in Russia. Towards the end of 1936 friends became aware that Stanislavski and Meierhold were meeting regularly. Neither was forthcoming about the content of their talks. Stanislavski would say no more than that they had discussed 'various matters connected with the theatre'. Meierhold was equally reticent. It would appear, however, that they mainly talked of the problem of repertoire both for the theatre and for opera. Stanislavski returned from his stay at Barvikha in February 1937, in better health and in a more positive frame of mind. Towards the end of his stay, a group of assistants had come to visit him to discuss the plays on which students were to work now that they knew the basics of the 'system' and were ready to start work on a role. Stanislavski insisted that they work on classics, because, 'in any work of genius you find an ideal logic and progression'. The plays he suggested were *Hamlet* and *Romeo and Juliet*. He was also visited by members of the Opera Theatre who presented extracts from *Evgeni Onegin*.

On his return, Stanislavski gave priority to the Studio, where he worked through March and April. On April 7 he met a group of directors and the singers who had performed *Onegin* at Barvikha. He did not feel they had understood Pushkin. Their eyes betrayed their lack of conviction. They had to learn how to get into a creative mood. Towards the end of the meeting Meierhold's name came up. Stepanova, one of Stanislavski's favourite young actresses, explained that the problem for young actors was that, Stanislavski apart, there was no one of any authority. They needed someone to take artistic charge. Possibly Moskvin, Leonidov or Kedrov. All three, Stanislavski replied, were stretched to the limit and, in any case, Moskvin and Leonidov were ill. When Meierhold was mentioned as a possibility, the young tenor Shchelov huddled in mock terror and laughed. Stanislavski's reply surprised him:

> 'Why do you do that? I'm not against Meierhold. I may share a common language with him, even the same language. He could come and stage an opera for us, provided he doesn't get up to his tricks. But even if he did that, it would change nothing. He can't take charge, he has his own theatre.' (K.S. Archive.)

For the next few weeks he worked with Rumiantsev on *Rigoletto*, with Kedrov on *Tartuffe* and with students at the Opera-Dramatic Studio on *Hamlet*, always applying the same method: the search for credible sequences of physical actions and the through-action which gave them dramatic unity and significance. He also insisted on students and professionals alike that they must rehearse a scene afresh each day, concentrating on their intentions, their tasks. They must avoid at all costs merely repeating the externals of what they had done the day before.

In late May Elizabeth Hapgood arrived in Moscow where she spent ten days, meeting Stanislavski every afternoon. Her hope was that he could give her the second half of *An Actor's Work* but very little was written and she had to return to New York empty-handed. In June he spent considerable time going through the revised Part One with the Russian editor, Semianovski. At the end of the month he fell ill again and his departure to Barvikha had to be delayed for three weeks.

At Barvikha he worked intensively on *An Actor's Work*. He was never seen without his pencil and notebooks, even on hot evenings, in the park. He was still worried by certain terms. He had been in correspondence with party officials who urged him to discard words like 'intuition' which could be replaced by 'artistic flair'. He must, he was told, use a language that would be accessible to the masses.

In late August Meierhold arrived in Barvikha and the two men discussed what Meierhold described as 'agonizing questions' about the artistic future of their own theatres and Russian theatre in general. The common language Stanislavski had mentioned to his young colleagues earlier in the year was being expanded and developed. It was evident to him as never before that Meierhold was the only person with whom he could discuss major artistic questions at a serious level, uncluttered by ideology. On his return from Barvikha he resumed work at the Studio but in November fell ill again and everything stopped, although he was able to help Lilina who was rehearsing *The Cherry Orchard* with the students.

In January 1938 Stanislavski was seventy-five. The occasion was marked by a flood of congratulations from all round the world and a series of newspaper features. One of the most touching letters was from Meierhold:

'My feelings towards you, my dear teacher, are such that no poor pen can express them.

How can I tell you how much I love you?!

How can I tell you how grateful I am for all you have taught me about the difficult art of directing?

If I have the strength to survive all the difficulties I have experienced in the last few months I will come and visit you and you will see the pleasure in my eyes that you are hale and hearty once more and that you are once again working for the good of our great country.'
(V.E. Meierhold, *Stati, Pisma, Rechi, Besedi*, vol. 2, p. 436.)

The difficulties to which Meierhold referred were the attacks to which he had been subjected, culminating in the closure of his theatre on January 8 after a matinée of *The Inspector General*.

Stanislavski saw an opportunity. Since Meierhold no longer had his own theatre, he was now able to take the 'artistic charge' Stepanova had asked for the previous April.

Meierhold, however, apart from his letter, made no attempt to contact Stanislavski. He did not want to jeopardize his situation. Guilt by association was all too common. It was by chance that Stanislavski learned Meierhold's telephone number. His granddaughter, Cyrilla, had gone into a flower shop to find Meierhold and 'a very beautiful lady', his wife. Meierhold asked if Stanislavski could ring him and gave her the number. Having nothing on which to write it down, she ran all the way back to Leontievski Lane to give it to her grandfather, repeating it over and over again lest she forget it.*

Stanislavski telephoned Meierhold at eleven o'clock one morning, inviting him to come over. Meierhold left home immediately. The discussions went on all day and well into the evening. A short while later Meierhold met the actor Chushkin at the main post office. As they walked back to Meierhold's apartment, he asked Chushkin for details about the work being done at the new Studio – what kinds of improvisations were being done? What were the experiments with the

---

* Personal communication by Cyrilla Falk to the author.

Method of Physical Action in the rehearsals for *Tartuffe*? He then let drop that he and Stanislavski would soon be working together and that they had met several times.

Rigoletto was not going well. Stanislavski was able to work closely with Kedrov on *Tartuffe* which was a small-cast, one-set play, and so the transition from Leontievski Lane to the theatre was smooth. But with a large-scale, complex work like *Rigoletto* the gap between his private work and the main rehearsals opened out again. It was the physical side that was lacking. Stanislavski had always acknowledge Meierhold's mastery of movement and staging. He now wanted him to realize the highly detailed production plan he had taken five years to write. He kept his intentions as secret as he had kept their earlier conversations. He had tried to point his colleagues in Meierhold's direction several times, suggesting that his expertise in physical staging would be useful and that he had a deep knowledge of the Renaissance which would be useful for *Rigoletto*. Nobody took the hint. Meierhold was the 'opposition'. Stanislavski, therefore, simply announced his decision. On March 7, 1938, Rumiantsev telephoned Stanislavski to tell him that there would be a full run of *Rigoletto* the following day. Would he be present? He can hardly have expected the response: 'No, I shall not be at the rehearsal but Vsevolod Emilievich Meierhold will see it in my place.' Stanislavski then gave strict instructions that his decision was only to be announced just before the rehearsal. It was greeted with stunned silence. Meierhold entered quickly and was shown to the chair specially reserved for Stanislavski. It was a symbolic enthronement. It did not, as could be expected, go down well with everybody. Meierhold was Meierhold. The leopard cannot change his spots. Stanislavski countered all objections with the curt reply, 'The theatre needs him.'

Meierhold was no mere passive recipient of favours. Like Stanislavski he possessed energy. His determination to create new opera was undiminished by the lack of imagination and understanding displayed by the authorities. When on May 25 Stanislavski came to the Onegin Room to see students' work on *The Merry Wives of Windsor*, he was not alone. Behind him were Meierhold and Shostakovich who had been friends for many years, once sharing a flat in Leningrad in the late 1920s. Shostakovich was just emerging from a period of disgrace. *Lady Macbeth of Mtsensk*, which Nemirovich had produced with such outstanding success in 1934, had suddenly been banned after more than two hundred performances. In January 1936 Stalin had finally attended a performance and had taken violent exception to the work. On January 28 a scathing attack appeared in *Pravda* under the title 'Muddle Not Music' and the work was taken off. Shostakovich withdrew his Fourth Symphony, one of his most advanced works, and set to work on the Fifth, 'An Artist's Response to Just Criticism', which, when performed in 1937, did something to restore him to favour. But he was still tainted with his reputation for 'Bourgeois Formalism'. Meierhold, disgraced himself, and with nothing to lose, felt it important to bring Shostakovich and Stanislavski together. A further meeting was arranged on June 12 when the two men found many points of agreement on the problems of staging opera, particularly crowd scenes. Meierhold also tried to arrange a meeting with Prokofiev but this did not come off.

Stanislavski remained as naïve about the true nature of Stalin's rule in 1938 as he had been in 1935. While he was an avid reader of newspapers and could keep up with events as they were reported, he had no way of assessing the truth or falseness of what was written. He was unaware of the growing atmosphere of terror in which his contemporaries lived. He was not caught up in the general panic. During the great show trials, he did not, like other leading members of the Art Theatre – with the honourable exception of Kachalov – sign letters, hysterically denouncing the accused. He was not asked to. He was, in fact, systematically and deliberately isolated from events.

In the case of a number of important figures – artists and intellectuals of international repute – Stalin followed the policy known as 'isolate but preserve'. Stanislavski's routine, his meetings, were carefully controlled by his doctors, who were under instruction from Stalin. He was not allowed out of the flat in Leontievski Lane, which was almost hermetically sealed, except to commute to the sanatorium in Barvikha. He was thus virtually living in internal exile in the middle of Moscow. After his death, Meierhold launched a bitter attack against his doctors, maintaining that their refusal to allow him fresh air and exercise had contributed to his decline. Possibly he did not know the real reason behind this enforced isolation.

Stanislavski was never in any personal danger, even when the Great Terror was at its height. Indeed, it would have been difficult to prosecute a man whose artistic ideas were being pressed into service as a cornerstone of the state's official policy. He could therefore continue his work in the privacy of his home and studio. Even his contacts with Meierhold went unopposed. A Meierhold guided and controlled by him was doubtless viewed as a Meierhold neutralized and therefore, for the moment, to be tolerated. There was no sense of Stanislavski protecting Meierhold, or registering a protest. He had in fact approved the decisions both to close the Second Art Theatre and Meierhold's theatre. His decision to work with Meierhold was purely artistic. He was now interested in the Meierhold who described himself as a realist, a stripped-down realist, a realist of sharply defined form. When he died, matters took a quite different turn.

In the last few months of Stanislavski's life the two men met and talked frequently. Despite the secrecy with which they surrounded their conversations, colleagues came to the conclusion that they were working towards a synthesis of Bio-mechanics and the Method of Physical

Action. Both were convinced that at a moment when drama was sterile, the only way forward was through opera. Much of their discussion centred on Meierhold's plan to stage Mozart's *Don Giovanni*. They were both concerned with the problem of how to break the work down. How many scenes, or episodes, would there be? Fifteen to eighteen, Meierhold suggested. No, twenty to twenty-five, Stanislavski responded. There was a creative excitement in their talk which Stanislavski had not experienced for many years. He was now fully convinced that, all differences apart, Meierhold was the only person who could take his place. One of his last instructions was, 'Look after Meierhold, he is my sole heir not only in our own theatre but in general.' Stalin's police did indeed look after Meierhold. Having allowed him to succeed Stanislavski and complete the staging of *Rigoletto*, they arrested him on June 20, 1939, as a German spy just as he was planning the production of *Don Giovanni* he had discussed a year before. He was tortured and shot at a prison near Moscow in February 1940.

The summer was approaching. At the end of June Meierhold went on tour with the Opera Theatre but kept in constant touch by telephone. Nemirovich was abroad. On the evening of August 2 preparations were almost complete for the annual departure to the sanatorium in Barvikha. Everything was packed, including the precious manuscripts which Stanislavski took everywhere with him. *An Actor's Work on Himself: Part One* was now finished and had been sent to the printers. He had reworked much of the material from the 1935/6 version, changing some of the metaphors. In particular he had restructured the last three chapters, moving material around. The greatest modifications occurred in the final chapter on the Subconscious. He had also written a special preface which is a coded message to his critics. He went through the points Gurevich had raised over the years: he admitted that some of the material was old-fashioned, that his vocabulary was unscientific but claimed, quite untruly, that it had come from students in the course of their studies. He simply asked that, with all its shortcomings, the present form of the book be accepted, as it was all he could manage at his time of life.

Stanislavski was still working on Part Two of *An Actor's Work*, dictating it in the hot summer days, but it was far from complete.

He seemed to be in good health. Lilina wrote a quick postcard, full of confidence, saying how cheerful he had been recently. When the moment came to leave, however, things went badly wrong. His doctor and his nurse have both left slightly different but not irreconcilable accounts of the events of that evening. Dr Shelagurov went into his room and found him, in his pyjamas, sitting in an armchair with his eyes closed. When he asked him how he felt his reply was slow and muted but he still expressed a desire to go. His pulse as arhythmic and his temperature had gone up to 39.2 degrees. There could be no question of making the thirty-kilometre journey to Barvikha. The stretcher men who were ready to take him downstairs and the two waiting cars were sent away. According to the nurse, at the moment they were due to depart, he had a sudden attack of nausea and collapsed on to the pillows. This would be consistent with a further heart attack. Later that evening further examination revealed:

> 'In the lungs at the back particularly on the left-hand side moist crepitations could be heard. In the area of the heart the usual factors – dull sounds and a fluttering arhythmia. No pain in the abdominal cavity.' (Dr Shelagurov in *O Stanislavskom*, Moscow, 1948, p. 523.)

It proved impossible to bring his temperature down. Camphor injections were prescribed to assist the functioning of the heart. Stanislavski's mind often drifted away but suddenly on the 7th he spoke of Nemirovich, quoting one of Lermontov's most famous poems:

> 'Who's looking after Nemirovich? You see how he's "a lonely white sail". Perhaps he's ill. Is he short of money?' (Dukhovska in *O Stanislavskom*, Moscow, 1948, pp. 550–1.)

It was a touching impulse towards a man for whom, in spite of everything, he still felt some loyalty and affection. Lermontov's verses seemed to sum up their early quest together:

> 'White now the one lone sail is gleaming
> There in the azure mist of the foam.
> Of what in far-flung lands is it dreaming?
> What has it lost in the land of home?'

But the end suggested their darker days:

> 'But it, like a rebel, begs for the storm.
> As though in storms it might find peace.'

Stanislavski's reference to money recalled times when Nemirovich had borrowed from him to settle his debts.

Nurse Dukhovska then asked if he would like to dictate something to his sister, Zinaïda. He looked at her and said, rather severely: 'Not something but a whole world of things. But I can't now, I get things muddled up so.' These were his last words. At 3.45 in the afternoon, when Nurse Dukhovska came to take his temperature, his whole body suddenly quivered, as if with fright. His face was convulsed, he turned deathly pale, his head dropped forward. He had already stopped breathing.

It had never occurred to Lilina during the preceding two months that he might die. His first books since *My Life in Art* were appearing. On June 15 his production plan for *The Seagull* had been published. At the end of July he had signed a proof copy of the Russian edition of *An Actor's Work on Himself: Part One* believing that what he held in his hands was the final copy. It had involved Stanislavski in one final ideological battle with the authorities. On receiving the proofs he noted that the word 'unconscious' had been systematically struck out. He was obliged to write to the Central Committee of the Communist Party to have the word restored. He also decided, wisely no doubt, to suppress the book's final paragraphs in which he had spoken once more of the Unconscious. The book was not actually ready until the autumn. On September 2, Lilina wrote:

'At three in the afternoon they sent an advanced copy of his book; the labour of his life, three weeks after his death. Why is fate so cruel? Who knows, if he had seen this book in his lifetime what a boost it might have been, what a stimulus to go on living.' (K.S. Archive.)

Such optimism was not justified. After being pushed and driven for fifty years or more the body had finally given out.

THE 'SYSTEM': THE LAST PHASE

Tributes flowed in from all over the world. Stanislavski's body was buried in the cemetery of the New Maiden Monastery where Russia's great are laid to rest. Nearby is Chekhov's grave with its symbolic cherry tree. That corner has since been reserved for the members of the original Moscow Art company.

Stanislavski left behind a mass of unrevised manuscripts. *An Actor's Work on Himself: Part Two* and *An Actor's Work on a Role* remained unfinished. Reconstructed versions of them did not appear until the 1950s and 1960s. The fact that so much remained fragmentary and incomplete is central to the continuous nature of his enquiries. In 1936 he remarked, 'I have been working for thirty-five years on the laws of organic creation, I have created the "system" and I am still revising it.' The notion that his findings could be confined within a set of narrow definitions was anathema to him. For Stanislavski, the 'system' was never more than an aid to the creative process. It is not, as Maria Knebbel, one of Stanislavski's most remarkable colleagues late in life, noted, a cookery book with a set recipe for every problem.

Yet, almost inevitably, Stanislavski suffered the fate of all those who try to confront artistic problems in their richness and complexity. It is, as he had stated at the time of the Revolution, much easier to be doctrinaire and tidy.

The 'system' has been used, rejigged and modified with varying degrees of intelligence and seriousness. Elements have been dragged out of context elaborated and presented as the 'system' itself. Alternatively it has been pressed into ideological service. After the Second World War the Soviet authorities, continuing the work begun in the 1930s under Zhdanov, forged it into an instrument of Socialist Realism. Stanislavski's practice was schematized, codified, transformed into a dogma and force-fed to students, who, if they had talent, secretly rebelled. Later generations came to regard the 'system' as part of the Stalinist machine. This has been sufficiently damaging for there to be, even now, talk of the 'rehabilitation' of Stanislavski.

A rediscovery of the 'system' must begin with the realization that it is the questions which are important, the logic of their sequence and the consequent logic of the answers. A ritualistic repetition of the exercises contained in the published books, a solemn analysis of a text into bits and tasks will not ensure artistic success, let alone creative vitality. It is the Why? and What for? that matter and the acknowledgement that with every new play and every new role the process begins again.

SELECT BIBLIOGRAPHY

Works in Russian

STANISLAVSKI

Works, documents by:

Sobranie Sochinenii, 8-volume edition, Moscow, 1951–64.
new 9-volume edition, vols 1–4. Moscow, 1988–91.
Rezhissiorskie Eksempliari K. S. Stanislavskovo, 6 vols, Moscow, 1980–1994.
Iz Zapisnikh Knizhek, 2 vols, Moscow, 1986.
'Chaika' v Postanovke, Leningrad/Moscow, 1938.
Rezhissiorskii Plan *Otello*, Moscow/Leningrad, 1945.
Stanislavski Repetiruiet (Ed., I. Vinogradskaia), Moscow, 1987.
Besedi K. S. Stanislavskovo v Studii Bolshovo Teatra v 1918–22gg. Noted down by K. E. Antarova, ed., L. Gurevich, Moscow, 1952.
Stanislavski Reformator Opernovo Iskusstva, Materiali, Dokumenti, Moscow, 1983.
Iz Perepiski K. S. Stanislavskovo i V. I. Nemirovich-Danchenko (1902–17gg), in Istoricheskii Arkhiv, No. 2, 1962.

Works on:

ABALINKA, N.
Sistema Stanislavskovo i Sovietski Teatr, Moscow, 1950.
(Ed.) Nasledie Stanislavskovo i Praktika Sovietskovo Teatra, Moscow, 1953.
GORCHAKOV, N. G.
Rezhissiorskie Uroki K. S. Stanislavskovo, Moscow, 1951.
K. S. Stanislavski o Rabote s Aktiorom, Moscow, 1958.
KLIMOVA, L. P.
K. S. Stanislavski v Russkoi i Sovietskoi Kritike, Moscow, 1986.
KRISTI, I.
Rabota Stanislavskovo v Opernom Teatre, Moscow, 1952.
NOVITSKAIA, L. P.
Uroki Vdokhnovenija, Moscow 1984.
POLIAKOVA, E.
Stanislavski Aktior, Moscow, 1972.
Stanislavski, Moscow, 1977
RADISHCHEVA, O.
Istorija Teatral'myklv Obmoshenij, 1897–1908, Moscow, 1997.
SOBOLEVSKAIA, O. S.
K. S. Stanislavski rabotaet, beseduet, otdikhaet, Moscow, 1988.

Stanislavski, 1863–1963, Moscow, 1963.

STROEVA, M. N.
Rezhissiorskie Iskaniia Stanislavskovo, 2 vols, Moscow, 1973, 1977.

TOPORKOV, V.
Stanislavski na Repetitsii, Moscow, 1950.

VINOGRADSKAIA, I.
Zhizn i Tvorchestvo K. S. Stanislavskovo, Letopis, 4 vols, Moscow, 1971–76.

VOLKENSTEIN, V.
Stanislavski, Moscow, 1922.

Works on individual productions:

CHUSHKIN, N.
Gamlet-Kachalov, Moscow, 1966.

NEKRASOV, V.
'Bezumnii Den Ili Zhenitba Figaro', Moscow, 1984.

Magazine articles:

TEATR
January 1983, Misli o Teatre, Iz Zapisnikh Knizhek, 1898–1936.
October 1983, Stanislavski Repetiruiet 'Molière'.

VOPROSI TEATRALNOVO ISKUSSTVA
1978, Maria Knebbel, K Voprosu o Metode Deistvennovo Analiza.

NEMIROVICH-DANCHENKO

Works by:

Iz Proshlovo, Moscow, 1936.
Rezentsii, Ocherkii, Stati, Interviu, Zametki (1877–1942), Moscow, 1980.
O Tvorchestve Aktiora, Moscow, 1984.
Izbranie Pisma.

Works on:

PROKOVIEV, V. N.
Dni i Godi Vl. I. Nemirovicha-Danchenko, Moscow, 1962.

SOLOVIEVA, I.
Nemirovich-Danchenko, Moscow, 1962.

MOSCOW ART THEATRE: Letters, Articles, Memoirs

CHEKHOV ANTON
Pisma, 13 vols, Moscow, 1974–83.
Perepiska, 2 vols, Moscow, 1984.

CHEKHOVA, MARIA
Pisma k Bratu, Moscow, 1954.

CHEKHOV, MIKHAÏL
Literaturnoe Naslednie, 2 vols, Moscow, 1986.

KNIPPER-CHEKHOVA, OLGA
Perepiska I (1934), II (1936)
Perepiska, 2 vols, Moscow, 1972.

FLIPPOV, BORIS
Aktiori bez Grima, Moscow, 1977.

GORKI, M.
  Perepiska, 2 vols, Moscow, 1986.
KACHALOV, V. I.
  Sbornik Statei, Vospominanii, Pisem, Moscow, 1954.
KEDROV, M.
  Stati, Rechi, Besedi, Perepiska, Moscow, 1978.
LEONIDOV, L. M.
  Vospominaniia, Stati, Besedi, Perepiska, Zapisnie Knizhki, Moscow, 1960.
LILINA, M. P.
  Maria Petrovna Lilina, Ocherk Zhizni i Tvorchestva, Moscow, 1960.
MARKOV, P. A.
  Dvenik Teatralnovo Kritika, 4 vols, Moscow, 1974–7.
  V. Khudozhestovonom Teatre, Moscow, 1976.
  Kniga Vospominanii, Moscow, 1983.
MOSKVIN, I. M.
  Stati i materiali, Moscow, 1948.
MAIAKOVSKI, VLADIMIR
  Sobranie Sochinenii, 12 vols, vols IX and XI, Moscow, 1978.
MEIERHOLD, V. E.
  Stati, Pisma, Rechi, Besedi, 1891–1939, Moscow, 1968.
ORLOV, YU. M.
  Moskovskij Khudozhesvenny, Teatr. Novatosotvo i Inaditsii v Organizatsun
    Tvozchestovo Protsessa, Moscow, 1989.
  Moskovskij Khudozhesvenny, Teatr, Legendy n Fakty, Moscow, 1993.
PIZHOVA, OLGA
  Fragmenti Teatralnoi Sudobi, Moscow, 1986.
POPOV, A. D.
  Tvorcheskoe Nasledie, Moscow, 1979.
PROFFER, E. (ED.)
  Neizdannie Bulgakov, Teksti i Materiali, Ardis, Ann Arbor, 1977.
SHVERUBOVICH, V.
  Ostarom, Khudozhestvennom Teatre, Moscow, 1990
SMYSHLJAEV, V.
  Pechal'no i Nekhorosho v Nashem Teatre, Moscow, 1996.
SULERZHITSKI, L. A.
  Povesti i Rasskazi Stati i Zametki o Teatre, Perepiska, Vospominaniia o L. A.
    Sulerzhitskom, Moscow, 1970.
VAKHTANGOV, YE.
  Materiali i Stati, Moscow, 1959.
  Evgeni Vakhtangov (eds., Vendrovskaia, Kaptereva), Moscow, 1984.

INDIVIDUAL BIOGRAPHIES AND AUTOBIOGRAPHIES

BEREZKIN, V. I.
  V. V. Dmitriev, Leningrad, 1981.
DURILIN, S. H.
  Maria Nikolaevna Ermolova, Moscow, 1953.
GIANITSOVA, S.
  S. Pamiatiu Naedinie, Moscow, 1985.
KOONEN, A.
  Stranitsi Zhizni, Moscow, 1985.
LIVANOV, B.
  Stati, Pisma, Vospominaniia, Moscow, 1983.

SELECT BIBLIOGRAPHY 381

NEKHOROSHEV, YU., I.
Dekorator Khudozhvenostovo Teatra Viktor Andreievich Simov, Moscow, 1984.
POLIAKOVA, E.
Sadovskie, Moscow, 1986.
RUDNITSKI, K.
Meierhold, Moscow, 1981.
SHCHEPKIN, M. S.
Letopis Zhizni i Tvorchestvo (compiled T. S. Grits), Moscow, 1966.
Mikhail Semeonovich Shchepkin, Zhizn i Tvorchestvo, 2 vols, Moscow, 1984.
SHCHEPKINA-KUPERNIK, T.
Ermolova, Moscow, 1983.
SIMIRNOV-NESVITSKI, YU.
Vakhtangov, Moscow, 1987.
VULF, V.
A. I. Stepanova – Aktrisa Khudozhestvenovo Teatra, Moscow, 1985.
ZOGRAF, N.
Aleksandr Pavlovich Lenski, Moscow, 1955.
ZORKAIA, N.
Aleksei Popov, Moscow, 1983.

THEATRE HISTORY

ALPERS, B.
Teatr Mochalova i Shchepkina, Moscow, 1979.
Iskaniia Novoi Stseni, Moscow, 1985.
BENEDETTI, JEAN
The Moscow Art Theatre Letters, Methuen, 1991.
Dear Writer . . . Dear Actress, Methuen, 1998.
EFROS, N.
MXAT 1898–1923, Moscow, 1924.
EZHEGODNIKI MXAT,
1943, 1944 (2 vols), 1945 (2 vols), 1946, 1947, 1948 (2 vols), 1949–50, 1951–52, 1953–8.
ISTORIIA RUSSKOVO DRAMATICHESKOVO TEATRA,
6 vols (of 7), Moscow, 1977–82.
ISTORIIA SOVIETSKOVO DRAMATICHESKOVO TEATRA, KNIGA,
1, 1917–45, Moscow, 1984.
KHAICHENKO, G. A.
Stranitsi Istorii Sovietskovo Teatra, Moscow, 1983.
Malii Teatr, 2 vols, Moscow, 1978, 1983.
MOROV, A.
Tri Veki Russkoi Stseni, 2 vols, Moscow, 1978–84.
MIKHAILSKI, F. H. (ED.)
Moskovskii Khudozhestvenii Teatr v Sovietskuiu Epokhu, Materiali i Dokumenti, Moscow, 1974.
SMELIANSKI, A.
Mikhail Bulgakov v Khudozhestvenom Teatre, Moscow, 1989.
SOLOVIOVA, INNA
'The Theatre and Socialist Realism 1929–1953' in A History of Russian Theatre (ed., Robert Leach and Viktor Borovsky), Cambridge University Press, 1999.

SOVIETSKII TEATR 1926–32, Part One, Leningrad, 1982.
STROEVA, M. N.
  Chekhov i Khudozhestvenii Teatr, Moscow, 1955.
ZOLOTNITSKII, D.
  Akademicheskie Teatri na Putiakh Oktiabr, Leningrad, 1982.

DRAMATIC THEORY AND CRITICISM

BELINSKI, V.
  Sobranie Sochinenii, 9 vols., vols I and VIII, Moscow, 1976, 1982.
  O Drame i Teatre, 2 vols, Moscow, 1983.
CHERNICHEVSKI, H. I.
  Izbrannie Stati, Moscow, 1978.
DOBROLIUBOV, N. A.
  Literaturnaia Kritika, Moscow, 1979.
FELDMAN, O. M., (ED.)
  Gore ot Uma na Russkoi i Sovietskoi Stsene, Moscow, 1987.
GOGOL, N
  Izbrannie Stati, Moscow, 1980.
GRIGORIEV, A. A.
  Teatralnaia Kritika, Moscow, 1985.
LUNACHARSKI, A.
  Sobranie Sochinenii, 8 vols, Moscow, 1966–69.
NINOVA, A. A. (ED.)
  Dostoievski i Teatr, Sbornik Statei, Moscow, 1983.
OSTROVSKI, ALEKSANDR
  Sobranie Sochinenii, 12 vols, vol. X, Moscow, 1978.
  O Literature i Teatre, Moscow, 1986.
PUSHKIN, ALEKSANDR
  Sobranie Sochinenii, 8 vols, vols VI, IX, Moscow, 1976, 1977.
TOLSTOI, L. N.
  Literature, Iskusstvo, Moscow, 1978.

ARTICLES

BELOOUSOVA A., AND LAMAN, N.
  Stanislavski i Dr Markov, Sovietskaia Kultura, January 30, 1988.
DYBOVSKIJ, B.
  Vilemu Predlagaemykh Obstojatel'stv, Minuvshee, 10.
LAMAN, N.
  Mali Khudozhestveni, Sotsialisticheskaia Industria, October 26, 1988.
SMELIANSKI, A.
  Ukhod, Teatr, 1988, No. 12.

Works in other languages

AMIARD-CHEVREL, CLAUDINE
  Le Théâtre Artistique de Moscou (1898–1918), CNRS, 1979.
BLAIR, FREDERIKA
  Isadora, Equation, 1986.

CRAIG, E. G.
  On the Art of the Theatre, Heinemann, 1980.
  Craig on Theatre (ed., J. Michael Walton), Methuen, 1983.
DIDEROT, DENIS
  Oeuvres Esthétiques, Garnier, 1968.
GARFIELD, DAVID
  A Player's Place, Macmillan, 1980.
HIRSCH, FOSTER
  A Method to their Madness, W. W. Norton & Co., 1984.
HOUGHTON, NORRIS
  Moscow Rehearsals, Harcourt, Brace & Co., 1936.
PAECH, JOACHIM
  Das Theater der Russischen Revolution, Scriptor Verlag, 1974.
RICCOBONI, LOUIS
  Réflexions Historiques sur les Différents Théâtres de l'Europe (Facsimile
    Edition), Forni Editore, Bologna, 1969.
  Observations sur la Comédie et sur le Génie de Molière (Facsimile Edition),
    Forni Editore, Bologna, 1978.
ROBERTS, J. W.
  Richard Boleslavsky, His Life and Work, UMI Research Press, Ann Arbor,
    1981.
SENELICK, LAURENCE
  Gordon Craig's Moscow Hamlet, Greenwood Press, 1982.
  Serf Actor, The Life and Art of Mikhail Shchepkin, Greenwood Press, 1984.
SANDER, HANS-DIETRICH
  Marxistische Ideologie und Allgemeine Kunsttheorie, Kylos-Verlag,
    Tübingen, 1975.
SAYLER, OLIVER
  The Russian Theatre under the Revolution, Little, Brown & Co., 1920.
  Inside the Moscow Art Theatre, Brentano's, 1925.
STRASBERG, LEE
  A Dream of Passion, Bloomsbury, London, 1988.

MAGAZINE ARTICLES

CARNICKE, SHARON M.
  An Actor Prepares, Theatre Journal, December, 1984.
HOBGOOD, BURNET M.
  Stanislavski's Books: An Untold Story, Theatre Survey, vol. XXVII, 1986.
SENELICK, LAURENCE
  Stanislavski's Double Life in Art, Theatre Survey, November, 1981.
  New Information on My Life in Art, Theatre Survey, May and November,
    1983.

APPENDIX

Productions directed or supervised and roles played by Stanislavski at the Society of Art and Literature, the Moscow Art Theatre, the Opera Studios and the Stanislavski Opera Theatre: 1888–1938.

Year & date	Productions directed or supervised	Role

THE SOCIETY OF ART AND LITERATURE

1888

December 8 — Baron, *The Miserly Knight* (Pushkin)

December 11 — Yakovlev, *Bitter Fate* (Pisemski)

1889

January 15 — Don Carlos, *The Stone Guest* (Pushkin)

January 19 — Don Juan (ibid.)

February 6 — Baron Oberheim, *A Cup of Tea*

February 9 — Obnovlenski, *The Rouble* (Fedotov)

March 11 — *Burning Letters* (Gnedich) — Krasnokutski

April 20 — Baron von Aldringen, *A Debt of Honour* (Paul Heyse)

April 23 — Ferdinand, *Kabale und Liebe* (Schiller)

November 26 — Imshin, *A Law unto Themselves* (Ostrovski)

1890

January 3 — Piotr, *Don't Live as You Wish* (Ostrovski)

January 6 — (For the Mamontov Circle) — Samuel, *King Saul* (Mamontov)

March 18 — Laviraque, *Honour and Revenge* (Sollogub)

April 5 — Paratov, *Girl Without a Dowry* (Ostrovski)

1891

January 3 — Taliski, *Why There was Strife* (Krilov)

February 8	*The Fruits of Enlightenment* (L. Tolstoi)	Svesdinstsev
November 14	*Foma* (Dostoievski/ Stanislavski)	Rostanev

1892
January 23		Moréaque, *Anna de Quervilliere* (Legouvé)
March 22	(With artists of the Mali)	Bogusharov, *The Lucky Man* (Nemirovich-Danchenko)

1893
October 31	(Mali Artists and the) Society)	Dulchin, *The Last Sacrifice* (Ostrovski)
December 10	(With junior members of the Mali)	De Santos, *Uriel Acosta* (Gutskov)

1894
February 7	*The Governor* (Diachenko)	George Dorci
April 20		Ashmetiov, *The Barbarian* (Ostrovski and Soloviov)
April 25	(Lyric Scenes)	Agesander, *Aphrodite* (Krotkov/Mamontov)
December 15	*Light Without Heat)* (Ostrovski and Soloviov	Rabachev

1895
January 9	*Uriel Acosta* (Gutskov)	Acosta
April 10		Smirnov, *The Bear* (Chekhov)
November 2		Police Officer, *Let's Keep it in the Family* (Ostrovski)
December 6	*A Law unto Themselves* (Pisemski)	

1896
January 19	*Othello* (Shakespeare)	Othello
April 2	*The Assumption of Hannele* (Hauptmann)	
November 19	*The Polish Jew* (Erckmann-Chatrian)	Matthias
December 19	*Girl Without a Dowry* (Ostrovski)	

1897
February 6	*Much Ado about Nothing* (Shakespeare)	Benedick
October 12		Morozov, *The Appointment*
November 17		Man with a Big Moustache, *A Burning Heat* (Ostrovski)
December 17	*Twelfth Night* (Shakespeare)	Malvolio

1898
January 27	*The Sunken Bell* (Hauptmann)	Heinrich

THE MOSCOW ART THEATRE

October 14	*Tsar Fiodor Ioannovich* (A. Tolstoi)	
October 19	*The Sunken Bell* (Hauptmann)	Heinrich
October 21	*The Merchant of Venice* (Shakespeare)	
November 4	*A Law unto Themselves* (Pisemski)	Imshin
December 2	*La Locandiera* (Goldoni)	Ripafratta
December 17	*The Seagull* (Chekhov)	Trigorin

1899

February 19	*Hedda Gabler* (Ibsen)	Lövborg
September 29	*Death of Ivan the Terrible* (A. Tolstoi)	Tsar Ivan
October 3	*Twelfth Night* (Shakespeare)	
October 5	*Drayman Henschel* (Hauptmann)	
October 26	*Uncle Vania* (Chekhov)	Astrov
December 16	*Lonely People* (Hauptmann)	

1900

September 24	*Snow Maiden* (Ostrovski)	
October 24	*An Enemy of the People* (Ibsen)	Dr Stockman

1901

January 26	(100th Performance)	Psaltery Player, *Tsar Fiodor*
January 31	*Three Sisters* (Chekhov)	Vershinin
September 19	*The Wild Duck* (Ibsen)	
October 27	*Michael Kramer* (Hauptmann)	Kramer
December 21	*In Dreams* (Nemirovich-Danchenko)	Kostromskoi

1902

March 26	*Small People* (Gorki)	
November 5	*The Power of Darkness* (L. Tolstoi)	Mitrish
December 18	*The Lower Depths* (Gorki)	Satin

1903

February 24		Consul Bernick, *Pillars of Society* (Ibsen)
October 2		Brutus, *Julius Caesar* (Shakespeare)

1904

January 17	*The Cherry Orchard* (Chekhov)	Gaev
October 2	Maeterlinck Triple Bill	
October 19		Shabelski, *Ivanov* (Chekhov)

December 21	Chekhov Triple Bill	
1905		
March 31	*Ghosts* (Ibsen)	
October 24	*Children of the Sun* (Gorki)	
1906		
September 26	*Woe from Wit* (Griboiedov)	Famusov
1907		
February 8	*The Drama of Life* (Hamsun)	Kareno
December 12	*The Life of Man* (Andreiev)	
1908		
September 30	*The Blue Bird* (Maeterlinck)	
December 18	*The Inspector General* (Gogol)	
1909		
December 9	*A Month in the Country* (Turgenev)	Rakitin
1910		
March 11	*Enough Stupidity in Every Wise Man* (Ostrovski)	Krutitski
1911		
September 23	*The Living Corpse* (Tolstoi)	
December 23	*Hamlet*	
1912		
March 5	*A Provincial Lady* (Turgenev)	Liubin
1913		
March 23	*Le Malade Imaginaire* (Molière)	Argan
1914		
February 3	*La Locandiera* (Goldoni)	Ripafratta
1915		
March 26	*The Siege During the Plague* and *Mozart and Salieri* (Pushkin)	Salieri
1917		Rostanev, *The Village of Stepanchikovo* (Adapted from Dostoievski) – Rehearsal only
December 25	*Twelfth Night* (Shakespeare) (First Studio)	
1920		
April 4	*Cain* (Byron)	

1921
June 9   *Rimski-Korsakov Evening*
July 14   *Pushkin Musical Evening*
August 2   *Werther* (Massenet)
October 2   *The Inspector General*
                   (Gogol)

1922
June 15   *Evgeni Onegin* (Tchaikovski)
November 17   On tour in Zagreb   Shuiski, *Tsar Fiodor*
                                                     Ioannovich (A. Tolstoi)

1924
January 7   (On tour in USA)   Metropolitan. *Tsar Fiodor*

1926
January 23   *A Burning Heart* (Ostrovski)
April 5   *Il Matrimonio Segreto*
                   (Cimarosa)
May 18   *Nicholas I and the*
                   Decembrists (A. Kugel)
June 15   *Les Marchands de Gloire*
                   (Pagnol/Nivoix)
October 5   *The Days of the Turbins*
                   (Bulgakov)
November 28   *The Tsar's Bride* (Rimski-
                   Korsakov)

1927
April 12   *La Bohème* (Puccini)
April 28   *Le Mariage de Figaro*
                   (Beaumarchais)
October 29   *Les Soeurs Gérard* (Ennery
                   & Cormon)
November 8   *Armoured Train 14–69*
                   (Ivanov)

1928
January 19   *May Night* (Rimski-
                   Korsakov)
February 17   *Untilovsk (Leonov)*
March 5   *Boris Godunov*
                   (Moussorgski)
April 20   *The Embezzlers* (Kataiev)
                                        (ACTING CAREER ENDS
                                           OCTOBER 1928)

1930
February 26   *Queen of Spades*
                   (Tchaikovski) –
                   Production Plan
March 14   *Othello* (Shakespeare) –
                   Production Plan
                   abandoned

1932
May 4   *The Golden Cockerel*
                 (Rimski-Korsakov)
November 28   *Dead Souls* (Gogol/
                 Bulgakov)

1933
June 14   *Artists and Admirers*
                 (Ostrovski)
October 26   *Il Barbiere di Seviglia*
                 (Rossini)

1935
April 4   *Carmen* (Bizet)

1936
February 11   *Molière* (Bulgakov)
May 22   *Don Pasquale* (Donizetti)

POSTHUMOUS PRESENTATIONS

1939
March 10   *Rigoletto* (Verdi) –
                 completed Meierhold
December 4   *Tartuffe* (Molière) –
                 completed Kedrov

INDEX